P9-BYX-630

Praise for

Harriet Jacobs: A Life

❧

"This is the book we've been waiting for, the life of the most important African American woman writer of the nineteenth century. Here for the first time is the full portrait: the public and private Jacobs, the author and the activist, the free woman as well as the slave girl. Impeccably researched, compellingly told, *Harriet Jacobs: A Life* is a milestone in American literary biography."

—William L. Andrews, E. Maynard Professor of English, UNC Chapel Hill, co-editor of *The Oxford Companion to African American Literature*

"...diligent scholarship has restored [Jacobs] to the front ranks of the champions of the abolitionist movement...Jacobs is the subject of a splendid biography of Jean Fagan Yellin...She emerges from Yellin's memorable biography as a quiet revolutionary, an authentic voice for the sufferings and aspirations of African Americans during the 19th century, and a person with 'a soul that burned for freedom.'"

—*Philadelphia Inquirer*

"Drawing upon years of original research, Yellin gives us the fullest portrait we've ever had of Harriet Jacobs, before, during, and after slavery. We see in Harriet Jacobs a woman who was unique and who at the same time represented the entire history of black people in the nineteenth century."

—Henry Louis Gates, Jr., W.E.B. DuBois Professor of the Humanities, Harvard University

"Yellin's fine reconstruction of an impressive personality should firmly embed Jacobs in American cultural history."

—*Kirkus*

"At last, the biography of Harriet Jacobs we have needed, by exactly the right author. Jean Fagan Yellin has given us the life not just of a slave girl, but of a remarkable woman."

—William S. McFeely, Pulitzer Prize-winning author of *Grant: A Biography* and *Sapelo's People: A Long Walk into Freedom*

"This scholarly account, woven in a reader friendly fashion, restores 'an heroic woman who lived in an heroic time' to history and to us."

—Publishers Weekly

"Jean Yellin, whose recovery of Harriet Jacobs' *Incidents in the Life of a Slave Girl* helped make it a national classic, now gives us as full a story of this amazing woman—writer, activist, humanitarian—as we are ever likely to have."

—Nina Baym, Jubilee Professor of Liberal Arts
and Sciences, University of Illinois, author of *Woman's Fiction*

"This biography stands on its own as the story of an oppressed slave turned engaged citizen."

—Booklist

"Long respected as THE expert on Harriet Jacobs and her classic narrative, Jean Fagan Yellin now offers a riveting biography. *Harriet Jacobs: A Life* brings the power of storytelling to impeccable scholarship. Yellin's dedication to Jacobs pays off beautifully—as history and as life story."

—Nell Irvin Painter, author of *Sojourner Truth:
A Life, A Symbol*, Edwards Professor of American History, Princeton University

"Twenty years of scholarship have resulted in this splendid biography, which gives us a sense of Jacobs' life beyond the events recounted in her own memoir."

—Times Picayune (New Orleans)

"A brilliant book...Combining two decades of intensive detective work with passionate and eloquent prose, Jean Fagan Yellin offers a masterful tale of slavery and freedom, kinship and friendship, personal survival and collective transformation."

—Nancy Hewitt, Professor of History and Women's
& Gender Studies, Rutgers University

"Yellin's biography reveals new details about Jacobs' life."

—The News and Observer (Raleigh, North Carolina)

"Few books have been awaited as impatiently for by so many in the past decade and a half as Jean Yellin's *Harriet Jacobs: A Life*. [It] rewards us with a superbly told tale that awakens us to the horrors of slavery and the majesty of the human will to transcend its evil."

—Nellie McKay, Professor of English and
Afro-American Studies, University of Wisconsin

Also by Jean Fagan Yellin

The Intricate Knot:
Black Figures in American Literature, 1776–1863

Women and Sisters:
The Antislavery Feminists in American Culture

Edited by Jean Fagan Yellin

The Abolitionist Sisterhood:
Women's Political Culture in Antebellum America
(with John C. Van Horne)

The Pen Is Ours:
A Listing of Writings by and About African-American Women
(with Cynthia D. Bond)

Uncle Tom's Cabin, by Harriet Beecher Stowe

Incidents in the Life of a Slave Girl, by Harriet Jacobs

INCIDENTS

IN THE

LIFE OF A SLAVE GIRL.

WRITTEN BY HERSELF.

EDITED BY

L. Maria Child.

PRICE ONE SHILLING

HODSON & SON

PORTUGAL STREET W.C. LONDON.

Cover of the pirated edition of *Incidents in the Life of a Slave Girl* showing Harriet Jacobs hiding in the attic as a slavecatcher confronts her grandmother. London, 1862. By permission of the British Library.

Harriet Jacobs
A Life

JEAN FAGAN YELLIN

BASIC
CIVITAS
BOOKS

A Member of the Perseus Books Group

Copyright © 2004 by Jean Fagan Yellin

Published by Basic Civitas Books,
A Member of the Perseus Books Group

All rights reserved. Printed in the United States of America. No part of this
book may be reproduced in any manner whatsoever without written permission
except in the case of brief quotations embodied in critical articles and reviews.
For information, address Basic Civitas, 387 Park Avenue South, New York,
NY 10016-8810.

Books published by Basic Civitas are available at special discounts for bulk
purchases in the United States by corporations, institutions, and other organizations. For more information, please contact the Special Markets Department at the
Perseus Books Group, 11 Cambridge Center, Cambridge MA 02142, or call
(617) 252-5298 or (800) 255-1514 or email special.markets@perseusbooks.com.

Designed by Bookcomp, Inc.

The Library of Congress has catalogued the hardcover edition as follows:

Yellin, Jean Fagan.
     Harriet Jacobs : a life / Jean Fagan Yellin.
        p.   cm.
     Includes bibliographical references (p.) and index.
        ISBN-13 978-0-465-09288-8 (hardcover)
        ISBN-10 0-465-09288-8 (hardcover)
     1. Jacobs, Harriet A. (Harriet Ann), 1813–1897.   2. Slaves—United
     States—Biography.   3. Women slaves—United States—Biography.   4.
     African American women authors—Biography.   5. African American women
     social reformers—Biography.   I. Title.

E444.J17Y45 2004
306.3'62'092—dc22   2003017256
ISBN-13 978-0-465-09289-5 (paperback)
ISBN-10 0-465-09289-6 (paperback)

This was to have been for Peter, David, and Benjamin
because it's their turn,
but instead it is
for Ed.
He earned it.

Contents

Acknowledgments

〜❦〜

Years ago, my early interest in Harriet Jacobs was encouraged by Sherman Paul, Jean B. Hutson, Dorothy B. Porter Wesley and Charles T. Davis—friends and scholars whose work lives on. Dorothy Sterling has proved a never-failing source of encouragement and inspiration. Despite misgivings, Elizabeth Vann Moore generously supplied crucial Edenton identifications. Most of what I have learned about Jacobs's life in slavery in the South is the result of the extraordinary work of George Stevenson and his colleagues at the North Carolina State Archives. My understanding of Jacobs's life in Rochester and her authorship of *Incidents* owes much to Karl Kabelac and Mary Huth, at Rush Rhees Library, the University of Rochester; to Nancy Hewitt, who is writing a biography of Amy Post; and to Anne Dealy. For insight into the Willis years, I am grateful to the late Robert B. Burnham, to Elaine Burnham, to Sylvia and Charley Burnham, and to Bundy and Bob Boit. For precious family records and memories, I am hugely indebted to the late Dr. William J. Knox. For Jacobs's English experiences and the British editions and reviews of Jacobs's book, I owe much to Claire Taylor, Allan D. Austin, Lee Chambers-Schiller, and to Philip Lapsansky of the Library Company of Philadelphia. For a sense of Jacobs's Cambridge, I am grateful to Reverend Jeffrey L. Brown. For an unforgettable view of Savannah, I am indebted to the impressive W. W. Law, and to Reverend Dr. Charles L. Hoskins. Others who helped along the way included Harriet Hyman Alonzo, Esme Bhan, Ron Buchart, Delano Copprue, Chris Densmore, Judith Downey, James Downs, Carol Faulkner, Henry Louis Gates, Jr., Kathryn Grover, Carolyn Karcher, Evelyn Leong, Catherine Mach, Margot Melia, Lauren Osborne, Marilyn Richardson, Roger Stein, Deborah van Broekhoven, Joyce Warren, and Judith Wellman.

Archivists and librarians have been crucial to my project, and I am grateful for the help I have received from the American Baptist Society; Antioch College Library; Beinecke Rare Book and Manuscript Library at

Yale; the Bentley Historical Library and Clements Library at the University of Michigan; Boston Public Library; British Library; Columbia University Libraries; Cornell University Library; Dr. Williams Library, London; Free Public Library of the City of New Bedford; Friends Historical Library; George Arents Library of Syracuse University; Georgia Historical Society; Library at the Harriet Beecher Stowe Center; Henry H. Huntington Library; Houghton Library at Harvard University; John Rylands University Library of Manchester at Deansgate, Deansgate, UK; Library Company of Philadelphia; Library of Congress; Local History/Special Collections, Alexandria Library; Martin Luther King Library, Washington D. C.;Massachusetts Historical Society; Missouri Historical Society; Moorland-Spingarn Library, Howard University; Mount Auburn Cemetery; National Archives; New York State Archives; Kendall Institute, Old Dartmouth Historical Society-New Bedford Whaling Museum; Onondaga County Public Library; Quaker Collection, Haverford College Library; Pace University Library; Bodleian Library at Rhodes House, Oxford, UK; Schlesinger Library, Radcliffe College; Schomburg Center for Research in Black Culture, New York Public Library; Sophia Smith Collection, Smith College; Southern Collection, University of North Carolina Libraries; Stanton-Anthony Papers; and William L. Perkins Library, Duke University.

I am deeply indebted to grants that made much of the research possible: an NEH Fellowship for College Teachers in 1986–87; a summer research fellowship from the Historical Society of Pennsylvania and the Library Company of Philadelphia in 1988; a Scholar-in-Residency at the Schomburg Center for Research in Black Culture of the New York Public Library, funded by the Ford Foundation in 1989–90; an Archie K. Davis fellowship granted by the Carolina Society at the University of North Carolina at Chapel Hill in 1991; and a fellowship at the W. E. B. DuBois Institute for Afro-American Research at Harvard University in 1993–94. I owe much to the scholars I met at these institutions and to my sisters in the Women Writing Women seminar at the City University of New York. While all of these made positive contributions to this book, its faults are mine alone. I am very aware that others view Harriet Jacobs with different eyes.

My agent Geri Thoma, my editor Liz Maguire, and dear colleagues, friends, and family helped me keep my eyes on the prize over the very long haul. I am particularly grateful to Thadious Davis and Frances

Smith Foster, who made important comments on an early version and offered steadfast encouragement. And I am much beholden to the students in my classes, to those who worked with me on Harriet Jacobs, and to the anonymous graduate students who have rushed up to me at meetings over the years to say how important Jacobs is to them, then vanished. My children and grandchildren—Peter, Lisa, Michael, David, Amelia, Mosé, Genevra, Benjamin, Sarah and Blaze—all have made room in their lives for Harriet. I am grateful.

Introduction

I have lived with Harriet Jacobs for a very long time and am eager to get her presence out of my head, her papers out of my house, and her story into the hands of readers. But I truly cannot imagine life without her. As "Hatty," as "Linda," and as "Mrs. Jacobs," she has enriched me with new angles of vision, new ideas, new words, new ways of being in the world. She has brought me deeply-textured relationships with cherished colleagues and has given me rich experiences throughout this country and beyond. Presenting her life story is as much a deep loss as a joy.

People ask how and why I have become involved in Jacobs's life—why I have spent days, nights and weekends over the last twenty years studying her life and work. The answer is easy: her story is compelling. She is the only woman I know of who was held in slavery, who was a fugitive both in the South and in the North, an antislavery activist who wrote and published her life story and then, during the Civil War, went back south to work with the black refugees behind the Union lines and report what she saw in the northern press. We know of the heroic Harriet Tubman and her work during the war as a Union spy. And we know of the heroic Sojourner Truth and of her relief efforts. But because of slavery's antiliteracy laws, neither Tubman nor Truth could write her own story, and instead produced only "as-told-to" narratives. Astonishingly, Jacobs managed both to author her own book and to get it published before Emancipation, and then during the war she used her celebrity to publish reports from the South and to gain support for her relief mission.

Raised in an Old Left family, I was taught about male chauvinism and thought I knew something about it, but at the beginning of feminism's "Second Wave" in the 1970's, I concluded that I needed to raise my consciousness. In my dissertation, published as *The Intricate Knot: Black Figures in American Literature, 1776–1863*, I addressed issues of "race" and class. I had not touched gender, even in discussing writers like

Lydia Maria Child and Harriet Beecher Stowe. Actually, I knew no way to write about gender. I had no usable language. Thinking about the new feminist criticism, I decided to try to teach myself how to use the perspective of gender by re-reading the female writers I had studied.

And so I began. While reading chronologically through the works of Lydia Maria Child, as my training demanded, I reached 1861 and *Incidents in the Life of a Slave Girl* [ILSG]. This Anne Frank-like story of a woman's struggle against oppression was a text I remembered well. I had discovered it while working on my dissertation, had found it absorbing—and then carefully omitted it from the list of books I would discuss. The reason was simple. On its face (actually, on its title page) *Incidents* presented problems that, as a graduate student, I did not have the tools to cope with. Yes, it had a title, but it didn't have an author, only an editor, Lydia Maria Child, who testified in her Introduction that she knew and trusted the pseudonymous author calling herself "Linda Brent." Further, although the title page listed a place and date of publication, it didn't name a publisher. The name of a Harriet Jacobs was somehow connected with *Incidents*, but the accepted academic opinion, most recently voiced by Yale historian John Blassingame, was that while a woman named Harriet Jacobs might perhaps have existed, the book's author was Lydia Maria Child. No sensible graduate student would include such a questionable text in her dissertation, and although I thought it fascinating, I left it out. But now, rereading my way through Child's works, I encountered it again as a book she had edited, and my interest in it grew.

Child names herself the book's editor and in her Introduction writes that she has revised the author's manuscript, "but such changes as I have made have been mainly for purposes of condensation and orderly arrangement." Expanding on her editorial role, she continues: "I have not added any thing to the incidents, or changed the import of her very pertinent remarks. With trifling exceptions, both the ideas and the language are her own. I pruned excrescences a little, but otherwise I had no reason for changing her lively and dramatic way of telling her own story." [ILSG p. 3] I took Child at her word. I remembered the scandal that had engulfed her friend John Greenleaf Whittier, the abolitionist poet-journalist who years earlier had edited *The Narrative of James Williams*. Whittier had been humiliated when he learned that the southern press documented a series of inaccuracies in the text and used these to argue that all of the slave narratives were false. The abolitionists withdrew the book from circulation, and Child was so concerned that she wrote Whittier a letter expressing her sympathy and lamenting that "The doubt thrown on his narrative is doing incalculable mischief" to the abolitionist cause.

Making my way through the shelf of Child's writings, I felt I knew her well. She had composed novels as well as pamphlets, but I was certain of her commitment to the antislavery cause and thought it highly unlikely that she would have permitted herself to write a novel using the first-person voice of a fugitive slave, for fear of harming the movement. I also recalled seeing at the Schomburg Collection of the New York Public Library, a Library of Congress card with the words "Negro author" neatly penciled in a librarian's professional hand. This further piqued my curiosity. Who had written *Incidents*?

Trying to solve the puzzle of authorship, I phoned the people at the University of Massachusetts where Child's papers were being edited for publication. I was told that they had acquired some interesting letters concerning *Incidents*. They suggested that I contact the archivists at the University of Rochester who were preparing the papers of Quaker/abolitionist/feminist Amy Post. When I called Rochester, they said yes, in the Post papers they had found a clutch of letters involving Harriet Jacobs.

I ordered copies of the letters, and when they arrived read in them the story of the conception, composition, and publication of *Incidents*. These letters convinced me not only that Harriet Jacobs had written a book, but that she had written the book that Child had edited. I was persuaded both by the content of the letters and also by their literary style. Their vocabulary—not monosyllabic but multisyllabic—is the vocabulary of *Incidents*, and their syntax—not a series of simple sentences, but a range of compound-complex structures—is the syntax of *Incidents*. To my mind, the stylistic characteristics of these letters, combined with their content and with Child's assertion that she had edited the book, solved the puzzle of authorship. I felt certain that the woman who signed the Author's Preface with the pen name "Linda Brent" was a woman named Harriet Jacobs.

But a second question remained. Had Jacobs's "Linda" written a book about her own life—as she claimed? Or had she written a novel? After all, her story of seven years in hiding is difficult to believe. And so I set out to determine whether the events narrated in *Incidents* corresponded to the events in the life of Harriet Jacobs—whoever she was. In this quest, I was joined by Dorothy Sterling, author of a dozen pioneering books about extraordinary women. Sterling was researching Harriet

Jacobs among the grouping of 19th century black women she would include in *We Are Your Sisters*, and she generously shared with me the bits and pieces she had gleaned about Jacobs from antislavery newspapers like *The Liberator* and *The National Anti-Slavery Standard*. Attempting to determine whether *Incidents* was fiction or fact presented serious problems. Child not only used fictitious names as she edited. She included no names, dates, or places in the southern sections of Jacobs's narrative. How to begin to try to determine whether the life of "Linda Brent" had been lived by the woman named Harriet Jacobs?

Energized by Sterling's findings and by the Rochester letters, I wrote to dozens of archives, asking for correspondence to, by, or about "Harriet Jacobs," "Linda Brent," or any combinations thereof. And I got very lucky. The Sophia Smith Collection at Smith College sent a letter from Harriet Jacobs to Ednah Dow Cheney. Dated "Edenton April 25th," it begins: "I felt I would like to write you a line from my old home. I am sitting under the old roof twelve feet from the spot where I suffered all the crushing weight of slavery." Reading this, I couldn't believe my eyes. Edenton—wherever that was—was Jacobs's hometown.

Reaching for my atlas, I learned that Edenton is in North Carolina. Then I began going through Jacobs's book as if it were gospel truth, extracting the histories of the two families intertwined in it. I listed everything *Incidents* reveals about each family: occupations and property owned, marriages, births, illnesses, and deaths. The first generation of "Family A" began with the narrator's grandmother, called "Aunt Martha" and described as one of the three children of a slave woman and a South Carolina planter. During the Revolutionary War he had set his family free and sent them to St. Augustine, but they were captured and separated by the Americans, and "Martha" was sold to the "keeper of a large hotel." [ILSG p. 5]. The first generation of "Family B" began with the hotel keeper who had bought young "Martha," and with the hotel-keeper's wife, who at his death continued to run the hotel after inheriting his property, including "Martha." [ILSG p. 6] After outlining four generations of these families, I sent off my genaeological listings to every North Carolina library I could locate.

All of my inquiries, it turned out, were forwarded to the same person: Elizabeth Vann Moore of the Edenton Historical Society. An extended correspondence followed, and ultimately—despite the fact that she did not believe that the stories in *Incidents* were true, or even that Harriet Jacobs had authored the book—Miss Moore graciously supplied the information necessary to name the families. The key to solving the mystery of authorship, I learned, appears in the book's very first paragraph. "Linda" writes that "during the Revolutionary War," her grandmother was bought by "the keeper of a large hotel." [ILSG p. 5] Miss Moore informed me that Edenton's only colonial hotel was owned by Joseph Horniblow, that Horniblow had a son-in-law named Dr. James Norcom, and that the papers of both men are in the state archives.

Visiting Raleigh, North Carolina, I examined the Horniblow and Norcom Papers. After reading through them, I thought I had identified the major characters in *Incidents*. Dr. James Norcom was "Linda's" nemisis, the wicked "Dr. Flint"; his wife Mary Matilda Horniblow Norcom was her jealous mistress "Mrs. Flint"; Molly Horniblow was her grandmother "Aunt Martha"; and her little brother John, loaned by his mistress Elizabeth Horniblow to her doctor son-in-law, was "William." This accomplished, I had pretty much done what I could do. As I was rushing through my work at the archives so I could catch my plane home, the copy machine broke down. Hurriedly leaving some dimes and requests to mail me copies of the documents I still needed, I left. Then I waited.

And waited. And waited. Finally, I phoned George Stevenson, *researcher extraordinaire*, and told him that I planned to go back to Raleigh, that I would return to the archives, and that I really wanted my copies. Oh, he replied, he had meant to get back to me. He had been searching around, and had found some things I might think interesting. When I arrived, he showed me a table loaded with documents he had unearthed.

It was years later when I learned that—while I was busily examining the materials Stevenson had collected—he was preparing a test to determine whether *Incidents* was a legitimate North Carolina-authored antebellum autobiography, and that if it was, he had decided to go to work documenting it. The test he created was to identify "Linda's" father, about whom we knew only what she had written: Although the son of "a white gentleman," he was a slave. He had taught his children to love freedom. He was a skilled house-carpenter whose master permitted him to hire his time. He died when "Linda" was about 12 years old, and "Linda" had named her daughter (who we knew was called Louisa Matilda) for his young mistress. With these scraps of information, Stevenson stayed up all night, searching for a skilled slave carpenter mentioned in the will of a man with a daughter named Louisa Matilda.

By morning, he had found him. The slave carpenter was named in the will of Dr. Andrew Knox, whose daughter was named Louisa

Matilda. Convinced that *Incidents* is authentic, Stevenson became committed. For the next six years he and I worked together (often by long-distance phone at one minute after eleven at night, when the rates went down) documenting Jacobs's text, incident by incident. (For example, we identified "Mr. Sands," the father of "Linda's" children, as the Hon. Samuel Tredwell Sawyer, Esq.; dated the resignation of St. Paul's Reverend Dr. Avery, whom she calls "Reverend Mr. Pike"; and identified the installation and the forced resignation of Reverend William D. Cairnes, who questioned the system of chattel slavery.) Although the answers to some queries still remained elusive, I decided that we had enough to publish an edition. Because the academic community judged *Incidents* an inauthentic slave narrative, it was important to find a prestigious academic publisher, and at the suggestion of the late Herb Gutman, I approached Harvard University Press. Finally in 1987, my edition appeared with the generous endorsement of Professor Blassingame.

Completing the Harvard edition of *Incidents*, I really thought I was done with Jacobs and that she was through with me. But as I was finishing work on the volume, Philip Lapsansky of the Library Company of Philadelphia sent me a couple of her letters that he found in periodicals published by relief groups during the Civil War. Then, exploring black and reform journals, I discovered more. I was amazed to realize that Jacobs had achieved some celebrity as the author of *Incidents*, and that it was only later that her identity was forgotten. I was more amazed to learn that she used her celebrity among northern reformers to win support for her relief mission among the black war refugees, and that she wrote back to her northern audience in the press, describing life behind the Union lines.

To embed her appropriately in American cultural history, I thought, there needed to be a biography of her life—which I now knew extended well beyond the freedom with which she had ended her narrative. And so I began work on a full biography of Jacobs, a project that took another decade. When I was well into this work, Professor William Andrews reminded me that my colleagues would want to examine the materials I was collecting, and—rather innocently—I conceived of the Harriet Jacobs Papers project. It seemed to me that an edition of Jacobs's papers would be a natural extension of research on her biography. (Recently, after having been relegated for years to my left hand, the Papers project has been awarded funding and established on a professional level.)

My life with Harriet Jacobs has lasted more than twenty years. Reviewing that life, I recall many memorable moments. One of them occurred when I drove up to Yale to discuss my findings with the late Charles T. Davis, founder of the university's Department of African American Studies. After a thoughtful interchange, Charley said, "Whether *Incidents* was written by a black woman or by a white woman, it is still a very peculiar book." He was right. Moving beyond the established patterns of black male-authored slave narratives and beyond the structures of white female-authored fiction, Harriet Jacobs told a story new to American letters. Another memorable moment occurred when Fred Stern, a dear friend and colleague, commented that despite its great interest, *Incidents* is, after all, not *Moby-Dick*. I have kept this in mind, but upon reflection, have concluded that he was wrong. *Incidents* is, like *Moby-Dick*, a work of American genius, and Harriet Jacobs's life is, in Emerson's sense, a representative life.

Jean Fagan Yellin
Goldens Bridge, New York

PART ONE

HATTY

Private Dreams of Freedom and a Home

1

So Fondly Shielded

I was so fondly shielded that I never dreamed
I was a piece of merchandise.
—Harriet Jacobs, *Incidents in the Life of a Slave Girl,* p. 5

S he did not know. Papa's pride, Mama's darling, Grandmother's joy—she did not know she was a slave. Not until she was six, and Mama died. And really not even then. But later, when she was willed to Little Miss, she had to find out. Hatty was a slave.

Harriet Jacobs was born a slave in Edenton, Chowan County, North Carolina, in 1813, twenty-four years after the adoption of the Constitution had firmly established slavery in the newly formed United States. It would be seven years before slavery's spread into new states would be limited by the Missouri Compromise, and a half century before Emancipation. At her birth, there was no reason to think that baby Hatty would live out her life as anything but a slave—yet she not only freed herself and her children, she became an activist and an author, a runaway whose narrative of her life was championed by the abolitionists and feminists and was a weapon in the struggle for emancipation. During the Civil War she went back south, working as a relief worker and an advocate on behalf of the black refugees behind the Union lines in Alexandria and later in Savannah, telling their story in the northern press. When racist violence engulfed the South, she retreated to Massachusetts and then to Washington, D.C., where she died in 1897. Harriet Jacobs was an heroic woman who lived in an heroic time. Committing herself to freedom, she made her life representative of the struggle for liberation.

Harriet Jacobs was born in Edenton because her grandmother Molly had been bought and brought there before the Revolution by a local tavern owner. Originally peopled by the Chowan tribe and settled early,

Edenton was an important port from 1771 to 1776, when North Carolina was a British colony. Trade boomed: 828 ships cleared the port, a quarter of them bound for New England and nearly half for the West Indies. They carried exports from the pine forests—barrel staves, shingles, tar, and deerskins; from the farms—corn, cane, tobacco, cattle, and hogs; and from the water—fish. The largest imports were rum, molasses, salt, and linen. After the Revolution, however, prosperity ended. In 1783 a traveler, eyeing the derelict ships in the harbor, doubted that Edenton would ever reclaim its trade. "It appears that most vessels entering the Sound pass by the town." He was decidedly unimpressed by Edenton's inhabitants—"The white men are all the time complaining that the blacks will not work, and they themselves do nothing. . . . We lived at a regular tavern where . . . half a dozen negroes were running about the house all day, and nothing was attended to, unless one saw to it himself." It was to just such an inn, Horniblow's Tavern, that the child Molly, Harriet Jacobs's grandmother, was taken as a slave.

Molly was one of three children of a slave woman and her South Carolina master. At his death during the Revolution, Molly's father had freed his black family and sent them under British protection to St. Augustine. On the journey, they were captured by Americans, separated, and sold. Edenton's John Horniblow bought Molly while he was traveling, probably in 1780, and took her back to his tavern. There she grew to adulthood, becoming, over the years, "an indispensable personage in the household, officiating in all capacities"[ILSG p. 6]. The tavern's central location next to the courthouse, and its role as a public house in a seaport, guaranteed that the observant slave girl knew whatever was going on.

When Molly could slip away—from dusting, sweeping, and making up the beds, from bringing in the water and wood, from peeling and chopping, clearing away, washing up, scrubbing, and scouring—she could run down to the harbor where piles of farm products were shipped out and manufactured goods were shipped in. On a bright June day in 1785, these were not the only cargoes. The port was astir with news that the brig *Camden* had arrived with a cargo of Africans in its hold, fresh from the Guinea coast after a seven-month voyage. A visiting London merchant commented, "a hundred slaves aboard in the state of nature (women and men). They talk a most curious lingo, are extremely black, with elegant white teeth. . . . They are all from twenty to twenty-five years of age." The slave girl Molly, like everyone in town, knew that they had been bought to dig a seven-mile canal and drain a lake across the Sound from Edenton, and that it was to be finished by Christmas, if the rain would stop.

Four years later, Edenton celebrated the adoption of the federal Constitution: at dawn, the Union flag was flown from a staff in the center of town, and the ships in the harbor hoisted their colors; at noon a salute was fired by a dozen "24 pounders"; and at sundown, the courthouse cupola was lighted by twelve lanterns suspended from the flagstaff. (Because Rhode Island had not adopted the Constitution, the thirteenth lantern was kept dark.) According to the census, in 1790 Edenton consisted of about 150 houses, and its population numbered about 1,000 black slaves—half owned by five large slaveholders—and 600 whites, a third of whom owned no slaves. (Most of the slaves were numbered as residents because their owners lived in town, although they themselves lived and worked on the farms nearby.) The unequal distribution of wealth among the whites occasioned complaints, and the local paper deplored both the presence of young men "lolling in tavern piazzas and . . . gaping and sauntering about the public rooms," and criticized the "fine fat hogs in our streets." With the adoption of the federal Constitution, shipping revived. But in 1795, a hurricane closed Roanoke Inlet, destroying the most direct passage from Albemarle Sound to the Atlantic. Then as the century closed, work began on the Dismal Swamp Canal from Redding (now Elizabeth City) through the Great Dismal Swamp, connecting the Albemarle Sound to the Virginia markets at Norfolk and Portsmouth. Opened to flatboats in 1805, this canal—"to North Carolina a *blood*-sucker at her very vitals"—impoverished Edenton as it enriched her Virginia rivals, and it guaranteed that a sea-lane would never be cut through the Outer Banks.

Like every slave, Molly was conscious of the violence of the slavery system, and the 1791 revolution in Santo Dominigo, today called Haiti, must have underscored that awareness. At the nearby island—with a population of 30,000 whites, 40,000 mulattoes and free blacks, and 400,000 slaves—the slaves rose, demanding the rights proclaimed in the French Revolution. The consequence was bloody. Although the revolt was put down, in 1793 Haiti became the first country in the Western Hemisphere to abolish chattel slavery. Whites fled, and Edenton, like other southern ports, experienced an influx of French-speaking refugees.

The refugee Haitians had reason to be terrified of rebellious slaves, and their fear was contagious. In the wake of the events on the island, Edenton, like other southern settlements, became increasingly aware of the potential threat posed by its slave population. In 1808, in an effort to end nighttime thefts by fugitive slaves hiding in the woods and the swamps (called "pocosin"), the town imposed a curfew and mounted a patrol to enforce it. The *Edenton Gazette* reported in March 1811 that "a party of men, in scouring . . . Cabarrus's Pocosin, came across a Negro Camp, which contained 5 runaway Negroes, 2 wenches and 3 fellows, who were armed." After capturing both women and shooting and killing two of the men—the third escaped—they found "a vast deal of plunder . . . together with a great number of keys" to houses and outbuildings. Their concern, the paper continues, was not only theft. "These fellows, we are credibly informed, had bid defiance to any force whatever, and were resolved to stand their ground: which resolution was exemplified by the resistance they were about to make. Each fellow stood with his musket pointed, watching a favorable opportunity." The report further charges that the fugitives' camps, called "maroons," were encouraged by "some of the dram-shop gentry on the wharf, that are suffered to vend their articles at an unseasonable hour of the night, and on the Sabbath."

In June 1812, when America declared war on Great Britain, Edenton's trade—like that of all American ports—collapsed. A year later, local militia units were mustered to prevent a British squadron from landing troops, but the enemy ships, unable to cross the shallow bar, never reached the town. The war intensified the fears of white Edenton concerning the danger their slaves represented. That summer, a worried resident urged that everyone "who has not arms in his house; immediately procure them." He feared, he explained, that in defending themselves against the foreign enemy they might ignore "that which may spring up in our bosom!"

Property lists reveal that by this time Molly had become the mother of five children. (They say nothing of the children's fathers.) After her master's death, she was owned by his widow, Elizabeth Horniblow. Over the years, as Elizabeth's daughters married, she would give each bride one of Molly's daughters as a wedding gift: Molly's Betty would go to Mary Matilda, and Becky to Eliza. To Margaret, an invalid who would never marry, Elizabeth had already given Molly's Delilah.

Delilah, according to her daughter Harriet, was "a slave merely in name, but in nature . . . noble and womanly." Hatty was only six when her mother died. When in adulthood she wrote *Incidents in the Life of a Slave Girl*, her autobiography, she offered her readers no memories of her mother's height or weight, posture, gesture, or expression, but she did specify her color. Both her parents were "a light shade of brownish yellow, and were termed mulattoes" [ILSG, p. 5]. Jacobs also writes that she often recalls her mother's last blessing. Unlike her brother John who, two years younger, kept merely "a slight recollection" of Delilah, Jacobs reports that "in many an hour of tribulation I . . . seemed to hear her voice, sometimes chiding me, sometimes whispering loving words into my wounded heart." It is her mother's voice—not her face—that lived in Jacobs's memory.

Of her father she wrote more. When, where, and how Delilah met and married Elijah, we do not know. But Jacobs mentions a ring and reports that—although for slaves, marriage had no legal force—their wedding was not without ceremony. Because Elijah lived on for six years after Delilah's death, Hatty and her brother had more time to know him, and both evoke a fuller sense of the man. Elijah was born on the Knox plantation in nearby Pasquotank County, probably to Athena, a slave of Dr. Andrew Knox. His father was apparently Henry Jacobs, an illiterate white farmer who owned no slaves and who lived with his wife and children across the county line in Perquimans, within a mile of the Knox plantation. Elijah grew up on the Knox place and, although illiterate, became a skilled carpenter. Trusted by his owners, he worked on houses in the country and in town, where he met and married Molly Horniblow's daughter Delilah. Even after Dr. Knox moved away in 1812, Elijah was permitted to remain in Edenton with his wife and children. Her father, Jacobs writes, was so "skilful in his trade, that, when buildings out of the common line were to be erected, he was sent for" [ILSG p. 5]. "By his nature," she recalls, "as well as by the habit of transacting business as a skilful mechanic, [he] had more of the feelings of a freeman than is common among slaves" [ILSG p. 9]. From their father, little John and Hatty learned to value themselves and to prize both education and liberty. His daughter writes that his "strongest wish was to purchase his children" [ILSG p. 5]. His son spells out his tortured life as the father of slaves. "To be a man, and not to be a man—a father without authority—a husband and no protector—is the darkest of fates. My father," he testifies, "taught me to hate slavery, but forgot to teach me how to conceal my hatred. I could frequently perceive the pent-up agony of his soul, although he tried hard to conceal it in his own breast. The knowledge that he was a slave himself, and that his children were also slaves, embittered his life, but made him love us the more" [TT in ILSG p. 208].

Hatty was proud of her father's carpentry skills, and as she grew old enough to explore the neighborhood, she perhaps recognized Elijah's expert workmanship in the federal portico at elegant Beverly Hall, or in the unusual drilled spiral molding on James Iredell's double porch. She was familiar with the barrel-vaulted ceiling and square bell tower and spire of St. Paul's, where she had been baptized, and with the impressive Georgian county courthouse, with its brick walls and handsome cupola at the end of the green. Yet Harriet Jacobs never describes the town's architectural beauty. What she does write is that her family "lived together in a comfortable home" [ILSG p. 5].

This home became a model she would spend her life trying to replicate for her own children. Jacobs probably spent her first "six years of happy childhood" with her father, mother, and little brother in one of the outbuildings behind Horniblow's Tavern on King Street, with kin all around her—her grandmother Molly, who through her decades at the tavern worked "in all capacities, from cook and wet nurse to seamstress," her uncle Mark Ramsey, her aunts Betty and Becky, and her uncle Joseph, only a few years older than she [ILSG pp. 5–6].

Nurtured by this extended family, little Hatty blossomed. Her eyes dazzled by the sunshine illuminating Albemarle Sound, her ears delighted by the arrival of the stagecoach driver, who came "tearing down . . . [Broad] Street, his horses in full canter, blowing his long tin horn, heralding his approach as he drew up in front of Horniblow's Tavern," Molly's cherished granddaughter led a charmed life. She knew no threatening master. Actually, neither her mother nor her grandmother had a master, but instead answered to a mistress. And because her mother was not, like Grandmother Molly, wet nurse to her mistress's baby, Hatty was not displaced at the breast, as her mother Delilah had been. Harriet Jacobs's later life testifies that her family successfully protected the bright-eyed little girl, whom they "fondly shielded" in these earliest years [ILSG pp. 5].

The most joyous season for all Edenton children, black and white, was Christmas, when the Jon Kuners appeared. Wildly costumed, complete with cow horns and tails, singing lyrics composed for the occasion and beating out exciting rhythms on the gumbo box, jawbones, and triangles, large troops of slave men from the plantations danced into town early Christmas morning. This was a gloriously liberating time. Openly confronting their masters, the Jon Kuners begged money and rum, and if denied, ridiculed the whites, sarcastically singing, "Poor massa, so dey say; / Down in de heel, so dey say; / Got no money, so dey say; / Not one shillin, so dey say; / God A'mighty bress you, so dey say." Like this song, the festival, perhaps imported from the West Indies, echoes African songs of derision. Jacobs later recalled that "every child rises early on Christmas morning to see the Johnkannaus" [ILSG pp. 118–119]. After noon, when they had gone, came the feasting and the presents.

Festival time lasted from Christmas to New Year's Hiring Day. On January 1, everyone went down to the Market House to watch the spectacle. Jacobs describes how, on New Year's Eve, the slaves "gather together their little alls, or more properly speaking, their little nothings, and wait anxiously for the dawning of day. At the appointed hour the grounds are thronged with men, women, and children, waiting, like criminals, to hear their doom pronounced" [ILSG p. 15]. Crowding around a master they thought kind, the people begged him to hire them for the year. Little Hatty, living at the tavern in the center of town, could not be shielded from such scenes—could perhaps not be shielded from much at all, except the knowledge that she herself was a slave.

But hiding that knowledge could not protect her from the fact that her entire life was shaped by the slave society in which she lived. She was only three years old when the Chowan County Court empowered the sheriff to raise a troop to capture eleven "runaway Negroes," ordering that if they did not surrender, "any person or persons may kill and destroy the said Slaves . . . by such means as he or they may think proper . . . without incurring any penalty." Next day, the grand jury indicted a number of slaveholders, accusing them of permitting their slaves to use the fugitives' stolen money to buy the runaways gunpowder or lead, and to steal guns for them out of the courthouse. Is it possible that the little girl underfoot in the tavern kitchen did not hear of this?

She was four when slavery intruded into her home, partially shattering her carefully fostered security. The family circle was broken on January 1, 1818, when Hatty's twelve-year-old uncle Joseph was moved out of the tavern after being sold to Josiah Collins the Younger. Like many other slaves, Joseph—who seemed "more like my brother than my uncle"—was sold because of events in his owner's family. Molly's master had left four heirs when he died, and by the time his estate was finally settled, Molly had five children. The heirs divided her older children among themselves, then sold off the youngest and split the cash. Hatty, who saw her invincible grandmother reduced to tears, understood that Joseph's sale was "a terrible blow" [ILSG p. 6]. The lesson was not lost on the little girl. No matter how strong the family, slavery could tear it apart.

There was no way that her protective family could shield Hatty from knowing Joseph was sold. Nor could they keep her from knowing about the slave sales held at the tavern. On the first of January 1819, Dr. James Norcom advertised that he would auction off a plantation, one or two men, and two women "with 8 children (3 of which are large enough to take into service) at Mrs. Horniblow's tavern." That spring another newspaper ad announced: "To be sold before Mrs. Horniblow's Tavern in Edenton 2 town lots, Negro woman Peggy & her three children Miles, Hardy & Rosetta, under a deed of trust given by Charles & Mary Bissell. Joseph B. Skinner, trustee." Try as her family might to make little Hatty's home "comfortable," the Horniblow Tavern functioned as a hub of Edenton's slave society.

The family could try to make the little girl feel safe, but they could not protect her from knowing the violence of the slave system. In February, an armed raid on a fugitives' camp in the swamp resulted in the capture of an outlaw the *Edenton Gazette* called "Dilworth," known as "General Jackson." This man, it claims, was "the noted ringleader of the band of runaway Negroes, who have for a long time been depredating upon the property of the good citizens of this Town and County." The same issue of the paper also reports a pitched gunbattle between "a number of gentlemen" and "another gang of . . . desperadoes." "Approaching their camp, which was in a hollow gum [tree], sufficiently large to contain six persons with much comfort, JACK (commonly called Jack Stump) late the property of Mr. Edward Haughton, dec'd, but now said to belong to Mr. John Bond, of Bertie [County], was shot, of which wound he died the following day. He had fired twice, and was in the act of loading again, when he received the contents of several charged pieces. He was in company with Bristol, belonging to the estate of Thomas Vail, dec'd, and fought with the but end of his musket until he was dragged out of the hollow nearly exhausted." No matter how "fondly shielded," certainly little Hatty heard this news.

That April, Edenton experienced a different kind of excitement. President James Monroe arrived with an entourage to investigate the possibility of revitalizing the harbor and invigorating the economy by building an outlet from Albemarle Sound to the ocean. Boarding the new steam ferry linking Edenton to Plymouth, the notables proceeded to Nag's Head and Roanoke Island, then returned for the festivities. That day—if her grandmother Molly was one of the cooks preparing the elegant public dinner served in the paneled upstairs room at the courthouse—Hatty had to finish her chores quickly and then stay away from the enticing smells of the kitchen, with pots simmering on the fire and fancy loaves baking in the hot ovens.

To many, the town's celebratory twenty-one-gun salute at the President's visit overshadowed the talk of gun battles in the swamp. But not to Edenton's blacks who, like Elijah, thirsted for freedom. In May 1819, the paper reported renewed terror: "On Tuesday evening last Negro *Shadrach*, formerly the property of Dr. Norcom, who had been a runaway for near two years, was shot near this town, and expired next morning. He had long been depredating upon property of the inhabitants of this town, and county; and was discovered lurking round the house of a widow lady . . . with a view, no doubt, of ascertaining whether she had any person to protect her, that he might plunder with impunity. She, however, unknown to him, had a boy about 14 years of age in the house . . . that pulled the fatal trigger. Shadrach, we believe, belonged to some person in the western country."

That year Harriet Jacobs's mother died, and the little girl's "fondly shielded" early childhood ended. On her deathbed, Delilah gave Hatty her blessing, and her mistress Margaret Horniblow promised the dying woman that her children "should never suffer for any thing" [ILSG p. 7]. It was then, at age six, that Harriet Jacobs discovered that she herself was a slave. At the time, however, this knowledge meant little. Hatty, who so sorely missed her mother, continued to live at the tavern with her nurturing family under the protection of Miss Margaret, who did indeed fulfil her promise to her dying slave.

Although only in her early twenties, Miss Margaret was a very sick woman. While the details of her illness are not known, its severity is clear. In a letter written the year before Jacobs's mother died, the doctor reports that Miss Margaret seemed somewhat better, "gaining flesh and Strength" on a new regimen. But later, at about the time she promised to care for little Hatty and John, she was "still unable to walk without pain & deformity." Nevertheless, under her protection and surrounded by family, Delilah's children grew finely, their lives enriched by the presence of their father Elijah, who was allowed to stay with them when working in Edenton, as when their mother was alive.

Prosperity returned to the town with the end of the War of 1812 and "it was common to see from twenty to sixty sail of vessels within the harbor, where the immense piles of staves, hundreds of hogsheads of sugar and molasses covered the wharves, and great quantities of produce filled the warehouses." Now the world of Delilah's children expanded. It is not clear whether old Miss Elizabeth herself did the daily shopping for the tavern kitchen, or whether each morning Grandmother Molly went down to the market on the wharf to bargain with the farmers for eggs, butter, fowl, and garden vegetables, then on to the fish market for the day's catch. (She could have bought fresh meat from the town's butcher, but might have preferred to shop for flitches of bacon and hams salted and cured in the country.) If Molly did the daily marketing, she could have taken Hatty with her on her daily rounds. As "grandmother's child," the little girl enjoyed a privileged place in the black community, where skilled house servants like Molly, who were owned by people of substance, had status.

Six times each year during "court week," Horniblow's Tavern was packed full. Then the judges sat, and everyone with legal business— plaintiffs, defendants, witnesses, and jurymen—crowded the streets. "Temporary booths for the sale of cakes, pies and other refreshments, mostly kept by Negro women, abound in the neighborhood of the Court House," a visitor noted, "and there are also numerous 'tobacco wagons,' which resemble, by their large size and huge canvas tops, the Western emigrant wains." In addition to those connected with the courts were "people who have no court business . . . [who] assemble for the purpose of paying and collecting debts, purchasing mules, harness, &c., 'making trades,' talking politics, and too many . . . to have a spree. There is generally a smart sprinkling of drovers, horse-jockeys, auctioneers of books and jewelry, gamblers [and] dentists." Whether or not Grandmother Molly kept a booth, to Hatty and the other children, court week was as good as the occasional visiting circus.

The little girl's world was expanding in other ways as well. During these years Miss Margaret taught her two skills that would shape her life. Sewing was a marketable skill Jacobs would later use to support herself and her children. Reading and spelling—knowledge that would soon become illegal to impart to slaves—gave her the ability to transform her world and to write about her life. In 1819, the year Miss Margaret assumed responsibility for Delilah's children, the trustees of the Edenton Academy announced the addition of "two accomplished Female Teachers to take charge of the education of young ladies." They offered "Spelling, Reading, Writing, Geography & Grammar" at $5.00 a quarter, and "The above with Needle Work $6." Miss Margaret did not attempt to duplicate the academy's entire curriculum for her slave girl.

She did, however, teach Hatty the rudiments—probably from her own "Blue Back Speller," used not only for spelling, but for reading and moral instruction. From her own prayer books, she taught Hatty "the precepts of God's word." More than thirty years afterward Jacobs, testing her writing skills by composing letters to the newspapers, commented: "the spelling I believe was evry word correct punctuation I did not attempt for I never studied Grammer there fore I know nothing about it but I have taken the hint and will commence that one study with all my soul." Later, writing her life story, she testified to her gratitude for Miss Margaret's extraordinary gift of literacy. "For this privilege, which so rarely falls to the lot of a slave, I bless her memory" [ILSG p. 8].

Despite the rare indulgence of her young mistress, however, and despite the loving presence of her family, the child could not be shielded from the bitter realities of slavery. In the spring after Mother Delilah's death, Grandmother's mistress celebrated the marriage of her daughter Eliza by giving away the third of Molly's daughters as a wedding present, and Aunt Becky vanished from Hatty's life.

After this loss an event occurred that Jacobs would later record in her autobiography. In the only story about either of her parents included in her book, she raises a crucial question: to whom did she and her brother owe allegiance and obedience? Whose—and ultimately, who—are they?

> One day, when . . . [my little brother's] . . . father and his mistress had happened to call him at the same time, he hesitated between the two; being perplexed to know which had the strongest claim upon his obedience. He finally concluded to go to his mistress. When my father reproved him for it, he said, "You both called me, and I didn't know which I ought to go to first."
>
> "You are *my* child," replied our father, "and when I call you, you should come immediately, if you have to pass through fire and water." [ILSG p. 9].

The lesson was not lost on Hatty and John. Nothing and no one comes before family.

In Hatty's twelfth year, everything changed. Grandmother's mistress Elizabeth Horniblow rented out the tavern and moved into lodgings, taking with her her sick daughter Margaret, her maid Nancy, and young Hatty, and sending nine-year-old John to work in the office of her son-in-law

Dr. James Norcom. Then, three months after the children were uprooted, they were separated from their father because Elijah's young mistress married a man who forbade him from hiring out his time. Determined to assert his mastery over his wife's carpenter slave, James Coffield ordered Hatty's father to leave his family and move out to Green Hall plantation. For Elijah, the move from Edenton must have been particularly hard, since it separated him both from his children and from his new wife Theresa, a free woman. Their son—named Elijah for his father—was born on December 15, 1824. Soon after, Grandmother's mistress gave up her rented town quarters and moved to Dr. Norcom's plantation, apparently entrusting to her sister Hannah Pritchard her daughter Margaret, who was doubtless too sick to be removed from her doctor's care.

Miss Margaret wrote her will that spring, when it became evident even to her slave girl Hatty that her health was failing. Grateful for the care and instruction she had received, the child loved her mistress and prayed for her recovery, but on July 3, Miss Margaret died. After the funeral at St. Paul's, Hatty was sent to her grandmother at the tavern. Recalling her mistress's many kindnesses, she "could not help having some hopes that she had left me free. My friends were almost certain it would be so. They thought she would be sure to do it, on account of my mother's love and faithful service" [ILSG p. 7]. They were mistaken. Decades later Jacobs recorded their profound disappointment. "So vanished our hopes. My mistress had taught me the precepts of God's Word: 'Thou shalt love thy neighbor as thyself.' . . . But I was her slave, and I suppose she did not recognize me as her neighbor. I would give much to blot out from my memory that one great wrong" [ILSG p. 8].

Margaret Horniblow had owned five members of Jacobs's family, but her will freed none of them. Instead, Miss Margaret left all of her surviving slaves to her mother Elizabeth Horniblow, Grandmother Molly's mistress—a decision that kept them together, but that also kept them enslaved. Then when her will was read, it was revealed that on the day she died, Miss Margaret had changed her mind. In the presence of her physician, Dr. James Norcom (who was also her brother-in-law), she had apparently added a codicil on behalf of her niece, Norcom's three-year-old daughter. It reads: "It is my will & desire that the foregoing device be so far altered, that my negro girl Harriet be given to my niece Mary Matilda Norcom Daughter of Dr James Norcom, and I further give & bequeath to my said niece my bureau & work table & their contents."

This deathbed codicil condemned twelve-year-old Hatty to enslavement in Dr. Norcom's house.

Although witnessed by Dr. Norcom and by one Henry Flury, the codicil was never signed. Still, it is clear that Miss Margaret did not free her young slave girl—and that Harriet Jacobs was justified when, at midlife, she wrote that she and her family felt betrayed. "Notwithstanding my grandmother's long and faithful service to her owners, not one of her children escaped the auction block. . . . As a child, I loved my mistress; and, looking back on the happy days I spent with her, I try to think with less bitterness of this act of injustice" [ILSG p. 8]. Miss Margaret had not only left Hatty a slave, she had left her a slave in Dr. Norcom's household. Or had she? Was it Miss Margaret who dictated—and then did not sign—that codicil? Or was it Dr. Norcom himself, who seized the opportunity to control his sister-in-law's bright young slave girl? Although no one contested the validity of the document, and it seems certain that Jacobs never even knew that it was not signed, it is possible that Miss Margaret died believing that after her death, Delilah's children would belong to her mother and that they would continue to stay with their Grandmother Molly and Uncle Mark. Surely Miss Margaret betrayed her slave girl's hopes by not giving her her freedom, but it is possible that she might not have committed that second betrayal, that she might not have sent her twelve-year-old favorite into the home of Dr. James Norcom, a man who would prove to be a lecher.

2

My Puny Arm Felt Strong

❧

When he told me that I was made for his use . . . that I was nothing
but a slave, whose will must and should surrender to his, never
before had my puny arm felt half so strong.
—Harriet Jacobs, *Incidents in the Life of a Slave Girl,* p. 18

Young Hatty came to think Dr. James Norcom a monster, and many of his neighbors might have agreed. Norcom, Chowan County born, was nearly fifty when his late sister-in-law's twelve-year-old slave girl entered his household. He was a quarrelsome, complex man, capable of both an intellectual's expansiveness and an egotist's bigotry. Committed and hard-working professionally, in his private life he was intense, controlling, and unforgiving. The town knew his scandalous history. In a community where divorce required the action of the legislature, in 1808 Norcom had petitioned the North Carolina legislature for a divorce from his first wife, Mary, charging her with "an imprudent and inordinate attachment to opium and intoxicating liquors," with domestic mismanagement, and with delivering a stillborn child that was not his. Although his wife was defended by her male relations, Norcom's divorce was granted. Two years later, he married old Mrs. Horniblow's daughter Mary, who at sixteen was only half his age. (Perhaps to blunt bitter memories of his first wife, he called his young bride "Maria.")

Among Norcom's papers is an undated fragment of musings on the "charming and bewitching Sex." Exclaiming that women are both "the pride the joy the Heaven of my existence" and "the bitterest of earthly curses," he wrote, "In the prime & vigour of life, & in the Zenith of my day, I never intently sought the favour of woman that I did not obtain it; and I glory in recollecting even now the transport of bliss that I have felt in the arms of pure & unadulterated love. But awful has been the reverse when the Scene has changed: when deceit dissim[ulation], & falsehood have taken the place of truth & Sincerity. . . . Then it is that you are made our most terrible tormentors & become demons incarnate. Oh! it is terrible, infinitely terrible to be hated by a woman. All is said that can be said when it is asserted that her hatred is as cordial & as strong as her love." Norcom's testimony to the force of his sexual passions and to the intensity of a woman's fury is perhaps rooted in his disastrous relationship with his first wife. But it certainly spelled trouble for the attractive young slave girl entering his household.

Hatty did not want to live under Norcom's roof, and she later recalled that "it was not without murmuring that I prepared for my new home" [ILGS p. 9]. Nonetheless, as the property of Miss Mary Matilda, age three, Hatty had no choice. In late July 1825, she fastened a pretty little pin—her most valuable possession—into her bundle, her mind filled with worry about her "spirited" brother, John. Willed by Miss Margaret to Elizabeth Horniblow and then loaned to Norcom, now he, too, must move into Dr. Norcom's household. There, she feared, he "was now to learn his first lesson of obedience to a master" [ILSG p. 9]. Carrying her things out to King Street, Hatty turned onto Broad and walked left. A year earlier, the doctor had moved his family into an old house in Eden Alley. Two rooms deep and two stories tall, with a double tier porch in front, the building housed Norcom, the pregnant Maria, and their six children. Their house slaves—Ben, Tom, Diver, Esther (the long-suffering cook), and most important to Harriet, her Aunt Betty, "the *factotum* of the household"—lived in the outbuildings.

At the Norcoms', Hatty and John "encountered cold looks, cold words, and cold treatment." Even the dog was unfriendly, "a nuisance in the house" [ILSG pp. 9, 12]. Despite Aunt Betty's presence, Hatty cried herself to sleep that first night. A few weeks later, she awakened to sounds that would ring in her ears for decades: the hiss of a whip, accompanied by the pitiful pleas of a slave. Next morning at the workhouse, the young girl saw the bloody wet lash, smelled its stench, and heard the people whispering that a man had been beaten for accusing the master of fathering his wife's light-skinned child. To the twelve-year-old girl, at the Norcoms' sex and violence seemed to clog the very air.

Hatty was uneasy. Although she quickly became fond of her three-year old Little Miss, after hearing Mrs. Norcom say that the child was afraid of her and only pretended affection, Hatty did not know what to think. Still, she began to find her place in the household. Dressing and caring for Mary Matilda was her responsibility, but when Little Miss slept, she was kept busy helping with household chores. Over the winter, Hatty learned from Aunt Betty the best ways to dust and clean, to polish silver and set the table, to do the churning and boil the laundry, and how correctly to answer the door when visitors came to call.

In spring, already shaken by a young friend's death, Hatty suffered a far greater shock. She had not even heard that her father was sick when Grandmother met her with the terrible news that he had died. Elijah's death ended his ceaseless effort to free his children. Both Harriet and John later testified to their father's determination to liberate them, and to his ongoing sense of outrage at his own enslavement. His master's order separating Elijah from his new wife and baby and from his growing children had dealt a devastating blow, and "added another link to his galling chain—sent another arrow to his bleeding heart." As a result, their father, "who had an intensely acute feeling of the wrongs of slavery, sank into a state of mental dejection, which, combined with bodily illness, occasioned his death."

Learning of Elijah's death, Hatty passionately "rebelled against God, who had taken from me mother, father, mistress, and friend." Inconsolable, she refused to listen when Grandmother tried to offer comfort by suggesting that perhaps God was sparing the dead from evils yet to come. (These words would echo later.) The Norcoms, she knew, condemned Elijah because they thought he "had spoiled his children, by teaching them to feel that they were human beings. This was blasphemous doctrine for a slave to teach; presumptuous in him, and dangerous to the masters" [ILSG p. 10]. Next day, following Elijah's body to the grave dug next to her mother's at Providence in the woods, Hatty angrily thought of her mistress, who had ordered her to decorate the house for a party "while the dead body of my father was lying within a mile of me" [ILSG p. 10].

Elijah's burial at Providence symbolized his independent spirit. Providence was perhaps the only place in Edenton where he had been able to give expression to his "feelings of a freeman" [ILSG p. 9]. Since 1787, the State of North Carolina had prohibited free blacks from entertaining slaves in their homes on Sunday or at night. The law was generally unenforceable—some families were part free and part slave. But black people could legally be punished for meeting together, and Edenton had at times mounted a nightwatch and cracked down on activities in Cheapside down by the water, where seamen could find liquor and companionship as well as food and lodging. Despite such surveillance, the people devised ways to meet away from the watchful eyes of the whites. Providence was their crowning effort to create their own space.

Providence was the name they gave the tract of land they bought communally, and the name they gave everything they built on that land: their graveyard, their "little church in the woods," and two or three small buildings they put up [ILSG p. 67]. It was created in 1818, when four men of Grandmother's generation—Alfred Churton, Thomas Barnswell, Jeffrey G. Iredell, and George Bonner, a cabinetmaker, a tailor, a barber, and a carpenter, two born free and two emancipated—had bought this block of lots on an isolated site at the edge of town. Bordered north and south by Carteret and Albemarle streets, the land ran down to the swamps and Filbert Creek on the west. When beavers built their dams, the creek flooded the eastern boundary on Mosely Street, leaving only a narrow path at the north. Here on this providentially inaccessible plot they built their meeting house and established their cemetery. This graveyard became the burial plot of dozens of black communicants of St. Paul's, and of many others—including an African American veteran of North Carolina's 10th Regiment, Continental Line in the Revolutionary War. Here Hatty's father had buried Delilah and planted a tree on her grave. Now, five years later, Hatty and John watched as he was laid beside her. (Providence would be forgotten and later, by the turn of the century, it would revert to wilderness. Then rediscovered, it was cleared and reconsecrated in February 2001.)

If the Norcom house had seemed cold to Hatty before her father's death, now it felt like ice. Nevertheless, her life settled into the routine of tending to little Mary Matilda and helping Aunt Betty with her endless work. Both she and John resented their positions in the crowded household. In particular she hated the coarse "linsey-woolsey" shift Mrs. Norcom issued each winter. In Hatty's eyes, it was a badge of slavery. She relied on Grandmother to provide better things, and when sent on errands, often stopped at Molly's kitchen for a treat. The first time Hatty was punished, one of Grandmother's gifts was the cause. It was snowing, and when Hatty wore the new shoes Molly had given her, they squeaked. Irritated by the noise, Mrs. Norcom ordered her to take them off and threatened that she would burn them up if Hatty wore them again. Outraged, the twelve-year-old slave girl obeyed, but then—instead of putting on the heavy slave shoes Mrs. Norcom issued—she angrily stripped off her stockings and defiantly marched out barefoot into the snow to run her mistress' errand. She came back sick and went to bed fantasizing that when she died of her cold, her mistress would grieve. But by morning, Hatty was well, and afterward, when she knew Mrs. Norcom better, she realized that her mistress would not have mourned the passing of "the little imp" [ILSG p. 19]. Years later, recounting this incident, she suggested that even as a young girl, she had demanded just treatment. She also suggested that at age twelve, she had not yet learned not to expect justice from her mistress.

Hatty and her brother were constantly thinking about freedom. At nearby Elizabeth City, it was reported that "twenty eight negroes belonging to the Society of Friends, and four who were free, left this place for Norfolk, to take passage in the brig *Doris*, Capt. Mathews, which sails shortly for Liberia." Such news spread quickly through Edenton's black community. In their preoccupation with freedom, Hatty and John were strongly influenced by Grandmother's youngest son. Only a few years older than Hatty, Joseph—although now owned by Josiah Collins the Younger and separated from the family—remained an important presence in their lives. Then one day, John brought catastrophic news. Joseph, whipped for obeying too slowly, had fought back, throwing his young master to the ground. Rather than submit to a public whipping, he decided to run. He managed to get away from Edenton, but unluckily a hurricane struck near Dover Beach, Princess Anne County, and his escape ship made for the port. There the captain, seeing a "wanted" ad, recognized Joseph and had him bound in chains. When the storm passed, the ship proceeded to New York. Joseph managed to get away in the city, but was later spotted by his master's lawyer, Joseph B. Skinner, captured, and returned to Edenton. Hatty was among the crowd watching as, "ghastly pale, yet full of determination," he was paraded in chains up Broad Street from the public wharf to the jail [ILSG p. 21].

Although Joseph was not allowed visitors, at midnight Hatty and Grandmother disguised themselves and were admitted by the sympathetic jailer. Writing at midlife, Harriet Jacobs vividly recalled the scene: the stripes of moonlight filtered through the barred window, the clanking of the chains, the coldness of Joseph's fingers when she clasped his hands. As months passed, his punishment was softened. The chains were removed, and Hatty and Grandmother were permitted to bring him warm suppers—along with treats for the jailer. But Joseph expressed defiance and was again chained. Confined in the dungeon, which was notorious for its "almost total exclusion of light and fresh air," and "almost always be-dewed with moisture," Joseph was quartered with men covered with filth and became infested with vermin. After several months, he was sold to a slave trader. "His face too pale, his form too thin," he said his good-byes to the family [ILSG p. 23]. Hatty gave him her precious pin as a keepsake and watched as the trader handcuffed her uncle while Grandmother clutched at him, pleading that he be spared. Then he was gone.

Later, the family heard that he had escaped from New Orleans and reached Baltimore, where—who could have thought?—he encountered his old master's neighbor. Northern-born Daniel McDowell did not betray the runaway, and when he returned home, he brought greetings from Joseph to his grieving mother. Still later, the family had another bit of news. Harriet's Uncle Mark, working on an Edenton–New York sloop, reported that he had met his younger brother in New York City. He told Joseph that their mother was trying to raise the money to buy him, but reported that his brother rejected the offer, saying that he would win his freedom for himself. Was it while rejoicing at the news that Joseph was in the free North that both Harriet and John decided that they would name any future sons for their uncle, to them an heroic figure?

If thoughts of Joseph inspired them, their condition as slaves was for-ever etched into their consciousness on January 1, 1828. Grandmother's mistress, Elizabeth Horniblow, had recently died. January 1st was the day that Norcom sold Elizabeth's slaves, along with her other property, at public auction. Among those put up for sale were three members of the fam-ily: Hatty's brother John, her Uncle Mark, and—unbelievably—Grand-mother. When the doctor told Grandmother he planned to sell her privately to spare her embarrassment, she objected. It was common knowledge that her dead mistress had intended to free her and, aware of the esteem in which she was held in the town, Molly insisted that everyone watch as he sold her off to collect the medical bills he claimed he was owed by Elizabeth Horniblow's estate. Seeing her on the block, the crowd hushed and, as Molly anticipated, refused to bid. Then the voice of Hannah Pritchard, the dead woman's sister, quietly offered $52.25, and later she bid $406.00 for Uncle Mark—the second highest price of the day. She was buying them with Grandmother's money. (For years, Molly had been putting aside the cash she earned by baking at night after she finished her daytime tasks, and before the sale, she apparently enlisted the help of old Miss Pritchard and the attorney Alfred M. Gatlin.) Later in the day, Norcom bought John, whom he had earlier borrowed from Elizabeth Horniblow's estate. Long afterward, John wrote from his home in England, "All of us, old and young, male and female, married and single, were sold to the highest bidder. . . . It would be in vain for me to attempt to give a description of my feelings while standing under the auctioneer's hammer: I can safely say that I shall not realize such feelings again" [ILSG p. 209]. His price, to be paid in six months, was $298.50.

Grandmother's strategy was completely successful. In the spring, Gatlin drafted Miss Pritchard's successful petition to the superior court to emancipate Molly. Her free papers issued, Molly moved into Gatlin's empty house on King Street, opened a bakery, and bought her son Mark Ramsey from Miss Pritchard. John later explained that Gatlin sold her his house and arranged for Mark's sale. "It may seem rather strange that my grandmother should hold her son a slave; but the law required it. She was obliged to give security that she would never be any expense to the town or state before she could come in possession of her freedom. Her property in him was sufficient to satisfy the law; he could be sold any minute to pay her debts, though it was not likely this would ever be the case."

Working for the Norcoms kept Hatty and her brother busy—John in Dr. Norcom's office next to Horniblow's Tavern, and Hatty, when she was not watching little Mary Matilda or running errands, in the Norcoms' kitchen and household. She felt some comfort at night sleeping in the outbuilding next to Aunt Betty, but now in her teens, Hatty was becoming a focus of Norcom's attention. She would later sketch two mutually exclusive, mutually complementary, inevitably intertwined models of womanhood:

> I once saw two beautiful children playing together. One was a fair white child; the other was her slave, and also her sister. When I saw them embracing each other, and heard their joyous laughter, I turned sadly away from the lovely sight. I foresaw the inevitable blight that would fall on the little slave's heart. I knew how soon her laughter would be changed to sighs. The fair child grew up to be a still fairer woman. From childhood to womanhood her pathway was blooming with flowers, and overarched by a sunny sky. Scarcely one day of her life had been clouded when the sun rose on her happy bridal morning.
>
> How had those years dealt with her slave sister, the little playmate of her childhood? She, also, was very beautiful; but the flowers and sunshine of love were not for her. She drank the cup of sin, and shame, and misery, whereof her persecuted race are compelled to drink. [ILSG p. 29].

According to this model, in which Edenton's teenaged daughters were either "young Misses" or "slave girls," Harriet Jacobs would inevitably live out her life as "Hatty." Norcom was repeatedly insisting that his slave girl obey his every command, and his most pressing command was that she submit to his sexual demands. Her later description of his methods of intimidation, alternating "stormy, terrific ways, that made his victims tremble," with "a gentleness that he thought must surely subdue," reads like a psychologist's study of the coercive personality [ILSG p. 27].

Although only in her teens, Jacobs already understood that while Norcom loved money, he loved power more. She later recalled her daily life in his house as a living hell and portrayed the doctor himself as a consummate devil. This view might seem exaggerated (and doubtless her later incarceration bred feelings of persecution), but her assertion that Norcom was implacable in his demand for obedience is borne out by his later treatment of her Young Miss, his beloved daughter Mary Matilda.

Norcom's personal correspondence testifies to his heartfelt affection for this daughter, but only one of her letters is among his papers. Written in her young adulthood, it is a pathetic plea begging her mother to prevail upon her father to forgive her. Mary Matilda had kept company with a man of whom her father disapproved and with whom her brothers quarreled. Although their dispute became violent—her brother horse-whipped her beau in the street, and court records mention shootings and a "riot"—she ran off with her suitor. In her letter, written two years later, she spells out her despair at the death of her baby (whom her family had never seen) and appeals to her mother to effect a reconciliation with her father. Despite this heart-rending plea, Norcom remained unrelenting. From the time Mary Matilda was very young, his letters to her had insisted on obedience: "Let me tell you, my dear, what it is to be a good girl: you must be affectionate & dutiful to your parents, obedient to their wishes & commands, & never do any thing that will displease them." "Surely you could not be so imprudent, so unfeeling, so ungrateful, or, to say all in one word, so undutiful, as to commit an act that would be displeasing to your father." A man who could not tolerate disobedience from his first wife or his beloved daughter, Dr. James Norcom certainly would not permit the open defiance of his slave girl.

Her master's efforts to gain Hatty's sexual compliance aroused her "disgust and hatred"—and her resistance [ILSG p. 27]. Of these years, she later declared: "The war of my life had begun; and though one of God's most powerless creatures, I resolved never to be conquered" [ILSG

p. 19]. Her hopes of finding an ally in her old mistress Mrs. Norcom, however, proved useless. Now in her early thirties and recently delivered of her seventh living child, Maria Norcom was all too familiar with her husband's sexual practices. Instead of offering the teenaged slave girl help, she vented her "jealousy and rage" [ILSG p. 28]. Countermanding her husband's order that Hatty move her bed to his apartment—ostensibly to be near little Mary Matilda—Maria ordered the slave girl to stay where Maria could keep a close watch. Now, waking at night to find her mistress bending above her to listen for any words she might mutter, and stalked by her master during the day, Hatty began to fear for her life. Like other domestic tyrants, Norcom succeeded in enforcing the isolation of his intended victim. He demanded her silence. Years later, Jacobs would write out her fury—breaking the convention that women should not feel passion of any sort, and most particularly should not feel anger. But now the harassed girl, ashamed and embarrassed, could not bring herself to tell her grandmother what was happening.

Then she had news she could tell. She was in love with a free-born black carpenter who wanted to purchase and to marry her. At Grandmother's suggestion, the love-struck Hatty appealed to a friend of her master to try to convince him to permit her lover to buy her. Norcom refused, scornfully asking, "'Do you love this nigger?'" After she said yes, he taunted her. "I supposed you thought more of yourself; that you felt above the insults of such puppies." When she asserted, "If he is a puppy I am a puppy, for we are both of the negro race," he struck her, warning that if he caught her young man "lurking" about the neighborhood, "'I will shoot him as soon as I would a dog'" [ILSG pp. 39–40]. This spelled the death of Hatty's girlish daydreams. Brokenhearted, she sent her suitor away, telling him that their situation was hopeless.

Only a lovelorn teenager could feel the intensity of her desolation. ("Why does the slave ever love?" Jacobs would ask, writing about this years later.) And only a teenager could know the urgency she felt when she heard that Norcom was actually building a house four miles outside of town—away from her watchful grandmother and from his jealous wife—where he planned to install her as his concubine. Desperate, she rehearsed her situation again and again, searching for an alternative to the role of despoiled slave girl.

The women in Harriet Jacobs's family had complex personal histories. In the years after her capture and sale to Edenton's Joseph

Horniblow, Molly had raised five children to adulthood, and Hatty had seen Grandmother win her freedom and buy and emancipate Uncle Mark. No one can be certain about the history of Molly Horniblow's relationships—surely her granddaughter did not know it—but everyone in town called her son Mark by two names, and his surname was not that of his earliest master, as was usual. Instead of being known as Horniblow's Mark or Mark Horniblow, he was called Mark Ramsey. Old-timers remembered Allan Ramsay as a prosperous dry goods merchant and haberdasher who, after being widowed for many years, had died without descendants. A few months after his death, Molly's Mark had been born.

Not only was the parentage of Molly's elder son perhaps a topic for speculation, but there may have been talk at the birth of her youngest. Documents suggest that Joseph, John and Hatty's heroic uncle, might have been fathered by one of the founders of Providence. Records show that when Joseph was twenty-one, Alfred Churton executed a deed leaving his old house on Gale Street in trust and directing that his son Joseph, by an unnamed slave woman, be allowed to use it rent free. But Churton's Joseph never enjoyed his property because he ran away from his master Josiah Collins; and Molly's Joseph ran from Collins at about the same time. Were there two fugitives named Joseph who escaped the Collins place that year? Or were Molly's and Churton's sons the same man?

Gossip or no gossip, through the years, Molly Horniblow had won the respect not only of the black community, but also of white Edenton. By "perseverance and unwearied industry," Grandmother "had become the mistress of a snug little home, surrounded with the necessaries of life." Hatty and her brother "longed for a home like hers. There we always found balsam for our troubles" [ILSG p. 17]. To her adolescent granddaughter, Molly Horniblow—a single mother denied legal marriage who had managed to raise five children and to free herself and her oldest son—certainly presented a model of successful womanhood. And Hatty knew other women who, like Grandmother, were neither ladies nor broken blossoms. Desperate to prevent Norcom from making her his sexual slave, she tried thinking beyond the usual options. Perhaps, she argued to herself, since it was her sexuality that Norcom coveted, she could use that sexuality to stop him. She could become involved with a member of the town's elite—someone with higher status than Norcom, a man he couldn't threaten, a gentleman who would treat his mistress well and perhaps even free any children he might father.

This adolescent fantasy did not seem so unrealistic when she thought of the Cabarrus family. She knew their story: Rose, their mother, had been owned by a member of Edenton's French community who had sold her to his bachelor brother. Auguste Cabarrus made Rose his mistress when she was sixteen, and after the birth of their son and daughter, he freed her and gave her both Charlotte and Leon. Cabarrus's high status eased his petition to emancipate his children through the North Carolina assembly, and more recently, he had made Rose a present of her mother, Mary Sue. By becoming Cabarrus's mistress, Rose had freed her entire family.

Hatty knew, of course, that they had had problems since their protector's death. When cataloguing Cabarrus's effects, the court had not found his gold watch with its chain, key, and topaz seal, and rumor was that Rose had taken it. Apparently furious at the thought that his father's watch might be seized from his mother, Leon stole jewelry from Faribault's store on Broad Street. He was jailed, and Hatty was old enough to remember when an angry crowd of black men had freed him from the prison. But Leon was recaptured, tried, convicted, and sentenced to thirty lashes, to be followed by two months' imprisonment and another whipping. He escaped after the first punishment, but was caught by a posse. Still, to Hatty, the life the Cabarrus family faced as free blacks in Edenton seemed infinitely preferable to what she believed she would suffer as Norcom's sexual slave. She could not bring herself even to think about the lives of any children she might have by him.

In her neighbor Major Sam, she thought she saw a way to stop Norcom and replicate Rose's triumph. Samuel Tredwell Sawyer was young, personable, and single. The oldest son of Margaret Blair and Dr. Mathias Sawyer—a descendant of a colonial governor of North Carolina and a relative of the current governor—he was the scion of a family that wielded both wealth and power. Major Sam had been educated at Edenton Academy and at the College of William and Mary (where he was judged "somewhat deficient in diligence"), then had read law and gained admission to the bar. Now back home, he was having some difficulties establishing a practice in Edenton, and—with time to spare—heard the neighborhood gossip about Mrs. Norcom's "open mouthed" jealousy of her daughter's teenaged slave girl. Sawyer was Grandmother Molly's neighbor, and he interested himself in the family, offering help and finding occasions to talk with her attractive granddaughter. Hatty was grateful for his concern and, impressed by the attention of such an "educated and eloquent" young gentleman, felt some warmth toward him [ILSG p. 54]. She was sure that Norcom would be furious to learn that she was involved with Sawyer—furious enough, she believed, to sell her. And she convinced herself that a man of Sawyer's caliber would, like Cabarrus, buy his mistress, treat her well, and free any babies he might father.

Her mind filled with schemes to escape Norcom and her flesh crawling with his touch, at fifteen, Harriet Jacobs became Samuel Tredwell Sawyer's mistress. Confessing this in her book years later, she revealed virtually nothing about their relationship, not even where and when they met. She only described one scene when they were alone together and she risked capture to beg him to free their children. But clearly they met often, and clearly she became pregnant. Ashamed and worried about Grandmother's response to her pregnancy, she could not resist the urge to tell her tormentor, Norcom.

But when, after Norcom ordered her to his isolated house, she revealed she was carrying another man's child, he left without a word. Amazed, Hatty walked over to Grandmother's to confess everything. She sat down to sew, struggling to compose herself so that she could speak, when Mrs. Norcom appeared and accused her of intimacy with Norcom. Grandmother, who had heard the neighborhood talk, turned upon Hatty. Wrenching Delilah's wedding ring and silver thimble from her hand, she ordered her out of the house. Tears streaming, Hatty left. As she heard the gate close behind her, she knew her childhood had ended.

This is the story that Jacobs's first-person narrator "Linda" tells in *Incidents*. It may seem impossible today to understand how a self-respecting teenager like Hatty could seek freedom through a sexual relationship with a man like Sawyer. It is, however, clear that at fifteen, she did not have the option of choosing virginity, nor did she have the option of choosing marriage with a young man she loved. Loathing Norcom, when presented with his demand that she become his sexual slave, she created an alternative option: to encourage and accept Sawyer, "thankful that I do not despise him" [ILSG p. 59]. His attentions, she later wrote, flattered her "pride," and while at first she felt only "sincere gratitude for kindness," soon "a more tender feeling crept into my heart" [ILSG pp. 55, 54].

And what was Sam Sawyer thinking and feeling? His relationship with Norcom's slave girl was typical of men of his time, place, and class.

He left no record of his liaison with Hatty, but perhaps a psychologist with an historical bent could speculate concerning his thoughts and feelings. Is it possible that they shared some version of love? Can that word be used in connection with a relationship that is so utterly unequal? Or is it enough to conclude that their relationship was such that it was not impossible for Harriet Jacobs—a self-respecting nineteenth-century enslaved black teenager—to sustain over several years?

Sawyer became involved with Hatty when he was building his political base and establishing himself as a significant presence beyond Edenton, and even beyond Chowan County. The only existing correspondence between him and Dr. Norcom is a letter he wrote on July 2, 1828. It is an apology that may—or may not—refer to his current involvement with Norcom's slave girl. It begins:

> This is to request that all that has passed between us of an unpleasant nature may be forgotten and buried in oblivion.—On my part, I regret it exceedingly, and being far your junior in years, am free to admit that you have not been treated by me with that decorum which your age, your character and your standing in society merited. . . . I hope that you will credit the assertion when I tell you, that though a difference has for sometime subsisted between us yet my feelings towards you were far from being inimical and all that I have said, or done was purely the offspring of a momentary passion.

It may be that his subject is politics—Sawyer and Norcom had held opposing views in the past, and Sawyer begins the next paragraph with a clear reference to his candidacy in an upcoming election. But the possibility that the issue is political is perhaps ruled out by Sawyer's comment that he would be stupid to think "that a confession of error on my part, would have any effect upon you in a matter of that kind, and when it is likewise known to us both, that at an anterior contest, (when we were upon friendly terms) you preferred my rival to myself."

Hatty was soon reconciled with Grandmother. When the jealous Maria forbade her to return to the Norcoms' house, Hatty moved her clothing and featherbed into Molly's bakery home and continued her liaison with Sawyer. Over the next five years, she had plenty of time to think about having drunk "the cup of sin, and shame, and misery, whereof her persecuted race are compelled to drink." Writing *Incidents* at midlife, she took full responsibility for her actions. "I know I did wrong. No one can feel it more sensibly than I do. The painful and humiliating memory will haunt me to my dying day" [ILSG pp. 55–56]. Then, reflecting that "still, in looking back, calmly, on the events of my life, I feel that the slave woman ought not to be judged by the same standard as others,"she vindicated herself, her grandmother Molly, and all of her neighbors who had not permitted their sexual experiences to prevent them from building lives as proud, upstanding black women [ILSG p. 56].

3

A Determined Will

My master had power and law on his side; I had a determined will.
There is might in each.
—Harriet Jacobs, *Incidents in the Life of a Slave Girl*, p. 85

I t was a difficult pregnancy, and through these months, Hatty grew closer than ever to her family, especially to Aunt Betty, who was also expecting a child. Hatty's son came too early, but grew stronger as the weeks passed. Her relationship with Sawyer continued as before. He arranged with Molly to support both mother and baby and was willing to have the little boy bear his name. But Hatty knew that this would incense Norcom, and she delayed the baptism.

With her mistress still adamantly opposed to allowing her in the house, arrangements were made for Hatty and her baby to continue to stay at Grandmother's. There she was busy with child care and housework, with the animals—Molly kept two cows who gave delicious cream—and with the baking. Under Molly's tutelage, Hatty perfected her domestic skills and learned how to produce the jams, jellies, preserves, and conserves that Grandmother put up and sold in her bakery-teashop. In Edenton, most daily bread was cooked in fireplaces on griddles and iron spiders. Although several houses in town had small "dutch ovens" on the hearth, many families got their loaves, crackers, and cakes from the bake house. The town apparently never had more than one baker at a time, and years earlier, when Tildsley Summers had closed his doors and stopped offering his loaf bread, crackers, cakes, pilot bread, butter biscuits, and rusks for sale, the way was made clear for Molly Horniblow to open her business. Although no bakery had been at that location before, after years of experience in the kitchens at Horniblow's Tavern, she apparently supervised the building of her new oven. Molly probably

30

offered daily loaves as well as various kinds of seamen's bread for sale, and every morning, she and Hatty made the regular corn and wheat breads. They also offered her famous crackers and snowballs and, on occasion, fancy cakes for weddings.

Life at Grandmother's was pleasant, but although Mrs. Norcom would not have her in the house, Hatty was still Norcom's slave. He persistently attempted to control her, appearing unannounced to demand her presence or to query her about her movements, and striving to restrict her acquaintance, even among the black community, to those he judged appropriate. The doctor was exceptionally sensitive to social position, but all of Edenton was hierarchical. While whites ranked above blacks, and free people above slaves, multiple levels existed within each grouping. Because he was a physician, Norcom's rank was high, but it fell well below that of a man like Sawyer, a descendant of the colonial aristocracy. The status of slaves depended on that of their masters, as well as on their color and their position as house slaves or as field slaves. While slavery was the crucial dividing line among people of color, many families, like Grandmother's, embraced members who were both slave and free.

The highest rank in the black community was enjoyed by prosperous men like Gustavus Adolphus Johnson, who were connected—often by "blood"—to the white aristocracy, and who had been freed. Grandmother belonged to the next social level, made up of the freed men who had been owned by moderately prosperous white families and the freed women who had been owned by the white aristocracy (although the women, of course, had fewer opportunities for prosperity than the men). A third group of free people of color had less status. These included descendants of eighteenth-century unions between black men and indentured white women, a small group whose very existence defied the entire legal and social structure of chattel slavery and was an embarrassment to white Edenton. Judith, the matriarch of the Burke family, had been born in Chowan County to a white woman by a black man, and had in 1771 appealed to the court to grant her freedom upon completion of her indentured servitude (obligatory for free children of color). At least two of her sons and several of her grandsons were carpenters; her grandson Henry owned a horse and gig and rented a family pew in St. Paul's before his early death in 1844. Like Judith Burke, Jane Banks was born in Chowan to a white woman by a black man, and after completing the terms of her indentured servitude, she, too, appealed to the court to win her freedom, moved to town, and bought a house. Her daughter married the Horniblow's slave carpenter Dick Pea, purchased a home, and raised a large family in Edenton. These free "mixed-race" families were a thorn in the side of the white town, and they were constantly in trouble with the authorities. The Banks women were indicted for disturbing the peace and for assault, and repeatedly accused of stealing—a window curtain, quantities of cheese and pork, a trunk of shoes and clothing, a "black Canton crepe shawl." The Burke brothers were at times arrested for brawling.

But brawling was not restricted to Edenton's free blacks. Men of every rank and color, from Hatty's aristocratic protector Samuel Tredwell Sawyer on down, were involved in public fracases. In the disastrous economy of the late 1820s, it didn't take much to provoke a quarrel between neighbors, much less between professional competitors. Late in 1829, Dr. Norcom vented his spleen in a long letter to the *Gazette*. Charging that he had been slanderously accused of setting exorbitant fees, he offered to match his colleagues' rates "if they are not absolutely mean and contemptible" and, using the third person, explained why he was writing. "Having been so long and so often the victim of malicious slanders and insidious calumnies, which he could never condescend to trace or to investigate, he deigns not to suggest an enquiry on the subject; but it is a duty which he owes to himself, and *perhaps* to the community, in which his conduct and views have been so often and so entirely misrepresented."

Two weeks later, Norcom placed an ad putting up for sale everything he owned except his livestock and his slaves. He listed virtually all of his real estate in Edenton and Chowan County—a 400-acre farm with house and barn; Kentucky farm, including 320 acres; his lots and house in town, as well as his "*Medical Establishment*, consisting of a commodious Shop, with all the Medicines, Furniture, Instruments and Books needed by a Practitioner in an unhealthy country." At the beginning of the new year, he repeated his offer to sell out, and asked those who owed him money to pay up. By the end of February, however, he apparently changed his plans, and the ads stopped.

Norcom's public quarrel with his colleagues supports Jacobs's view that he was an angry man, but in the terrible economy of the late 1820s, he was not alone in considering a move from Edenton. In 1824, some southerners had supported a tariff, arguing that it would protect not only northern-produced textiles but southern cotton as well. They were wrong. Under the tariff, the price of exported goods remained low while prices on imports became prohibitive, and in 1828, a new tariff granting further protection to northern manufacture weighed even more heavily on southern agriculture. When, condemning that "Tariff of Abominations," South Carolina's John C. Calhoun reasserted the argument that a sovereign state could nullify a federal law, nullification and secession became a topic of discussion thoughout the South, and in Edenton as well.

Like every other southern port, the town was hurting. But Edenton's economy was hit even harder than most because of the new Dismal Swamp Canal which, by expediting shipping from Albemarle Sound to the James River, was diverting shipping away to Elizabeth City. The *Gazette* lamented, "We are going down-hill daily. . . . Our Shipping will soon have to *weigh anchor* and *about*, to some other harbor for employment, or lie in our docks to *rot*." A few weeks later, the editor announced the unthinkable:

> We have to present our papers to our readers to-day . . . completely destitute of Marine intelligence, and almost without a new advertisement. It is a fact, which has seldom occurred before, that there has been but one arrival and no departures, during the past week. . . . Business is at a complete stand.

Adding to the town's problems were the banks. Although most local borrowers were agriculturists with annual incomes, financial institutions required payment not yearly but quarterly. With foreclosings becoming widespread, in March 1829, the grand jury of Chowan County joined those of Duplin and Wayne counties in asking the governor to call an extra session of the General Assembly to explore means of relief. It was in this terrible economy that the *Gazette* ran an ad unlike the usual rewards for fugitives or the usual notices of slave sales accompanying bankruptcy proceedings. This ad was different: "NEGROES WANTED. The highest Cash price will be given for likely *Young Negroes* of both sexes, from 12 to 25 years of age by the subscriber, who is now situated at Mr. Hoskins, where he intends to remain for 15 to 20 days." A slave trader had come to Edenton.

Jacobs's nemesis Norcom was among those in desperate need of relief. He borrowed largely and often, and when he failed to pay his debts, the court authorized the sale of his property, including his slaves. Jacobs's brother John and her Aunt Betty were among those repeatedly itemized for sale and reprieved when Norcom paid up. Then on August 26, 1830, Harriet and her baby were included in a writ issued listing the slaves to be sold to satisfy Norcom's debts. It was the closest thing to a birth certificate that Jacobs's son Joseph would ever have.

But then, Norcom managed to satisfy his creditors, and Hatty and her little Joe were not put up for sale. There is no way of knowing whether—if Sam Sawyer was aware that his mistress and his infant son faced public auction—he made plans to buy them. In August 1830, the month they were marked for sale, he was reelected to represent the town of Edenton in the state legislature. Sawyer moved to Raleigh, between legislative sessions returning to Edenton and to Hatty's bed.

A few months earlier, a worried Edentonian wrote to the *Gazette* and signed himself "Santo Domingo," making an ominous reference to the Haitian revolt. In response, the editor advised his anxious reader that he should focus his concerns on "the *northwest* of our Town, where *perhaps*, he may find some real cause of complaint." This was apparently an allusion to the gatherings of the black community at their Providence meeting house where, Jacobs later remembered, "they had no higher happiness than to meet . . . and sing hymns together, and pour out their hearts in spontaneous prayer" [ILSG p. 67].

The political climate worsened when it was discovered that copies of *Walker's Appeal . . . to the Colored Citizens of the World but in Particular and Very Expressly to Those of the United States of America* had somehow reached North Carolina. David Walker, born free in North Carolina, had ended his *Appeal* by quoting the Declaration of Independence to assert that slaves were justified in using force to win their freedom. Alerted to this "inflammatory" document, Governor Owen wrote to the senators of the thirty-two eastern counties—including Chowan—warning them "to the necessity of arresting the circulation" of Walker's pamphlet. Then in September, the *Gazette* editorialized at length against another "inflammatory"publication, *The Rights of All*, a New Jersey newspaper published by black activist Samuel Cornish. Warning that "emissaries have been dispersed, *for some time*, throughout the Southern States, for the purpose of disseminating false principles and infusing the poison of discontent," the paper concluded, "there is now no doubt in our minds, that a conspiracy for exciting insurrection in the South is carrying on, by the free colored people of the North, under a sense of imaginary wrongs and privations."

Two weeks later, the *Gazette* printed an extraordinary letter in which Rigdon M. Green, a free man of color, wrote to clear his name, complaining that his character had been "unjustly and wantonly impugned and grossly censured" because he was accused of receiving copies of *The*

Rights of All. Acknowledging that he had been sent two copies of the paper, Green denied that he had ever supported it, and he included a letter from Cornish verifying that he "is not nor ever was" a subscriber. (Green's disclaimers raise some interesting questions. Who else in Edenton read those two issues as Cornish's paper passed from hand to hand? Could Harriet Jacobs's first contact with organized abolitionism—with the demand of equal rights for all, a demand she would assert all of her long life—have come as early as 1830?)

Responding to the threats presented by "inflammatory publications," the North Carolina legislature of 1830 created a storm of repression that changed the social climate of the state. In Edenton, the *Gazette* spelled out the new legislation that was aimed to control not only slaves, but free people of color and whites as well. There were laws and more laws: "to prevent the gaming of Slaves, and to prevent free persons from gaming with them"; "to direct the Sheriff to sell any slaves . . . confined in jail as a runaway"; to prohibit free people of color "from peddling and hawking out of the county in which they reside"; more effectively to prevent them from migrating into North Carolina; "to prevent all persons from teaching Slaves to read or write"; "to prevent the circulation of seditious publications"; to order county courts to establish patrols; "to prohibit the trading with Slaves"; to provide "further punishment for harbouring or maintaining runaway slaves" and "to regulate the emancipation of Slaves within this State"—requiring an emancipating master to file a petition with the court and to post a $1,000 security bond, and requiring an emancipated slave to leave North Carolina "within ninety days and never return." One act, entitled "More effectually to prevent intermarriages between free negroes or free persons of color and white persons and slaves" might have given Sawyer pause—although of course he had never dreamed of marrying the slave girl whose bed he shared.

Certainly Sawyer had no public quarrel with the institution of chattel slavery. After the close of the session, answering charges by his political opponents that he was "a *nullifier*, a *Traitor* and a *disunionist*," he affirmed his patriotism in the *Gazette*. He explained, however, that he of course could not persevere in his allegiance to the federal government if Congress were to trample on basic rights—by establishing an aristocracy, or suspending habeas corpus, or denying trial by jury, "or emancipating our slaves, &c." He then rhetorically inquired, "Is there an individual in this community . . . [who would propose, if Congress passed such legislation] that the sovereign State of North Carolina should fold up her arms in apathy and indifference and *submit?* If any, speak; for him have I offended."

Less than three weeks after Sawyer's affirmation of his allegiance to the system of chattel slavery, the bloodiest slave insurrection in American history took place. On August 21 and 22, 1859, in Southampton County, Virginia, rebel Nat Turner and his men killed fifty-five whites. In Edenton, sixty miles downstream, the weekly *Gazette* published nothing about the revolt until nine days after it occurred. When finally the newspaper broke its silence, it attempted to reassure its readers that they were in no danger from Nat Turner's men:

> It seems that the insurrection was entirely local in its character, and originated with a few misguided and desperate slaves, who . . . were enabled to increase the strength of their forces to about the number of forty, and not two hundred as was represented. It commenced without any general previous concert or matured design. . . .
>
> In two *short days*, they were nearly all killed to a man, and the insurrection completely suppressed! An awful warning to that class of our population, of the folly and madness of ever engaging in similar hopeless attempts.

The editor continued to calm Edenton's white community:

> Let then the fate of the foolish and deluded insurgents of Southampton, be a solemn memento to the black population throughout the land; and let them remember, that every similar attempt, instead of alleviating, serves only to increase and rivet the rigour of their chains.

Still, he urged caution:

> With us we have detected no signs nor symptoms of an insurrectionary spirit; the slaves appear quiet, peaceable and unoffending, and while we recommend *vigilance* to our citizens, we would likewise respectfully suggest, that they should not suffer the present excitement, to cause them to deviate from their accustomed mild and moderate treatment to the slaves. The innocent should not suffer on account of the wicked— nor the just be confounded with the unjust.

But this admonition came too late. The repression had begun nine days earlier, when news of Nat Turner first reached the town.

Protected by Sawyer and by Molly's patrons, Hatty was forewarned that a special muster was called and that Grandmother's house, like the homes of the rest of Edenton's black population, would be searched by patrols. She of course could not protest openly against the reprisals being planned against the black community. Nevertheless, Hatty devised a way to express her contempt for the patrollers. Aware that "nothing annoyed them so much as to see colored people living in comfort and respectability," deliberately, as an act of resistance, she spent the day making the house as attractive as she could. "I arranged every thing in my grandmother's house as neatly as possible. I put white quilts on the beds, and decorated some of the rooms with flowers" [ILSG p. 63]. Then, defiantly, she sat at the window to watch.

She had seen musters, but never anything like this. On the Green, to the sounds of fifes and drumming, white men, both uniformed country gentlemen and poor whites, some without hats or shoes, were organizing into groups of sixteen. Josiah Coffield—the brother of her father's last master, a man Jacobs knew as "notorious for his cruelty"—led the patrol to Molly's house. While he stood guard outside, his men pushed their way in and rummaged through "every box, trunk, closet, and corner," grabbing silver coins from a drawer, turning linens and bedding out of a trunk, breaking into the buffet and opening up jars of Molly's preserves [ILSG pp. 64–65]. Alarmed, Hatty asked a white neighbor to step inside. When the patrollers became excited at finding writing in the house, Coffield interrogated her. Hatty saucily acknowledged that she could read, but in response to his command to produce letters, said she had none. Finally the men left, whacking at the bushes in the garden. As they moved on, Coffield turned back to curse Molly's home and everyone in it. When night fell, Jacobs heard worse than Coffield's curses. Alarmed by the shouts and screams coming from outside, she was afraid to go to the door, but peeked under the window curtain to see people being dragged to the Green by the armed mob.

A week later, the violence continued, and Edenton remained under martial law, the day patrol ending only with the coming of the night guard. On September 1, a local slaveholder wrote a friend, "ten likely fellows were brought to town from the northern region of Chowan County and jailed, the 'proof' being 'strong against them.'" After another week, the *Gazette* acknowledged some of the violence: "Since our last 19 negroes in this County have been taken up and committed to jail in this place. We understand a large number of citizens from the several counties bordering on the Dismal Swamp, commenced yesterday to scout this great rendezvous for runaway slaves &c. It is hoped their efforts will not be in vain." Hatty and her friends began to hear the whispered stories that circulated in town about atrocities committed against the blacks out in the country, as the unsanctioned reprisals continued, never to be documented.

The state-sanctioned reprisals, however, are recorded in court papers. On September 1, when Small's Jim was questioned under oath at Edenton, he described a conspiracy "to kill the whites" and named more than a dozen names. That same day, seven warrants were issued. Within a week there were five more, and by the end of the month nineteen men—the property of ten local slaveholders—were in the old jail behind the courthouse. Eight of them were indicted for conspiring "to rebel and make insurrection," and on October 12, Charles Johnson's slave Godfrey went to trial. When he was found innocent the other indictments were dropped, and on November 10—eleven days after Nat Turner was captured and the day before he was executed—the *Gazette* reported that "not the slightest evidence was adduced to warrant the belief of their participation in any plot." Later that fall court term one of the informers, "not having the face of God before his eyes, but being moved and seduced by the devil," was accused of lying about Godfrey and indicted for perjury. But even then it was not over. "People felt," one white man wrote, "as if rattlesnakes were under their beds and hidden in the shrubbery."

Like Santo Domingo, it would never be over. In the wake of Nat Turner's insurrection, both military repression and everyday surveillance intensified, and naked violence increased. The *Gazette*, announcing "those persons who went from this county to aid in searching the Dismal Swamp, have returned," noted that while the results of other patrols had not yet been reported, the Gates County posse "succeeded in capturing 12 negroes." In Edenton, the military presence was inescapable: a cavalry company assembled at the courthouse parade ground on Saturday mornings at 11, and the Chowan Guards drilled there at 3:30 on Saturday afternoons "armed and equipped according to law."

Despite the decline in maritime commerce, there really was no way to seal off the town from knowledge of what was happening in the larger world; really no way that the *Gazette* could be the only—or even the major—source of information about that world. Edenton's black seamen, both slave and free, could not be prevented from communicating, as they always had, with their free brothers and sisters in New England,

Haiti, Central America, Mexico, and Bolivia—where slavery had ended—as well as in other regions of the American South, and in Argentina and Brazil—where the struggle continued. And these men could not be prevented from telling what they had seen and heard to the folks back home. Still, the white South could try to control the channels of information. In the wake of Nat Turner's insurrection, the *Gazette* noted that a Columbia, South Carolina "Vigilant Association" was offering "a reward of *fifteen hundred dollars* for the apprehension and prosecution to conviction, of any white person who may be detected in distributing or circulating within that State the newspaper, called 'The Liberator,' printed in Boston, or the pamphlet called 'Walker's Pamphlet,' or any other publication of a seditious tendency." At Raleigh, a grand jury indicted Boston's William Lloyd Garrison and Isaac Knapp for breaking North Carolina law by circulating *The Liberator*, "a seditious publication." (The *Boston Courier*, while agreeing that *The Liberator* was "inflamatory" and "dangerous," replied that as long as it did not break Massachusetts law, it could not be stopped from publication.)

The violent atmosphere and the effort at censorship were intended to control the black population. Even after the military presence ended, the masters, still fearful that any congregaton of blacks signaled a possible insurrection, tightened their control. They forbade visiting on the plantations, and in town, when the people asked to be allowed to resume their meetings at Providence, not only denied their plea but pulled down the slaves' church, leaving its wreckage to molder as a testament to their power. Members of the Providence congregation were told that some space would be set aside for them in the galleries of the white churches, and for a few weeks, St. Paul's rector held a Sunday service for them in the home of one of his black members. Hatty, who was invited because she could read, attended twice. Reluctantly, she sat through the minister's rebukes against the slaves' evil ways: lying to their masters, practicing divination with coffee grounds and roots, stealing master's corn and selling it at grog shops for rum, pitching pennies in back streets and down on the wharf. But the reverend's missionary spirit soon faded. When he offered to preach to the black members of the congregation if they came to his kitchen, Jacobs heard that he made them wait so long that they went off to a Methodist shout.

In this charged atmosphere, it was good to have the protection of a man like Major Sam Sawyer—especially since Hatty was pregnant again. The day Norcom noticed her body rounding, he became furious and, dashing out of the house, returned with a pair of scissors and cut her hair close, to mark her as a whore. When she dared protest, he beat her and then, seeing she was hurt, left swearing not to hit her again. In his eyes, her pregnancy was an intolerable affront to his authority, and all summer he stopped in at Molly's bakery almost every day, spewing out verbal abuse.

Hatty's child was born in the fall. She had hoped for another boy, and was distressed when she learned the baby was a girl. "Slavery is terrible for men; but it is far more terrible for women," she later wrote. "Superadded to the burden common to all, *they* have wrongs, and sufferings, and mortifications peculiarly their own" [ILSG p. 77]. Her own "wrongs, and sufferings, and mortifications" were now daily orchestrated by an infuriated Norcom. One day, goaded by his constant pressure, Grandmother asserted herself. Norcom had beaten Hatty, and Molly, indignant and angry, ordered him out of her house. Astonished, Norcom responded that his slave girl was "insolent" and accused Molly of sanctioning Hatty's wayward behavior [ILSG p. 82]. Grandmother answered back that he himself was the cause, and he left in a rage. Another day, recognizing in the baby's tiny face the features of Major Sam's late mother, Norcom cursed his slave girl, her infant, and the dead grandmother alike.

On a Sunday morning when they knew Norcom was away, Molly and Hatty walked over to St. Paul's carrying the baby and leading Joseph by the hand. Among the congregation were father Elijah's old mistress Mrs. Knox and her daughter Louisa Matilda. Before the ceremony, Miss Louisa offered to serve as godmother. The baby was christened with her given names, and after the service, old Mrs. Knox gave tiny Lulu a golden chain—an emblem too symbolic of slavery for Hatty's insurgent taste. Hating all chains and with rebellion in her heart, she had resolved that her children would never use "Norcom," although it was the name of their first master. Nor would they use "Knox," the name of the owner of their maternal grandfather. Determined to honor her father, she had decided that they would take "Jacobs," the name her father had been denied, although it belonged to the white man who had sired him. It was the name Hatty planned to adopt if and when she could.

At Grandmother's, the days melted into each other. In addition to caring for Joseph and little Lulu, doing housework, and helping with the baking, Hatty kept busy with her needle, learning embroidery and dressmaking, and making clothes for the family and for others. (She never used the hated linsey-woolsey, but instead, sewed the "Satinetts of various qualities; Brown Sheetings & Shirtings" shipped in by schooner and advertised in the *Gazette*.) But the family was never free of Norcom's persistent intrusions, and as months—then years—passed, the climate of repression in the town failed to ease.

Then one Sunday, horror: in a canoe tied up about a mile from Edenton, in a cove up John's Island Creek near the Pembroke estate, the decapitated body of a black man was found. George Cabarrus had met a grisly end. He had been born the slave of Stephen Cabarrus, but after his master's death, the property had been sold. George, his washerwoman's son, was bought by a local man who lost everything in 1829 and sold him to another local man, who in turn sold him to a slave trader. Somehow, George had escaped from the trader's coffle and was heading home to his wife at Pembroke when he was spotted by bounty-hunters. Apparently thinking him outlawed, they shot him dead and, assuming that to collect their prize money they need only show his head, decapitated him. In town, however, they discovered that the reward money was offered for capturing and confining George in a North Carolina jail. To avoid being accused of murder, they disposed of his head and left. Decades later, Harriet Jacobs would remember the grisly sight and the sickening stench: "This slave man was brought to the wharf, placed in a small boat . . . early in the morning, with his head severed from his body, and remained there in an August sun until noon, before an inquest was held."

Neither Harriet nor her brother could forget George, and such remembrances made their lives bitter. Working in Norcom's office, John used every means at his disposal to resist his master. One strategy was to leave as often as possible, a tactic that elicited Norcom's complaint that "no persuasion, no menaces, no punishment, can confine [John] to the scene of his duty!" In retaliation, John later testified, Norcom's sons were explicitly "instructed . . . to see that I did not learn to write."

Although Norcom consistently refused to sell her to Sawyer, Hatty was not without influence over Major Sam. Together, they evidently devised a plan to buy her by commissioning a slaveholder, who was planning to leave for Texas, to purchase her for Sawyer. The jealous Norcom flatly refused to sell and accused Hatty of a sexual liaison with the prospective buyer, then taunted her with the news that in Raleigh, Sawyer had been courting a heiress who possessed "beautiful black eyes, and black hair, and . . . a beautiful form . . . worth about eight thousand dollars." He

began haunting Molly's house. The idea that another man wanted to buy
Hatty spurred his determination to control her every movement, and
learning that she visited a friend, he expressed astonishment that Sawyer
permitted her to socialize with people he believed beneath her. Then, as
if to show that he cared about her well-being, he again proposed that he
himself provide her with both freedom and a home.

All she need do to achieve her long-desired goal, he coaxed, was agree
to become his mistress, move into the cottage he would provide, and
never see Sawyer again. She later recalled his very words: "If I have been
harsh with you at times, your willfulness drove me to it. You know I exact
obedience from my own children, and I consider you as yet a child"
[ILGS p. 83]. If she refused, he warned, he would send her and her children out to Auburn, the plantation he had bought as a wedding gift for
his son James Jr., who was about to be married. Hatty was convinced
that Norcom's offer was a trap and that he would never make good on
the promise to free Joseph and Louisa Matilda. When she rejected him,
Dr. Norcom, furious at her audacity, swore that he would put her son to
work and sell him, and that he would raise her daughter for sale as a
fancy girl. Molly tried to intercede, even offering to pay Dr. Norcom for
Hatty's time, but was told that her granddaughter's "feelings were
entirely above . . . [her] situation," and that out at the plantation, she
would soon learn how to behave [ILSG p. 85].

Leaving Joseph (who was sick) at Grandmother's, Hatty climbed into
Norcom's old wagon and rode the six jolting miles out to Auburn with
Louisa in her arms. It was a beautiful April day, but Hatty did not hear
the birdsongs or see the greening fields. Her mind was elsewhere. "I had,"
she writes, "a woman's pride, and a mother's love for my children; and
I resolved that out of the darkness of this hour a brighter dawn should
rise for them" [ILSG p. 85]. The plantation was as she remembered: bleak
and flat, its large fields running off into the woods. Behind the Big House
stood the slaves' cabins made of rough logs chinked with clay, their chimneys sticks piled "cob-house fashion." When she was told that instead of
staying in the quarter she was to sleep in the Big House, she was glad she
had brought along her featherbed, for James Norcom Jr., her young master, had provided nothing for her and her child.

Two-year-old Lulu was not used to being left alone. After settling her
onto the kitchen floor and telling her she could go out as far as the yard,
Hatty had to follow her young master up the stairs. Handing her the
housekeys, he instructed her to get the house in order. Surrounded by

piles of household linens, she sewed until noon, then went searching for Lulu, who had cried herself to sleep. All week, Hatty worked from sunup until dark getting the household ready for James Jr.'s bride—hemming bed sheets and table linens, sewing draperies for the windows, and binding carpeting for the floors. Neglected, little Lulu cried herself sick, and seeing the fieldworkers' children feeding on thick sour milk from a wooden trough, an iron spoon in one hand and a piece of hoe cake in the other, Hatty knew she had to get her daughter away from there. Another day, as she sat sewing by the window, she heard in the yard below "that weary cry which makes a mother's heart bleed," then silence [ILSG p. 87]. Putting down her work, Hatty looked under the great porch, which was raised a couple of feet above the ground, and found Lulu curled up asleep. Carrying her daughter out, without thinking she said aloud that it would be better if she never awakened, then saw James Norcom Jr. watching. That night, he sent Lulu some sweetened milk and a biscuit, and Hatty learned that a few hours earlier, he had killed a large snake under that porch. Next morning, without asking anyone's permission, she stopped a cart loaded with shingles for town, put Lulu on it, and sent her home to Grandmother.

Then, like the others, Hatty began to use night as what was called "the slaves' holiday." With a fieldworker friend, again and again she walked the six miles to Edenton to see her family, trudging back the six miles to Auburn by daybreak. Grandmother, she knew, was consulting with Sawyer, trying to win freedom for her and the children. But she also knew that Dr. Norcom was determined to keep her his slave. Every day, supervising household arrangements or sitting sewing endless stitch after endless stitch, she rejected one plan after another. Then it all became clear. If she ran off, why wouldn't Dr. Norcom be willing to sell her? And—rather than incur the trouble and expense of raising the children— why wouldn't he be willing to sell them, too? And wouldn't Major Sam buy the doctor's worthless escaped slave and her children?

On the Sunday before the new Mrs. James Norcom Jr. was to arrive at Auburn, Hatty gained permission from her young master to spend the day in Edenton. She had decided exactly what she would do. She had determined to act to save her children from slavery, and she believed today might be the last she would ever have with Grandmother, little Joe, and Lulu. Jacobs would always remember the tumult she felt on this calm spring day. At sundown, she left Grandmother's house and walked over to Providence burying ground. She found her parents' graves, though the name on her father's wooden headstone was almost obliterated, and the tree he had planted over her mother had rotted to a stump. Hatty was always profoundly moved by the silence and the sacredness of the place. Now, deeply committed to rescuing her children—or to die trying—at twilight she knelt and kissed the faded letters of her father's name, passionately praying for guidance and for grace. As she passed the ruin of Providence Meeting House on her way back to King Street, she thought she heard her father's voice, urging her on.

That night she slept with Grandmother who—sensitive to her impulsive granddaughter's moods and fearing she might be planning to escape—voiced a warning: "Stand by your own children, and suffer with them till death" [ILSG p. 91]. Back at Auburn on Monday, Jacobs continued the preparations for the appearance of young Mrs. James Norcom Jr., and on Wednesday she joined the slaves thronging to greet their new mistress. At the wedding dinner, Hatty waited on table for the first time in her life. She felt humiliated when ordered about by Dr. Norcom, and his wife, who would not speak to her, smiled triumphantly when she handed her her plate. The next week, Hatty overheard that arrangements were being made for Joseph and Louisa to be sent out to the plantation. Old Mrs. Norcom knew that she would be chained to Auburn if her children were there, and the Norcoms had decided that "it was a good place to break us all in to abject submission to our lot as slaves" [ILSG pp. 93–94]. That night, as always, Hatty's last task was to lock up the house. At half past midnight she felt her way down the stairs, opened the front window, stepped over the low frame, and walked out of her life.

Soaked by large drops of rain and bewildered by the intense darkness, Hatty dropped to her knees in prayer, then stumbled toward the road. She half-ran, half-walked the six miles to town and stole into Grandmother's house. There, after making hurried arrangements and offering a fervent prayer, she kissed her sleeping children and left again. She found shelter—she never told how or with whom—but knew that she wouldn't be safe anywhere in Edenton.

In the morning, James Jr.'s bride was dismayed to find her valuable house slave gone. Dr. Norcom was immediately notified, and he angrily marshaled the entire resources of the slave power—sheriff, patrols, courts, and the press—to catch her. The patrols searching Molly's house discovered that Hatty's trunk was empty, and (as she had forseen) concluded that she would run north. By mid-morning, they had ordered a stop to all northward vessels. By afternoon, arrangements were in place for a night watch on the town. Next day, posters went up warning any who might aid her escape, and offering a reward for her capture. For years, this "wanted" ad, composed by the furious Dr. Norcom, was the only description of Harriet Jacobs: "She is a light mulatto, 21 years of age, about 5 feet 4 inches high, of a thick and corpulent habit, having on her head a thick covering of black hair that curls naturally, but which can be easily combed straight. She speaks easily and fluently, and has an agreeable carriage and address. Being a good seamstress, she has been accustomed to dress well, has a variety of very fine clothes, made in the prevailing fashion, and will probably appear, if abroad, tricked out in gay and fashionable finery." Then—as if condemning her children to plantation slavery was not adequate motivation—"As this girl absconded from the plantation of my son without any known cause or provocation, it is probable she designs to transport herself to the North."

Edenton long remembered 1835 as "the year of the whirlwind." One resident recalled "standing in the street, watching the ugliest cloud I think I ever saw, rising in the west about sunset . . . preceded by a thick scud, that looked like black smoke, which speedily formed a large column apparently through the center of the cloud. The blinding flashes of lightning, the frequent peals of heavy thunder, and the awful roaring of the wind were singularly appalling." But for Harriet Jacobs and her family, 1835 marked the start of her years in hiding.

For a week the search was intense. We will never know how Hatty managed to get word to her family who, terrorized by Norcom, urged her to return and beg for mercy. But she vowed not to go back. One night, shrinking in the bushes after being driven from her hiding place by her hunters, she felt a sharp pain in her leg. She struck out at the slimy thing that had bitten her, and after trying to draw out the poison, got word to the family that something must be done. Distressed and in tears, Molly took a desperate risk and confided in a neighbor she had known all her life. Though a slaveholder, Martha Hoskins Rombough Blount was a woman "who studied the welfare of her whole household both black and white." Now, apparently moved by Molly's recital of Norcom's sexual threats, she offered to shelter Molly's granddaughter until the patrols were lifted and she could escape from Edenton.

At first dark, before the night patrol began its watch, Hatty disguised herself and went to the meeting place. There she met Nancy, Mrs. Blount's cook, whom she followed to her mistress's house on Queen Street. Nancy locked her into a small room above the mistress's bedroom.

Nancy and her mistress visited the fugitive, but hid her from members of
the household who—like the housemaid Jenny—they feared untrustworthy. Hatty spent the summer weeks reading and sewing, and in the mornings, lying atop a pile of unused featherbeds, peeked out the window to
watch Dr. Norcom walking to work. She felt proud of outwitting him. But
she was terrified when one day Nancy, fearing the house would be
searched, led her downstairs and outside to the kitchen, then pulled up a
floorboard, told her to lie down on the buffalo skin beneath, and replaced
the board. She did not resurrect Hatty until after dark.

After a time, Hatty was delighted to hear that Dr. Norcom had borrowed money to travel to New York City to retrieve her. He of course
returned empty-handed, but kept up the pressure. Upon learning of her
escape, he had immediately jailed Hatty's children, her brother, and her
aunt Betty—all of the members of her family he owned. When she learned
that her children were in jail, Hatty was beside herself, but remained in
hiding after her brother sent a note saying they would be worse off if she
returned. Norcom continued to harrass Grandmother, demanding to
know Hatty's whereabouts. The family wondered whether he was behind
the town's decision that summer to repair Molly's well—an action that
kept men posted just outside the bakery, day after day, all summer long.

Behind the scenes, Sam Sawyer was trying to negotiate to buy the
children and John. Masking his role in the transaction, he sent a speculator to offer high prices. Norcom at first refused, but then—strapped for
money—changed his mind. After a quick sale, he tried to get assurances
that the speculator would sell them out of the state, but it was too late.
Sawyer had already bought them. John later described how, maintaining
the charade, they were made part of the speculator's coffle, and he was
put into irons. "The chain was thirty or forty feet long, with handcuffs
every two or three feet. The slaves were handcuffed right and left on each
side of the chain. . . . We were all snugly chained up, the children in the
cart, and the women walking behind; friends weeping, and taking a
farewell shake of the hand—wives of their husbands, and parents of their
children" [ILSG p. 214]. The slave coffle set off, but stopped at J. B. Skinner's farm a mile outside Edenton. There George Lamb, the jailer, took
blacksmithing tools out of the cart and began to hammer at John's chains.
When Lamb got them off, he told John to take the children to Grandmother's house, then to go on to his new master, Major Sam Sawyer.

In hiding, Harriet knew none of this. But she would always remember that day, because after sundown while listening to someone in the

street below singing "Home, Sweet Home," she thought she heard children moaning. Kneeling near the window, she saw a band of moonlight and, within it, Joseph and Louisa Matilda. They vanished, and she heard the sound of the key. When she turned and saw Nancy, she begged frantically to hear what had happened. Were her children dead? Were they sold? Nancy, trying to calm her, stayed all night, and next day, the news came. Her desperate plan was working: Joseph and Louisa were safe from Norcom.

Still, she remained in danger, and Norcom remained dangerous. One morning, Hatty heard the scraping of keys in the lock. Had the house slave Jenny become curious when Nancy appeared wearing a new dress that Hatty had sewed? Grandmother was somehow consulted, and it was decided that she must leave her cell immediately. To clear her path, Mrs. Blount went to visit her late brother's family at Clement Hall in the country, taking the treacherous Jenny with her. Nancy brought Hatty a sailor's jacket, pants, and tarpaulin hat and, after warning her to put her hands in her pockets and "walk ricketty, like de sailors," sent her outside [ILSG p. 112]. At the gate, she was met by her father's former apprentice, who led her to the wharf where Aunt Betty's husband, her seafaring uncle, waited with a rowboat. He handed her in, rowed her out to a moored ship, and hoisted her on board, explaining that Uncle Mark was preparing a hiding place for her. Until it was ready, they would sleep on the ship at night and conceal her in the pocosin during the day.

Cabarrus Pocosin lay near the Great Dismal Swamp, for two centuries the largest hideout for fugitive slaves in North Carolina and Virginia. In Jacobs's day, the area was "inhabited almost exclusively by run away negroes, bears, wild cats & wild cattle." It was virtually impossible to find a fugitive in its depths, and within its dense growth, the runaways had built maroons. In North Carolina, the eastern and coastal counties were commonly understood to attract fugitive slaves, as one of Norcom's neighbors testified. Advertising for his slave Jerry, he wrote: "It is very likely he is lurking in or about Edenton, a place more noted, they say in the state, for the concealing and harboring of runaways." Added to the attraction of the swamp was the presence of the port, which offered runaways access to vessels that could carry them out of North Carolina. By 1840, Chowan County would contain more slaves than whites, and even before the organization of Providence proclaimed the autonomous spirit of Edenton's black community, the size of the town enabled fugitives to blend into the black crowds in the streets.

Before first dawn, her uncle rowed three miles into the swamp with Harriet and a friend. (For his protection, she never identified him, and we still don't know who he was.) They moored the boat in the shallow brown water, slashed a path through the thick undergrowth, and Hatty's friend carried her to a hummock dry enough to sit on. She was devoured by mosquitoes, then as the light increased, saw that they were surrounded by snakes. She became terribly frightened. Almost a century earlier, a traveler describing the pocosin, with its "great numbers of cypress trees, tall, straight, and lofty, in many of the swamps and low grounds; besides multitudes of singular excrescences, named cypress knees . . . [growing] out of the most miry places," voiced amazement at "the numbers of large serpents, lying upon logs and fallen trees in the river, basking themselves in the sun. . . . Most of them were of the kind called moccosson snakes, as large as the rattle-snake, but thicker, shorter, and destitute of rattles, which renders them more dangerous." The snakes were still thriving in Hatty's day, and by late afternoon, she was frantically flailing a stick to keep them away. Just before dark, she and her friend made their way closer to the passageway entering the pocosin and heard her uncle's low whistle. She was sick with fever that night on board the ship, but before sunup went back out into the swamp. They tried burning tobacco to keep the mosquitoes off, but the smoke made Hatty sick. In the evening, her uncle got word that a hiding place was ready in Molly's house. Blackening her face with charcoal and again putting on her sailor's clothes, Hatty was rowed ashore. She mingled with the seamen at the wharf, went up Broad Street to King Street, turned the corner, opened Molly's gate, and walked in. It would be almost seven years before she walked out again.

4

Cunning Against Cunning

I resolved to match my cunning against his cunning.
—Harriet Jacobs, *Incidents in the Life of a Slave Girl*, p. 128

Quickly, as Hatty stepped in Grandmother's door, Uncle Mark urged her to climb up into the corner cupboard he had built in the storeroom while she was in the swamp. Using its shelves as a ladder, she pushed open a trapdoor he had cleverly cut in the ceiling and passed up into a space under the roof. There they had laid her bedding. It was dark and the air was stifling, but there were no snakes, and Hatty slept, awakening at intervals to the reassuring sound of her children's voices downstairs. After a time—it must have been day, but no light entered her cell—Molly opened the cupboard doors to set a plate of food on the shelves, then closed them.

Crawling on her hands and knees, Jacobs reached down for the plate and measured her hiding-place. It was, she reckoned, about nine feet long, seven feet wide, and, at the peak of its sloped roof, some three feet high. When she lay down and turned over, she bumped her head on the roof. The family was doing everything they could to guarantee her safety—and their own. They well knew they were all at risk. If Hatty were discovered, she would of course be sent back to Norcom. If Grandmother and Mark were found guilty of concealing a fugitive slave, they would be fined and prosecuted by the state. If they were found guilty of assisting a runaway to escape from North Carolina, they would be subject to the mandatory death penalty. As a precaution against suspicion, they decided to keep the storeroom door unlocked and its window uncurtained, carefully advertising to passers-by that they had nothing to hide.

Feeling her way around the tiny space, Hatty found something sticking out of the boards above her and, in the darkness, grasped a gimlet

49

her uncle had left behind. She felt her way to the wall she thought was next to the street, and after figuring evening must have come, began boring rows of holes and poking out the spaces in between. When she finished, she had made a peephole an inch square, and she sat up late, delighted to breathe in the fresh air and peer out into the darkness of King Street. Seen from her loophole, the town took form. Next morning, there was a patch of blessed light, and she could read. And read she would, deeply from Molly's well-worn Bible and when she could, from snippets of newspapers. Still, the next six years and eleven months would become a blur. Most of what she learned of the life of the town would come from the lips of her grandmother, her uncle, and her aunt. What she knew was only the life within her cell: the summer's heat, the winter's cold, the creatures skittering under the eaves, the tiny red insects that made her skin burn.

In this cramped space, Hatty began experiencing classic symptoms of sensory deprivation. Experts write that when people lack an environment with normal stimulation to the senses—sight, hearing, touch, taste, smell—they experience "massive free-floating anxiety . . . perceptual distortions and hallucinations, illusions in multiple spheres (auditory, visual, olfactory)." These are accompanied by acute confusion, sometimes by "mutism, and subsequent partial amnesia." Notions of persecution arise, and simple hallucinations become more complex, with an accompanying loss of the sense of reality. These symptoms, psychologists explain, have been observed in individuals subjected to conditions of sensory deprivation for short periods. Harriet Jacobs would remain in the crawl space for years. Later, in *Incidents*, she would reluctantly recall "those long, gloomy days, with no object for my eye to rest upon, and no thoughts to occupy my mind, except the dreary past and the uncertain future!" [ILSG pp. 116–17].

The family tried to keep her connected to life. At first, their news was of the efforts to catch her. Norcom, furious at her escape, was wreaking his vengeance on them all. After selling John and the children, he was still determined to punish someone and forbade Aunt Betty to see her sailor husband when he was in port. With this tie broken, Uncle Stephen, attached to Edenton only by love for his wife, did not return from his next voyage north. Hatty had always found Norcom's behavior a mix of terrible storms and furious silences. But even Hatty would have been surprised if she could have read a letter her master penned to his daughter that autumn. He instructed her not to "indulge in passion or ill-humour to any one, even to servants, for, though they wait on us & we have a right to their labour, humanity & decency require [that we treat] them with gentleness & forbearance." With this behavior, he wrote, "they will be made to love[and s]erve us better."

Now Aunt Betty—functionally widowed by Norcom's vengeance—began to serve her erratic master "better" by assigning to herself the role of spy in his household. (Whether she realized that Norcom used morphine—a drug he could not tolerate—is unclear. Somewhat later, in his correspondence he revealed himself a man struggling to maintain physical and mental health, writing of "that horrible & almost insupportable sense of weariness and restlessness which forced me to my seducing & dangerous nostrum [the morphia].") To the family, Betty announced that Norcom was leaving for New York where, he had heard, Hatty had been spotted. Peeking through her loophole, Jacobs feasted her eyes on the sight of the doctor heading down Broad Street toward the *Bravo* (recently converted to steam), on the first leg of his pointless journey north. Back from his trip, he persisted in his efforts to catch her, one day even walking Joseph and little Louisa to the shops in Cheapside and trying to bribe them with shiny silver coins and bright kerchiefs for news of her whereabouts.

They were all relieved when winter came and the town finally stopped working on Molly's well—and, the family feared, spying on them. But with the winter, Jacobs's cell grew cold. On milder days, she wrapped herself in blankets and huddled by her loophole, watching for people in the street and listening to their conversations. Her spirits rose before Christmas, when Molly brought home cloth and thread for her to sew into clothes and toys for the children. But Grandmother's decision to invite the constable and his lackey for a holiday dinner frightened her. Hearing them talking on the piazza, she thought her "heart almost stood still," and she was terrified when, after leading them through all the downstairs rooms, Molly took them upstairs, saying she wanted them to see a mockingbird Mark had tamed. Afterward, they were sent home with Grandmother's famous puddings for their wives—and with the clear impression that she had nothing to hide. That first winter up in her cell, Jacobs's distress was physical as well as mental. She suffered from frost-bitten shoulders and feet and "longed to draw in a plentiful draught of fresh air, to stretch my cramped limbs, to have room to stand erect, to feel the earth under my feet again." Fearful that she would lose the use of her legs, she determinedly stretched her muscles and crawled around the tiny space each day [ILSG pp. 119, 121].

The family made a consistent effort to bring her news of the town. Before the holidays, the word had been that the Reverend Dr. Avery—whom they despised—was leaving for Greensboro, Alabama. Now they learned that a Dr. Cairnes would be St. Paul's new rector. Cairnes was a man they grew to admire. He arranged for the slaves to use the church gallery for special meetings on Sunday evenings, and he gave them serious sermons, but he was not to prosper in Edenton. Only a year after he arrived, the family reported that he had offered his resignation.

Everyone knew that the congregation had become divided over Dr. Cairnes's ministry because he had voiced grave doubts about spiritual authority for slavery. A few months after he arrived in Edenton, a wealthy parishioner, the widow Mary Bissell, had fallen sick. Reverend Cairnes visited Mrs. Bissell in her home, across from Mrs. Blount's house (where Hatty had hidden), and a week before she died, he wrote out Mrs. Bissell's will for her and witnessed her signature. Mrs. Bissell left all seven of her slaves to the American Colonization Society to be freed and sent to Africa. The news swept Edenton from parlor to cabin, then up to Hatty's attic. Everyone, black and white, could recall that years earlier, the *Gazette* reported that Quakers had sent their slaves from Norfolk to Liberia. And everyone knew that their prominent neighbor, the Hon. James Iredell Jr., had served as president of the Edenton Auxiliary Colonization Society. But no one in white Edenton knew anybody who had actually freed any slaves and sent them to Liberia or Sierra Leone, and no one in black Edenton knew anybody who had actually gone there to live.

Nor would they. Despite Mary Bissell's dying wishes, her will was immediately challenged by distant cousins and remained in the courts for years. In 1837, the family house was sold, and the slaves were moved into cheap rented quarters. Instead of being freed and sent to Africa, they were hired out. In 1838 Maria, one of Mrs. Bissell's slaves, was hired by Dr. Norcom. A few years later, Maria would be indicted by the court for hiring out her time "as if she were a free woman," and the master who had hired her would be convicted for permitting Maria to keep house "as a free woman" and for committing fornication with her. (Despite this, the following January, he would hire her again.) Then in 1843 Dr. Norcom, owed money by the Bissell estate, would be awarded a judgment of $90.00 and $8.00 in damages, a writ leviable not, as usual, on "lands and tenements," but only on "goods and chattels"—and Maria would be seized by the sheriff. On July 22, 1843, seven years after Mary Bissell tried to free her, Maria would be sold to the highest bidder for $175.00. Neither Maria, nor any of the other Bissell slaves, not even those who

had been children at the time of their mistress's death, would ever live to
see Africa.

Whether Dr. Cairnes had influenced the dying Mary Bissell to free
her slaves and send them off to Africa, or whether he had simply recorded
her wishes and witnessed her signature, white Edenton held him responsible for her decision. When the vestrymen, Dr. Norcom among them,
divided over his ministry, Cairnes announced that he would stay only if
he had their unanimous support. Instead, they voted unanimously
against him. Three days later, Dr. James Norcom was appointed senior
warden of St. Paul's.

This—like all other news—came to Hatty's attic from the lips of her
grandmother, her aunt, and her uncle. What she heard was not always
accurate, and some of it she later misremembered, confusing Mrs. Bissell's death with the death of Reverend Cairnes's wife a few months earlier. But Hatty remembered clearly that, shortly after she had run from
Dr. Norcom, an Edenton slaveholder had made a singular effort to free
her slaves, and that—as Hatty's days and weeks in the attic multiplied into
months and years—the people remained enslaved. If in her mind, Hatty
had tried to pattern herself on Rose Cabarrus, a "slave girl" who had
managed to win freedom for herself and all her family, then Maria Bissell must have presented her with an alternative model that she was determined not to replicate: a "slave girl" who remained the helpless subject
of the actions of others.

The stories the family brought her told not only of betrayal, but of
violence. In summer, there was ghastly news: their friend Abby (owned
by Martha Blount) was walking near the Chinquapin Chapel when she
saw the constable shoot his gun and heard human groans. He had killed
Tom Hoskins, who three days earlier had run from Auburn, James Norcom Jr.'s plantation. Although Abby testified to what she had seen and
heard, the coroner's jury concluded only that "a certain person, or persons unknown; fired a Gun or some fire arms at the said negro man Tom,
which gun was loaded with Powder and lead, and did enter the body of
said Tom about the right shoulder, which Caused his death against the
piece and dignity of the State." Harriet's brother John later angrily commented, "There was no pay for this—only a feast of blood. Tom's crime
was running away from one whom I know to be an unmerciful tyrant."

During the second winter, the weather was unusually bitter, and even
the brackish water in Edenton harbor froze over. Hatty suffered unbear-
ably. In her icy attic, she later wrote, her "limbs were benumbed by inac-
tion, and the cold filled them with cramp. I had a very painful sensation

of coldness in my head; even my face and tongue stiffened, and I lost the power of speech." She lay unconscious for sixteen hours, and after John brought her around, became delirious. They drugged her to keep her quiet, and then, burning charcoal for warmth, almost suffocated her in her airless den. (When finally her brother brought up an iron pan with burning coals, "I was so weak, and it was so long since I had enjoyed the warmth of a fire, that those few coals actually made me weep.") During her slow recovery, her mind was overwhelmed by dark thoughts. "I tried to be thankful for my little cell, dismal as it was, and even to love it, as part of the price I had paid for the redemption of my children." Sometimes she managed to believe that "God was a compassionate Father, who would forgive my sins for the sake of my sufferings. At other times, it seemed to me there was no justice or mercy in the divine government." Through all this, she somehow was able to survive and to persist in the belief that she would "get out of this dark hole some time or other" [ILSG pp. 122–23, 131].

Inside her cell, each day seemed like the last. Sometimes she could judge the passage of time only by the growth of her children, whom she glimpsed through her peephole when they played outdoors. But beyond those cramped walls, the town was changing. The Dismal Swamp canal had absorbed most of its commerce. Although 5,000 bales of cotton could be shipped from Edenton each year, and although the town had a charter for a railroad, a visitor commented that with "a suicidal perverseness the citizens will not build it, for the very politic reason, that though it could not but benefit Edenton it would also help Norfolk!" While the rest of the economy stagnated, however, the fisheries were thriving, and from mid-March until mid-May, worked around the clock.

The following summer, Sam Sawyer announced he would run for Congress. Predictably, Dr. Norcom—who had not forgiven Sawyer for outwitting him—supported Sawyer's opponent. Although the doctor was usually a "staunch Whig," and although the Whigs had joined the coalition backing Sawyer, Norcom broke ranks. After making another futile trip to New York searching for Hatty, he returned in time to try to influence the election outcome. Fourteen years earlier, he had bolted his party to help defeat Sawyer's uncle and had triumphed, bragging that he entertained "290 persons in my own house & thereby secured to our friend the decisive . . . vote." Since then, both the *Gazette* and a citizens' group had denounced "the practice of treating with intoxicating drink at . . . elections . . . with a view of influencing votes." Norcom nevertheless flouted public opinion by again supplying his neighbors with election-day food and drink. But his effort was useless. Although Major Sam was dogged by what he saw as "certain malign influences, the cry of nullification and the influence of the baptists," he won handily.

Now Hatty, trapped in her cell, had new worries. Sawyer was making plans to leave North Carolina for Washington—and to take her brother John with him—but he had never set into motion the involved legal process of executing free papers for Joseph and Louisa. Hatty had always assumed that she could somehow reach Sawyer in an emergency. But what if he should die far from home? What if the children became the property of his heirs? Frantic with worry, she nerved herself to take a wild risk. She felt certain that Sawyer would not leave Edenton without stopping at Grandmother's to make arrangements for the children. Knowing that the *Fox* would cast off between ten and eleven, she lowered herself down into the storeroom sometime before nine. It was clumsy work. Her ankles gave out when she reached the bottom of the shelf-ladder, and she fell to the floor, but managed to crawl to the window and huddle behind a flour-barrel.

She heard the clock strike, and then Major Sam's voice was outside the window asking a companion to wait while he spoke with Molly. A few minutes later, when she heard him leaving, she summoned all her courage. Pushing the shutter open as he passed by the window, she said, "Stop one moment, and let me speak for my children" [ILSG p. 126]. She saw him falter, then continue down the walk and out the gate. Crouching in the dark, she felt shocked, devastated to learn that she meant nothing to him, that the children meant nothing. Writing later, she described her emotions as intense—and not all of them concerned the children. "Had he so little feeling for their wretched mother," she asked, "that he would not listen a moment while she pleaded for them?" Overcome by "painful memories," it was only when she heard the shutter opening that she realized she had forgotten to hook it [ILSG p. 126]. Then she looked up.

She had not even seen Major Sam since she had climbed up into her cell, and they had not spoken for years. Now their words were whispered and rushed. He was appalled to find her huddled there, fearful that her presence would endanger Molly and the family. She was determined to exact his promise to free the children. Quickly, he gave her his word—adding that if it could be arranged he would buy her as well—when footfalls interrupted them. As Hatty stretched up to close the shutter, he stepped back into the house to tell Molly of their talk, then moved quickly down the walk, out the gate, and toward the wharf. Too weak to climb back up the shelf-ladder, Hatty called to Uncle Mark for help. He gently carried her up and left her in her cell with her musings, "starless as the midnight darkness around me" [ILSG p. 127].

Writing her book years later, Jacobs would describe this dramatic scene, spelling out the only conversation that she would record between "Linda," her pseudonymous narrator, and the man with whom she had had a five-year relationship, the father of her children. Perhaps what she wrote is a record of her memories. Or perhaps it is a sketch of her fondest fantasy: that Sawyer was concerned for her safety and that he readily agreed to her demands. Sawyer left no record. Jacobs, like all slave narrators, would shape her book with both a public agenda—to forge her story as a weapon against the slave system; and with an autobiographer's private agenda—to convince her readers to understand and sympathize with her. To her targeted audience of free women schooled in nineteenth-century sexual conformity and female domesticity, this was a memorable passage.

Now she began disguising her hand to correspond with her brother, whom Sawyer had taken to Washington. Perhaps this letter-writing is what prompted her to begin waging psychological warfare against Dr. Norcom. Summoning the trusted friend who, years earlier, had protected her in the swamp, Hatty again climbed down into the storeroom and, as Mark guarded the gate, revealed her plan. To convince Norcom that she had left the state, she would write to him using a northern address. Could her friend find her an old New York newspaper so she could locate an address that would look legitimate, and could he arrange for her letter to be mailed from New York? Pulling a scrap of the *New York Herald* from his pocket—it had been used to wrap a cap he had bought the day before—he assured her that he knew a trustworthy seaman on the New York packet who would mail her letters. Next morning at first light, she studied the *Herald* to find a plausible street and number and, reckoning the time needed to carry a letter to New York and mail it from there to Edenton, copied out an address, postdated the page, and began. She drafted one letter to Norcom and in it enclosed another, addressed to Molly. After delivering these to her friend, she told her aunt and her grandmother what she had done and asked Betty to report on Norcom's response.

Four days after her letters were to be sent from New York, Aunt Betty reported that Norcom had picked them up at the post office and carried them home to Eden Alley. Hatty warned Grandmother to expect Norcom the next morning, and asked her to place a chair for him where Hatty could hear their conversation. Next day she heard Norcom slam the gate, make his way up the walk, come into the house, and make himself comfortable.

Enthralled, Hatty listened, breathless, as he played out the scene she had scripted. Over the years, the *Gazette* had run stories about antislavery sentiment in Massachusetts. Remembering these stories, in her letter to Molly, Hatty had asked that Joseph and Louisa be sent north to Boston, where she said she now lived. But Norcom had destroyed her note and had substituted instead a counterfeit letter that he had signed with her name. In his version, she was ashamed of running away and wanted to come back to Edenton, although not as a slave. Only if this was impossible did she ask that the children be sent north to her. To Molly, Norcom proposed that he pay Mark's fare to Boston to bring Hatty home, and he gave assurances that he would sell her to Grandmother, who could then free her. Baiting the trap with Hatty's lifelong dream, he said he assumed that the children were already free, and when she returned, they could be a happy family in their own home.

Hearing him, Hatty felt a rush of excitement. Not only had she enmeshed Norcom in her design, he was even embroidering on it, using her fabrication as the basis for his own forgery. It was delicious to realize that she could play mindgames with the man who for years had tried to control her consciousness. She no longer felt herself Norcom's victim, but his enemy. By convincing Norcom that she was in Boston and that he could slacken his surveillance in Edenton, Hatty felt that she had won the first skirmish in her war against him. She now knew she could not only act on herself—she had already learned she could strike at her enemy this way—but by manipulating him. This tiny triumph over her enemy became the occasion for her to begin to regain control of her body, to prepare herself for the battles to come. She persuaded Molly to agree that, in the earliest dawn, she could lower herself down into the storeroom and begin to exercise to try to regain the use of her legs. And with this small victory, she opened an ongoing bogus correspondence from the North.

In August 1838, the town learned that Sam Sawyer had married Miss Lavinia Peyton of Virginia, a niece of the woman he boarded with at Washington. The bride wanted to be married in Chicago, where her married sister lived, and despite his fear that, once on free soil, John might claim his freedom, Major Sam took Harriet's brother to accompany him on his wedding journey. They traveled to Baltimore and Philadelphia, then on to Niagara Falls and Buffalo, and by boat to Chicago. Five weeks after leaving Washington, they made their way back, stopping in Canada and in New York City before arriving in Edenton.

In Molly's bakery home on King Street, the family eagerly awaited John's arrival. Grandmother invited some of his friends, cooked a special dinner, and lovingly set his place at the table. At the first blast of the stage's horn, Mark walked over to the tavern to welcome his nephew, but when the passengers climbed down, John was not among them. A neighbor asked where he was, and Major Sam said that he had been decoyed away by the abolitionists.

Molly wept when Mark brought her the news. She was certain that, like her beloved son Joseph, her grandson John was gone forever. Hatty, in her attic cell, also mourned—selfishly, she later concluded. Years afterward, she would hear of John's escape from his own lips: how in Canada, on the trip home, he had thought he might gain his freedom by obtaining a British seaman's protection, and how later in New York, urged on by old Edenton friends, he had decided to run away before his master left the city. Major Sam and his bride were staying at the Astor House Hotel near New York's City Hall. John told how he had taken his clothing from the hotel in small parcels as if to have it laundered, and boldly carried his trunk out to be repaired at Johnson's, nearby on Fulton Street. Then, after waiting on his master and mistress at table until 4:00, he arranged for a note to be delivered informing Major Sam that he was escaping. Shouldering his trunk, he simply walked down to Pier 1, Battery Place, boarded the 4:30 boat to Providence, and went on to New Bedford.

In her cell, Hatty was now plagued by a new fear. Would the loss of his valuable slave make Major Sam more reluctant to sign papers emancipating the children? On Sunday morning, Grandmother led little Joe and Lulu out onto the piazza so Hatty could be cheered by the sound of their voices. When a neighbor stopped by to visit, she wept her sorrow at losing John, but her friend rebuked her. Clapping her hands, she exclaimed that Molly should not bewail her grandson's absence, but instead thank God that he had taken his freedom. And Hatty, listening, rejoiced that John was saved and prayed for forgiveness.

Major Sam and his bride returned to Washington for the final session of the Twenty-fifth Congress, and in the spring, brought Laura, their new baby, home to Edenton. Sawyer ran for reelection that summer. He was not a compelling speaker. "His style," one listener wrote, "is pretty, fanciful and chaste—his voice is weak and unmusical which detracts much from oratory." Attacked in the *Gazette* for his voting record, Sawyer responded with a circular defending his position. But he lost the contest.

That summer Hatty watched through her peephole as baby Laura was carried about in her nurse's arms—and felt uneasy. She worried when Aunt Betty brought the news that Dr. Norcom's wife planned to tell the young Mrs. Sawyer that Joseph and Louisa were Major Sam's children. Her anxiety increased the afternoon Joseph came home upset because the major's wife, seeing him in the street, had called him "a pretty little negro" [ILSG p. 137]. A few days later, Major Sam stopped by to inform Molly that he had told his wife that the children were his, and that their mother was dead. Now he wanted to take them home so that his wife could see them. This so troubled Hatty that Grandmother did not tell her when she sent them off to Sawyer's house. The result of their visit was that Lavinia Sawyer decided to raise Joseph and that her sister, who was visiting, wanted to adopt Louisa. Hearing this, Hatty was beside herself. The notion that her children would be given good homes seemed fine, but she feared that—at some point, in some crisis—Joseph and Louisa might be sold by their "protectors." Almost frantic with worry, she convinced Grandmother to remind Major Sam of his promise and to beg him to emancipate the children legally. Finally, Molly went. She reported back that Sawyer was surprised by her message and assured her that as far as he was concerned, the children were free. Sawyer then announced that their mother could decide their futures—but, he warned, Norcom was still claiming them, asserting that their sale was illegal because they were his daughter's property, not his. He urged that they be sent north.

Hatty felt completely powerless. Negotiating with Major Sam through Grandmother, she finally agreed to send Lulu to Washington with her father until the time he could take her to be raised and educated by his cousin in Brooklyn. She mourned the prospect of losing her daughter—not to freedom, as she had lost her brother and her uncle, but to some indeterminate status. And she particularly hated the idea of her beloved Lulu playing the traditional slave girl's role of "colored" nursemaid to her "white" half sister Laura in Washington. She hated it even more when she reflected that this was happening because Major Sam had not bothered to legalize the children's emancipation. Despite her fury and foreboding, however, Hatty knew that she had no choice. She asked only to spend the night with her darling child before they took Lulu away.

Five years after climbing up into her cell, Hatty felt her way down the cupboard-ladder into the storeroom, walked across the piazza, and climbed the stairs to the room where she had given birth to her babies. Uncle Mark brought the little girl to her, then left mother and daughter together to enact a scene of high emotion. Tearfully, Harriet revealed herself to her beloved child, and little Lulu, believing and incredulous, wept and promised secrecy. The night passed quickly. Back in her cell, Hatty sobbed alone in the dark and vowed that somehow she would get to Brooklyn.

Days, then months, passed. Hatty had continued writing letters to Norcom, some of which were posted from as far away as Canada. Now she wrote to Brooklyn, then to Washington in Molly's name, asking whether Louisa had arrived safely. Finally, after a half year, a letter came from a daughter of Sam's Brooklyn cousin announcing that Lulu had arrived and commenting that Sawyer had given her to the writer as "my little waiting maid" [ILSG p. 142]. Hatty was stunned. Had Major Sam actually made his daughter a present to his young cousin? If Louisa could so easily be disposed of, what did this imply for Joseph? Their son thought he was free. Could he, too, be made to live as a slave?

January came, and with it, the usual slave hirings and sales. This year, among the "likely and valuable negroes" auctioned off to pay their masters' debts was Aunt Sue Bent's daughter. "Fanny"—the name Jacobs calls her in her narrative—was bought by a local man, but her four little girls were purchased by a master who lived far from Edenton. Like many slaves whose lives were shattered by sale, she ran, and like many, when she ran she went to family. But this situation proved unique. Hatty's Joseph, playing in Grandmother's yard one afternoon, spotted the fugitive and told Grandmother. All that spring, two women were in hiding in King Street.

Hatty had somehow managed to keep her spirits up after the loss of her brother, but now she felt deprived of her little girl and became increasingly depressed. Then there was worse news. She heard Dr. Norcom tell Grandmother that Aunt Betty was sick and that Molly—who had not entered his house for years—must come immediately. Hatty was frantic because she could not go to her. Aunt Betty had nurtured her since she was six, had carried her last, doomed baby while Hatty was carrying Joseph, and had unfailingly supported Hatty's determination to resist slavery and to create a home in freedom for her children. At the Norcoms' home, surrounded by the Norcom family, for two days Molly sat by the bed of her only living daughter, looking into her eyes and watching her die, unable to speak freely. On the first day, Betty, struggling with paralysis, tried to comfort her. On the second, she lost the ability to speak. Hatty fainted when Uncle Mark brought the news that Aunt Betty was dead. He revived her, warning that she must not permit her grief to add to his mother's. It did not help matters that Norcom—who, following the recent death of his devout son Benjamin Rush, had become a communicant of St. Paul's—suggested that Harriet be persuaded to come back to Edenton and return to his household to "supply her aunt's place." Now when Hatty peeked downstairs, she saw that Molly was aging visibly. More often than before, Grandmother was knocking out the signal for her to come to the trapdoor so she could speak of her dead daughter. But Hatty knew that her presence was not a comfort, but a constant source of stress.

Increasingly restless, Hatty determined to go north to meet her daughter and her brother, north where she could arrange for Joseph to be sent to her. She was worried thinking that her children—like Maria Bissell's Mary and John, who had been promised freedom in Liberia—would be trapped forever in southern slavery. Then in this crisis, a way was opened by Providence: not solely the divine power guiding human destiny, but also the force of the combined efforts of Edenton's black community. The faithful friend who had helped her survive in the swamp appeared at Molly's door with word of a ship that could prove a means of escape to free soil.

The news was electric. Hatty consulted with Uncle Mark, and he promised to convince Molly—who ever since Joseph's reenslavement, was terrified of the consequences of escape. She knew that the passage of time had not lessened the dangers fugitives faced. Only the previous year, Charles W. Mixson had advertised in the local paper offering a fifty-dollar reward for Penny Howcott, "about 40 years of age," run away "two months since." Announcing that the fugitive had a mother and son five miles above Edenton at Howcott's plantation, one daughter at Coffield's plantation, and a second daughter in town at Mrs. Ward's, in addition to a son in Perquimans, a brother in Edenton, and another in Bertie, Mixson speculated that she might have been "lurking about some of her acquaintances or relations in Edenton." He ended by announcing: "I will give the above reward for the said negro Penny, if delivered to me, or confined in any jail, so that I get her again—or I will give the same reward for her *head* alone."

Despite Molly's fears, the family began to make hurried secret preparations for Hatty's escape. Then news circulated among the slaves of the murder of a fugitive, the son of Grandmother's friend, who had run off after a whipping. Captured and returned to his master's plantation, the young man was again whipped, then imprisoned within the mechanism of a cotton press, where he remained until he died, gnawed by rats.

Molly was terrified that her granddaughter might face a similar fate, and her panic was infectious. Hatty abandoned her escape plan, proposing that Aunt Sue Bent's "Fanny" take her place. Molly still could not stop worrying. The escape ship, instead of weighing anchor, remained in the harbor, and on the third day, when the foul weather had not broken, Molly signaled for Hatty to come down into the storeroom, where she poured out her fears. What if Aunt Sue Bent's daughter should be discovered? What if "Fanny" were tortured and implicated them all? She and Mark would be ruined. It was not enough that she had lost her last daughter. . . . Then, as she wept and cried, a voice called out to her from the piazza, and into the storeroom stepped Mrs. Blount's untrustworthy housemaid Jenny, sent by her mistress for some crackers.

Hatty hid behind a barrel, and Grandmother hastily led the woman to the piazza, this time locking the storeroom door, which she had forgotten to do earlier. After a few minutes, when the crackers were counted out and the woman was sent on her way, Molly returned in despair. Afraid that her forgetfulness had destroyed her granddaughter, she urged Hatty to make her escape immediately.

Hatty spent the hours until nightfall locked in the storeroom with her son. They had not spoken for almost seven years, and both were choked by emotion. She was astonished when he told her he had known of her presence. He had once heard her cough, had awakened to see Lulu's bed empty the night before she left, and had listened as Grandmother whispered a warning—but had never voiced his suspicions to anyone. She told him she was now going north, that she would arrange for his passage, and that she would see him there. While they spoke, Molly appeared with her savings, which she pressed upon her granddaughter.

Then, for a last time, Jacobs climbed up into the cupboard. Despite her conviction that freedom was in her future, she felt sad. At the appointed time, she lowered herself into the storeroom. Grandmother clasped her hand, and together they knelt with little Joseph while Molly poured out a fervent prayer. Then, stepping up the walk, Hatty opened the gate and moved quickly toward the wharf. She did not look back.

5

Sometimes Like Freedom

❧

I called myself free, and sometimes felt so;
but I knew I was insecure.
—Harriet Jacobs, *Incidents in the Life of a Slave Girl,* p. 166

Harriet Jacobs never divulged the details of her escape. She revealed only that after almost seven years, an opportunity for freedom presented itself. But she left a few clues, and—as with other mysteries in her narrative—it is possible to document aspects of her flight. There was an appealing scenario. The sea captain who agreed to carry her to freedom was perhaps James Wright—the same man who, after hiring Maria Bissell, was indicted for permitting her to live as if she were free, and who later was indicted with her for fornication and adultery. This man could have seemed approachable to Jacobs's friends, and they could have made the necessary arrangements for her passage with him. Then when it was learned that a Captain James Wright was master of the schooner *Skewarkey*, and that early in June 1842 a change in ownership caused the schooner to be delayed in the port of Edenton for three days, the riddle of Jacobs's escape seemed solved. But further investigation established that Maria Bissell's temporary master was a Captain James O. Wright of Gates County, in 1842 only twenty-four years old—not the "elderly" sea captain of Jacobs's narrative, and that the master of the *Skewarkey* was a Captain James A. Wright. This information ruined a wonderful story, but it kept the details of Jacobs's escape a mystery—as she wished.

Some things, however, are clear. It was probably on June 7, 1842, that "Fanny" boarded the vessel in Jacobs's place, expecting to sail from Edenton the next morning. But Wednesday dawned dark and cloudy, with contrary winds, and the ship remained in dock. On Thursday, "the wind and weather remained the same" [ILSG p. 152]. This marked the beginning of six weeks of rain that left the crops rotting in the fields. At Edenton, "the earth was so full of water that no trees except those having the largest and longest tap roots could withstand the storms. With a half dozen exceptions, every shade tree in town was blown down. . . . Transportation and travel were entirely arrested." It seems almost preternatural, but Jacobs had entered the attic in "the year of the whirlwind," and now was leaving it at the onset of "the wet year."

It was on Friday morning, June 10, that the faithless Jenny barged into Grandmother's for her mistress's crackers. By then the wind had shifted enough for the vessel to leave the dock, and she was beating down the harbor channel when Jacobs's friend ran to the wharf and paid two boatmen a dollar apiece to catch up with her. Seeing a light-skinned man being rowed toward his ship by two darker oarsmen, and fearing a search for runaways, the captain hoisted sails. But the boatmen caught up with the vessel, and Hatty's friend clambered aboard. After a hurried conference, the captain was convinced that a second woman needed his help, and he agreed, at a steep price, to wait at a specified spot until evening when she could come aboard.

At dusk Hatty went with her friend to the meeting place, where she was met by Uncle Mark—and in a surprise move, her son—and climbed into the waiting rowboat. Once she was aboard ship, the captain introduced himself and showed her into the tiny cabin, where "Fanny" was waiting. In the arms of her old friend, Hatty could no longer control herself. She sobbed so loudly that the captain came to warn them against making noise. With the wind against them, they were still in sight of town, and Hatty worried that the constable would chase them down. Frightened of the sailors around her, she soon conceived of more fears: since the captain had already been paid, might he not give them up to make even more money?

Yet after "Fanny" reassured her, saying she had been well treated during her three days on board, Hatty became more calm. She climbed up on deck and, after years spent in the fetid attic crawl space, found the spring night magical. Next morning, squinting against the brightness, she was enchanted by the light and air. She described her delight when they reached the Chesapeake: "O, the beautiful sunshine! the exhilarating breeze! and I could enjoy them without fear or restraint. I had never realized what grand things air and sunlight are till I had been deprived of them" [ILSG p. 158]. She spent the next days on deck, trying to recover the use of her legs by exercising and rubbing them hard with salt water. Finally on Sunday evening, the ship entered the harbor.

Next morning, Hatty was up before dawn to see the sun rise over free soil. From the water, the city loomed gigantic. She had heard, of course, that Philadelphia was big, and had listened to Uncle Mark's descriptions of New York, even bigger. But her reference point was Edenton. She was not prepared for this metropolis. After saying her goodbyes and making sure a message would be delivered to the family back home, she was handed into a rowboat with the captain, and in a quarter of an hour, she and "Fanny" were deposited on a wooden wharf.

She had come to Philadelphia with the names of black folks from Chowan County who had settled in the city, and with the knowledge—repeatedly condemned by the *Edenton Gazette*—that "the poor slave had many friends at the north." Now, standing on the wooden dock in the morning sun, Hatty was overwhelmed by the sights and sounds and smells enveloping her. She steadied herself, then felt the captain tap her shoulder. Turning, she saw him gesture at a black man behind them. After pointing her toward a shop on the wharf, the captain began asking the stranger about trains to New York. She made her way to the store, but buying the double veils and gloves she had planned as a disguise was frightening. She had not set foot in a shop for years, and when the clerk named the prices in levys—which she had never heard of—she almost panicked. Thinking fast, she handed him one of Grandmother's gold pieces, then counted the change: a levy was worth eleven cents. Focusing carefully to blot out the city's noise and confusion, Hatty walked back to the captain, who introduced the stranger to her as Reverend Jeremiah Durham. The man took her hand like an old friend and, explaining that she and "Fanny" had missed the morning train to New York City, invited her to his home. His wife, he said, would make her comfortable, and friends nearby would welcome "Fanny." Her eyes blurred with tears as she said good-bye to the captain and his men and turned to follow Durham though the busy morning streets.

Making their way along the wharf, they turned into East Pine, then walked block after block to Durham's home between Tenth and Eleventh on Barley. As they walked, he introduced himself as a minister at Bethel, one of Philadelphia's black churches, and told her something about the city. In 1842, Philadelphia housed 19,000 African Americans, the largest free black population in the country. The community supported fifteen

churches, twenty-one day schools, sixty-four Mutual Relief or Benevolent Societies, and a Vigilant Committee, into whose protective hands
Jacobs and "Fanny" had luckily fallen. Routinely placing themselves at
risk by helping fugitives, the Vigilant Committee lived up to its name by
aiding "colored persons in distress" and regularly sent its members to the
city docks looking for fugitives. Today was Durham's turn.

At the house, Jacobs was greeted by the reverend's wife. (Was it now
that she first introduced herself using the name "Jacobs," as she had long
dreamed?) Meeting Mrs. Durham, Hatty was deeply struck by the realization that here was a black woman whose home and family were protected by law, whose daughter spent her days at school—not, like Lulu,
as waiting-maid to her white cousins. Gratefully, she accepted her hostess's invitation to dinner, then went with her host to search for her Edenton friends. They were not at home, but on the way back to the Durhams'
she began to feel enough at ease to look around her, noting with pleasure
the clean streets and neat stoops. As they walked, she responded to
Durham's inquiries about her past, but when, in answer to his persistent
questions, she revealed her children's parentage, she was shaken by his
response. Counseling her against divulging her sexual history, he warned
that some might treat her with "contempt" [ILSG p. 160]. This upset her
deeply. It would be years before she could confide in anyone again.

Later that day, a Vigilant Committee representative came to the
house to meet her. The group was hard-pressed to help the large numbers of fugitives from slavery arriving in the city. Forty-six refugees had
passed through their hands between January 20 and June 9, and over the
summer months, they would somehow manage to help 117 more men,
women, and children. It cost the committee about $3.00 to move each
refugee through Philadelphia, and its members were constantly raising
money—from sympathizers, from special collections at churches like
Bethel and the First Presbyterian below Shippen, from public celebrations
commemorating the August First abolition of slavery in the West Indies,
even from a "soiree." The activists offered Hatty money, but she told
them Grandmother had given her enough to get to New York. She was,
however, glad to accept their invitation to stay in the city a few days until
they could find someone to go on with her. Back home, Edenton had
fought against building a railroad, and like many of her townspeople, she
felt nervous about the idea of riding on a train for the first time.

The next few days were an education. "I verily believed myself to be
a free woman," Jacobs later wrote. "All this was new to me. . . . Philadelphia seemed to me a wonderfully great place" [ILSG pp. 161–62]. From

her startled reaction to the noise of a firebell in the night—she jumped up and dressed, thinking that as in Edenton, black women and children would have to drag the engine down to the water and fill it—to her delight at the sound of the morning street cries of women selling radishes, berries, and fish, she absorbed the life of the city around her. Mrs. Durham took her in hand, walking her through the neighborhood and even to 54 Mulberry Street, where the artist Robert Douglass Jr. was exhibiting miniatures and portraits. She had never seen the likenesses of black children before and found them particularly beautiful.

During these few days she met Elizabeth Chew, who would become a close friend. Both Elizabeth and her sister Hester were members of the Philadelphia Female Anti-Slavery Society, a group working with the Vigilance Committee. To stay current with rescue efforts, the women had asked the committee to "furnish us a report of their proceedings at our stated meetings." One of these was scheduled for June 23, while Jacobs was in the city, although it is very doubtful that she risked attending. She did, however, meet prominent activists. These included Joshua Coffin, a founder of the American Anti-Slavery Society, and Reverend Daniel A. Payne, who had just been received as a preacher by the Philadelphia Conference of the African Methodist Episcopal Church. (Reverend Payne was so taken by the story of Hatty's seven-year imprisonment that he suggested she write her narrative, and Coffin reached Lydia Maria Child, urging her to tell the story in the antislavery press.)

She also met Robert Purvis, chairman of the Vigilance Committee. Years later, he still remembered the "beautiful creature" who, after being "confined for seven years, . . . was brought in a vessel to Philadelphia." It was not Jacobs's beauty, however, that struck him so deeply as her cast of mind. He was moved by her obvious effort, after years of isolation and imprisonment, to embrace life. "Her long confinement so effected her in feeling that she repeatedly expressed to me a desire to return to the 'little dark place' as she called it—in which she had been in-mured." Jacobs's psychological state struck him as a subject for a poet: "Hers was a truthful representation of Byron's 'Prisoner of Chillon' when he declares upon being set free that: 'My very chains and I grew friends / So much a long communion tends / To make us what we are! Even I / Regained my freedom with a sigh.'"

Jacobs was struggling hard to leave that darkness behind her. On Friday, she and "Fanny" were introduced to Lymas Johnson, a Vigilance Committee member who had helped other refugees reach New York. Handing them their train tickets, he warned that he feared they would be uncomfortable in the Jim Crow cars. To Hatty, the railroad was exciting, but its noise and smoke overwhelmed her, and she was indeed shocked by the "dirt car," her first experience with northern segregation. She had not known that black passengers, denied the right to travel first-class, were relegated to "a large, rough car, with windows on each side, too high for us to look out without standing up," where drinking and smoking were permitted [ILSG p. 163]. (In Philadelphia, activists were demonstrating against the railroad's discriminatory practice, and for the rest of her life, Jacobs would join protests against segregated transportation in railroads, trolleys, and ships.) They reached Jersey City in only four hours, then boarded a ferry across the Hudson River and arrived at Courtland Street Station in New York. Everything was chaotic, with people scrambling to collect baggage and hail cabs, and after a tussle with an Irish cartman, Jacobs and "Fanny" paid twelve shillings to be taken to 33 Sullivan Street, the boardinghouse recommended by the Vigilance Committee.

Jacobs's first priority was to see her daughter. Prepared, as in Philadelphia, with the names of Edenton people in the city, she immediately contacted an old neighbor for help. He took her to the foot of Fulton Street, where they crossed the East River on the ferry—a double-ended steam vessel unlike Edenton's *Fox*—and disembarked in Brooklyn. Walking up Myrtle, they saw two young girls, one of whom Hatty recognized as the daughter of an old friend of Grandmother's. Only then did she realize that the other girl was her own Lulu.

It upset Jacobs to see how two years had changed her daughter, now almost nine years old. It was wonderful that she had grown so tall, but she was obviously suffering from neglect. Louisa had to complete an errand for her mistress, so after hugs and kisses, mother and daughter promised firmly that they would be together the next day. Jacobs spent the rest of Saturday in a warm reunion with old Edenton friends—laughing, crying, and thanking God for her deliverance. Early next morning, she wrote a careful note to Louisa's mistress, Mary Bonner Blount Tredwell (the wife of Major Sam's first cousin). Anxious not to endanger Grandmother by revealing that she had just come from Edenton, she wrote that she had arrived from Canada, and she asked permission for her daughter to visit her. Mary Tredwell sent Louisa to Hatty with reassurances that she need not worry that Norcom would be informed of her presence, and she invited Jacobs to visit.

The afternoon Jacobs spent with Lulu did not ease her mind. While Louisa maintained that she was well treated, her mother found her too quiet and submissive. She was particularly troubled to learn that the Tredwells had not sent her to school, as agreed—although Brooklyn had two African Free Schools, and the city had developed "a plan for the better education and moral culture of the Negro population." Jacobs became even more troubled when she visited the Tredwells' house. Although Mary Tredwell greeted her personally, she looked her straight in the eye as she stated that Major Sam had given Louisa to her teen-aged daughter Margaret as a servant.

This shook Jacobs deeply. She remembered James Tredwell's bankruptcy and his term in debtor's prison in Edenton. In Brooklyn, she saw hints that the family's fortunes were shaky—not like their cousins the Seabury Tredwells who, all Edenton knew, were living in Manhattan in a Greek Revival row house with a marble-framed fanlight doorway, handsome parlor ceilings, and wall-to-wall carpeting. If James Tredwell again failed and returned south, Jacobs realized, her Lulu could again become a North Carolina slave—or could even be sold. (Her worries were well-founded. A dozen years earlier, when Tredwell was facing ruin, he had planned to spirit his slaves away from the creditors and sell them: "I am determined to sell under the Trust or remove the negroes out of the state and try to get them to Louisiana where they are worth something.") Desperate to ensure her daughter's free status, that night Jacobs wrote to Norcom and to his daughter Mary Matilda, asking them to name the price of her freedom.

Having found Louisa, she tried next to locate her brother. She went to Boston after hearing he was there, but was told that he had moved on. In New Bedford, she learned that he had shipped out on a whaler two years earlier and would not return for months.

Back in New York at the Sullivan Street boardinghouse, Jacobs had a chance to look around her. Like other southern newcomers, she found the city astonishing. One visitor wrote, "What an empire, or rather what a world is New York City, and how insignificant do all other places appear when compaired [sic] to this, with its thousand omnibusses thundering through the streets eighteen hours out of the twenty four, its many thousand hacks, and countless drays, with its hundreds of magnificent hotels, crowded with traveling millions, with its numerous steam boats constantly moving loaded with passengers, also the railroads that radiate from the city with their long train cars." Here, as in Philadelphia, Jacobs met antislavery activists. Although the Ladies' New York City Anti-Slavery Society was notorious for excluding people of color, the city's free black population—over 16,000 strong—supported thirty-three of its own philanthropic and benevolent associations, many organized by women. These addressed their members' needs, raised funds for their churches, helped widows and orphans—and also actively aided fugitives. The all-black New York Ladies Literary Society collected money for the male New York Vigilant Committee, and shortly before Jacobs arrived in the city, black women formed the Manhattan Abolition Society and the Colored Female Vigilance Committee.

When Jacobs began looking for work, however, she did not approach any of these groups. Made wary by Reverend Durham's warning that information about her children's origins might cause her to be held in "contempt," she later wrote, "when I first came North I avoided the Anti-slavery people as much as possible because I felt that I could not be honest and tell the whole truth." Instead, she searched for work on her own, and when she heard of a job as a baby nurse, applied immediately.

This job interview was fortunate for Jacobs, who needed work. It was also fortunate for Mary Stace Willis, an Englishwoman who, after a brief courtship, had married the American writer Nathaniel Parker Willis, "poseur and poet, city dandy and country gentleman." Mary Willis had followed her new husband to Owego Creek in upstate New York six years earlier. At Glenmary, their country house, she had delivered a still-born daughter. Then in June—while Jacobs was in Philadelphia—Mary Willis gave birth to a healthy baby girl. Her husband's *American Scenery* had recently been published, and now he was busily churning out magazine pieces for the *Mirror*, *Graham's*, *Godey's*, and *The Ladies' Companion*. His biographer asserts that at the time, Willis was, "beyond a doubt, the most popular, best paid, and in every way most successful magazinist that America had yet seen." Nevertheless, finances were tight. Willis liked to live well. His father-in-law had not left him any of his fortune, his publisher had failed, and he had reluctantly sold his country estate and moved his wife and their new baby, Imogen, down to the city.

Mary Willis decided to trust her judgment. She hired Hatty without references, and they agreed on a trial period of a week. That week become a month, and the month became a year. Jacobs's relationship with the Willis family was to continue into the next generation. Caring for little Imogen enabled her to begin to heal the wounds—physical, emotional, and psychological—that she had suffered over the past seven years.

It would take time to heal. Most obvious, Jacobs's legs were causing her serious concern. After years of enforced inactivity, she was unable to run up and down the steep stairs at the Astor House without their swelling up. Instead of firing her, however, Mary Willis reorganized the baby's schedule to save Hatty steps and called in a doctor. Jacobs's psychological wounds were not so easily treated. Although finally in the North, she was unable to find peace of mind because she could not forget, even for a minute, that she and Lulu were vulnerable to Norcom's claims. Mary Willis proposed that the child come live with them, but Jacobs was afraid of offending the Tredwells. "Sweet and bitter," she later wrote, "were mixed in the cup of my life, and I was thankful that it had ceased to be entirely bitter" [ILSG p. 170]. She cheered herself with the thought that now, for the first time since Lulu was tiny, she was able to be with her often, and with the awareness that she was setting aside her wages to fulfil her dream of making a home in freedom for her children. Day by day, as she tended little Imogen, her spirits lifted.

And then they soared. Harriet's brother John appeared, back from the sea. As the *Frances Henrietta* dropped anchor in New Bedford, his friend Robert Piper boarded with the news that his sister Hatty had come north, was searching for him, and was working for a family at the Astor House. Hearing this, John drew his pay and came down to New York. One morning, playing with Imogen near the window, Jacobs saw her brother in the street below. He was shocked at the sight of her. "At first she did not look natural to me; but how should she look natural, after having been shut out from the light of heaven for six years and eleven months!" [ILSG p. 221]. Reunited, they laughed and cried, John recounting the details of his escape from Major Sam, and Hatty describing the family's anticipation of his arrival and Grandmother's distress at hearing that he had run off; John telling his experiences at sea, and Hatty narrating her maritime escape. Then together they took the ferry to Brooklyn to reunite Lulu with her uncle. With their transplanted Edenton friends, they shared the latest from home. The most important news was that Grandmother had petitioned to free Uncle Mark, and had managed to have her appeal signed by most of the prominent men in town.

John stayed for a week, and together he and Harriet discussed the Norcoms' replies to her letters. The doctor had written that she would have to come back to Edenton before he would even consider selling her. The answer to her plea to Mary Matilda, ostensibly written by her mistress's brother, was an urgent invitation to return to Edenton. It attempted to play upon her feelings for "your old grandmother, your child, and the friends who love you" and claimed that the doctor, "by

our persuasion, will be induced to let you be purchased by any person
you may choose in our community" [ILSG p. 172]. Reading this, Jacobs
thought she recognized Norcom's devious hand, which she could not
trust.

In the spring when the weather broke, Jacobs felt anxious about taking
little Imogen outside to play. Everywhere, she saw Southerners who had
come north seeking cooler weather, and she was terrified that she might
be kidnapped. This was not an idle fear. Only months earlier George
Latimer, a Norfolk runaway, had been arrested and jailed in Boston. In
response to the huge protest that followed—in addition to a legal defense,
black and white abolitionists organized a Latimer Committee, held mass
meetings, mounted a petition drive, and even published a newspaper, *The
Latimer Weekly and North Star*—Latimer's owner agreed to sell him for
$400. In this frightening climate Jacobs, hearing that Norcom was again
coming to New York, abruptly asked Mary Willis for two weeks off,
arranged for a friend to care for little Imogen, and fled to John, living in
Boston. With her brother she felt safe, and she immediately wrote Grandmother asking that Joseph be sent to her. Molly, who had been the children's ostensible owner ever since Major Sam had bought them, sent
Joseph on the New York packet with a note asking a friend to send him
on to Boston. Jacobs was thrilled, one morning, to hear her son—now a
teenager—knocking at John's door, excited and proud to have made the
trip all by himself.

Joseph brought good news. With the heavy weight of Harriet's con-
cealment lifted, Grandmother and Uncle Mark had begun picking up the
pieces of their lives that they had laid down on Harriet's behalf seven long
years before. Finally able to bring a wife into the house, Mark was planning to marry Ann, a daughter of the late Gustavus Adolphus Johnson.
And—her conscience finally freed of secrets—Grandmother had become
a communicant of St. Paul's. Jacobs arranged for her son to stay in Boston
with her brother. After a few days, when she heard that Dr. Norcom had
returned to Edenton, she went back to her job with the Willises.

In New York, however, the influx of southern tourists was a constant
worry. She was relieved to leave the city when the Willises decided to
vacation in Saratoga. Harriet Jacobs's trip to Saratoga as Imogen's nursemaid in the summer of 1843 was memorable not for the relief it offered
from fears of kidnapping, however, but for the racial insults she experienced. When Jacobs was refused service onboard the Troy line's new

steamboat *Knickerbocker*, her employer, true to her English upbringing, insisted that she receive equal treatment. During the season, Saratoga was a popular destination for distinguished Southerners, and the hotels were filled with "the rich merchants from New Orleans, and the wealthy planter from Arkansas, Alabama, and Tennessee, with the more haughty and more polished land-owner from Georgia, the Carolinas and Virginia." To Jacobs's employer Nathaniel Parker Willis, Saratoga was "a neutral ground, where the south discovers that the north is not a Mont Blanc, and the north perceives that the south is not a Vesuvius!" But to Jacobs, the presence of the Southerners posed a threat. At the hotel, she studied the faces of the guests "with fear and trembling, dreading to see some one who would recognize me" [ILSG pp. 175–76].

Saratoga's United States Hotel was nothing like Horniblow's Tavern. The family stayed in a cottage on the extensive grounds, and Willis puffed the establishment in his columns as "a superb hotel indeed, in all its appointments." He regaled his readers with descriptions of "the springs and colonnades, the woodwalks and drives, the sofas and swings," and of the views from the pillars of the colonnade, looking down toward Congress Hall. His audience was charmed by his description of life at the spa, and of the Saratoga belle. She was, he wrote, up at six to drink the "metallic" medicinal waters, then joined "the crowd of fashionables at the Congress spring, where the band played every morning," breakfasted with five hundred people, then promenaded in the drawing-room until eleven, when she sought out the bowling alleys. After dinner at two, when the men took their chairs out onto the grass to smoke and listen to the German band, she again joined "the full-dress crowd" until tea, and from then on was busy with "hops" and balls until midnight. (Willis, however, did not detail for his readers Jacobs's day—which was spent tending to the needs and whims of little Imogen.)

Later that summer, the family vacationed at the Marine Pavilion at Rockaway which, Willis instructed his audience, was "the favorite and regular resort of many of the best families of the city, the society . . . of a more refined quality and on a more agreeable footing than that of any other watering-place." Jacobs later wrote that she agreed that the shore was wonderful and the Marine Pavilion excellent. But "every where I found the same manifestations of that cruel prejudice, which so discourages the feelings, and represses the energies of the colored people" [ILSG p. 176]. When hotel staff told her she would have to eat in the kitchen, she refused to comply, and Willis ordered room service. Then when the

white staff complained that they would not "wait on negroes," Jacobs
stood her ground, and ultimately, she was allowed to eat in the dining
room. "Finding I was resolved to stand up for my rights," she writes,
"they concluded to treat me well."

Back in New York, Jacobs hurried over to Brooklyn to see her daughter. There she encountered Joseph Blount, Mrs. Tredwell's ne'er-do-well
brother (who, she later learned, was routinely sending Louisa out for
liquor and asking her to pour it, then whispering "vile language" into the
preadolescent's ears). Visiting one Sunday morning in late October,
Jacobs found Lulu upset. The child explained that she had found a torn-
up letter while sweeping the yard. She took it to the other children, who
laughed when she said she was afraid it might concern her mother. But
when they pieced the scraps together, they saw it was the draft of a note
Blount had written to Dr. Norcom in Edenton, telling him how he could
seize Jacobs. They carried the fragments to Mary Tredwell, who confronted her brother. He denied the accusations, then left hurriedly.

Clearly, Jacobs had been betrayed. In Edenton, it was gossiped that
Dr. Norcom was having financial difficulties, and now Blount had written to help Norcom seize his runaway property. Distraught that she must
again run, Jacobs became further upset when she realized that she had
never explained her situation to Mary Willis. She hurried back to Manhattan and that night revealed that she was a fugitive.

Early next morning, Jacobs sent word to her brother in Boston, and
Mary Willis contacted New York's antislavery Judge Arent Van der Poel
and the abolitionist attorney John Hopper. She then went with Jacobs to
a friend's home, where Hatty could hide until John's arrival. Jacobs
pleaded with Louisa's mistress to let her daughter accompany her, and
Mary Tredwell agreed after demanding that the child return in ten days.
She sent Lulu to her mother wearing outgrown clothing and carrying her
few things in a school satchel. Seeing Lulu in her thin summer dress,
Jacobs took off her own flannel skirt, which she quickly cut down for her
little girl, and Mary Willis brought the child a warm shawl and hood.

John reached New York on Wednesday. Taking Lawyer Hopper's
advice, they went north by the Stonington route, less traveled by Southerners. Hopper, full of suggestions and good wishes, met them on the
Sound steamer *Rhode Island* and put in a word with the stewardess on
their behalf. But when Jacobs tried to buy cabin tickets, she was refused
because of her color. With Louisa by her side, she appealed to the captain as Hopper had counseled, and was able to arrange for them to sleep

below deck out of the weather. At Stonington, they found the train wait-ing. Although ordered to sit near the engine, they protested and moved back away from the noise.

New York had been cold, but Boston was colder still. Norcom had again torn up her life, but this time, Jacobs was not voyaging alone toward a "city of strangers" [ILSG p. 158]. This time, she had her daughter with her, and her brother was taking them to his home. Boston's black com-munity, centered at the base of Beacon Hill, included only 2,000 people— fewer than Philadelphia's or New York's—but it seemed larger than its numbers. Mostly New England born and literate, black Boston embraced a rainbow of people, including seamen from around the globe, refugees from the South, and foreign-born blacks who had been freed when slav-ery had been abolished in Haiti, Central America, Mexico, and the British Empire. They centered their lives around their households, and families expanded to take in boarders like Harriet's brother John.

Their organizations were as varied as their accents and colors. Most important were the five churches, but secular groups thrived as well. By 1843, when Jacobs's brother John settled in the city, the African Society and the African Lodge # 459 had been joined by a cluster of cultural and mutual-aid societies: the Adelphic Union Library Association, the Histri-onic Club, the Boston Philomanthean Society, and the Young Men's Lit-erary Debating Society. The public lectures of the racially integrated Adelphic Union Society, unlike most, welcomed women. But women had their own groups, including the Colored Female Union Society, the Afric-American Female Intelligence Society, the Colored Female Charitable Society, the Daughters of Zion, the New England Temperance Society of People of Color, and the Garrison Society, as well as the Mutual Lyceum and racially integrated groups such as the Boston Female Anti-Slavery Society.

John now signed himself "John S."—an apparent compliment to his last master, Sam Sawyer. His path north had been worn smooth by ear-lier black migrants from the southeastern states. It may be that he chose to make his home in Boston because during his months in New Bedford or his three years at sea he read David Walker's "incendiary" *Appeal*. Or perhaps he saw copies of William Lloyd Garrison's newspaper *The Lib-erator*, which for a dozen years had made "abolition" synonymous with "Boston." Possibly he recalled when, in 1831, the *Edenton Gazette* had reported the $1,500 reward offered by the Vigilant Association of

Columbia, South Carolina, for "the apprehension, prosecution and conviction of any white person" distributing Walker's *Appeal* or Garrison's *Liberator*. And he might also have remembered that the *Edenton Gazette* had publicized Garrison's indictment, by the Wake County North Carolina superior court, for circulating a "seditious publication." Certainly among his black shipmates were several of the young Bostonians who in the 1840s were creating a distinctive new militant urban culture within the diverse and vibrant population of what white Boston called "Nigger Hill."

An escaped slave himself, John would have been drawn to the struggle to save the fugitive George Latimer from being sent back to his Norfolk master. The black and white activists had organized their massive protests while John was still at sea. Just as he returned from his whaling voyage, Latimer's freedom was bought, and the community delivered petitions to lawmakers in Washington and Springfield. The following month, this mass protest resulted in the passage of the Massachusetts Personal Liberty Act, which forbade sheriffs from detaining fugitive slaves and state judges from taking part in their capture.

That winter and spring, *The Liberator* ran notices headed "Aid the Fugitive," which publicized the efforts of the New England Freedom Association, organized a year earlier and committed to "assisting all persons in making their escape from slavery." Later, the association presented public talks by leading abolitionists Wendell Phillips, Samuel J. May, and William Lloyd Garrison. All summer, the community was buzzing with talk about the National Convention of Colored Citizens planned for Buffalo.

To John S., the Boston community's focus on self-education was as appealing as its rescue work and its politics. Members of the Aldephic Union could borrow books from its library and were invited to join an elocution class, and Edward B. Lawton and William C. Nell helped organize a series of public lectures by black and white antislavery activists William Lloyd Garrison, Edmund Quincy, and Frederick Douglass. Just a year younger than John, the Boston-born and -educated Nell served as a model of commitment to the movement, not only becoming John's important friend, but also befriending both Harriet and Louisa. One evening—although the lecture's focus was educational, not political—Nell introduced Dr. H. I. Bowditch's speech on "the evidences of design as exhibited in man and the lower animals" by referring to his efforts on Latimer's behalf, and after the talk, Henry W. Williams read a poem on science, and Messers. Howard and Holmes presented instrumental music—all for a seventy-five cent ticket "admitting a lady and gentleman."

John S.'s decision to live in Boston gave him access not only to events within the black community, but also to the interracial organizations his friend Nell favored. If he is indeed the "John Jacobs" of Boston who donated thirty-six cents to help defray the expenses of the Tenth Annual Convention of the New England Anti-Slavery Society, then less than four months after coming ashore, he had found his way to the Garrisonians. In this heady company, the young man who four years earlier was unable to write the note to his master declaring himself free must indeed have found Boston "the hub of the universe."

To his sister Harriet, 1844 Boston was heaven: "I felt as if I was beyond the reach of the bloodhounds; and, for the first time during many years, I had both my children together with me" [ILSG p. 182]. Added to this was her pleasure at having her brother nearby. Quickly she found someone to share the rent and set up housekeeping. Jacobs had arrived in the city as activists were beginning to organize a campaign to integrate public education in Boston—a campaign close to William C. Nell's heart. He had never forgotten that at age thirteen, because of his color he had been denied the school prize he had earned, and now he was leading the fight for equal schooling. Jacobs enrolled Joseph in the segregated Smith School and, aware that ten-year-old Louisa was embarrassed by her illiteracy, began tutoring her daughter at home. (Two years later, the activists' petition for the integration of all Boston schools was denied by the Primary School Committee, which judged that the distinction of race was established by "the Almighty . . . founded deep in the physical, mental and moral natures of the two races." Undaunted, the community organized a Negro School Abolition Society, and in addition to demonstrating and picketing, mounted a lawsuit. Although the abolitionist Charles Sumner argued that segregation in public education denied all children "those relations of equality which our constitution and laws promised to all," the court found that separate schools were not necessarily unequal. In response, the community boycotted the Smith School. Finally in 1855, responding to a petition signed by nearly 1,500 people, both black and white, the Massachusetts legislature abolished school segregation.)

With her children apparently safe under her roof, Jacobs needed a job to support them. One notice in *The Liberator* advertised: "Colored Help. Persons wishing for colored help in their families can be supplied by calling on Mrs. NANCY PRINCE, Belknap-street, second door from Myrtle-street, where those wishing for situations can be provided with them." Twenty years earlier, the deeply religious Prince had followed her husband to Russia's imperial court, then in 1840 and 1842 had traveled to Jamaica, hoping to convert and educate the island's emancipated slaves. Back in the United States, she was in Boston planning to establish an employment agency. Of this effort Prince later wrote, "I labored with much success, until I hired with and from those with whom I mostly sympathized, and shared in common the disadvantages and stigma that is heaped upon us, in this our professed Christian land."

Looking for work, Jacobs may have called on the Willises' many Boston relatives. Certainly she searched out Edenton folks, including George, the son of Grandmother's neighbor Polly Lowther. George, ten years younger than John, had been freed by his master and sent to Boston, where he was now working as a hairdresser. But while Jacobs was eager to find friends from home, she deliberately distanced herself from her brother's attempts to introduce her to the new people he was meeting in the community activities that were absorbing more and more of his energies. She was still humiliated by Reverend Durham's comment about her sexual history and felt that she could not become involved with the activists because she could not "be honest and tell the whole truth" about her life. Despite repeated sessions with John S., who "would mingle his tears with mine while he would advise me to do what was right," she could not bring herself to confide in anyone.

How involved Harriet Jacobs became with abolitionist Boston is unclear. Did she share with John S. the seventy-five cent admission price for a gentleman and lady to attend the eighth course of Tuesday evening lectures sponsored by the Adelphic Union Library Association at Tremont Chapel? If so, she heard speeches by prominent reformers like Wendell Phillips, Dr. Walter Channing, Reverend Samuel J. May, Edmund Quincy, and William Lloyd Garrison. If she chose to pay the twenty-five-cent fee, the day before Christmas she went to Amory Hall to visit the Eleventh Massachusetts Anti-Slavery Fair, with its displays of knitting and netting, tapestry work, dolls, wax-fruit and shell-work, drawing-room gloves and purses, as well as dozens of American and English books and writing materials, all for sale to raise money for *The Liberator*.

On a cold Monday in February, Boston's "Colored Citizens" held a mass meeting at the Belknap Street Meeting House. They were protesting the imprisonment of free black sailors in southern ports and the mistreatment of Massachusetts representatives Samuel Hoar and Henry Hubbard, who had gone south in the sailors' behalf. If John S. was present, he must have been particularly moved when "several colored seamen came forward to testify to the sufferings and cruelties they had experienced in southern prisons."

After the new year, the "colored" ladies of the First Independent Baptist Female Society announced their intention to organize a fund-raising fair for the church, and a few months later, they advertised that the event would be held at Marlboro Chapel. Harriet Jacobs's faith had been deeply shaken by her experiences with the religion she had seen practiced at Edenton's St. Paul's, and perhaps she did not attend this event. Doubtless, however, she would have been interested when, in the spring, women of the New-England Freedom Association announced that they were collecting donations for "three fugitives from the Southern prison-house" who had just appeared in Boston. But by then, Jacobs had left the city.

PART TWO

LINDA

Public Dreams of Freedom and a Home

6

A Great Millstone Lifted

For the first time in my life I was in a place where I was treated
according to my deportment, without reference to my complexion. I
felt as if a great millstone had been lifted from my breast.
—Harriet Jacobs, *Incidents in the Life of a Slave Girl*, p. 183

Harriet Jacobs's life changed again on March 25, 1845, the day
Mary Stace Willis died delivering a stillborn baby. Willis, bereft,
wanted to take little Imogen to visit her mother's grieving family in England and went to Boston to ask Jacobs to accompany the child.
Later, writing her book, she explains that her heart went out to Imogen,
"the little motherless one." Certainly she well remembered what it felt
like to be a "little motherless one." Willis was offering more money than
she was earning, and doubtless she was finding it extremely difficult to
feed herself and her children on the wages she could make as a seamstress. It must have been hard for her—when she finally had both of her
children under her roof—to decide to accept Willis's offer. But accept it
she did. Preparing to leave, she made careful arrangements for her children. Boston's printing trades were generally closed to blacks, but a few
years earlier a black printer had established a small shop for their training, and some abolitionist presses hired African Americans. After apprenticing Joseph to "a good place" and making provisions for Louisa to stay
with her housemate and continue her schooling, Jacobs began readying
Imogen for the trip.

They sailed for Liverpool in early summer. The Boston–Liverpool
steamship *Britannic* had little in common with the vessel in which Jacobs
had escaped from Edenton, and now she was not huddled in a tiny cabin
to hide from slavecatchers, as she had been three years earlier. Now she

was traveling in style—albeit as a servant—as one of an international grouping of passengers that included the citizens of a dozen countries.

Their destination was an England widely praised by African Americans as a place of refuge, a country where increasing numbers of fugitive slaves and abolitionist activists were finding community with black Britons who had a long history. The African slave trade had supplied not only laborers for the West Indian sugar plantations, but also domestic servants for the planters who, over time, moved to England with their slaves—and sold some of them in Bristol, London, and Liverpool.

Some 14,000 or 15,000 black people were living in England by 1772, when judges in the historic Somersett case ruled that "a foreigner cannot be imprisoned *here* on the authority of any law existing in his own country. . . . No master ever was allowed here to take a slave by force to be sold abroad." Although this decision did not emancipate Great Britain's black slaves, it was hailed as an important victory for the antislavery cause. A dozen years later African American loyalists—who had fought on the British side during the American Revolution after Lord Dunmore proclaimed that he would "arm my own Negroes & receive all others that come to me who I shall declare free"—arrived in London as free men. In 1787, the Society for the Abolition of the Slave Trade had been organized, and twenty years later, the British slave trade was abolished. After continuing resistance and struggle, an 1833 Act of Parliament freed the slaves throughout the entire British Empire. The date the West Indian Emancipation Act took effect—August 1, 1834—was celebrated annually by abolitionists in Britain and in America.

In England, Jacobs felt herself a free person for the first time since—at age six—she had learned she was a slave. Jacobs's arrival was preceded by that of a number of African Americans. Some, like the freeborn Nathaniel Paul and Charles Lenox Remond, came to raise money and support for the abolitionist movement. Others had professional goals, like James McCune Smith, who enrolled at Glasgow University, and Robert Douglass Jr., who studied art at the British Museum and National Gallery and whose paintings Jacobs had admired in Philadelphia. Still others came as fugitives, seeking safety and the opportunity to work as political activists. The year that Jacobs fled Auburn plantation, another North Carolina fugitive, Moses Roper, had shipped out from Boston and in England, his *Narrative* had found a wide audience. The year that Jacobs escaped north, Moses Grandy had come to Great Britain to raise money to buy his family out of slavery. Only months after Jacobs's arrival, the most famous African American fugitive, Frederick Douglass, fled to England to escape slave hunters. During the rest of Jacobs's stay, Douglass was touring the British Isles, lecturing, organizing, and raising money for the cause.

Jacobs came, however, not as an abolitionist activist but as a baby-nurse. When the *Britannic* docked at the historic slave port of Liverpool, she had no time to tour its streets and wonder at the sculptured heads of African elephants—and of African slaves—decorating the facade of its city hall. Instead, she kept Imogen quiet and fed while Willis fumed as their baggage slowly made its way through Customs, then raced to catch the 4:00 train to London. Here there was no Jim Crow car. Willis bought two first-class train tickets—one for Jacobs and Imogen, one for himself—and five hours later, they had traveled the 220 miles to the capital. He took rooms at the Adelaide Hotel and there fell into bed, ill with fever. While Willis convalesced, Jacobs, tending Imogen, had little chance to explore London. From her hotel window and her walks with the child down in the park, however, she glimpsed "the tide of life that flowed through the streets," which she judged contrasted dramatically with "the stagnation" in southern cities [ILSG p. 183].

Jacobs treasured her memories of the next two weeks—not because of the hotel, which was attractive enough, although the food was somewhat "less luxurious" than in New York, Saratoga, or Rockaway. She found these weeks memorable because, "ensconced in a pleasant room, with my dear little charge, I laid my head on my pillow, for the first time, with the delightful consciousness of pure, unadulterated freedom" [ILSG p. 183].

Jacobs's relieved response to the apparent lack of British racism contrasts sharply with Willis's shocked reaction to the presence of black people in Britain, and to the natives' interactions with them. Recovered from his illness, he sent back a series of "Pencillings" about his travels for his American readers: "I see, daily, blacks, walking with white women, and occupying seats in the dress-circle of theatres, quite unnoticed by the English." At the London colosseum, he thought it noteworthy to describe "three ladies, dressed with the most respectable elegance . . . *surrounding a negro!* It was a lad of nineteen or twenty, in a jacket and trowsers, entirely black, and as ugly and ill-shaped a negro as you could easily find. His hands showed that he had been used to hard work, and he had evidently newly arrived in London. The ladies were making a pet of him. . . .These ladies were probably enthusiasts in anti-slavery, and had got a *protege* who was interesting as having been a slave."

After a few days in Oxford Crescent, where Willis had friends, they went on to Steventon, near Abingdon in Berkshire. There they stayed in the home of Mary Stace Willis's sister Anne and her husband Reverend William Vincent. Willis wrote little about tiny secluded Steventon, instead regaling his audience with a description of the picturesque old church at nearby Abingdon, "a tumbled-up, elbowy crooked old place, with the houses all frowning at each other across the gutters, and the streets narrow and intricate." Depositing Jacobs and his daughter with his in-laws, he took the train back to London, then went on to the Continent. Earlier, at Liverpool, he had written that he was struck by what he saw as "the *utter want of hope* in the countenances of the working classes—the look of dogged submission and animal endurance of their condition in life," and concluded, "I would prefer being an English horse to being an English working-man." But at Steventon, Jacobs reached quite a different conclusion. Although staying in a small town said to be the poorest in the county, she was favorably impressed. "The people I saw around me were, many of them, among the poorest poor. But when I visited them in their little thatched cottages, I felt that the condition of even the meanest and most ignorant among them was vastly superior to the condition of the most favored slaves in America" [ILSG p. 184].

During these months at the vicarage, Jacobs received "strong religious impressions." At Edenton's St. Paul's, she had been disgusted, repelled by the "contemptuous manner" in which African Americans were offered communion, revolted by the fact of Dr. Norcom's church membership, sickened at seeing ministers of the gospel buying and selling slaves: "The whole service seemed to me a mockery and a sham." Now she found herself profoundly moved by the realization that at Steventon, everything was different. In contrast to Edenton's slave-trading clerics, she judged Reverend Vincent "a true disciple of Jesus" and, impressed by the "beauty" of his life, was filled with faith. Jacobs later testified that this visit to England signified not only her freedom from slave catchers and racists, but also her profound spiritual rebirth. "Grace entered my heart, and I knelt at the communion table, I trust, in true humility of soul" [ILSG p. 185].

Willis had initially planned on leaving Imogen with her aunt to be sent to school in England, and in November, after reporting that his little girl might stay on for a year, he added that "Harriett, her maid, is still here, & will return with me probably." It was hard for Jacobs to decide to go home, back to the daily racism and—worse—to Norcom's unending harassment. In England, not only was she a free woman, but she "never saw the slightest symptom of prejudice against color. Indeed," she later wrote, "I entirely forgot it, till the time came for us to return to America" [ILSG p. 185]. Still, her children were on the other side of the Atlantic. After ten months abroad, Jacobs returned to the United States with Willis and Imogen. (In the end, he, too, could not bear to be separated from his daughter.)

Back in Boston, Jacobs thought she could pick up the threads of her life, but much had changed while she was gone. Joseph, not yet eighteen, had run away from his apprenticeship, furious at the abuse he received from his fellows when they discovered that he was not white. Then, proudly determined not to be dependent on his uncle, he had shipped out to sea. When Jacobs learned that he had signed on for a whaling voyage, she mourned, knowing it would be years before she saw him again. Still, settling back into her two rooms at 87 Charter Street with Lulu—now suddenly taller than her mother—she was glad to be back. She quickly found work. Willis's niece was to be married, and her trousseau had to be finished by early May. Jacobs was not looking for excitement, and she drew satisfaction from watching her daughter's steady progress at school, and from their small pleasures at home.

Her brother's life, however, had become anything but routine. During the months she was away, John S. had developed into a full-fledged activist, increasingly committed both to the community and to the anti-slavery cause. Now a member of the Lecture Committee of the Adelphic Union Library Association, he was working with men like William C. Nell and Edward B. Lawton to put together the ninth annual lecture series, featuring both white and black speakers. In addition, he had taken on the position of corresponding secretary of the beleagured New-England Freedom Association, and he had joined the Garrisonian faithful in donating money to the Massachusetts Anti-Slavery Society. Since his arrival in Boston three years earlier, John S. had become one of the up-and-coming young community leaders Nell described in his report on the Young Men's Literary Society: "the members of this Society, unlike those of the more favored in the city, have not enjoyed the aid of teachers; but are mainly indebted for their improvement to the mutual suggestions and criticisms imparted within their own little circle. Those among them in any way prominent, to their honor be it spoken, owe it to their perseverance and self-denial, under circumstances unfavorable to mental cultivation."

Jacobs had experienced a sense of political and spiritual liberation in England. Unlike Frederick Douglass, however—who would find his years abroad transformative—she had returned to America a fugitive. Now she decided to settle in Boston because "my old master was rather skittish of Massachusetts. I relied on her love of freedom, and felt safe on her soil" [ILSG p. 187]. Still, she continued to distance herself from the abolitionists. She might have felt comfortable hearing the talk on "The Life of Queen Esther" that was organized "for moral and religious purposes" by the Colored Female Societies at the May Street Church, or attending the Free Meeting, late in May, on "Social and Mental Improvement." But though her activist brother joined the executive committee of the Monument Association organized to commemorate Charles Torrey—who had died in jail while serving time for helping slaves escape—it is doubtful that Jacobs accompanied him and the other "colored citizens of Boston" who met at the Zion Chapel in June to plan the memorial. More likely, she and Louisa Matilda joined him at the Fourth of July "Rural Fair and Anti-Slavery Pic Nic" at Dedham to hear the band music and the speeches by William Lloyd Garrison, Wendell Phillips, and Ralph Waldo Emerson. John S., who had already signed the "Anti-Slavery Peace-Pledge" condemning the Mexican War, perhaps was among those collecting signatures, and it is easy to imagine that Harriet helped the women with the food.

Later in July, the Belknap Street Church opened its doors to honor Garrison, who was sailing for England. There he would join Douglass and others who—in an effort to isolate proslavery churches from the international Christian fellowship—were pressuring the Free Church of Scotland to return money they saw as tainted because it came from churches in the American South. After a prayer by Reverend W. T. Raymond, speeches by John T. Hilton and Garrison, and resolutions by William C. Nell, Jacobs's brother John S. took the floor. Speaking "in the name of three millions of American Slaves against the Free Church of Scotland," he offered a series of resolutions in the harsh language of the Scriptures:

> Whereas, the Free Church of Scotland has taken sides with the oppressor, in defiance of the laws of Him who is the founder of the only true Church. . . . Resolved, that we regard them not as Christians, but wolves

in sheep's clothing; their places of worship as not being the temples of the living God, but dens of all manner of unclean beasts. . . . Resolved, that it is the duty of all true Christians to pray earnestly to God . . . that the traffickers in the blood and souls of men be driven from the temples. Resolved, That we, the oppressed of these United States of America, do entreat our anti-slavery friends in Scotland to hear us through our beloved Garrison, and in the name of God and humanity let their watchword ever be, *No Union with Slaveholders.*

If they heard John S. speak in the crowded church that spring evening, his sister and his niece sat straight and proud. The last day in July, the "levee" at Tremont Temple was organized by John S. and the other members of the Torrey Monument Association. After the speeches, everyone was invited to "partake of the luxuries of the table," and at midnight, when the bell of Park Street Church rang out, all knelt in prayer celebrating the abolition of slavery in the West Indies. Jacobs's experiences in England made this event deeply meaningful—as was the parade the next day, when the Union Brass Band, carrying antislavery banners, paraded through the streets to celebrate British Emancipation.

Not a man to limit himself to public speaking, a few weeks later when John S. heard that a Boston merchant was about to send a fugitive back to New Orleans, he decided to act. After vainly trying to convince others to join him, he went out by himself and spent the night alone, watching the islands in the harbor in a fruitless rescue effort. When the runaway (named Joseph, like their lost uncle) was sent back into slavery, doubtless the entire Jacobs family joined with prominent Boston citizens at the huge Faneuil Hall meeting protesting the illegal seizure of a slave on Massachusetts soil and appointing a Vigilance Committee of forty to prevent future captures.

The determination of eminent Bostonians to stop slaveholders from kidnapping fugitive slaves from the city was important to everyone in the audience at Faneuil Hall, but it had special significance for Jacobs. With Joseph at sea and Lulu in Boston with her, she was feeling some relief about her children, but she had been wise to refuse to leave her daughter with the Tredwells. James Tredwell died that summer, and his widow moved back to North Carolina. If Jacobs had not insisted that Louisa come to Boston with her, her daughter would now again be a North Carolina slave.

And still Jacobs was not free of the Norcoms. Shortly after returning from England, she had received frightening letters from Edenton. One was a report that Norcom had written to the New York police describing her in detail and offering a $100 reward for her capture. Another was from Norcom's son John, now a born-again Christian, who urged her to return to Edenton and professed concern that she was lonely far from her grandmother, her uncle, and her friends. A third was from the Edenton newcomer Daniel Messmore, who had married Mary Matilda Norcom, and the fourth and most upsetting was from her young mistress herself.

Mary Matilda's marriage had followed a series of episodes that polarized the Norcom family and the entire Edenton community. Her husband had been excoriated by her father as "a man whose origin & history nobody knows, who has not character amongst us; who is alike destitute of manners, morals & education, who in fact, is nothing less than an impersonation of impudence lewdness & obscenity! a reckless desperado." Before the wedding, Messmore had assaulted Mary Matilda's brother Caspar Wistar with a stick and cowhide; two days later, young Norcom shot and wounded Messmore, who shot back. The violence continued when, a few months later, another of Mary Matilda's brothers and a dozen other young men mobbed Messmore. Caspar Wistar Norcom was imprisoned, Messmore was indicted for perjury—and Mary Matilda and Messmore left Edenton. Cut off by her family, Mary Matilda needed money. Signaling that she had been tracking Jacobs's whereabouts, she timed her letter to Jacobs so that it would coincide with Willis's return from England. Now writing to remind Harriet that she had never consented to her sale, Mary Matilda urged her to return, or, alternatively, to purchase herself.

Jacobs drew courage from the 5,000 Bostonians who crowded Faneuil Hall to protest the practice of kidnapping fugitives from the city, and from the presence of ex-President John Quincy Adams, who served as chairman of the meeting. More important, John S.'s involvement with organized abolition had prompted him to report the threats she received to Sydney Howard Gay, resident editor of *The National Anti-Slavery Standard*.

Informing the abolitionists of his sister's danger, John S. displayed both his lack of formal education and his characteristic wit:

> they have let the cat out of the bag and I thort that I would tell you that it proved to be a devel in disguise my sister received a very affectionate letter lass week from her young mistress Mrs Mesmore she writes of her having married and also of having heared that my sister had gone to England she has been waiting the arrival of Mr. W and now reminds

my sister of her former love and in that affectionat manner so peculiar to this no soul Nation she want to know if she wont COME HOME that she had never consented for her Father to sell her becaus she did not wish her to be the slave of anyone but hirself who had always loved her and been kind to her—. . . . the newly made Mrs Mesmore wants her to return home or buy her self but as my sister has not the means of buy her self and finds these cold regons more healthy than the suny South they will have to love each other at a distance the sweetest love that can exist betweene master and Slave.

Jacobs was confident that, once warned, the Boston abolitionists would be able to prevent her kidnapping. She felt relatively safe in her Boston home.

In December, a Belknap Street Church reception welcomed Garrison back to Boston. At the holidays, Faneuil Hall hosted the Antislavery Bazaar, and in the spring, an overflow crowd at the Belknap Street Church celebrated "the successful career abroad, and safe arrival home" of Frederick Douglass. His speech, with its references to the contrast between the humiliation he was subjected to in America and the respect he was accorded across the Atlantic, where "every mark of esteem was tendered," surely resonated in Harriet Jacobs's ears, flooding her with warm memories of her own experiences abroad.

In August, the entire Jacobs family may have watched as the city again celebrated West Indian Emancipation, with 150 black Bostonians parading on horseback through State Street, and they may have all attended the *soriee Musicale* featuring the eight-year-old black prodigy Cleveland Lucas at the piano—a performance *The Liberator* judged an antidote to "those who caricature the colored man by their Banjo minstrelsys." In September, it seems likely that Harriet was among the women who collected clothing for sixty-six Virginia slaves who, emancipated in their master's will and then cheated by his managers, arrived in Boston seeking refuge and jobs. Surely Harriet, John, and Louisa were all at the Belknap Street Church in the fall to see a banner presented to the Young Men's Literary Society and, later in the day, to hear the members present "Declamations, Dialogues, &c." to the public. In late October, John S.'s friend William C. Nell reported on the National Convention held at Troy, New York. The meeting, held at Belknap Street Church, featured a spirited debate over integration, as well as speeches by leaders such as Henry Highland Garnet and Frederick Douglass debating the value of physical force and moral suasion in ending slavery and racism.

During these months, when she was not working or involved with her family, Harriet Jacobs was exploring the city. Now in her middle thirties, Jacobs was a woman whose life had been largely determined by her sexuality—her adolescence blasted by Norcom's predatory attentions and her young womanhood defined by her five-year liaison with Major Sam, then blighted by her years in hiding. Did she now find a partner to share the pleasures of her life in freedom? If she did, she left no record. Nor did anyone else, and William C. Nell, who relished sharing personal tidbits, would have noted any gossip circulating. Readers interested in Jacobs's attitudes toward sexuality doubtless would see a text for analysis in the three cloth dolls she later sewed for the Willis children. Two are little girls, one fashioned from brown cotton, one from black. Both are simply but carefully dressed, their neat feet sticking out under full petticoats and gathered skirts. The third, larger than the others, is a black mama doll embroidered with staring eyes, a neat nose, and a small unsmiling mouth. Wearing an elaborate tignon (traditional headscarf) and earrings, she is dressed in a large bright print, but under her lace-trimmed petticoat she has no feet at all. Nor does she have any legs. Instead, her body has been stitched closed across her hips. A psychologically oriented critic might make much of this, reading the doll as a sign of Jacobs's rejection of female sexuality. Alternatively, a specialist in toy making might see the doll as an example of a common type often constructed by nineteenth-century seamstresses. (Certainly, however, the psychological critic would also have something to say about that.)

To this discussion of Harriet Jacobs's personal life, one bit of information should be added. When she was a very old woman, Jacobs was annually confronted by a man knocking on her door gathering information for the city directory. Each year, she identified herself as the widow Harriet Jacobs. But her answers varied in response to the query, whose widow was she? Usually, she named Samuel; once Elijah; and once George. It is easy enough to deduce that when she answered Samuel, she was thinking of Samuel Tredwell Sawyer, her children's father; and that she was thinking of her own father Elijah Knox Sr. when she answered Elijah. But who was George? Could this be the name of the young man she had so passionately loved at sixteen, the suitor she had sent away after Norcom made his threats? Could this George be a figment of her vivid imagination, plucked from the air to hush a questioner intruding into her privacy? Or could he be some other man—perhaps someone she met in Boston—who had enriched her life?

Recently, questions have been raised concerning Harriet Jacobs's relationship to Sawyer. On December 1, 1993, the Church of the Latter Day Saints sealed a record listing their marriage in 1828 at Edenton. But certainly no such marriage took place. Nowhere in any North Carolina records is this marriage recorded, nor—given the laws prohibiting interracial unions—could it have occurred. But if it had, it would have legitimatized Jacobs's claim, in her old age, that she was the widow of Samuel.

While Jacobs was building a life in Boston, John S. was becoming more deeply immersed in antislavery work. One of the reformers' key issues was the case of Jonathan Walker, a middle-aged white Massachusetts sea-captain who was arrested in Florida for aiding seven escaping slaves. Walker had been convicted, jailed for a year, displayed on the pillory, and branded on the hand with the letters "SS" (slave stealer). Now back in Massachusetts, the captain began a lecture tour, and in November John S., deciding his apprenticeship on the platform was complete, joined him. Their public appearance was announced in *The Herkimer Freeman*: "That well-known sufferer for righteousness' sake, Capt. Jonathan Walker, an honest-hearted weather-beaten Christian sailor . . . arrived here on the 25th instant . . . and, after one more meeting here on New Year's night, expects to 'show his *hand*' among the people of the other sections of the county. He is accompanied from Boston by John S. Jacobs, 'a noble man of sable brow;' who, though but nine years since a Carolinian slave, has well improved his self-gained freedom, and speaks with fluency and depth of interest scarcely excelled by any of his predecessors—even by *Douglass* himself."

The two men spoke at meetings in western Massachusetts and then went to central New York, where they lectured for a month in Herkimer, Oneida, and Madison counties before moving on to the western part of the state. After two months on the road, Walker described their tour in a letter to *The Liberator*: "It is seldom an evening passes in which we do not have a meeting, and, with few exceptions, in different towns and villages each evening. We have travelled several hundred miles on foot, through cold and storm, slush and mud. . . . Though few seem willing to take a decided stand either for or against the system of slavery, there is much anxiety to know what is to be the result of the present agitation of this subject."

Arguing both "against slavery and oppression, and consequently against this plundering and murdering government," and also against religionists who wanted to restrict Sabbath activity to churchgoing and Bible-reading, John S. and Walker encountered fierce opposition, especially to their Sunday lectures. Describing one Sunday when, after walking "11 miles through the snow, with our bag of books on our backs, and no dinner," they were reduced to holding their meeting in a schoolroom rather than in a church because they were condemned as Sabbath breakers, John protested: "Let us suppose this charge true—that we are Sabbath breakers. . . . I have yet to learn that I have not as good a right to get up, or go to, an anti-slavery meeting on Sunday, as they have to get up, or go to, their meetings."

After four and a half months spent speaking to hundreds of audiences from Boston to western Massachusetts and in central and western New York State, John S. and Walker ended their tour. They had, Walker reported, experienced some of the antiabolitionist "mobocratic spirit"— drums were beaten and bells rung to disrupt their meetings, and once "a gun [was] fired at the door, &c.; and while speaking, I was sprinkled with a shower of musket shot, but as they were not buried in powder, they fell harmless." Although they raised money by selling antislavery publications, after paying their expenses, each netted only $51.14 for their "hard service in the cause of suffering humanity." Despite this, Walker thought that they were correct in their decision not to pass the hat at their meetings. "After one has been tearing off the mask of hypocrisy, exposing religious and political inconsistencies, and handling roughly the people's gods, to shove a contribution box in their faces, expecting to receive money for it, is quite preposterous."

As their tour wound down, John S. began lecturing alone. His itinerary took him to Rhode Island and Massachusetts, then home to Boston in the middle of April. By summer, however, he was back on the road, speaking in the Western Series of the abolitionists' "100 Conventions" along with antislavery stalwarts Adin Ballou, Dr. E. D. Hudson, and Stephen and Abby Kelley Foster. Taking their texts from antislavery resolutions, from biblical passages, and from newspaper accounts of current events, they addressed "thin" crowds of twenty-five to 125 on weekdays, and larger audiences on Sundays. John S. joined their team at Winchendon Village and spoke at Waterville, Winchendon, Ashburnham, and Westminster—where he was challenged by a minister who said that rather than witnessing the immediate abolition of slavery, "he would prefer to see the slaves in their bondage millions of ages." Ending their tour at Princeton, Ballou judged their work only partially successful.

Attracting farmers to meetings at haying-time was difficult, and "the urgency of business, the long warm days, the short evenings, and the usual exhaustion of our best friends, the working people, after a hard day's toil, all operated against us."

Before the month was over, John S. was featured at two more events. The first—an "Anti-Sabbath Convention" proposing that instead of observing the Sabbath solely by going to church, "it is lawful to do well on the Sabbath day"—was savagely ridiculed in the *Boston Daily Atlas*. Although not identifying John S. by name, the reporter noted his use of humor and of his personal experiences on the platform. "Next, rose a mulatto man, a fugitive slave, who kept the moderator on the grin by his witty allusions to the love he used to bear his old master, a North Carolina lawyer, and a member of Congress, and by his playful remarks upon the manner in which he escaped from bondage. His massa, while doating upon a newly married wife, whom he became acquainted with at Washington, and with whom he came North to be joined to, was sufficiently in love to be a little *blind* in one eye, while the mulatto's suavity of manner pulled the wool over the other. Thus he escaped. He said he had been in the Sandwich Islands, and damned our churches for sending the Bible there, when it was so much more needed at home in the South."

Two weeks later, John S. rejoined Ballou and the Fosters, along with May and Johnson, at a convention at Milford near the utopian community of Hopedale. Once again, the press reported his distinctive style, autobiographical comments, and attacks on pro-slavery Christians and Sabbatarians. "John S. Jacobs came forward, and in a modest and unassuming, yet manly and dignified manner, proceeded to address the audience. He spoke of his condition as a slave, of his unsuppressible love of freedom, of his escape from bondage. . . . And he remarked, there are those being assembled to what they suppose the worship of God, by the bells sounding around us, who are ready to sanction that act, to blame the abolitionists, for endeavoring to wake up the public mind. . . . He thought theirs could not be Christian worship, for it was *Christian* to feel for *all*."

In mid-September, John S. joined movement stalwarts voicing the most radical of the "ultra" Garrisonian ideas. At the quarterly meeting of the Essex County Anti-Slavery Society, held at Lynn, they condemned Amcrican churches for sanctioning and condoning slavery, condemned political parties for operating under the pro-slavery Constitution, condemned political antislavery in general, and condemned American

churches for sanctioning and condoning slavery and the clergy for prey-
ing on the people.

In December, Harriet and Louisa welcomed John S. back home in Boston,
where he helped members of the Boston Female Anti-Slavery Society decorate the hall for their annual fair. While he had been living the transient
life of a movement activist, Harriet and Lulu were hard at work. Jacobs's
skills as a seamstress kept her in demand by the Willis family and current
with their news. She learned that Willis's sister Sara, now a penniless
widow, was living in a boardinghouse on Columbia Street and trying to
support her little girls by sewing for a living, and that Willis had remarried and taken Imogen to live with him and his new wife in New York.

Jacobs maintained her ties to the Willis family, but she was finding a
wider life in Boston. Here she could take Louisa to gatherings such as the
meeting of "colored citizens" supporting the rights of black Canadian
expatriates, and contribute clothing to the fugitives appearing in Boston
in increasing numbers, "from the necessity of the case, almost utterly destitute." When summer came, she and Lulu could visit Amory Hall to see
"Bayne's Gigantic Panoramic Painting of a Voyage to Europe," and she
could tell her daughter more about her travels. On the Fourth of July,
they could join the "three to five thousand people" at Abington Grove
listening to abolitionist speakers, both men and women, both black and
white. On everyone's lips that day was the plight of the Edmondson family, seized escaping from slavery in Washington, D.C., on the schooner
Pearl. Their seizure was a double-edged reminder of Jacobs's successful
escape and of her vulnerability to recapture. Later that summer at the
Lynn celebration commemorating West Indian Emancipation, the newest
topic was the upcoming National Colored Convention, to be held at
Cleveland in September. And in August, there were published reports in
The Liberator by John S.'s friend Nell—now in Rochester working with
Frederick Douglass—on the recent "Woman's Rights Conventions," held
at Seneca Falls and Rochester.

Lecturing had opened up John S.'s life, and now he wanted to
broaden his niece's perspective as well. Perhaps it was the feminists'
strong statement about women's education, or the controversy over
Boston's segregated Smith School—or perhaps it was simply because
John S., who was planning to move to Rochester to continue working for
the movement, had discovered an educationally sound seminary nearby
that would accept a "colored female" as a student. For whatever reason,

late that fall, John S. urged his sister to prepare to send her daughter away to study at Hiram H. Kellogg's Young Ladies Domestic Seminary in Clinton, New York.

It was hard to let Lulu go. Harriet could never forget that she had missed most of her daughter's childhood, and even their short years together in Boston had been interrupted by her trip to England. She prized each day they could spend together. Still, she knew she must not stand in Lulu's way. She must not put her needs above Lulu's chance for a brighter life. Jacobs tried to focus on practical tasks: sewing, mending, ironing, and packing her daughter's clothes for the trip west. But she was plagued—not only by worries about loneliness and by apprehensions about how Louisa would manage at the school—but by a deeper dread. For years, she had known that someday she must explain her liaison with Major Sam. But how to begin? She had been silenced by the fear that her daughter would condemn her. Now Lulu was about to leave. What if Harriet should die, and someone else revealed her secret? Jacobs remained mute until the night before the scheduled departure. Then, with Lulu's ticket bought and her trunk packed, she forced herself to speak.

Beginning quietly, she was telling her teen-aged daughter about her own adolescence—about Norcom's threats, her frantic efforts to prevent him from forcing her into concubinage, her relationship with Major Sam, and her terrible unending guilt—when Louisa hugged her, pleading that she stop. She already knew it all, she said, had known since she was a little girl in Washington, Miss Laura's nurse had told her, then forbidden her to speak of it. Back then, she confided, she had wondered why her father lavished attention on Laura and had no smiles for her. But she was little then. Now, she assured her mother, the fact that he had left their lives forever didn't matter. It was her mother she loved. Listening, Harriet Jacobs felt physical relief. She need not have smothered her feelings. While she had been attempting to save Lulu pain, Lulu had been trying to spare her embarrassment. Secure in her daughter's love, she held her tightly. Then she let her go.

The Reverend Kellogg's school, established more than a dozen years earlier, was grounded on the idea that "the education of Females is especially important and worthy of the attention and support of the church" because of women's role as mothers and teachers. Both Kellogg's use of a work-study program to limit expenses and his rigorous intellectual curriculum had influenced Mary Lyon's Mount Holyoke, famous for training women beyond puddings and nurseries. Kellogg's catalogue announced that tuition and board cost $100.00 for an academic year of forty weeks, divided into three terms. Students studied "Reading, Spelling, Writing, Geography, Arithmetic, Grammar, Natural Philosophy, Chemistry, Geology, Mineralogy, Botany, Algebra, Geometry, Trigonometry, Astronomy, Natural History, Physiology, Rhetoric, Mental Philosophy, Moral Philosophy, Butler's Analogy, Vocal Music, Latin and Greek." (Optional were "Music on the Piano Forte, French, German, and Drawing.") A committed abolitionist, Kellogg not only admitted African American students along with Anglo-Americans, but when they could not pay, he reduced their fees and solicited money from wealthy reformers to help with their expenses.

When Jacobs's daughter joined the young women walking up the broad front steps of the seminary building at the corner of Mulberry and Kellogg streets, she found herself among more than a hundred students, a few of them black. At first, Louisa hid her mother's status as a fugitive slave, hoping to avoid becoming the object of well-meaning sympathy. But when by chance it was discovered, Kellogg reduced her fees. The transition she had already made in Boston from home schooling had not been easy, and now, entering Kellogg's Young Ladies' Domestic Seminary, Louisa was painfully aware of her limitations. But she was determined to succeed, and at Clinton she did well, making her uncle and her mother proud. Although she knew she was "not blessed with poetical abilities," Louisa wrote a poem as her uncle asked, and she struggled to produce a composition fit for the school paper. Stimulated by the course of study, happy in the company of the other girls, and impressed by her teachers, Louisa enjoyed the seminary mightily. "It seems to me," she confided to her uncle, "as though time never flew so rapidly."

After escorting his niece to Kellogg's school in Clinton, John S. continued on to Rochester, his new base of operations. At the end of January, Harriet Jacobs read with pride the first announcement of his lectures in *The North Star*. The next month, the paper was running two speaking itineraries: one for her brother, and one for a series of joint lectures by her brother and Frederick Douglass. In his account of their two-week tour, Douglass spells out their perils: "the lecturing field is the stage upon which to get a more vigorous idea of the monster of slavery: You get here the real 'bar-room' bluster—'tar and feathers'—'ride him out on a rail'— 'ought to be hung'—the '*niggers*' ought to be sent out of the country—

they are only fit for slavery, &c. . . . [But] we meet not only the roughest forms of pro-slavery in the country but the most thorough and whole-souled Abolitionists, to commune with whom, is worth all the labors, and even the insults to which the Anti-Slavery advocate is subjected."

The men left Rochester in the February snow, and their lecturing took them to fourteen hamlets, villages, and towns, where they delivered twenty speeches in sixteen days and sold twenty subscriptions to *The North Star*. Of their meeting at Henrietta, Douglass writes: "Friend Jacobs spoke first, in his usual calm but feeling manner, with respect to the 'foul treachery and ruinous wrongs' connected with the whole sys-tem of slavery," and was heard by an "attentive audience." From village to village, their reception varied. At Madison, the local abolitionist was sick and had been unable to make arrangements for their meeting; at East Mendon, "strange to say," they were hosted by a man who had voted for President Taylor; at Avon "there was not Anti-Slavery enough in town to give a lecturer on slavery a night's lodging." They had to compete for audiences with a religious revival hostile to abolition at West Bloomfield, but at Canandigua drew good crowds, thanks to a Baptist minister who, ejected from his pulpit by pro-slavery parishioners, had opened his own small antislavery meeting house. Despite a disruption by "a recreant *black*" at Penn Yan, John S. "evidently made a deep impression upon the listening hundreds," and although defamed as heretics, they also com-manded a large audience at Prattsburgh. But at Bath, all the churches were closed against them, and they found the twenty-six miles to Branch-port in melting snow "hard walking. . . . Considering the state of the roads, and the inclemency of the weather." Their Sunday evening meet-ing at Rushville was a success, however, and after a good crowd at Hopewell, they ended their tour at the Canandigua Anti-Slavery fair.

After two weeks in Rochester, John S. went back on the road. In *The North Star* he reported that at Southbarr, where a religious revival was being held, the Presbyterian minister refused his request to open the meet-ing, saying "he would object to the offering a prayer at those meetings, for the deliverance of three millions of his countrymen from chains and slavery." Disgusted to hear the same attitude voiced at Oakfield, John S. bitterly concludes, "The cause of bleeding humanity finds but few friends at protracted meetings and revivals of religion. They are all so busy in trying to save that invisible and undefined part of man called the soul, that they will see his body, the image of God, trampled in the dust unheeded." Things were even worse at Albion and West Gaines, where no arrangements had been made for his meetings; and at Eagle Harbor, the "streets were so muddy that the people could only get to the Meeting House in wagons." Denied the use of the church at Johnson's Creek, he spoke angrily in the schoolhouse, commenting, "The idea of a church being dedicated to God, that bars its doors against humanity, is absurd. . . . 'is not this the fact that I have chosen to loose the bonds of wickedness, and let the oppressed go free, and that ye break every yoke'!"

At Lockport, he met a fifty-one-year-old fugitive who had just escaped from the South, and at Lindonville, he spoke to a full house. Monday evening, after walking more than six miles to set up his next day's meeting, John S. entered the hall tired and feverish, but was revitalized when he heard some little girls singing an antislavery song. "The change was so great I soon felt like another man, knowing I was among friends, though they were small ones. I got them to open the meeting with an antislavery song; their choice was 'I am an abolitionist, I glory in the name,' &c. . . . I told those little girls how little slaves were treated, I was heard with apparent interest." Then at Eagle Harbor, he faced a "disorderly" audience, "being in part made up of some boatmen, whose highest idea of manliness seemed to be disturbance." Summing up his tour for his *North Star* readers, John S. voiced exhaustion. "At no time during my laboring in the cause as a lecturer, have I found so few friends, as on the present occasion. In some of these towns, it has been more than a year since the slaves of this land have had any one to tell of their wrongs."

By the time her brother's discouraging report was in print, Jacobs had heard his sad stories from his own lips. Lonely in her small Boston apartment with Louisa gone, in March she moved her few things west to Rochester. There she could be nearer her daughter's boarding school and could work with her brother on his new project: running the Anti-Slavery Reading Room.

7

My Mind Became Enlightened

❧

The more my mind had become enlightened, the more difficult it
was for me to consider myself an article of property.
—Harriet Jacobs, *Incidents in the Life of a Slave Girl*, p. 199

After Boston, Rochester didn't look like much, but the busy man-
ufacturing city on the lake changed Jacobs's life. During her ten-
month stay, she learned to enjoy working with others for social
change. Although she had put down some roots in Boston's black community, she had remained distant from the reformers John increasingly
chose as friends. But in Rochester, Jacobs immediately joined her
brother's activist circle. Centered in the Sophia Street home of the white
Quakers Amy and Isaac Post, the group included a number of antislavery Friends. They had recently formed the Yearly Meeting of Congregational Friends (later the Friends of Human Progress), because the
Genesee Yearly Meeting—although sharing their antislavery sentiment—
rejected their social activism and reserved the right to judge actions that
individuals took in matters of conscience, such as abolition. The Posts'
intimates were pillars of the Western New York Anti-Slavery Society,
pacifists and followers of Garrison's demand for the immediate abolition
of slavery. Staunch supporters of *The North Star*, the weekly newspaper
that Frederick Douglass had just launched in town, they were outspoken
defenders of the Douglass family's challenge to school segregation. Only
months before Jacobs came to Rochester, Amy Post and her friends had
participated enthusiastically at the Seneca Falls Woman's Rights Convention, and they were central to the follow-up convention at Rochester
two weeks later. According to historian Nancy Hewitt, in their public
involvement in social issues, Post and her circle "reshaped the landscape
of female activism in Rochester." Joining them, Harriet Jacobs joined the

most radical women in the nation, the initiators of the women's rights movement.

The year before Jacobs arrived in the city, the abolitionists, taking seriously the responsibility of making Rochester a regional hub of the movement, had opened an Anti-Slavery Office and Reading Room "where our friends from the surrounding country can gain information in regard to the progress of our cause, and supply themselves with books and pamphlets." In addition to free reading materials, they raised money for the cause by selling "a rich variety of Fancy and useful articles made by the Ladies' Anti-Slavery Society."

The women met on Thursdays in the Anti-Slavery Office and Reading Room downtown at 25 Buffalo Street on the floor above *The North Star* (and here Jacobs met the charismatic Douglass). They gathered "to sew, knit, read, and talk for the cause," and in the fall of the year, to organize their annual fund-raising bazaar. Amy Post declared, "The pleasure of meeting once a week with the cheerful spirits of such men and women as are engaged in this holy and unselfish cause, is sufficient recompense for the loss of our labors at home. . . . Indeed, I can scarcely wait from one Thursday to another." Despite her enthusiasm, however, the Society complained at the end of 1848 that their reading room "had been visited by but few."

Harriet Jacobs's move to Rochester coincided with the Society's decision to hire her brother to revitalize the room: beginning with its March 23, 1849 issue, *The North Star* carried an ad announcing:

Antislavery Office and Reading Room,
No. 25 Buffalo St. Rochester, opposite the Arcade.

This office has been newly stocked with the latest and best works on slavery and other moral questions. Among them are the Young Abolitionist—Poverty its illegal causes and legal cure—The Power of Kindness—The Branded Hand—History of the Mexican war—Theodore Parker's Sermon on J. Q. Adams—do on the Mexican war—do his letters to the People of the United States—The Church as it is or the Forlorn Hope of Slavery—Despotism in America, and Archy Moore.

I intend to have in connection with office a Circulating Library, as soon as I can get a sufficient number of useful and instructive books of a moral and scientific character.

JOHN S. JACOBS

With John S. often away lecturing, however, it was his sister who unlocked the office door weekday mornings at 9:00 and closed it at 6:00, and it was Harriet Jacobs who was listed in the 1849 *City Directory* as "Agent Anti-Slavery Reading Rooms, over 25 Buffalo."

All that spring and summer from Mondays through Fridays, sitting at her desk in the reading room, with her daughter studying at the boarding school nearby and her brother intermittently lecturing on the road, Harriet Jacobs was free to read her way through the abolitionists' library, probably taking time out on Thursday afternoons to work with the other women on the annual fair. In Rochester, Jacobs had both the time and the opportunity to undertake a crash course in the theory and practice of organized reform.

By fall, John S. had given up the reading room and decided to make his living by opening "a spacious oyster saloon" in the Waverly buildings on State Street. He had worked hard for the movement that summer. He represented Rochester at the August First celebration commemorating British Emancipation at Auburn, along with antislavery workers from the host city and Elmira, Pen Yan, Canandigua, and Fort Plain. A crowd applauded the antislavery resolutions and afterward marched from the Methodist Episcopal Church on Washington Street to city hall to hear the "eloquent" and "thrilling" speeches by Reverend Samuel R. Ward and Reverend Henry Highland Garnet, and the songs by the Gaera Choir.

When Jacobs first came to the city, instead of settling into the black community and working closely with Union Anti-Slavery Society leaders like E. W. Walker and Mary Gibbs, she had stayed in the Sophia Street house of John's friends Isaac and Amy Post. There, she was surprised to find herself feeling at home. Although she was ten years younger than her hostess, her beloved Joseph bore the same name and was the same age as Amy's first-born (and both young men gave their mothers cause to worry). And she immediately made a pet of Amy's youngest, two-year-old "dear Willie," who learned to call her "Dah."

The Posts were awash with "the newness": not only antislavery and women's rights, but spiritualism. Like many reformers who, disillusioned with traditional beliefs, were still eager to assert the immortality of the soul, they were drawn to seances. Here, in what were termed "scientific demonstrations," mediums exhibited their ability to contact people who were not present—often those who had died—through spirit communications such as table-rappings. When in the spring, Amy Post visited her family on Long Island, then went on to New York for the American Anti-Slavery Society annual meeting and impulsively traipsed up to Boston for the New England Society anniversary, back in Rochester her husband Isaac tried to keep abreast of her activities both by mail and by mediums. Table-rappings not only brought him news of his wife, but also assured him that it was acceptable for their son to eat his pudding with "as much Molasses as he *likes*."

Living at the Posts', Jacobs was conscious that for the first time since her return from England, she was among white people who did not look down on her color. Isaac Post was well aware of his radical egalitarianism. Writing to his wife of an aunt's planned visit, he asked, "Did you frighten her with your talk about eating with coloured persons so that she will not like to come[?] I think she would not be troubled long for I wish our family all behaved as well as Harriet for I dont believe she would object sleeping with her after three days acquaintance." To Jacobs, the Posts' ability to turn antislavery theory into antiracist daily practice made friendship seem possible. Soon Amy Post's warmth invited an intimacy that Jacobs—who sorely missed her grandmother—hungered for. And so it was to Amy that Harriet, after years of tormented silence, finally told her story—not all at once, but in snatches, and never without agonized tears. Her friend later remembered her anguish: "Though impelled by a natural craving for human sympathy, she passed through a baptism of suffering, even in recounting her trials to me. . . . The burden of these memories lay heavily upon her spirit." Listening, Amy sensed that "her story was too sacred to be drawn from her by inquisitive questions, and I left her free to tell as much, or as little, as she chose."

In May, Jacobs received a letter that left her too excited to eat. She was "in an exticy," Isaac Post wrote, because she heard from her son. Joseph, home from the sea, announced that he would come to Rochester in two weeks. It was while awaiting his arrival that Jacobs composed the earliest of her writings that has survived. She wrote to her friend Amy on two scraps of paper, forming her letters carefully in a spidery hand—she had learned Miss Margaret's lessons well—but leaving the small spaces between letters that betrayed her copybook model. In her letter, Jacobs shares with her friend her eagerness for Joseph's visit—"I feel so happy daily expecting to see my Son"; reassures Amy—"things seem to go on smoothly at home"; and reports on local happenings—"went to hear Mr. Louis Lecture last night and I can assure you that he did not forget to hold up the name of Isac and Ammy Post as the Coloured Man &

Womans friend." Then, after voicing her abiding sense of the loss of family ties—"I know that if you are at Long Island you are happy for it is a great blessing to have parents to visit"—she relays the latest movement news. "The Office go on as usual   had a few here to meeting on Sunday." Commenting on the visit of Douglass's British supporters Julia and Eliza Griffiths, she continues, "I suppose we shall have Frederick and the Miss Griffiths here on Sunday to draw a full house." Jacobs's use of metaphor to end her letter expresses the delight she was discovering in putting words on paper: "Rochester is looking very pretty   the trees are in full Bloom and the earth seems covered with a green mantle."

Joseph disappointed his mother in a second letter by asking her to meet him in New York. She left Rochester instantly, and when she returned a few days later, had revised her view of the future. After more than three years at sea, Joseph, now twenty, was planning an independent life. Never again would he live under his mother's roof. He had grown up before Harriet could realize her dream of making a home in freedom for her children.

Abolitionists were of several minds concerning the traveling minstrel shows that descended on Rochester that summer. Julia Wilbur, an antislavery activist Jacobs met at the reading room, angrily recorded in her diary that at Campbell's concert, "(9 white men with blackened faces) a Colored man was refused admittance." Frederick Douglass routinely condemned any refusal to seat African Americans, and when Gavitt's Original Ethiopian Serenaders came to town, he wrote in *The North Star* that he was unsure his readers would approve of his reviewing their performance, "so strong must be their dislike to everything that seems to feed the flame of American prejudice against colored people; and in this they may be right." Then, countering the standard antislavery view that blackface minstrelsy fed white racism, he continues, "we think otherwise." While asserting that performers "must cease to exaggerate the exaggerations of our enemies, and represent the colored man rather as he is, than as Ethiopian Minstrels usually represent him to be," Douglass argues that "it is something to be gained, when the colored man in any form can appear before a white audience; and we think that even this company, with industry, application, and a proper cultivation of their taste, may yet be instrumental in removing the prejudice against our race."

Throughout the summer, Douglass used *The North Star* to promote the Rochester women's Anti-Slavery Fair. Amy Post—who, with her co-workers, was organizing multiple fund-raising fairs throughout the countryside—had initiated the campaign for the Rochester bazaar six months in advance of its December 1849 date, and surely Jacobs, living in the Posts' home and working at the reading room, was intimately involved in the diligent efforts of the Sewing Circle. At times the women moved their Thursday afternoon meetings from the reading room to the Douglass family home on Alexander Street, perhaps to accommodate Anna Murray Douglass, whose baby Annie had been born in the spring. Despite the women's industrious labors, however, the bazaar was postponed. When it was finally held after the new year, Douglass expressed disappointment with the small amount of money raised. Post, however, voiced satisfaction, seeing the event as a successful demonstration against racism. "One hundred people, of all classes and colours sat down to one table, and the most perfect decorum and order prevailed, to my views and feelings of equality, it was exceedingly gratifying and for our cause in Rochester a glorious achievement, I thought."

Executive sessions of the Western New York State Anti-Slavery Society were frequently held in the Posts' home, and Jacobs may have responded to the Society's open invitation to attend their annual convention early in January. That winter, the abolitionists and the black community were mounting public protests against school segregation, and at one courthouse demonstration, after hearing speeches by local leaders including Douglass, the crowd passed resolutions charging that the board, in establishing separate schools for "colored children . . . misrepresented the sentiments of the community, violated the rights of colored citizens, and needlessly inflicted a wound upon the feelings of the least protected part of the inhabitants of this city." They appointed Isaac Post to an interracial committee to draft "a remonstrance" to the Board of Education.

More pressing than the problem of local school segregation, however, was the threat of a national compromise on the slavery issue. The vast lands won in the Mexican War—Texas, New Mexico (including Arizona), and Upper California—ignited the national dispute over the South's "peculiar institution." Throughout the country, abolitionists and proponents of slavery argued over whether Congress had the right and the duty to prohibit slavery in the territories, or whether it was duty-bound to protect slavery and powerless to prohibit it there. At Rochester in the autumn, a mass meeting had been held to oppose the extension of slavery. Now in early spring, Isaac Post was again standing among the men, both black and white, on the platform at Corinthian Hall, proposing resolution after resolution against a compromise with the slave power.

> Resolved, Compromise or no compromise, constitution or no constitution, whether the escaping fugitive from slavery shall have his trial of freedom before a jury, a pro-slavery post master, & whatever tribunal, that no testimony short of a bill of sale from Almighty God can establish the title of the master to his slave, or induce us to lift a finger to aid in his return to the house of bondage.

Their militancy did not, however, change the political reality. Congress passed the Compromise of 1850, which included a new fugitive slave law presuming guilt, not innocence, denying an alleged fugitive the right to testify in his or her own defense, and denying the right to a trial by jury. President Millard Fillmore signed the new legislation empowering slave masters to use United States marshals to organize posses, arrest suspected fugitives, and carry them to special commissioners who could send them back into slavery. In free states as well as slave states, Americans were liable to trial and punishment for hiding or aiding fugitives.

As the bill was being debated, protests erupted throughout the North. Among them was a convention of fugitive slaves and their supporters called by the New York State Vigilance Committee for late August in Cazanovia, Madison County. John S. had lectured in Madison County, and it is likely that he and his sister were among the group of "close to 50 fugitives" who joined the 2,000 demonstrators at Cazanovia. Advertised as a protest against the new Fugitive Slave Law, the convention quickly constituted itself a defense committee after hearing that the general agent of the New York State Anti-Slavery Society, William Chaplin, had been captured by the District of Columbia police while trying to help two slaves escape from their masters. On the first day, the audience—including a number of women and "a smart sprinkling of blacks"—crammed into the Free Congregational Church to listen to the speeches and debates. They also heard antislavery songs sung by fifteen-year-old Emily and seventeen-year-old Mary, the famous Edmondson sisters who, after being seized while attempting to escape from slavery, had been freed through Chaplin's efforts. On the second day, the crowd adjourned to Mrs. Wilson's orchard, where their protest was photographed. The highlight of the Cazanovia meeting was the "Letter to the American Slaves from those who have fled from American Slavery," a radical document in the tradition of the appeals by Garnet and Walker: "You are prisoners of war, in an enemy's country—of a war, too, that is unrivaled for its injustice, cruelty, meanness—and therefore, by all the rules of war, you have the fullest liberty to plunder, burn, kill, as you may have occasion to do to promote your escape." A month later, John S. was preaching the same militant message at a protest rally in New York City.

On the day President Fillmore signed the new Fugitive Slave Bill into law—September 18, 1850—John S. decided to light out for the West. California had been admitted as a free state a week earlier, and he thought the law could not be enforced there. Before heading west to try his luck in the gold fields, however, John S. threw himself into the demonstrations denouncing the seizure of James Hamlet, the law's first New York victim. After hearing him at a meeting at Zion Chapel, abolitionists praised his "resistant spirit," and the antislavery press reported John S.'s passionate denunciation of the new law word for word:

> My colored brethren, if you have not swords, I say to you, sell your garments and buy one. . . . They said that they cannot take us back to the South; but I say, under the present law they can; and now I say unto you, let them only take your dead bodies. . . . I would, my friends, advise you to show a front to our tyrants, and arm yourselves; aye, and I would advise the women to have their knives too. But I don't advise you to trample on the laws of this State, but I advise you to trample on this bill, and I further advise you to let us go on immediately, and act like men.

John S. did not limit himself to arousing the crowd. He proposed concrete collective action, suggesting that they organize "a registry" so they could aid refugees threatened by the new law.

It is likely that his sister was among the fugitives in his audience that Tuesday evening, for Harriet, too, had returned to New York. Although sorry to leave her Rochester friends, she was sharply aware that leaving them did not mean that they could not continue to be part of each other's lives, because unlike slaves who were kept illiterate, they could be in touch through the mails. Thinking of Grandmother Molly, she wrote to Amy Post, "many far more deserving than myself has been debared from this privilege."

Back in New York City, Jacobs visited Imogen Willis. She had not forgotten the little girl who "had thawed my heart, when it was freezing into a cheerless distrust of all my fellow-beings" [ILSG p. 190]. Her fondness for the child did not, however, extend to Imogen's father, who had become "one of antebellum America's best paid and most prolific poets, editors, and 'magazinists.'" Life in his household led Jacobs to believe that Nathaniel Parker Willis held pro-slavery views. In *The North Star* a year earlier, Douglass had critiqued pro-slavery Northerners by republishing an item taken from Willis's *Home Journal*. "The Night Funeral of a Slave" concerns a visitor to the South who, after seeing a master mourning a slave's death, judges he has been wrong to condemn slavery. The abolitionists had republished this piece to argue that what appears to be a master's generosity is actually his self-interest: "The painted coffin, and the shroud of finest cotton, are highly profitable investments, as they suggest the idea of favors and privations to minds which might otherwise be occupied with the thought of that justice which is denied them." Is not, the abolitionists queried, the master's apparent kindness actually "a proof of intolerable impudence and hardness of heart, that he can use the occasion of his victim's funeral to say solemnly and with much feeling, to the survivors, that their souls' welfare depends on their patient acquiescence in his usurpation of ownership over them?" Douglass's analysis of Willis's pro-slavery apology reinforced Jacobs's distrust of her former employer.

The affection she felt for his daughter, however, was real. And now, meeting the new Mrs. Willis, she was favorably impressed. A romantic story was attached to Willis's second marriage. Long before Willis met Cornelia Grinnell, her father, a New Bedford manufacturer making the Grand Tour, had commissioned a sculptor to chisel a statue of his little daughter, and somewhat later, when Willis was living abroad, the remainder of the same block had been used for his portrait bust. When Jacobs made her visit, both marbles were on display in the parlor: the likeness of Willis with the curling locks he had affected in young manhood, and Cornelia as a demure little girl, with a bird in one hand and a cup in the other.

A dozen years younger than Harriet Jacobs and two decades younger than her husband, Cornelia Grinnell Willis was personable and bright, a woman with "a penetrating mind and an uncommon energy and firmness of will." To Jacobs, most important was that she was "an American, brought up under aristocratic influences, and still living in the midst of them; but if she had any prejudice against color, I was never made aware of it; and as for the system of slavery, she had a most hearty dislike of it" [ILSG p. 190]. Cornelia Willis had two young children, two-and-a-half-year-old Grinnell and five-month-old Lilian. At her visit,

Jacobs learned that Cornelia had been ill ever since Lilian's birth. Letting her sympathy outweigh prudence, she agreed to become the baby's nurse—although even before the new Fugitive Slave Law she had felt insecure in New York, and now was certainly more threatened. John S. shared her fears. Leaving for California, he solicited Cornelia Willis's promise "as a lady" that she would not permit the Norcoms to seize his sister.

It was a fearful time, "the beginning of a reign of terror to the colored population" [ILSG p. 191]. Through the antislavery press, Harriet Jacobs kept track of attempts to capture fugitive slaves. At Boston, in October a Georgia slaveholder obtained a warrant for William and Ellen Craft; in February, Fred Wilkins (called "Shadrach") was seized and dragged into court; and, two months later, Thomas Sims was arrested. But there was fight-back. At Christiana, Pennsylvania, the slave catchers who tried to return William Parker to slavery were met with guns; and at Syracuse, an outraged crowd rescued Jerry McHenry after he had been taken into custody at the police office.

These news reports underscored the terror all around her in New York, where Jacobs saw

> many a poor washerwoman, who, by hard labor, had made herself a comfortable home, was obliged to sacrifice her furniture, bid a hurried farewell to friends, and seek her fortune among strangers in Canada. Many a wife discovered a secret she had never known before—that her husband was a fugitive, and must leave her to insure his own safety. Worse still, many a husband discovered that his wife had fled from slavery years ago, and as "the child follows the condition of its mother," the children of his love were liable to be seized and carried into slavery. [ILSG p. 191]

In the Willis house on Fourth Street, fear was stifling her, weighing down her every movement. "When I took the children out to breathe the air," she later wrote, "I closely observed the countenances of all I met. I dreaded the approach of summer, when snakes and slaveholders make their appearance" [ILSG p. 193]. To Amy, she confided, "I never go out in the day light accept I ride insite."

Yet in the face of the terror, African Americans and their friends were organizing. For decades, vigilance committees in northern cities had been aiding fugitives: "boarding and lodging them for a few days, purchasing clothing and medicine for them, providing them with small sums of money, informing them as to their legal rights and giving them legal protection from kidnappers," then helping them establish themselves in a new place. Now their work multiplied. Jacobs's role in the vigilance movement will never be fully known. But we do know that every day, she checked the daily papers, searching the listings of "Arrivals at City Hotels," looking for the names of Southerners who came slave-catching, and hoping against hope that she would not find "Norcom" among them.

Then in the spring of 1851 she had frightening news from the South. It was known in Edenton that Jacobs had returned to New York, and there was a plan to seize her. Quickly she conferred with Cornelia Willis. Little Lilian loudly objected to being parted from her nurse, and her mother proposed that Jacobs take the child and go to Cornelia's parents in New Bedford. If Jacobs were caught alone, she reasoned, no one would know. But if she had Lilian with her, the authorities would have to return the child, and Cornelia could try to rescue her.

Gratefully, Jacobs went, and at New Bedford, the Grinnells sent her and little Lilian out to their country house. Jacobs wrote to her old friend William C. Nell, explaining her plight and speculating about the future: perhaps she had made a mistake by returning to New York. Perhaps she should seriously think about following her brother—as her son had—to California? Despite her misgivings, however, a month later she took Lilian home and returned to her job—perhaps because Cornelia Willis needed her and she did not want to disappoint the woman who had given such meaningful evidence of her friendship.

Back in New York, Jacobs lived in a state of siege. She was exhausted, and the physical tension she had known during her years in hiding returned. Then—belatedly—came news that Dr. Norcom was dead. Characteristically, Molly Horniblow sent a letter expressing the Christian hope that the old man had found peace. But Jacobs could never forgive him. Years later, she remained adamant: "There are wrongs which even the grave does not bury. The man was odious to me while he lived, and his memory is odious now" [ILSG p. 196]. Embittering her recollections of Dr. Norcom was her awareness that his death had not ended her danger. She could still be seized by his heirs. Norcom had left only a small estate, and in Edenton his widow was openly saying that her daughter could not afford to lose such a valuable slave as Jacobs.

To complicate Jacobs's situation, now Cornelia and Nathaniel Willis found themselves at the center of a sensational scandal. They had long been friends of the celebrated Shakespearean actor Edwin Forrest and his wife Catherine, but when Forrest charged adultery and filed for divorce, they took Catherine's part. In January, a furious Forrest had accosted Willis, and the next day, Cornelia Willis received an anonymous letter accusing her husband of adultery with Catherine Forrest. The story hit the newspapers in the spring when the *Herald* published Forrest's application for divorce, complete with accusations against Willis and his brother. Willis responded by defending both his brother and his wife (accused of having encouraged illicit behavior), and then published a vindication of Catherine Forrest. In June, as the convalescent Willis—who was recovering from rheumatic fever—was out walking in Washington Square, Forrest, shouting, "Gentlemen, this is the seducer of my wife," knocked him down and whipped him with his cane. When the police came, Forrest ranted that if they had not arrived he would have "cut his damned heart out." Willis sued Forrest for assault, and Catherine Forrest, who was awarded an injunction to stop her husband from proceeding with his suit, then herself filed for divorce on grounds of adultery. When Jacobs had returned from Rochester to visit little Imogen, the Willises's role in the widely publicized Forrest divorce was just beginning.

Late in 1851, the Willis household was being thrown into an uproar by the Forrest divorce trial. Every day for six weeks, jurors heard evidence in the sensational case. And every day for six weeks, in court next to her friend Catherine Forrest, sat Cornelia Willis. Much of the testimony incriminated her husband: The Forrests' waiter testified that he had seen Willis with Catherine Forrest on the back piazza, "lying on each other"; and a former servant swore that he had heard Willis saying, "Goodnight, dear," and had seen him in his stocking feet, coming out of the room where Mrs. Forrest had stayed, presumably to help nurse Cornelia during her postpartum illness. Then Cornelia Willis herself took the stand, testifying that she had set aside the room in her home for her friend, that Catherine Forrest had come to her at Fourth Street after leaving her husband, and that often, after Lilian's birth, she stayed overnight. Explaining that her friend's room was next to little Imogen's and that her husband usually went upstairs to wish the child a good night, she testified that from the stairs, it was impossible to tell which room her husband had come from, or to which room he directed his "Goodnight, dear." According to one report, "No one could believe that a spirited and refined lady, like Mrs. Willis, would have consented, for an instant, to put herself into such a position, without a full assurance of her husband's innocence; and no one who listened to her testimony could have thought her a woman likely to be deceived." When Willis was sworn, he flatly denied all accusations.

After six weeks of testimony, both the prosecution and the defense rested, and on January 26, the press reported that "thousands and thousands of the anxious public thronged the park," hoping to be admitted into court to hear the verdict. The jury was unanimous. It voted in Catherine Forrest's favor, clearing Willis's name and the names of the others accused of adulterous relationships with her and, finding Forrest guilty of adultery, granted her her divorce. According to Willis's biographer, "the one circumstance which more than all else influenced the decision of the jury was the constant presence in court of Mrs. N. P. Willis, side by side with Mrs. Forrest, and the brave, clear, and simple way in which she testified in her friend's behalf."

Now everyone in the Fourth Street household could breathe more easily—everyone, that is, but Harriet Jacobs. Although the family's lives were no longer being disrupted every day by the trial, she knew that she was still threatened by kidnapping. To her friend Amy Post, Jacobs wrote that she was trying to feel hopeful. She had, she said, burned two earlier letters "filled with trouble and care," but now, feeling "some encouragement," could share her concerns. Her brother John had abandoned California and moved on. Six months earlier, a miner who had bottomed out in California had returned home to Australia, where he discovered a "vast gold-field." Within months, "a thousand diggers were tunnelling, cursing and exulting on the banks of Summerhill Creek, and the road over the Blue Mountains was choked with a footsore, sluggishly winding column of men . . . trudging beneath the weight of tents, blankets, crowbars, picks, shovels, pans and billycans hastily bought at gougers' prices, stumbling toward unheard-of wealth in mud-balled boots under the driving rains of the Australian autumn." Among them were African Americans and men of color from the West Indies. In Australia, they were sheltered by British law, more colorblind than the American legal system.

Joseph had joined his uncle in the rush to Australia, and now Harriet was agonizing, trying to decide whether to follow them. John's first claim was a bust—the claim below his had paid each man $2,000, and he had turned down an offer of $500 before starting, but after three months of hard labor, he had nothing to show. He started over, joining four others at dry diggings on the Muiron Islands off the western coast, where, he wrote, he thought the mines looked promising: "there is five in the party and they have gone so far under the hills that they work by candle light . . . there has been a good many new discoveries where persons never thought of looking for gold and it has given new life to mining." John was, Jacobs explained to Amy, "very anxious to have me go. He thinks that I could do well out there." He proposed, however, that Louisa wait a year before joining them, and Louisa was "much opposed to being left behind." Jacobs paused for a moment, then spelled out her lifelong dream: "I could do any thing for the sake of a little shanty to call home and have my Children to come around me."

But before she could finalize her plans, Harriet Jacobs's world cracked open. On Sunday morning, February 29, recalling that she had neglected to examine yesterday's paper, she searched for it in the parlor and found the boy about to use it to kindle the fire. Running her eye down the column listing "Arrivals at City Hotels," she saw, at Taylor's Hotel, "D. Missmore & 1. Edenton." Norcoms's son-in-law had come to catch her.

Jacobs had never met her young mistress's husband—she did not even know what he looked like—but she knew that Mary Matilda had been left without a legacy after her father's death and was determined to catch her valuable slave Hatty and Hatty's valuable children. Jacobs rushed to Cornelia Willis, who ordered a carriage. Quickly bundling up little Lilian, grabbing her shawl, and swathing her face in veils, Jacobs carried the child outside. Cornelia Willis ordered the coachman to drive them around and around until finally, convinced they were not being followed, they stopped in front of the home of a friend. Harriet carried Lilian inside, and Cornelia went back to Fourth Street to deal with the strangers who began appearing at her door asking for Jacobs. (One even claimed to have a letter from her grandmother to deliver in person.) All were told that she had gone, no one knew where.

It was a terrifying day. From her hiding place, Jacobs got word to an Edenton friend, asking him to go to the Messmores at Taylor's Hotel. Knowing they were after Louisa upset her deeply. Joseph was out of their grasp, but Louisa was visiting friends in the city. Sitting in the Manhattan kitchen with two-year-old Lilian on her lap, when she thought of what could happen to her own daughter, now nineteen, "my heart was like a tiger's when a hunter tries to seize her young" [ILSG p. 199]. In late morning her Edenton friend, fearful of being followed, sent a note. He had seen Messmore, who asked about her whereabouts and claimed that he would permit her to buy herself, then got angry at hearing that she believed she had a right to her freedom. When afternoon came Cornelia Willis returned, reporting that her house was being watched and begging Jacobs to leave the city.

She would not. Disheartened and bitter, Harriet Jacobs felt as trapped as she had fifteen years earlier. The summer she was hidden by Grandmother's slaveholding friend, the terrifying days in the pocosin, the six years and eleven months of living death under the shed roof, the escape by ship, the week with the Durhams in Philadelphia, her life in New York with Mary Stace Willis, then in Boston and Rochester and now back in the city—all had been for nothing. She was still running and hiding from the Norcoms. Listening to the sound of the church bells tolling the afternoon service, she gave vent to her fury at the hypocrisy of the Christian United States of America: "Oppressed Poles and Hungarians could find a safe refuge in that city; . . . but there I sat, an oppressed American, not daring to show my face" [ILSG p. 198]. More hours passed. Cornelia Willis sent Louisa to plead with her mother to flee. When at ten o'clock Louisa had not returned, Cornelia came back in a carriage with a trunk she had packed. Finally, Jacobs agreed to run again.

Next morning, a double series of events began to unfold. The public drama was played out before Judge Bosworth and the press in the superior court, where Cornelia Willis went to sit and watch the argument in her husband's assault and battery case against Forrest. The private drama began when Jacobs dressed Lilian warmly and, in a heavy snowfall, again carried her to the Grinnells' New Bedford home. But in Massachusetts, she did not feel much better than she had in Manhattan. Fearing that the mails were being watched, Cornelia used an assumed name to send news. Willis, she wrote, had won his suit, but Messmore was still searching for Jacobs, and to end his harassment, Cornelia had decided to buy Jacobs's freedom. Harriet felt grateful—but knew that this was not the resolution she had in mind. She could not think of herself as a commodity, and "to pay money to those who had so grievously oppressed me seemed like taking from my sufferings the glory of triumph." She wrote back thanking her friend but rejecting the offer, explaining that "being sold from one owner to another seemed too much like slavery; that such a great obligation could not be easily cancelled" [ILSG p. 199]. She had decided to defeat the Norcoms herself by joining her brother.

But the matter was out of her hands. By the next mail, Cornelia Willis wrote that she had contacted the Colonization Society and authorized an agent to offer Messmore $300 to relinquish all claims on Jacobs and her children, and that Messmore had agreed. Reading this, Jacobs became dizzy. When one of the family, misinterpreting her apparent lack of response as skepticism, said he had seen the bill of sale, Jacobs began to shake uncontrollably. She felt as if she had been thrown to the ground. It was impossible to grasp. In the free city of New York, she had been sold as property. Then her head cleared. Her mind told her she was finally free, and she thought of her father, whose strongest wish was to free his children. "I hoped," she later recalled, "his spirit was rejoicing over me now" [ILSG p. 200].

Still, she did not feel free. She felt like merchandise. Better to have defied the vile law than to have complied with it, and shameful to be beholden to the racist Colonization Society. Better to have gone to California, or Canada, or Australia—anywhere until that terrible law was repealed, until slavery was ended in America. But the next day, when she dressed Lilian for the trip back to New York, Jacobs felt buoyant, physically lighter, "as if a heavy load had been lifted from my weary shoulders" [ILSG p. 200]. In the train, she kept her face unveiled, looking squarely at everyone around her, wanting one of them to be Messmore, wanting him to see her and know her and curse his luck at having sold her for a mere $300. But if, in the sound of the railroad wheels, she heard, freedom, freedom, freedom, a little later—when she stepped inside the door of the Willises' house on Fourth Street and found herself weeping gratefully in the arms of the tearful Cornelia—she knew it was not over.

8

Let Me Come Before the World

~❧~

*Only let me come before the world as I have been
an uneducated oppressed Slave.*
—Harriet Jacobs to Amy Post October 9 [1853]

She did not feel free. Although no longer legally a slave, Harriet Jacobs needed to act in order to feel liberated. But what could she do? John, she was sure, would be able to advise her, but John was on the other side of the world. It sometimes took as long as five months for his letters to reach her, and her need was urgent. She really could not wait for his counsel.

Certainly she experienced relief. But knowing that the Norcoms could no longer seize her and her children did not prevent her from feeling anguished by the means by which her freedom had been won. She confessed her conflicted emotions to Amy Post: gratitude for Mrs. Willis's help, real pain that her freedom had been gained by purchase. "The freedom I had before the money was paid was dearer to me. God gave me *that* freedom; but man put God's image in the scales with the paltry sum of three hundred dollars." Contrasting herself with her biblical prototype, she voiced profound disappointment. "I served for my liberty as faithfully as Jacob served for Rachel. At the end, he had large possessions; but I was robbed of my victory; I was obliged to resign my crown, to rid myself of a tyrant."

While Jacobs was hiding out in Massachusetts, Louisa had gone west in search of a teaching position. Now, with her daughter away and her brother and son chasing a phantom gold strike across the Pacific, Jacobs was troubled. To Amy, she apologized for her distressed tone: "it is hard for me to write while things remain as they are they burden me so heavily that my letters can afford you no pleasure. . . . situated as I am my

117

Brother and son away no home for Louisa to come to it makes me very unhappy for their sakes." True, she had steady work—the only one in the family who did—and her wages were enabling her to pay off Louisa's school expenses and the debts John had left behind. But she saw no way to unite the family.

Further, Jacobs felt infinitely beholden to her benefactor. Cornelia Grinnell Willis had paid $150.00 cash down for Jacobs. She needed an equal amount to pay off Messmore, and all spring she tried to raise the money. To one of her friends, she penned an extraordinary note: "I came this morning to ask your friendly assistance in buying a Slave. A woman in whom I have felt great interest . . . this spring was very nearly taken by her master." Explaining that she had hidden her and then arranged for her purchase, Cornelia ends this plea with a coda expressive of the chasm between the privileged social position she and her correspondent enjoyed, and Harriet Jacobs's status: "The woman is an intelligent and excellent person, quite above her position in some respects, and it seems to me a legitimate charity."

Jacobs was aware that Mrs. Willis, already burdened with small children, also had a very sick husband. Willis had returned from his "Health Trip to the Tropics" coughing up blood every night. In a desperate effort to recover, he decided to make his home in the Hudson River highlands where, he believed, the temperate climate would restore his health. At summer's end, instead of returning to Fourth Street, the Willises stayed on in the country, boarding at the Sutherlands' Glenbrook farm on the road to Newburgh while ground was broken nearby for the "cottage" Calvert Vaux had designed for them.

But how Jacobs wished that she had gone with her brother! "I have regreeted it so often that I did not go with him   if it were not for the many deep obligations that I am under to my kind friend Mrs Willis and it would be very ungreatful to leave her while her Husband health is so feeble for some times he is taken so sudenly that one dont know what the next day may bring forth   if it was not for this I would now gladly go." Her daughter's experiences made Australia seem doubly appealing: "Louisa who is still out West feel so disappointed   I felt she might there be enabled to support herself by teaching   I have done all that I could to fit her for the situation."

Perhaps it was to lift the depression deepening these letters that Amy Post suggested that—despite Jacobs's isolation from the activists' centers—she could make a contribution to the movement by writing the story of her life. At first, Jacobs responded that this was impossible. How could she tell her story when just thinking about the past was so painful? How could she write about her life when she was not a writer? How could she divulge her secrets to strangers, when it was all she could do to sob them into her friend's ear? She could not write her story. Write it? After being warned it might cause some to feel contempt, for years she had been unable even to speak it. Struggling to explain herself to Amy, she confessed that her brother had urged her to reveal her secrets, and "my conscience approved it but my stubborn pride would not yield." Yes, she finally had managed to whisper her story to her friend, but she suffered too much pain—too much shame—to tell anyone else. "dear Amy if it was the life of a Heroine with no degradation associated with it   far better to have been one of the starving poor of Ireland whose bones had to bleach on the highways than to have been a slave with the curse of slavery stamped upon yourself and Children."

She could not write the book. But neither could she not write it. Now that she was legally free, she felt she must help the antislavery cause. Writing her narrative, she could transform her experiences into a life representative of her oppressed people and build support for antislavery. Determined to triumph over her anguish, Jacobs vowed somehow to conquer her pride for the sake of the Cause. "I feel that God has helped me or I never would consent to give my past life to any one for I would not do it with out giving the whole truth   if it could help save another from my fate it would be selfish and unchristian in me to keep it back."

Jacobs had wrestled with her decision, but once it was made, immediately began exploring how to begin. She conferred with Cornelia Willis, who suggested that she leave the project for her children to undertake after her death. But Jacobs disagreed. "Now is the time when their is so much excitement everywhere." She considered with Mrs. Willis the possibility of somehow gaining the ear of an author who could tell her story. The obvious choice was Harriet Beecher Stowe, whose *Uncle Tom's Cabin* was rapidly becoming America's best-selling book. But contacting Stowe presented a problem. Jacobs was reluctant to request a letter of introduction from Mrs. Willis because her husband was "too proslavery" and would disapprove. Reaching for an alternative, she asked Amy to speak with the Anti-Slavery Society about approaching Stowe.

Thinking that she saw a way to proceed, Jacobs quickly sketched an outline of the book she was envisioning. "I should want the History of my childhood and the first five years in one volume and the next three and my home in the northern states in the second." Might it be possible, she asked Amy, to convince Mrs. Stowe to agree to let her visit for a month, so that she could become familiar with the story? Jacobs would make it worth her while: "I could give her some fine sketches for her pen on slavery." Conceiving this project, Jacobs felt a surge of energy. She actually could, she felt, be of value to the cause. "Dear Amy since I have no fear of my name coming before those whom I have lived in dread of I cannott be happy without trying to be useful in some way."

Post wrote to Stowe as Jacobs asked, but before she could receive an answer, the papers reported that the famous author would soon leave for England, and Jacobs decided to act quickly. Louisa had returned home with splendid memories of America's vast spaces, but without a teaching job. Despite Mrs. Willis's offer to include her daughter in the household, Jacobs knew Louisa wanted another kind of life: "she wants to seek her own livlihood where she thinks she can be most useful." Now, reading about Stowe's projected English trip, Jacobs saw an opportunity both for her daughter and for the book she had begun planning. Travel abroad, she was sure, would be wonderful for Lulu. It would give her a chance at the experience of living, as Jacobs had a few years earlier, free of American racism. Perhaps, her mother fondly thought, it would even enable her to make a name for herself in the international antislavery movement, as the Georgia fugitive Ellen Craft was doing. And if Louisa were traveling with Stowe, she might be able to convince the famous author to write Jacobs's life story.

Excited, Jacobs reported to Amy that she had proposed her plan to Mrs. Willis, who offered to write to Stowe suggesting that she add Louisa to her traveling party. Jacobs gladly reported that she had saved enough from her wages to pay her daughter's expenses, and "I thought if I could get her to take Louisa with her she might get interested enough   if she could do nothing herself she might help Louisa to do something   besides I thought Louisa would be a very good representative of a Southern Slave she has improved much in her studies and I think that she has energy enough to do something for the cause. she only needs to be put in the field."

But hope soon turned to outrage. Writing furiously, her pen stumbling in the effort to keep pace with her racing mind, Jacobs poured out her indignation to her friend: "as it is I hardly know where to begin for my thoughts come rushing down with such a spirit of rivalry each wishing to be told you first so that they fill my heart and make my eyes dim therefore my silence must express to you what my poor pen is not capable of doing." Stowe, she reports, had answered Mrs. Willis that "it would be much care to her to take Louisa   as she went by invitation it would not be right and she was afraid that if her situation as a Slave should be known it would subject her to much petting and patronizing which would be more pleasing to a young Girl than useful and the English was very apt to do it and she was very much opposed to it with this class of people." With her rejection, Stowe had enclosed Amy Post's letter and asked Mrs. Willis to verify its description of Jacobs's life. If the story were true, she suggested, she would incorporate it into *The Key to Uncle Tom's Cabin*, which she was rushing to complete before sailing to England.

To Post, Jacobs angrily condemned Stowe's behavior as both disgraceful and threatening. "I had never opend my lips to Mrs Willis concerning my Children—in the Charitableness of her own heart she sympathised with me and never asked their origin   my suffering she knew   it embarrassed me at first but I told her the truth but we both thought it was wrong in Mrs Stowe to have sent you letter   she might have written to enquire if she liked." Mrs. Willis, she continues, responded to Stowe in "a very kind letter beging that she would not use any of the facts in her key saying that I wished it to be a history of my life entirely by itself which would do more good and it needed no romance but if she wanted some facts for her book that I would be most happy to give her some." Receiving no answer, Jacobs reports, Mrs. Willis wrote again, and she herself wrote twice. Then Jacobs spells out her condemnation of the famous author: "it was not Lady like to treat Mrs Willis so   she would not have done it to any one."

Judging Stowe, Jacobs voices a sensibility schooled by a lifetime of experience serving a master who demanded not only obedience, but acquiescence. "I think she did not like my objection   I cant help it." Then, smarting from the racial insult in Stowe's dismissal: "think dear Amy that a visit to Stafford House [a center of British reform] would spoil me as Mrs Stowe thinks peting is more than my race can bear   weell what a pity we poor blacks cant have the firmness and stability of character that you white people have." Instead of concluding that Stowe's rejection spelled defeat for her project, however, Jacobs explores alternatives. Perhaps—recalling her brother's activism—she should consider approaching the Boston abolitionists "Mr Garrison Philips and Miss Weston"?

In mid-June, with Cornelia Willis "feeble" from another pregnancy, the burden of moving the family into the new house at Cornwall fell on Jacobs's shoulders. In the city to pack up the Fourth Street house, she saw an item in an old newspaper that moved her to insert herself into the international debate on American slavery. Written by former First Lady Julia Tyler, it was a defense of chattel slavery composed in response to the Duchess of Sutherland, whose "Stafford House Address" had appealed to the white women of the South to end chattel slavery. In "The Women of England vs. the Women of America," Tyler recites standard endorsements of the domestic role of American women and presents a series of stock apologies for slavery—including the argument that England, who had proved repressive in Ireland and the British West Indies, was responsible for American slavery; and the claim that the households of Southern women include "well clothed and happy domestics" who, although slaves, are better off than many free Englishmen and, contrary to abolitionist propaganda, are not denied access to Christian teachings. In addition, she asserts that the separation of slave families is "rare" and occurs only under "peculiar circumstances." Reading this, Jacobs flushed with outrage, and as soon as the household went to bed, took up her pen.

She wrote all night. In the morning, taking time only to check her spelling and to sign herself "A Fugitive Slave," she sent her letter off to the *Tribune*. Then she caught the early boat back up the Hudson to Cornwall.

Jacobs begins her first public letter by presenting her credentials for entering the discussion of "Mrs. Tyler's Reply." She is, she announces, an unschooled slave, but—still smarting from Stowe's rejection—is nevertheless writing her letter herself: "poor as it may be, I had rather give it from my own hand, than have it said that I employed others to do it for me. The truth can never be told so well through the second and third person as from yourself." She flatly states that what she reports will be factual: "As this is the first time that I ever took my pen in hand to make such an attempt, you will not say that it is fiction, for had I the inclination, I have neither the brain or talent to write it." Jacobs then describes the situation of a fourteen-year-old—identified as a younger sister—who was forced into concubinage by her master and at twenty-one sold away with her children to appease her mistress's jealousy. Arguing that southern women like Mrs. Tyler are aware of "the evils of slavery, and that the mistress as well as the slave must submit to the indignities and vices imposed on them by their lords of body and soul," she appeals to her readers as Americans, as Christians, and as mothers to remember "the millions of slaves they have at home, bought and sold under very peculiar circumstances." Ending with a reference to Harriet Beecher Stowe, Jacobs spells out her newfound literary aspirations. "Would that I had one spark from her store house of genius and talent, I would tell you of my own sufferings—I would tell you of wrongs that Hungary has never inflicted, nor England ever dreamed of in this free country where all nations fly for liberty, equal rights and protection under your stripes and stars." Then—indulging her delight in language: "It should be stripes and scars, for they go along with Mrs. Tyler's peculiar circumstances, of which I have told you only one."

When the letter was printed two days later, an author was born. Jacobs could only glance at her publication, however, because the *Tribune* was delivered while Willis was at dinner, and afterward he took it with him. Nevertheless, Jacobs was emboldened by seeing her words in print and dared hope *The North Star* might copy her work. She immediately began a second letter for the press. Then, writing "in the midst of all kind of care and perplexities," she snatched a few moments from readying the new house to tell Amy about her letter and to ask her to send two copies of the paper. "I cannot ask the favor of any one else with out appearing very Ludicrous in their opinion I love you and can bear your severest criticism because you know what my advantages have been and what they have not been. . . . I have another but I can not offer it before I can read over the first to see more of its imperfections." A week later the *Standard* reprinted her letter under its *Tribune* headnote explaining that the piece was published "exactly as written by the author with the exception or corrections in punctuation and spelling, and the omission of one or two passages." Post evidently discussed its appearance with William C. Nell, and he sent a copy of the *Standard* to Louisa, who was staying with friends. But when Nell questioned Jacobs, she was embarrassed and denied the piece was hers. Post had not yet responded to her revelation that her letter was in print, and she was uncomfortable disclosing her authorship to anyone else—even her friend or her daughter.

But her courage returned. A month later she sent the *Tribune* another letter signed "Fugitive." Now, as before, she was responding to an article in print and asserting that her experience authorized her participation in public debate. Now at issue was the practice of outlawry in North Carolina. In this letter, Jacobs recalls the 1833 murder of George Cabarrus, the runaway slave killed in Edenton by bounty hunters who, assuming he had been outlawed, murdered him, took his severed head into town

to claim their reward, and then, discovering that he had not been outlawed, fled, leaving Cabarrus's decapitated body in a canoe, rotting in
the sun. Emboldened by the appearance of this second letter, Jacobs composed a third. This time she wrote to condemn the Colonization Society
and their program of sending African Americans to Liberia—a practice
that most African Americans believed was a racist effort to deny them
their American birthright and to claim the United States as a "white
man's country."

In July, the Willis family moved into Idlewild, their new home at Cornwall up the Hudson, but summer was over before Jacobs heard from
Post. When she did, she wrote a "hasty" response. After hurriedly noting the pressures on the household occasioned by the birth of Cornelia
Willis's new baby and voicing her sorrow at not hearing from her son
and brother, she began her letter again with the announcement of a terrible loss: Molly Horniblow was dead. "dear Amy I have lost that Dear
old Grandmother that I so dearly loved oh her life has been one of sorrow and trial but he in whom she trusted has never forsaken her her
Death was beautiful may my last end be like hers." This distressing news
is the prelude to a major declaration. Without breaking her line on the
page, Jacobs continues, "Louisa is with me I dont know how long she
will remain I shall try and keep her all winter as I want to try and make
arrangements to have some of my time."
    Opening a new paragraph, she recalls the Stowe debacle and her
"Fugitive Slave" letters before finally naming the project she has decided
to undertake: "I must write just what I have lived and witnessed myself
dont expect much of me dear Amy you shall have truth but not talent
God did not give me that gift but he gave me a soul that burned for freedom and a heart nerved with determination to suffer even unto death in
pursuit of that liberty which without makes life an intolerable burden."
The death of her revered grandmother has freed Harriet Jacobs to write
her life story.

Jacobs was making the decision to write her narrative at a unique
moment in African American literary history. To establish an independent voice in the abolitionist movement, some black leaders were discussing the value of separate black institutions, which they called
"complexionally distinct." In the spring, "Ethiop" (William J. Wilson)
wrote in Douglass's *North Star*, "at present what we find around us,

either in art or literature, is made so to press upon us, that we deprecate, we despise, we almost hate ourselves, and all that favors us. . . . We must begin to tell our own story, write our own letters, paint our own picture, chisel our own bust . . . acknowledge and love our own peculiarities if we have any." In the autumn, *The North Star* published a specific appeal for an African American literature. The writer comments that "upon happier shores, the achievements of our brethren in the department of letters have fully demonstrated the fact that the descendants of Africa are not wanting in poetic power, nor in the brilliant imagination which characterizes the novelist." Recalling the black heritage of Europe's Alexander Pushkin and Alexandre Dumas, and of America's Phillis Wheatley and George Horton, he notes that the work of his contemporaries—Frederick Douglass, Charles Lenox Remond, Samuel Ringgold Ward, and Henry Highland Garnet—is mainly in "the narrow limits of pamphlets, or the columns of newspapers." He then calls for the creation of a more permanent literature: the appearance of new authors "should be the earnest and increasing prayer of all who desire the literary advancement of our people."

Actually, the creation of a permanent literature was already underway. Douglass's *Narrative*, which had appeared in 1845, had been followed by a number of slave narratives within the decade, and now the unparalleled sales of *Uncle Tom's Cabin* were opening the gates not only to fictional treatments of slavery, but also to autobiographies and biographies of American slaves. When Jacobs sat down to write in the evening after work, Frederick Douglass was penning his *My Bondage and My Freedom*, and William Anderson was also writing his life, as were William Green, William Grimes, Daniel Peterson, Austin Steward, John Thompson, Levin Tilmon, and Samuel Ringgold Ward; Josephine Brown was working on her biography of her father William Wells Brown, and William C. Nell was completing his ground-breaking history, *The Colored Patriots of the American Revolution*. The call for a more lasting African American literature was being answered.

Neither *The North Star*'s appeal nor the presence of others at work creating this literature, however, was what moved Jacobs to write her life. Her letter to Amy Post signals a deep connection between her decision and Molly Horniblow's death. On some level, the death of the grandmother she had last seen eleven years earlier now freed Jacobs—a forty-year-old former slave—to write her life. Every day that dawned, she knew that in liberating her children, she had accomplished what Molly could not. And every day that dawned, she knew that she could never have done it without Molly. But she also knew that, while Molly lived, she could not write it out. Although her conscience told her that she must write to help free others enslaved as she had been, she could never tell her whole story—she could never reveal her troubled sexual history—while her proud, judgmental grandmother lived.

Now Molly was gone, and she permitted herself to remember it all: Mama's scent, Papa's voice, Grandma and Uncle Joseph and John of course; the horn sounding curfew, the wind among the graves, his sickening insinuations, smiles, and threats, Major Sam and her beautiful babies; the road from Auburn, the snakes, and her loophole. She remembered the ship, the city, the railroad, and finding Lulu, then Joseph, finally John. Using some other woman's voice, she would find a way to tell some of it. But she also remembered what she would never tell: the filth he spewed at her, her hours with Major Sam, the endless dark.

Jacobs began writing at the Willises' home up the Hudson. Idlewild had been conceived as a famous writer's retreat, but its owner never imagined that it was his children's nurse who would create an American classic there. For his fourteen-room "cottage," Willis had picked a romantic spot on the shore of Moodna Creek, where the plateau suddenly drops 200 feet into a gorge. He carefully planned each gable, pinnacle, and piazza to take advantage of the dramatic site, and his architect Calvert Vaux proudly announced that "extensive views of the river and mountain scenery are gained from the various windows, each view being a separate picture set in a frame of unfading foliage." *Harper's*—publishing sketches on the homes of American writers—enthused, "there is every where embellishment enough for comfort, and elegance . . . choice little treasures in marble and bronze for mantle, bracket, and table. . . . Books there are, too—pleasant books, but not too rich for use."

Willis himself often rhapsodized about his country place in his weekly *Home Journal* column, describing its seventy acres and making famous the noisy brook cascading over the cliffs and crags of the ravine behind the house before dropping into the quiet meadow below—its dramatic fall surprising guests who entered from the front, where the broad lawn overlooked the Hudson River. Picturesque Cornwall stood high on the bluff above the water. Busy Newburgh lay four miles to the north. The Willis family often took afternoon outings there, making their way through streets crowded with farmers' wagons and the handsome carriages parked outside Chapman's Bakery. Impressive West Point, home of the nation's military academy, was four miles to the south. Only a mile from Idlewild was the rural village of Canterbury, but the nearest post office was at Moodna, off the main road on the banks of fast-flowing Moodna Creek, where bells ringing the shift change at Leonards' cotton factory and at Carson & Ide's papermill called 300 men, women, and children to their work. (Idlewild's guests were deprived of the spectacular waterfall on weekends, when the mills dammed up the flow of water.) In poetic language, Willis regularly pointed out the proximity of the Hudson highlands to Manhattan, which enabled them to offer both "rural tastes and metropolitan refinements." "From the promontory on which stands my cottage, I see the lake beneath my lawn traversed daily by a hundred craft of one sort and another—steamers, tow-boats, sloops, rafts, yachts, schooners and barges—makes a different thing of solitude. I presume five thousand people, at least, pass daily under my library window."

The river boats and their passengers passed, too, beneath Harriet Jacobs's window upstairs in the servants' quarters. At the Willises' country estate, she was surrounded by a natural environment chosen to touch a writer's soul. Yet her days were destined not for the study, but for the nursery. While Willis wrote by day, she undertook her project in secret, and at night.

Although Jacobs did not discuss her Newburgh or Cornwall neighbors in her letters to Post during these years, her comparative isolation at Idlewild was a consequence of her determination to write, not of the absence of a black community around her. All five of the Willises' servants were African American, and among the rural characters Willis described to his *Home Journal* readers was "broad-featured, simple, kindly, and cheerful" Black Peter, bought and sold three times in slavery days. Moving up the Hudson, Jacobs had joined a hundred black residents living in Cornwall. Although many of these, like their white neighbors, often went from one river town to the next, some—like the Adams and the Boles families—remained in Cornwall for generations. The historic local black presence is acknowledged by Angola Road, named for the African slaves brought to New Netherlands in the seventeenth century. And Cornwall was not lacking white opponents of slavery. Here, as elsewhere, the Quakers traditionally opposed the South's "peculiar institution." The local woman who later reminisced about her parents' home as "one of the stations of the 'underground railroad,'" recalled her mother trying to teach reading to a fugitive who stayed all winter working as a servant, and she remembered her father taking a runaway "in a sleigh across the Hudson on the ice not any too safe."

Nearby Newburgh, the site of the pre-Revolutionary estate of Hector St. John de Crèvecoeur—who though an owner of slaves, had included a passionate condemnation of southern slavery in his *Letters from an American Farmer*—was also the birthplace and burial site of Bishop James Varick, father of the African Methodist Episcopal Zion Church. Shortly before Varick's death, he had become a founder of the first African American newspaper, *Freedom's Journal*. In the 1830s, Newburgh had sent delegates to the first National Negro Conventions, and now in the 1850s, the town had a small but thriving African American community. There was even a black dancing master, Dubois Alsdorf, who instructed the Willis children in ballroom etiquette each week. Across the river, Poughkeepsie was home to Uriah and Violet Boston, strong supporters of the black press, whose barbershop was a center of the struggle to expand black suffrage in the state.

Nevertheless, Jacobs's letters from Idlewild convey a sense of isolation. Absorbed in writing her memoirs, she missed the face-to-face encouragement of the Posts' circle and of Nell's activists, and she reached out to her friends through the mails and infrequent trips to New York and Boston. Even more than encouragement, Jacobs needed time. Aware that she could not possibly finish her book without some relief from her twenty-four-hour, seven-day-a-week job, she turned to her daughter. In October, when Louisa visited her mother, Jacobs proposed that she stay on at Idlewild, and she agreed.

But everything seemed to be conspiring against Jacobs's efforts to concentrate on her manuscript. For ten days, she had to go down to the city to do the Willis' winter shopping. She took along Imogen, now almost thirteen, to have her portrait painted. As she explained to Post, this meant that she was forced to walk three miles to and from the studio, because the streetcar conductors and drivers discriminated against people of color. "I had a long distance to go to the Artist and they refused one day to take me in the cars." This outraged Willis's brother Richard, with whom Jacobs and Imogen were staying. In his journal, *The New York Musical World and Times*, he protested: "Occasionally, in the evening when completely exhausted, doubling her veil she could succeed, by the help of the little white, cherub face at the side of her, to gain admittance to a car or omnibus unchallenged. At other times, when she stood at the corner of a street and beckoned, the driver would pass her by unheeded or the conductor would seem not to see her. . . . It is a great question, whether our Northern intolerance and practical disgracing of a dark skin, or the slaveholder's subjection of the colored man . . . is the greater injustice and wrong of the two." (A few months later, when the black teacher Elizabeth Jennings was physically ejected from a horsecar, local African Americans demonstrated, and Jennings sued the Third Avenue Railroad Company of New York City. Jennings's treatment was protested by blacks as far away as San Francisco, and her victory in the courts prompted African Americans to organize a Legal Rights Association.)

Back at Idlewild, Jacobs wrote all winter—but still only in the evenings after the children were in bed, and then only when they were not wakeful. Instead of writing her book, her hands were busy sewing dolls for the Willis children. To Amy, she spelled out a writer's frustration: "if I was not so tied down to the baby house. . . . poor Hatty name is so much in demand that I can not accomplish much. if I could steal away and have two quiet Months. to myself. I would work night and day though it should all fall to the ground." She believed that if she told Mrs. Willis why she needed time off, it would be granted, but could not bring herself to reveal her project. Jacobs's need for secrecy was caused by embarrassment. "I have not," she writes, "the Courage to meet the criticism and ridicule of Educated people." But it was also an author's assertion of control. Mrs. Willis had bought her freedom, but Jacobs alone would tell her story.

When finally she did confide in the Posts, and in her old friends the Bracketts (with whom Louisa had stayed on school vacations years earlier), both offered their homes as writer's retreats. She considered finding Mrs. Willis a baby nurse and taking refuge in Boston: "as yet I have not written a single page by daylight. . . . with the care of the little baby the big Babies and at the household calls I have but a little time to think or write." Her arms encircling the Willis children, Jacobs's head was swirling with literary imagery: "the poor Book is in its Chrysalis state and though I can never make it a butterfly I am satisfied to have it creep meekly among some of the humbler bugs." Yet her letters to Post, often written at odd moments, testify that she was also maintaining her interest in the political events that were rushing the nation toward its crisis. Commenting on Isaac Post's stand on the Nebraska Bill (which functionally repealed the Missouri Compromise by mandating that popular sovereignty would determine whether Kansas and Nebraska entered the

Union as slave or free), she jokingly imagines him as a candidate and herself as enfranchised: "he shall have my vote 1856."

In mid-June, Nell visited Jacobs and gave her an eyewitness account of the fugitive slave case that has been described in the history books as "the rendition of Burns." In Boston on May 24, 1854, when a United States marshal seized the fugitive Anthony Burns, the city erupted. Despite a huge Faneuil Hall protest meeting, despite even an attack on the courthouse in which a man was killed, Burns was taken before a U.S. commissioner and—denied *habeas corpus,* denied bail, denied a jury trial, and denied the right to testify—was turned over to his master. On June 2, under orders of President Franklin Pierce, state and federal troops enforced the Fugitive Slave Law in Boston by joining local militia to escort Anthony Burns through angry crowds to the ship that took him back to slavery in Virginia. To Post, Nell wrote, "The past two weeks have been crowded with events unparalleled in the anti slavery history of the Nation—a whole volume I could fill with their narration. I need not tell You that from the first to the last I was up and doing and almost wore myself out."

During his visit to Idlewild, Nell and Jacobs rehearsed the Stowe disaster, and he urged her to complete and publish her book, "pledging any service in my power for its promotion." But Jacobs fell sick, and the evening Nell left, she went to bed for three weeks. "The trouble dear Amy" she explained, "is with my womb I cannot tell you how much I have suffered during my illness   Louisa tried to fill my place and with the extra care of me she got entirely run down." Arrangements were made for Louisa to take a few days off in Boston. Then she returned to Idlewild to assume her mother's responsibilities, and Jacobs, following doctor's orders, left to convalesce.

In Massachusetts, Jacobs began to feel better. She relished the abolitionists' political and cultural climate, and that autumn, Nell included her among the dozens of black and white activists—William J. Watkins, Charles and Amy Remond, Wendell Phillips, N. P. Rogers, William Lloyd Garrison, Lewis Hayden, Eliza Follen, Thomas W. Higginson—whose names crowd his letters. One Sunday, he reports to Post, Jacobs was among the congregation inspired by the great Unitarian minister and abolitionist Theodore Parker. Her health was improving, and he attributes her recovery to her changed environment and her distance from "*Idlewild* associations." Up the Hudson, Jacobs had not only been isolated from the movement, but her workload had become much too heavy.

In addition to the family, Willis routinely filled Idlewild with guests, and on Independence Day, her life had become even more difficult when, in a grand gesture, he opened his estate to a hundred local children. Nevertheless, in October Jacobs returned to Idlewild and resumed her days with the babies and her evenings with her pen.

Somehow she managed to write, for at year's end, Jacobs reported that "Louisa has some business in the city to attend to for me which cannot weell be done unless she was in some quiet place." Confiding to Amy that she has news—"I will tell you all that I have done for myself during the past six months"—and confessing that she is unsure of herself—"I begin to want courage my strongest Motto seems to fail me some times"—Jacobs suggests that she might be ready to hand some of her manuscript over to Louisa for copying. She is, however, apprehensive. "I shall miss Louisa very much when she leaves for she has been with me so long and I have felt so anxious about my Son and Brother not hearing from them it makes me feel that she is all that is left to me in this World." Then, signaling the value she places on sisterhood and their past activism, she ends by indulging in political nostalga. "I wish we were both at the Boston Bazar with busy hands doing much good."

As Willis's health deteriorated, Cornelia Willis was becoming more and more dependent on Jacobs. But Jacobs's health, too, continued to trouble her. "I have been very poorly for the last month with my old complaint. The Doct examined me this summer an say that I have a Tumer on my womb and that my womb have become hard as a stone I can never get well while I am at service." Still, she worked on.

In the spring, Harriet and Louisa managed to get away to attend the American Anti-Slavery Society meetings in New York. William Wells Brown touched a chord for them both when he declaimed, "Those of us who have lived in slavery could tell you privately of the degradation in the domestic circle of the master." Perhaps it was after these "anniversaries"— annual meetings ranging over several days and embracing a series of agendas from tract societies to peace groups to prison reformers to abolitionists—that Jacobs began dabbling in the spiritualists' seances that her Rochester friends found so compelling. A few years earlier Isaac Post, writing that he found his pen "moved by some power beyond my own . . . and believing it to be by the spirits of those who have inhabited bodies, and passed from sight," had authored *Voices from the Spirit World*. Now Jacobs, feeling unsettled about her family, and finding the mails from Australia sparse, found it appealing to try to contact her son and her brother through the spirit world. (When finally she did receive a letter through the mails from John S. and Joseph, she reported to Amy that their message was "just as the spirits told me it would be even the very Language was in the letter. . . . I was so happy to know that they were living.")

With confirmation that her brother and son were safe, and with her health somewhat improved, Jacobs could now acknowledge that her daughter needed to be out on her own. In July 1856, Louisa moved to Oxford Street in Brooklyn, where Willis's sister Sara and her new husband, James Parton, had bought a home. It seems likely that it was Jacobs who arranged for Lulu's position as governess to Sara Payson Willis Parton's twelve-year-old Ellen. Sara owed Harriet a debt. Years earlier, Jacobs had offered emotional support and friendship when Willis had abandoned his sister after she had been abruptly widowed, made destitute, then publicly denounced by an abusive second husband. Despite Willis's refusal to publish any of his sister's writings—by which she hoped to support her little girls and herself—Sara had managed to transform herself into the popular columnist Fanny Fern. She then divorced her abusive husband, reclaimed her older daughter from relatives, and established herself in New York. Fern could never forgive her brother. A public family feud was ignited when she published a scathing indictment of a thinly disguised Nathaniel P. Willis in brother Richard's *New York Musical World and Times*. Then, in 1854, she brought out *Ruth Hall*. Fern's roman à clef—which includes the Jacobs-like figure of a nurturing black woman who aids the besieged heroine—centers on the struggles of a mother like herself. Although widowed, destitute, and rejected by family and friends, Ruth Hall nonetheless succeeds in establishing a career and nurturing her children. Fern's book excoriated the character everyone recognized as her prominent brother, and brother and sister ended all contact. Nonetheless, Nathaniel's wife Cornelia made Fern's daughters welcome at Idlewild. Jacobs and Louisa of course saw them there, and to Jacobs, Louisa's need for employment and Fern's need for a governess must have seemed a perfect match.

But they were not. Of Louisa, Fern's young English friend Thomas Butler Gunn wrote that her position in the "pleasant, handsome" home Fern and her new husband established in Brooklyn seemed ambiguous at first. Learning her history from Fern, Gunn devoted three tightly written pages of his diary to "the handsome Creole."

This girl, Louisa Jacobs is intelligent and handsome. . . . No European would suspect the African blood in her veins; probably she would be considered a trifle Jewish. Most likely the *name* was selected for that purpose. She has the most beautifully silky black hair I ever saw without exception, on human head. Only a rich glossy ripple—such as young ladies produce artificially, now a days—hints at the dreaded *kink*, the wool characterizing the unhappy race. Her nose is aquiline and delicate, her eyes fine and lustrous, her teeth white, her complexion a warm yellow. Looking at her full face, you think it perfect—that it could not be bettered, but the profile is a little too thin—it lacks fullness, and suggests haggardness towards the decline of life. The girl has a sweet, soft, contralto voice, was kind, modest and self respective, and I do believe would make any man a good, loving wife. I've never seen any one *white* American girl whom I'd have chosen in preferences, and I've seen hundreds every way her inferior. . . .Well, this girl can never be married and admitted in to society on this side of the Atlantic. Her poor black mother would come and sit at her husband's table, her relatives, too. And this, in republican America, would taboo them. . . . Had I loved such a girl, that shouldn't have stopped me, nor all the Americans in this unchristian sham-republic.

Later Gunn, no longer a friend or even a fan of Fanny Fern, spelled out Louisa's sorry situation in his diary, writing that Fern had wanted to be rid of her because she feared that Louisa was competing with her daughter for the attentions of young men. "Louisa Jacobs—poor girl! With her soft, timid voice, beautiful hair and gentle demeanor. . . . Altogether the girl was humiliated insulted, the house made a hell for her." Years later, he noted that he had just "got some particulars" about the circumstances of her dismissal. Fern, he wrote, had actually imagined Louisa a threat to her marriage to James Parton. "Inventing some transitory spasm of jealousy against the girl and Jim in the course of some household round game, Fanny abused the girl like a very drab, calling her all the whores and bitches she could lay her tongue to; finally attempting to strike her, which Jim prevented. 'Woman! If you *do*,' said he,—'I shall do you a mischief.' In consequence of this row, Louisa Jacobs was sent off."

Gunn was not Louisa's only admirer. Two years before he met her, during a brief vacation in Boston she had attracted the attentions of William C. Nell. To Post, Nell had reported that he met Louisa on Sunday "and after tea crossed the Charles River in a Ferry Boat (the Bridge being repaired) with her and Mr. & Mrs. Lowther = had a pleasant chat = free and easy = hope to enjoy her company at the Abington celebration tomorrow = and perhaps more in *future*." Then—anticipating the grin on Amy's face as she read the message he was sending between the lines— he had asked, "What are you Smiling at? Mum's the word." Two days later, he and Louisa attended the celebration together, and on their return joined friends for tea, and "thence to Boston Common," where they found a band playing "sweet Music by Moonlight." The next day he escorted Louisa to visit his sister, then planned to accompany her on "a pleasant Moonlight sail across the river to Cambridge where an evening party will tender thier good wishes" as she left the city to return home. But Nell, at thirty-eight, was too old for the twenty-one-year-old Louisa, and his attentions had come to nothing. Nor would Gunn's. Nor would anyone else's. Perhaps too black for white men, too white for black men, and too feminist for either, Louisa would remain single.

At Idlewild, Jacobs was still tightly bound to the nursery. In early spring, she wrote Amy of her efforts to stay in touch with the movement. "I have followed you all as well as I could through the Liberator—and Standard. . . . I shall endeavor to leave home this time—if nothing happens— to prevent—a day or two before the Convention—. . . . I cannot remain more than two or three days at farthest—as we are in expectation of a little Stranger near that time—and those little important ones—make much ado in household affairs—."

But the pressures of family matters were overshadowed when in March 1857, the United States Supreme Court handed down the Dred Scott decision. Limiting the authority of free states to exclude slavery, and allowing the spread of slavery into the territories, the majority of the Court held that blacks could not be American citizens and that the Constitution presumed them "so inferior that they had no rights which a white man was bound to respect." Jacobs, despairing, permitted herself to express her emotion more fully to Post than in the manuscript she was writing:

> When I see the evil that is spreading throughout the land my whole soul sickens—oh my dear friend this poor heart that has blead in Slavery— is often wrung most bitterly to behold the injustice the wrongs—the oppression—the cruel outrages inflicted on on my race—sometimes I am almost ready to exclaim—where dwells that just Father—whom I love—and in whom whom I believe is his arm Shortened—Is his power

Weakened—that all these high handed outrages reign supreme law throughout the land—God does not permit it—Man is following the evil devices of his own heart—for he is not willing even to acknowledge us made in Gods own Image—have not the decision of the last few days— in Washington—decided this for us—I see nothing for the Black Man— to look forward to—but to forget his old Motto—and learn a new one his long patient hope—must be might—and Strength—Liberty—or Death—

In this urgent mood, Jacobs finished a draft of her manuscript. Despite Cornelia Willis's pregnancy, despite Willis's precarious health, despite everything, she made a quick trip down to New York to attend the Anti-Slavery Society's annual meeting. There she managed to hear Douglass and Remond and to visit briefly with Lucy Coleman (but not with Post, who missed the anniversaries for the first time in years). Disappointed that she had been unable to see her friend, back at Idlewild Jacobs wrote that she wanted to ask a tremendous favor:

> I have thought that I wanted some female Friend of mine to write a Preface or some introductory remarks for my Book—and there is no one whose name I would prefer to Yours—you know me better than most of my friends. . . . you must not hesitate to answer exactly—as you feel about it as much pleasure as it would afford me and as great an honor as I would deem it to have your name associated with my Book—Yet believe me dear friend there are many painful things in it—that make me shrink from asking the sacrifice from one so good and pure as your self—.

Post answered with a series of questions designed to help her write the requested Preface. In response, writing "in the only spot where I can have a light—and the mosquitoes have taken possession of me," apologizing for her "unconnected scrawl," and complaining "I have been interrupted and called away so often—that I hardly know what I have written"—Jacobs composed the clearest statement of intent that has survived from an American slave narrator. "I have My dear friend—Striven faithfully to give a true and just account of my own life in Slavery—God knows I have tried to do it in a Christian spirit—." She recognizes that her story will be read largely by a white audience that may be resistant to her voice. She knows that her book differs from other slave narratives in its focus on the sexual oppression of women in slavery—although, with the runaway popularity of Stowe's book, this has become a theme of popular novelists. Still, what she has written is not fiction, but her life story.

there are somethings that I might have made plainer I know—Woman can whisper—her cruel wrongs into the ear of a very dear friend—much easier than she can record them for the world to read—I have left nothing out but what I thought—the world might believe that a Slave Woman was too willing to pour out—that she might gain their sympathies.

She continues:

I ask nothing— I have placed myself before you to be judged as a woman whether I deserve your pity or contempt—I have another object in view—it is to come to you just as I am a poor Slave Mother—not to tell you what I have heard but what I have seen—and what I have suffered—and if their is any sympathy to give—let it be given to the thousands—of of Slave Mothers that are still in bondage—suffering far more than I have—let it plead for their helpless Children that they may enjoy the same liberties that my Children now enjoy—.

Jacobs cautions her friend against mentioning Willis's name, but asks her to note that she has been in service while writing. She does not, she explains, want her readers to think "that I was living an Idle life—and had got this book out merely to make money—." Still, she reminds Amy that "housekeeping and looking after the Children occupy every moment of my time we have in all five Children—three Girls—and two boys."

Jacobs was already planning her next move, speculating about the possibility that her book might be welcomed abroad. The writings of William Wells Brown and several slave narratives—including John Brown's *Slave Life,* Frederick Douglass's *Narrative*, and Moses Roper's *Narrative of the Adventures and Escape*—had been published in England, and each had won support from a prominent figure in the abolitionist movement. Living in a literary household had made her aware of the absence of an international copyright, and Jacobs was thinking of trying to get away to establish copyright and to sell her book both at home and in England. Perhaps, she speculated, "by identifying myself with-it I might do something for the Antislavery Cause."

Presenting this not as an idle fantasy but as a feasible project, she mapped out a plan to obtain letters of introduction from American antislavery leaders to their English comrades. Now it is no longer Louisa, as she had dreamed four years earlier, but Harriet herself who, she thinks, might become an international activist.

9

The Slave's Own Story

~❦~

It must be the Slaves own story which it truly is.
—Harriet Jacobs to Amy Post [October 1860]

Jacobs began to implement her plan at summer's end, after bringing the Willis children home from their visit with their New Bedford grandparents. She appealed to William C. Nell who, acting "as a brother should," agreed to escort her and Louisa to meet with the prominent abolitionist Maria Weston Chapman. At Chapman's Weymouth home, Jacobs explained her ideas about publishing her book abroad, and after a thorough discussion, gained Chapman's support.

In November, John S. wrote asking Harriet and Louisa to join him in England, where—having abandoned his gold mining hopes—he was working as a seaman. This seemed the perfect opportunity not only to see her brother but also to sell her book, and Jacobs began making arrangements to travel in the spring. Worried about "going so far from Louise," before she sailed, she saw her daughter safely settled among the activist circle of old friends in Boston.

She had set aside the winter for final work on her manuscript, but Willis became so ill that she felt she must remain at Idlewild until he was mending. Then, after making some hurried revisions, Jacobs again traveled to Weymouth, and on May 26, sailed for England "under the protection of Mr Mosses Grinnell," Cornelia Willis's uncle. She was armed with letters of introduction from Chapman to Garrisonian activists in England, Scotland, and Ireland, and with a letter from Mrs. Willis verifying that her freedom had been purchased. She would, she dreamed, return home a published author.

The crossing went without incident, and again in a country untainted by the stench of slavery, Jacobs felt reinvigorated. England must have seemed even more appealing this time, for she came not as a domestic servant but as an abolitionist activist. The manuscript she carried was complimentary to her prospective English public. Like other African American visitors, in it she praises Britain for its absence of racism and discusses the immeasurable superiority of the condition of even the most oppressed British "wage slaves" compared to the situation of chattel slaves in America. In addition, she testifies that it was while breathing England's free air that she felt able to renew the religious faith that gave her strength to tell her story.

Using Chapman's letters of introduction, Jacobs quickly reached people influential in the transatlantic antislavery community who should have been able to help her find a publisher. Although Chapman's sister was away on the Continent, Jacobs was warmly greeted by Hannah Waring Webb and her husband Richard Davis Webb, the prominent Irish editor of the Garrisonian *Anti-Slavery Advocate*. When Jacobs reached them, the Webbs were guests at Stafford House, home of the Duchess of Sutherland and meeting place of Britain's prominent reformers. The Duchess was so taken with Jacobs and her story that she invited "the dusky stranger" to join her house party.

These were weeks to remember. One member of the group (Garrisonians all) even read through her manuscript and judged Jacobs "one of the truest heroines we have ever met with." But Jacobs's hopes for an English publication were dashed, and it is not entirely clear why. Possibly the British abolitionists advised her to publish her book first in America because they feared British prudery. Certainly her story of her liaison with Sawyer challenged Victorian sexual practices. (William and Ellen Craft, legally married after escaping to the North, had fled to England in 1850, and by the time of Jacobs's visit, already had established an English following. But they would wait another two years before the story of their escape—with the light-skinned Ellen cross-dressing and masquerading as the young master of dark-skinned William—would see print.)

Not only did Jacobs fail to arrange for the publication of her book, but the randomness of her brother's sailor life prevented her from seeing John S., who had shipped out to the Middle East before she arrived. She did, however, become acquainted with some of his important colleagues in the movement. George Thompson, Britain's most prominent Garrisonian abolitionist, judged John S. "'a good fellow,'" writing, "I have as much confidence in him, as I have ever had in any colored refugee who has come to our shores. He is modest, disinterested, and I believe truthful honest and with a deep and lively concern for his brethren in bonds." Now, visiting the ailing Thompson, Jacobs met his daughter and son-in-law Amelia and Frederick Chesson, both antislavery activists.

She was often with the Chessons that warm, dry summer. In late July, they went together to the fifth Opera Concert at the Crystal Palace and were "delighted with everything." A few days later, Amelia Chesson noted that she met Jacobs at Mrs. Brown's for tea. (It is unclear whether their hostess was the wife of the black abolitionist lecturer John Brown—a fugitive from Georgia whose dictated narrative the Chessons' friend I. A. Chamerovzov had edited a few years earlier; or the wife of Henry "Box" Brown—who, after escaping from slavery by having himself crated up and shipped north, was exhibiting his box and his panorama "The Mirror of Slavery" throughout Britain. In either case, this visit signals that Jacobs had found her way into the circle of African American expatriates in London.) It would be surprising if, while in the city, she did not visit William and Ellen Craft, now living in Hammersmith, West London, and keeping open house for African American expatriates and their supporters. Their three little boys—Charles, now six, William Jr., three, and baby Brougham—would have been a magnet for Jacobs, who loved children. And it is likely that she tried to contact Julia Griffiths, whom she had known in her old Rochester days and who had returned to England.

It is not clear why Jacobs visited Liverpool, but it is clear that she left the city, rich with its profits from the slave trade, still without a patron or a publisher. Back in London, Jacobs went shopping with Amelia Chesson before returning to America. Recording the day in her diary, Chesson wrote that she had bought "a cheap dress for house wear." Then—permitting herself a rare personal note—added, "Sorry to lose Mrs. Jacobs to whom I have become really attached."

Jacobs returned to America and to Idlewild embarrassed by her failure and proudly determined to say nothing more about her book until she had somehow succeeded in bringing it out. Then in the fall, she had terrible news from Edenton: Uncle Mark Ramsey had died. Now everyone in her mother's generation was gone, and Harriet was the oldest in the family. She felt alone in the world as never before. Idlewild was bleak that winter, but in the spring, she managed to get down to New York City to attend the American Anti-Slavery Society Convention. Both emotionally and financially, it was a hard time. Jacobs had risked her pride and her savings in the belief that she could arrange for her book to be published, and she had failed. "I felt," she later wrote Amy, "that I had cut myself of from my friends and I had no right to ask their Sympathy—."

Jacobs was shaken out of her melancholy on October 16, 1859, when John Brown and his men seized the federal arsenal at Harper's Ferry. In the battle that followed, Brown was wounded, and five U.S. soldiers and ten of Brown's men—including two of his sons—were killed. African Americans and militant abolitionists hailed Brown for firing the first shot in the fight for freedom, and up the Hudson at Idlewild, Jacobs tried to find a way to register her support for the insurrectionists. She could not— like the prominent abolitionist writer L. Maria Child—pen a public letter to Governor Henry Wise of Virginia, offering to go south during the trials to nurse the wounded Brown. But she could, and she did, go back to her desk, and at the end of her day's work in the nursery she composed a new conclusion for her book: a tribute to Brown.

Jacobs submitted her manuscript to the Boston house of Phillips and Samson, and they agreed to publish it if she could arrange for a preface by Stowe or Willis, names well-known to the reading public. Jacobs had always been reluctant to expose herself to Willis, and his recently published "Negro Happiness in Virginia"—an unashamed apology for slavery—certainly did nothing to change her mind. She did, however, again approach Stowe, and again suffered rejection. Then Phillips and Samson failed. "Difficulties seemed to thicken," Jacobs later wrote, "—and I became discouraged."

Still, she made another determined effort. This time, she took her book to the publishers of James Redpath's best-seller, *The Public Life of Captain John Brown*. Thayer and Eldridge read her manuscript and said they would bring it out if she could supply a preface from L. Maria Child. Jacobs was familiar with Child's reputation as a longtime activist, the former editor of the *National Anti-Slavery Standard*, and the author of a shelf of antislavery pamphlets. But she had never met Child. Jacobs wrote Post that Stowe's devastating rejections made her "tremble at the thought of approaching another Sattellite of so great magnitude," but "I tried to fan the flickering spark that was left and resolved to make my last effort." She appealed to Nell, who arranged a meeting in Boston at the Antislavery Office at 21 Cornhill. Much to her relief, she found Child "a whole souled Woman" who not only agreed to supply a preface, but offered to edit her manuscript.

To a friend, Child explained that she was willing to help Jacobs "because she tells her story in a very intelligent, spirited manner, and the details seem to me well calculated to advance the cause I have so deeply at heart. It involves the reading of a good many M.S. pages, and the writing of a good many; but to help the slave is about all my life is good for now." Child wrote that she had "abridged, and struck out superfluous words sometimes, but I don't think I altered fifty words in the whole volume." A practiced and conscientious editor, Child kept the author informed as she worked on her manuscript. She was, she explained to Jacobs, "copying a great deal of it, for the purpose of transposing sentences and pages, so as to bring the story into continuous *order*, and the remarks into *appropriate* places. I think you will see that this renders the story much more clear and entertaining." Working with the section describing the violence wreaked on Edenton's black population after the Nat Turner insurrection, she queried: "What *were* those inflictions? Were any tortured to make them confess? and how? Were any killed? Please write down some of the most striking particulars, and let me have them to insert." Child reconfigured Jacobs's book by advising that its final chapter—the addendum on John Brown—be omitted. "It does not naturally come into your story, and the M. S. is already too long. Nothing can be so appropriate to end with, as the death of your grandmother." Following her suggestion, Jacobs restored the manuscript to its original shape.

In addition to editing the text, Child supplied an introduction and assumed the role of Jacobs's agent. In late September, she wrote that she had signed a contract and instructed Thayer and Eldridge to take out the copyright in her name—commenting (apparently in reference to the decision to publish the book pseudonymously), "Under the circumstances *your* name could not be used, you know"—and she enclosed a document for Jacobs to sign establishing the book as her property, in the event of Child's death.

Feeling certain that now her book would come out, Jacobs finally wrote to Post, apologizing for her long silence while searching for a publisher—"I am truly ashamed of it." She had, she explains, told Child how important Post's role had been—"of the feeling that had existed between us—that your advice and word of encouragement—had been my strongest promter in writting the Book." Then Jacobs updates Post on plans for its promotion. Although she thought that Post's introduction and the testimonial by George Lowther (an Edenton friend now in Boston) should appear as letters following the text, Child has suggested that they also be published in *The Liberator*, *The Standard*, and *The Anglo-African*. Sending on her editor's letters detailing the publishing arrangements, Jacobs includes a brief note pleading for secrecy: "I am pledged to Mrs Child that I will tell no one what she has done as she is beset by so many people and it would effect the Book." But the word was out. Nell had already heard of the publication plans and was looking forward to the appearance of the volume he called *Incidents in a Slave Girl's Life, or Seven Years Concealed in Slavery*, and a promotional blurb in the *Anti-Slavery Bugle* announced its "especial interest to every woman, and to all who love virtue."

With the book due to appear in November, Jacobs and Child scheduled a final meeting before publication. Then suddenly Jacobs's hands were full—not with her manuscript, but with caring for the Willis family. On October 11, Cornelia Willis, pregnant, ill, and bedridden for the past month, prematurely delivered a baby girl. With no doctor available, Jacobs abruptly became, in her words, "both accaucher and nurse." The birth did not go well. To Post, Jacobs reported that the baby died "from the effects of its Mothers illness" but that she managed to save Cornelia. When finally the doctor arrived, "he pronounced all right for for which I was very thankful." After describing this crisis to her friend, Jacobs permitted herself the lament of a writer who has been prevented from editing her final text: "I know that Mrs Child Will strive to do the best she can more than I can ever repay but I ought to have been there that we could have consulted together—and compared our views—although I know that hers are superior to mine yet we could have marked her great Ideas and my small ones together." The publishing date, she notes, has been pushed back to December.

Jacobs spent the holidays awaiting the appearance of her book, but Thayer and Eldridge were failing. Quickly, Child appealed to Wendell Phillips, suggesting that the American Anti-Slavery Society get the book out. When he judged this unfeasible, she urged that the society underwrite its publication, using the Hovey Fund, established to "change public opinion, and secure the abolition of Slavery in the United States." She asked Phillips to convince the Hovey Committee to take a thousand copies for society agents to sell, and to persuade Thayer and Eldridge to double their initial run of a thousand. Phillips negotiated with the publishers on Jacobs's behalf, and they demonstrated their belief in the manuscript by spending extra money to have it stereotyped—a more expensive process than typesetting. Nell wrote gratefully to Phillips, "My acquaintance with John S. Jacobs and his Sister Harriet and her Daughter Louise have established the trio as my adopted Brother and Sisterhood. I know you will feel recompensed for your promotion of the work by its merits and the authors worth." But after casting the stereotype plates, Thayer and Eldridge went bankrupt before printing a single copy. Then, apparently using what was left of her savings, Jacobs paid half the price outright and bought the plates. Somehow—doubtless with Child's help, perhaps with the aid of Cornelia Willis's publisher friend James T. Fields—she arranged to have her book printed and bound.

While Jacobs was working to get her book into print, the country was ripping apart. The day after Lincoln's election in November, defiant Charleston had run down the stars and stripes. In December, President Buchanan sent a State of the Union message to Congress which, although declaring Secession unjustified, blamed the abolitionists for the crisis: "the long-continued and intemperate interference of the Northern people with the question of slavery in the Southern States has at length produced its natural effects." Buchanan proposed a constitutional amendment to protect slavery in the territories and guarantee the return of fugitive slaves. While in Washington Congress was searching for a compromise, in Charleston, to the chime of church bells, the roar of cannons, and the cheers of the crowds in the streets, a South Carolina Convention unanimously resolved, "that the union now subsisting between South Carolina and other States, under the name of 'the United States of America' is hereby dissolved."

Although the Garrisonians had for years urged "No Union with Slaveholders," events were developing in ways that they had not predicted. In response to the national crisis Jacobs, unable to attend their annual meeting, sent the Anti-Slavery Society a $2.00 contribution to demonstrate her support in the face of the anti-black, anti-abolitionist mobs gathering in the streets. In Boston on December 3, the Tremont Temple meeting to commemorate the anniversary of John Brown's execution was mobbed, and when it reconvened at the Joy Street Church to denounce the violence, some black members of the audience were attacked. Two weeks later, Wendell Phillips was mobbed at the Music Hall, and when he spoke to Theodore Parker's congregation, the street was "lined by crowds of genteel ruffians." The violence was not limited to the big cities. Up the Hudson near Idlewild, during Watchtower Service on New Year's Eve, a white mob attacked the AME Zion church at Newburgh, "broke down the door and committed other depredations."

In January 1861, the most perilous new year in the history of the nation, Jacobs traveled to Philadelphia to launch her new career as an author-activist. Escaping Edenton nineteen years earlier, she had thought Philadelphia "a wonderfully great place" [ILSG p. 162], but even then, understood that it was not really safe. Mrs. Durham's prudence walking with her in the streets and her experiences traveling to New York in a Jim Crow car had suggested even to Jacobs's overwhelmed consciousness that all was not well. Actually, Philadelphia had spawned a number of anti-black, anti-abolitionist riots. Only a few months after Jacobs's visit, a crowd—perhaps incensed by a Young Men's Vigilant Society banner that showed a rising sun behind a slave with broken fetters—had attacked a black temperance parade commemorating British Emancipation. When the blacks fought back, a race riot ensued. The mob set fire to the Second African Presbyterian Church and Smith's Beneficial Hall, and white fire companies refused to save the black-owned buildings from the flames. Later the court, acquiescing to whites who condemned the black reformers' temperance hall in Moyamensing as a nuisance, ordered its destruction. With this, the African American abolitionist Robert Purvis, whose Lombard Street home had been targeted by the mob, became furious and despairing. "Press, Church, Magistrates, Clergymen and Devils—are against us," he wrote. "And the bloody Will, is in the heart of the community to destroy us." Convinced that the violence was not over, Purvis moved his family out of Philadelphia. His fears were well grounded. When in December 1859—only days before John Brown was hanged—the prestigious author and lecturer George William Curtis spoke on slavery at National Hall, the building was stormed and threatened with fire. And now Jacobs had come to the city to promote abolition by selling her narrative.

Traveling to Philadelphia, she weighed the book in her hand. It felt solid. The Boston Stereotype Foundry had done a professional job, and its more than 300 pages were neatly printed with *Incidents in the Life of a Slave Girl: Written by Herself* displayed on the title page. The volume looked lovely, bound in dark green, with a floral design and border embossed on front and back covers and "Linda" in gold on the spine. Harriet Jacobs had become "Linda Brent," but not to hide behind a pseudonym or to disappear under a fictitious name. As "Linda" she had empowered herself to write about a life that as "Harriet," she could neither speak nor write. But now that her book was actually published, she was eager to identify herself as its author.

What she had written, she had promised her reader, was true. But looking at her work, she knew that she had made a great many choices about what incidents she would not—could not—bring herself to tell the whole truth about, and so had decided not to write about at all. She had composed her story with a reader in mind, a free woman who had no experience with a sexual history like her own—a woman who had never in girlhood shuddered at the touch of a master's grating fingers, who had never been sickened by the smell of his old flesh as he leaned over her, his breathy whispers promising obscene delights, a woman who had never been harassed by his notes demanding her compliance, who had never had to listen as his voice changed from smooth to rasping. She had chosen not to dwell on his torture, but on her defiance. She had acknowledged that she must record her liaison with Major Sam, but she would not discuss their complex relationship and would certainly never dramatize their days and nights together. Nor would she tell the complicated story of her father's second wife and their child. No. She would strip her narrative, clearing it of all the extras. Everyone had a story, from Grandmother to Aunt Sue Bent, and she could not tell all of them. Instead, she would carefully restrict herself not to what she had heard, but to what she herself had seen. And she would omit most of that. She would, in fact, omit everything that might detract from the story of her freedom struggle. (A century later, scholars would verify the accuracy of many of her recollections, some granting her an autobiographer's authority to tell her story, and others not.)

Her reading had been a help. All of it enriched and shaped her book—from the biblical passages she had pored over in her attic hiding place, to the political writings John and his activist friends had introduced her to in the North, to the weekly antislavery press. Slave narratives, like those by Frederick Douglass and William Wells Brown, which had been circulated among the abolitionists in Rochester and Boston, were very important. Useful, too, were the dime novels flooding the market. And very helpful were the books in the Willises' library that taught her the conventions of fiction—works like *Uncle Tom's Cabin*, with Cassy's desperate drama of sexual slavery, and *Jane Eyre*, with its story of a woman's struggle for autonomy.

In Philadelphia, Jacobs established herself in the busy South Ninth Street home of John and Charlotte Chew. The house was crowded with their seven children, but she felt very comfortable there. One of her first stops was at the offices of *The Christian Recorder*, which noticed her book "most cheerfully." Commending it "as worthy of perusal," the *Recorder* suggested that its readers contact Jacobs, "in this city for a few days."

Before coming to Philadelphia, she had readied herself with an introduction to a young Quaker woman who could help her market her book. Mary Rebecca Darby Smith was apparently scandalizing her family by leading the frivolous life of a belle. But despite her frivolity, Smith retained her father's hatred of slavery, and Jacobs found her "the Slaves true Friend." Smith provided her with entree to local activists, and Jacobs spent days calling on members of Philadelphia's antislavery circles. (After one such meeting, the veteran abolitionist Sarah Pugh judged Jacobs "a faithful and true witness, a worthy and noble representative of her race.") By mid-January, Jacobs had sold fifty copies of *Incidents*. Despite encouragement to stay on in Philadelphia, however, she decided to travel to the surrounding areas to peddle her book.

Jacobs was working hard to promote *Incidents*, and she had help. In February, she went to Boston to meet with the Garrisonian leader Francis Jackson, who paid her $100 for copies to be sold by antislavery agents. Child, at home in Medford, was writing letter after letter, trying to push the book. (The problem, she explained to her friend, the poet John Greenleaf Whittier, was that "the Boston booksellers are dreadfully afraid of soiling their hands with an Anti-Slavery book; so we have a good deal of trouble in getting the book into the market." *Incidents* retailed at $1.00 but if a dozen copies were ordered, she wrote, the price would drop to sixty-eight cents.) Nell, too, was publicizing the book. Still using as its subtitle *Seven Years Concealed in Slavery*, he wrote a review in the form of a letter to *The Liberator* that focused on the book's appeal to women:

> "Linda" . . . presents features more attractive than many of its predecessors purporting to be histories of slave life in America, because, in contrast with their mingling of fiction with fact, this record of complicated experience in the life of a young woman, a doomed victim to America's peculiar institution . . . surely need[s] not the charms that any pen of fiction, however gifted and graceful, could lend. They shine by the lustre of their own truthfulness—a rhetoric which always commends itself to the wise head and honest heart. . . . [From it] all, especially mothers and daughters, may learn yet more of the barbarism of American slavery and the character of its victims.

Two weeks later, he advertised the book for sale.

Other Garrisonians also came through. In Ohio, Abby Kelley Foster's *Anti-Slavery Bugle* praised the book's "simple and attractive" style:

"you feel less as though you were reading a book, than talking with the woman herself." In New York the *National Anti-Slavery Standard* ran an ad, and under "Our Boston Correspondence" noted, "The book has a vivid dramatic power as a narrative, and should have a wide circulation." A week later, under the heading "New Publications," the *Standard* reprinted Jacobs's "Preface by the Author," L. Maria Child's "Introduction by the Editor," and the letters by George W. Lowther and Amy Post, adding that:

> if this narrative of the experiences of a noble woman in slavery could be read at every fireside in the free States, it would kindle such a feeling of moral indignation against the system . . . as would put an end, at once and forever, to all those projects of compromise by which politicians are now endeavoring to "reconstruct" the broken Union between North and the South.

The *Weekly Anglo-African* was equally supportive. In March, it published "The Loophole of Retreat" as an excerpt, and in April, writing that the book was for sale at Anti-Slavery offices in Boston, New York, and Philadelphia, announced that it could also be bought from editor Thomas Hamilton at the *Anglo-African* office. Like the *Standard*, the *Anglo-African* urged the book's relevance to the current struggle:

> No one can read these pages without a feeling of horror, and a stronger determination arising in them to tear down the cursed system which makes such records possible. Wrath, the firey messenger which goes flaming from the roused soul and overthrows in its divine fury the accursed tyrannies of earth, will find in these pages new fuel for the fire, and new force for the storm which shall overthrow and sweep from existence American slavery.

Particularly pleasing was the serious notice in the *London Anti-Slavery Advocate*. Its author (doubtless editor Richard D. Webb), wrote of having met Jacobs during her visit to England and testified that her published book was "substantially the same" as the manuscript she had brought with her.

> This book shows as forcibly as any story we have ever read the moral pollution and perversion inevitable in a community where slavery is a recognised institution. . . .[The author] will be sure to effect more good for her brethren and sisters still in bonds, by the diffusion of her story

amongst the people of the Free States, whom it is above all others important to inform, since they alone are able, by witholding their support
from it, to shake down the whole system of chattel slavery.

Reading this made it seem that there was now a chance for a London edition. This possibility seemed even more likely with the appearance of her
brother John's narrative in the London journal *The Leisure Hour*.

The first of the four installments of John S.'s serialized narrative appeared
on February 4, 1861, the day the representatives of the Confederate
States met in convention. Before his final chapter was published on February 28, the Confederates had adopted a constitution and inaugurated
Jefferson Davis as their provisional president. (Lincoln would not be
sworn in for another week.) In London, John had again become an
activist, as in his Rochester days. With the African American fugitives
William and Ellen Craft and the expatriate Sarah Parker Remond, he had
joined the London Emancipation Committee, which in the crisis was
working to persuade the British public not to support the secessionist
Confederacy—despite the ties binding the mills at Manchester to the
southern cotton fields.

John S. published his "True Tale of Slavery" in Britain's Religious
Tract Society's *The Leisure Hour: A Family Journal of Instruction and
Recreation*. The journal proposed to improve its "lower to middle class"
audience by presenting British history, popular science, and miscellaneous extracts, as well as poetry and advice, each week to its audience of
servants, workingmen, housewives, and the poor. In keeping with its
stated policy of avoiding controversy, it followed popular opinion in
post-Emancipation Britain by taking a generally antislavery tone. When
John S. submitted his manuscript, members of the London Emancipation
Committee doubtless judged *The Leisure Hour* a potential ally in their
effort to win the hearts and minds of working-class Englishmen.

Like the short fiction *The Leisure Hour* was serializing in February
1861, John S.'s "A True Tale of Slavery" is instructive. As a first-person
account of a good man who is trying to behave morally in difficult circumstances, it conforms not only to popular uplift fiction but also to the
model of the slave narrative epitomized by Frederick Douglass's 1845
Narrative. But its shape is unique. After recording his own successful
efforts to escape from slavery, the narrator turns to his sister's story—
although nowhere does he mention her sexual history. He does not refer

to her master's harassment and threats of concubinage, to her desperate decision to become another man's mistress, to her later commitment to save her infant daughter from sexual bondage in slavery, or to her belief that if she runs away her master will sell the children to their father, who will free them. In "A True Tale," John S. erases his sister's sexual experiences while presenting their consequences. He notes the existence of her children, her exile to the plantation, her escape and the resulting punishment of the family, her years of hiding in Edenton, her escape to the North, and her master's efforts to catch her. In his version, she runs away because she fears whipping. This is no hero tale of a mother who liberates her children; nor is it the confession of an anguished "fallen woman." By inserting his sister's story into his narrative, John S. suggests that it is very important. But without his sister's sexual history—without the narrative of the tormented girl, the shamed woman, and the devoted mother—her story is virtually untold. In his telling, the unique center of her narrative is lost.

John S. had developed a polished rhetorical manner years earlier, declaiming his story from platforms throughout New York and New England, and "A True Tale" echoes the hortatory style of those speeches, especially in its final pages. Announcing that his purpose is to punish his oppressors, he writes: "If possible, let us make those whom we have left behind [in the United States] feel that the ground they till is cursed with slavery, the air they breathe poisoned with its venom breath, and that which made life dear to them is lost and gone." He ends "A True Tale" with an unspeakable vision of horror: "When I have thought of all that would pain the eye, sicken the heart, and make us turn our backs to the scene and weep, I then think of the oppressed struggling with their oppressors, and have a scene more horrible still. But I must drop this subject; I do not like to think of the past, nor look to the future, of wrongs like these" [TT in ILSG pp. 227, 228].

Across the Atlantic, the horror was approaching day by day, as the United States moved toward civil war. When Lincoln was inaugurated on March 4, he announced, "I have no purpose, directly or indirectly, to interfere with the institution of slavery in the South where it exists," and he asserted that each state had the authority to control its domestic institutions. Then, on the morning of April 12, Fort Sumter was fired upon. Lincoln declared this an "insurrection" and called for troops—while promising "to avoid any destruction of, or interference with, property," including property in slaves. A few weeks later, in a move calculated to secure the capital, federal troops crossed the Long Bridge and occupied Alexandria, Virginia.

All that summer, the federal position on slavery was debated. In July, Congress passed the Crittenden Resolution stating that the war was being waged to save the Union, not for the purpose "of overthrowing or interfering with the . . . established institutions of . . . southern States." As fugitive slaves sought refuge behind the Union lines in Washington, D.C., Alexandria, and elsewhere, the debate over their status seesawed back and forth. In August, after the Confederates burned Hampton, Virginia, claiming General Benjamin Butler was using the town as a safe haven for fugitive slaves, the federal secretary of war instructed Butler that while the Fugitive Slave Law must hold within the Union, the situation was different in states that were in insurrection. Yet when federal Major General John Charles Fremont, declaring martial law in Missouri, issued an order confiscating all Rebel property and thus emancipating the slaves, Lincoln repudiated it.

At Idlewild, Harriet Jacobs received a letter from her brother in London. Describing British public opinion about America's war and commenting on the failure of the federal government to abolish slavery, John S. sounded the notes of a jeremiad: "You that have believed in the promise, and obeyed His word, are beginning to see the moving of His hand to execute judgment and bestow mercy. Those who have long sown chains and fetters will reap blood and carnage." Commenting that many Londoners are ill informed about the war, he notes that despite "all the blood and guilt on the slaveholders' souls, there are Englishmen here that dare express sympathy for them." As to his own plans, "I shall wait to see what course the North intends to pursue. If the American flag is to be planted on the altar of freedom, then I am ready to be offered on that altar, if I am wanted; if it must wave over the slave, with his chains and fetters clanking, let me breathe the free air of another land, and die a man and not a chattel." Jacobs had become one of the Garrisonians' circle with the appearance of *Incidents*, and now she took her brother's letter to editor Oliver Johnson. Johnson excerpted it, along with a letter John S. had written to Isaac Post, for publication in *The Liberator* and the *Standard*.

On August 1, the abolitionists again held their annual celebration at Abington to commemorate West Indian Emancipation. Despite threatening skies and heavy rain the night before, Jacobs joined the crowd that overflowed the town hall, listening to Garrison, Samuel J. May, and Wendell Phillips extol British Emancipation and free labor, condemn England's recognition of the Confederacy as a "belligerent," and prophesy that "if we do not make that civil war end in the abolition of slavery, it will inevitably be followed by a servile war." Next day, L. Maria Child stopped in at *The Liberator* office, seeking relief from Boston's steaming streets. In the afternoon, she later recalled, the rooms became crowded. "Many Anti-Slavery friends were returning from the celebration of the 1st at Abington, so that quite a levee was held at the office." Child was pleased to see Jacobs, who had with her a testimonial from Cornelia Willis attesting to the truthfulness of her narrative, and "whom every body agreed in declaring to be a very pre-possessing person." How Harriet Jacobs felt, anticipating that she would need Cornelia Willis's letter to authenticate her life—how she felt working with the abolitionists while anticipating that although they might not believe her, they would believe her elite white employer—we cannot know. But we can be certain that Jacobs had thought carefully before deciding to carry that testimonial.

At year's end, the pacifist Garrisonians were still debating what course they should take in relation to the war. They had questions. What was the Union's position on slavery? What was to be the fate of the black refugees behind the federal lines? Would the Army permit black men to fight? Perhaps to underscore the concerns expressed at Abington about the response of "the great body of the English people . . . in our day of trial," perhaps to address the controversy among British abolitionists about whether to condemn the South as a slavocracy or to support the Confederacy's right to self-determination, or perhaps to respond to John's comment that the British public needed more information about slavery—Jacobs decided that now was the time to try to publish *Incidents* in England.

Earlier, she explained to Amy Post, her brother had been critical, writing her "scolding lines—because I had not sent my book to different people in England. . . . I have taken it very patiently—but I don't give up as I used to. The trouble is I begin to find out we poor women have always been too meek." Now no longer seeking guidance, Jacobs assertively took charge and sent a copy of her book to Frederick Chesson, who was deeply involved in the work of the London Emancipation Committee. She followed this with a letter informing him that she had already shipped the stereotype plates to him, and asking him to find a publisher on the best terms he could. Chesson received the plates on January 18, and promptly took them to the London publisher William Tweedie, who had gotten out the Crafts' narrative. Within weeks, Jacobs's book appeared, renamed *The Deeper Wrong; or, Incidents in the Life of a Slave Girl. Written by Herself*. With the exception of its new title page, it had been reprinted from Jacobs's plates. When it was bound, Chesson called on Tweedie to discuss sending out review copies.

Less than a month later, the London publisher Hodson and Son produced a pirated edition. Chesson fumed: "This is the act of another hungry publisher stooping to take the bread from another's mouth. How much do we need a copyright treaty with America." Although Tweedie informed his attorney, it was as Chesson feared, and nothing could be done. "The title is probably the Publisher's copyright but Hodson has only taken a part of it—'Incidents in the Life of a female slave;' & as he has a copy of the American edition we shall not be able to get an injunction." "However," he notes with satisfaction, "we have got the advantage of the Reviews, which have been very satisfactory."

They certainly had. Amelia Chesson wrote a major review in the *London Morning Star and Dial* that got to the point immediately. "This perfectly truthful and simple history of the life of a woman born a slave and reared in that condition till she had reached the prime of life and had given birth to two children, is, we believe, the first personal narrative in which one of that sex upon whom chattel servitude falls with the deepest and darkest shadow has ever described her own bitter experience." Then, with an eye to the London Emancipation Committee's fears that the English public was not exerting enough public pressure on Britain to support the Union: "We would have every English matron exposed to the insidious influence of high-bred visitors from the Southern Confederacy, be armed beforehand with an insight into the precise nature of the wrongs which are inseparable from slavery in its outwardly most inoffensive and harmless guise. We can imagine nothing better calculated to affect such a result than this thrilling history of a slave girl's experiences."

That same morning, the *London Daily News* wrote: "We have in this country a vague notion of the wickedness of slave-holding. . . . It is necessary, in order to give practical definitiveness to this loose sentiment . . . that our theoretical notions of the gigantic iniquity should be illustrated by its personal desecration of our common nature, and the wreck it makes of hearts and minds like our own. We have never read a work better calculated to effect this than the volume before us." Naming Jacobs's Linda Brent a "heroine," the reviewer continues, "she is deserving of the title in its higher sense. Almost unconsciously, in her artless memoir, she sets before us a picture of endurance and persistency in the struggle for liberty, of strong natural affection, and at the same time of moral rectitude, according to her lights, which it would not be an easy matter to match."

The British abolitionists were able not only to harness the mainstream London press, but also to arrange for reviews in Newcastle ("has all the interest of romance and the instruction of history. . . . every one who reads 'The Deeper Wrong' will all the more rejoice that the Slave Power in America, fighting for its foul existence, is threatened with destruction"); in Plymouth ("Uncle Tom's adventures were not nearly so tragic as Linda Brent's. . . .There is nothing so like a hell upon earth, except, perhaps, an Austrian dungeon, as a plantation in the Confederate States"); even in the Irish *Londonderry Standard* ("the heart of every female reader especially is sure to rise in holy indignation while perusing the touching episodes in which the 'Perils of Girlhood' are so vividly described, while the religious world at large must blush for the humiliating uses to which professing Christianity often degrades itself in the Slave States. . . . We earnestly commend this absorbing history to all classes amongst our readers, since no man, who thoughtfully ponders the terribly significant facts here detailed, can avoid adding his signature in the death warrant of a system, which not only outrages human nature, but daringly perverts God's own economy of salvation into an instrument of Satan's work.") In April, the *Anti-Slavery Reporter* concurred. ("This is a most simple and touching narrative, which goes direct to the heart. . . . 'a romance of thrilling interest.' We cordially recommend this little volume to our friends.") Almost a dozen years earlier, Jacobs had written, "since I have no fear of my name coming before those whom I have lived in dread of I can not be happy without trying to be useful in some way." Publishing her book in Boston and in London, she had made a way where there was no way.

PART THREE

MRS. JACOBS

Public Demands for Freedom and Homes

❧

10

Spared for This Work

~✿~

The good God has spared me for this work. . . .
I pray to live . . . life has just begun.
—Harriet Jacobs to Amy Post, December 8 [1862]

In the spring of 1862, the abolitionists were feeling hopeful. The war seemed to be going well; the United States signed a treaty with Great Britain for a more effective suppression of the African slave trade; and both the House of Representatives and the Senate passed bills abolishing slavery in the District of Columbia. Equally encouraging was the news about the Port Royal experiment. The slaveholders on South Carolina's sea islands had fled early in November when the U.S. Navy sailed into Port Royal Sound. They left behind them piles of burning cotton bales and all of their property—including 10,000 slaves. Soon after, fifty-three young antislavery missionaries from Boston and New York landed at Beaufort (the only sizeable town) and "the abolitionists and the slaves confronted each other on slave territory for the first time."

Harriet Jacobs understood that it was in places like Port Royal that the future of her people would be worked out. Writing and publishing her life story, she had created herself as a representative woman, shaping her past from a private tale of shame of a "slave girl" into a public testimony against a tyrannical system. In the process, she had liberated her mind and spirit and now felt herself one of the freest women in America. Her self-liberation could not have been more timely. As the nation began to grapple with the issue of the future of thousands of men, women, and children who had been held in slavery, she knew what she would do. Instead of mounting the platform in the antislavery cause, as she had planned, she would return south to help the refugees. Instead of building a private refuge for herself and Louisa, she would help her people create homes in freedom.

Although the Fugitive Slave Law was still in force in the slave states that remained loyal to the Union, that summer Congress designated as "contrabands of war"—not to be returned to slavery—those fugitives who had run from disloyal owners. Because numbers of these people had fled to the nation's capital, Jacobs now decided that instead of Port Royal, she would go to Washington. In the District, the pro-slavery city council protested that Washington was becoming "an asylum for free negroes, a population undesirable in every American community," but the black press urged its readers to help. Daily, refugees were appearing among them—men, women, and children who, escaping from war and slavery in the South, were seeking a new life: "Thousands of contrabands . . . are in a condition of the extremest suffering. We see them in droves every day perambulating the streets of Washington, homeless, shoeless, dressless, and moneyless. And when we think of the cold freezing days of coming winter . . . our sensibilities of humanity sink under the dreadful apprehensions consequent upon such direful privations."

In early spring, Harriet Jacobs went down to Washington, taking with her bundles of clothing, blankets, and shoes that she had been collecting from sympathetic supporters over the winter. Then in June, she took three days to attend the tenth annual meeting of the Progressive Friends at Longwood, Pennsylvania. Jacobs may already have been acquainted with the group through Amy Post's Rochester circle. The Progressive Friends, one of the assemblies that had formed out of Hicksite Quakerism (itself a splinter group), were part of the "moral earthquake" shaking American Protestants at midcentury. Members came together to address the evils of the day—chattel slavery, the "slavery" of women to men, liquor, tobacco, capital punishment, and war. Their annual meetings at Longwood farm generally attracted large crowds, and this year, in addition to prominent reformers like Oliver Johnson (sometime editor of the *Anti-Slavery Bugle*, the *Pennsylvania Freeman*, and co-editor of *The National Anti-Slavery Standard*), their "visiting artists" included J. Sella Martin, Jacobs's pastor from her Boston days, Lucretia Mott, and William Lloyd Garrison.

Profoundly disappointed that Lincoln had not issued an emancipation proclamation, the meeting decided to depart from custom by sending a delegation to urge the President to abolish slavery. (When in late June the committee met with Lincoln, he dismissed them, commenting that a presidential emancipation decree would not be binding on the

South. Even the Constitution, Lincoln pointed out, "cannot be enforced in that part of the country now.")

At Longwood, Jacobs spoke with Garrison about her relief work, and he asked her to write a piece for *The Liberator* about Washington's black refugees. Initially housed in the old Capitol building, the people had been moved by the government across the street into an Army barracks called Duff Green's Row, and all summer, Jacobs divided her time between ministering to their needs and creating a support network that would enable her to fulfil her relief mission.

In September, Harriet Jacobs recorded her summer's experiences in a 40,000-word response to Garrison's request for information. Headlined "Life Among the Contrabands," Jacobs's letter is, as Garrison notes, "a very interesting and touching account." What she describes is chaos. First visiting the refugee headquarters at Duff Green's Row, "I found men, women and children all huddled together, without any distinction or regard to age or sex. Some of them were in the most pitiable condition. Many were sick with measles, diptheria, scarlet and typhoid fever. Some had a few filthy rags to lie on; others had nothing but the bare floor for a couch. . . . The little children pine like prison birds for their native element. It is almost impossible to keep the building in a healthy condition. Each day brings its fresh additions of the hungry, naked and sick. In the early part of June, there were, some days, as many as ten deaths reported at this place in twenty-four hours." The government-appointed superintendent of the "contrabands" spent his time registering the people. His office functioned as an employment agency where men were hired to work for $10.00 a month, single women for $4.00, and women with one child, $2.50 or $3.00. Almost as terrible as the condition of the people was the general lack of concern among Washingtonians about their need. Jacobs began her morning's work by looking into a small ground-floor room "covered with lime. Here I would learn how many deaths had occurred in the last twenty-four hours. Men, women and children lie here together, without a shadow of those rites which we give to our poorest dead. There they lie, in the filthy rags they wore from the plantation. Nobody seems to give it a thought. It is an everyday occurrence, and the scenes have become familiar."

By midsummer, however, a new superintendent had made improvements, enlarging the rooms, creating hospitals for men and for women, and arranging for cots and mattresses by working with the newly established Freedmen's Association, one of the groups organizing throughout the North to provide emergency relief for the refugees. To help volunteer nurses Hannah Stevenson and Julia Kendall—who were, Jacobs notes, "the first white females whom I had seen among these poor creatures, except those who had come in to hire them"—Jacobs asked a "true and tried friend of the slave" in New York for "such articles as would make comfortable the sick and dying." The same day that cots arrived, a large box from New York was delivered. "Before the sun went down, those ladies who have labored so hard for the comfort of these people had the satisfaction of seeing every man, woman and child with clean garments, lying in a clean bed. What a contrast! They seemed different beings. Every countenance beamed with gratitude and satisfied rest. To me, it was a picture of holy peace within. The next day was the first Christian Sabbath they had ever known."

In addition to her concern about the Washington refugees, Jacobs felt herself drawn to the people who had fled to Union-occupied Alexandria, "where the poor creatures seemed so far removed from the immediate sympathy of those who would help them." Working with two local women who "felt the wrongs and degradation of their race," she surveyed the men living in the open in the shell of an abandoned foundry, and the women, who were housed in an old schoolhouse. "This I thought the most wretched of all the places. Anyone who can find an apology for slavery should visit this place, and learn its curse. Here you see them from infancy up to a hundred years old. What but the love of freedom could bring these old people hither?" In Alexandria, Jacobs distributed "large supplies of clothing, given me by the ladies of New York, New Bedford, and Boston. They have made many a desolate heart glad. They have clothed the naked, fed the hungry." For her curious northern readers, Jacobs describes Birch's slave pen—famous for having transported more than 1,000 slaves down the Mississippi River each year, now used in part to house "contrabands" and in part to jail Secessionist prisoners. (Each group, she writes, is sharply aware of "the change in their positions.") She comments with pleasure on the schools quickly being established. Recording her visits to "what the people call the more favored slaves," she touches on a major theme of *Incidents*—the sexual abuse of black women by white men and the resulting population of light-skinned slaves. "Here I looked upon slavery, and felt the curse of their heritage was what is considered the best blood of Virginia."

In this letter, Jacobs sounds a new voice. No longer writing as the "slave girl" Linda, conflicted but nonetheless telling her forbidden story, here she writes without explanations or apologies, addressing her audience as equals, an audience with whom she shares the values of hard work, literacy, cleanliness, and Christianity. She assumes that Garrison and his readers know who she is and that they value her words. In the deliberate, compassionate manner of a teacher, she informs her readers of the plight of the less fortunate—the tortured fugitive who reached free land only to die with his ankles still bound by the master's rope, the orphaned child taken in by an already overburdened mother—and she instructs them in their duty toward their fellow men and women.

Writing her own story of her years in slavery, Jacobs had presented herself not as a victim but as a woman fighting for freedom. Now she presents the refugees as active agents capable of learning to build lives in freedom for themselves and their children. "Some of them have been so degraded by slavery that they do not know the usages of civilized life; they know little else than the handle of the hoe, the plough, the cotton pad, and the overseer's lash. Have patience with them. You have helped to make them what they are; teach them civilization. You owe it to them, and you will find them as apt to learn as any other people that come to you stupid from oppression."

Featuring her report, *The Liberator* ran a short paragraph announcing it as an account "by Mrs. Jacobs, the author of 'LINDA.'" Apparently recognizing Jacobs's new tone, in the reformers' writings from this time forward, she becomes "Mrs. Jacobs." To them, "Mrs." was a significant honorific. Using it, they conferred on her all of the respectability of a married woman—despite the fact that they knew she had acknowledged herself a mother who had never been a legal wife.

As word spread of Lincoln's impending Emancipation Proclamation, Jacobs's dreams were expanding. Sharing the abolitionist vision of an angel who, "entering the hovel of the slave, transformed it into a HOME," she now transformed her dream of a haven for herself and her children. Grandmother's refuge in Edenton could become the model of homes for all of the free men and women in a free South. Throughout the fall, Jacobs had traveled to Massachusetts, New York, and Pennsylvania, gaining the support of religious groups and of the freedmen's aid societies being organized, to build the network she would need to sustain a mission among the refugees. She had met with Quaker groups and with elite women readers of her book—longtime abolitionists like Sarah Shaw, Elizabeth Neall Gay, and Hannah Haydock. (Her editor, L. Maria Child, testified that "while she was here she harrowed up my soul.") Most important, she had sought out the refugee aid organizations that black women were beginning to form.

Since early 1862, when the African American *Christian Recorder* urged its readers to support refugee relief, black people had been organizing across the North. In Boston, black women decided to establish a permanent aid organization. Meeting each Tuesday evening in the vestry of the Twelfth Baptist Church, they collected twenty barrels of clothing and $25. Other Boston groups were also organizing. The Fugitives' Aid Society collected four or five barrels of goods and $25, as well as $45 for the wounded soldiers, and ran a series of fund-raising concerts and talks. Still another group of Boston's black women ran a fair at Mercantile Hall for the benefit of the widows and orphans of "colored soldiers." New Bedford, Stockbridge, Hartford, Oberlin, Brooklyn, Troy, Geneva, Albany, and Syracuse followed—all potential resources of support for Jacobs's mission.

One of the strongest organizations was the Ladies' Contraband Relief Association in Washington, D.C., founded by Elizabeth Keckley, a self-emancipated slave who had become Mary Todd Lincoln's modiste and friend. Keckley and her colleagues were gathering monthly contributions from members and supporters, including Frederick Douglass and "Mrs. President Lincoln," and they were collecting barrels of clothing and money from black churches and the Freedmen's Relief Association. To raise more funds, they organized a festival and presented concerts at the Presbyterian Church, and they also reached out to activists and church circles in Boston, Brooklyn, New York, Trenton, Philadelphia, Baltimore, New Haven, and even England and Scotland.

Energized by all of this activity, Jacobs decided to spend the winter in Washington. Excitedly, she wrote to Amy Post in early December 1862. Lincoln's promise of a general Emancipation Proclamation, made a half year earlier, had seized her imagination. "if ever I craved more than one pair of hands & money it is now not for myself my friend but to assist those that are so much worse of than myself." Her health was good, "better than it has been for years. . . . the last six months has been the happiest of all my life. . . . Our prayers & tears have gone up as a memorial of our wrongs before him who created us—and who will judge us— Man may desire to stand still but an arm they cannot repel is leading them on. . . . a just God is settleing the account."

Harriet Jacobs would write a great many letters over the next four years. Assuming her new role and embracing her new identity as "Mrs. Jacobs," she would help her people articulate their dreams—for freedom and equality, for land and homes—as public demands. But in no other letter that has been found would she permit herself such a personal expression of feeling. She would fill most with accounts of life in the camps, not with her responses to that life. To activists like L. Maria Child, she would pen affirmative comments clearly intended for the movement press. To the Quakers who became her sponsors, she would compose positive reports for publication in their journals. To co-workers like Elizabeth Neall Gay, Sarah May, and Hannah Stevenson, she would write professional correspondence. In all of these, she would voice her clear agenda: the refugees' dreams should be realized. They are warm-hearted, decent, intelligent people, eager to attain the Protestant virtues of literacy, Christianity, hard work, and cleanliness—virtues that Jacobs and her co-workers, as well as her readers, need to teach them.

Typically, writers for the mainstream press in the North and in England were noting not the similarities among themselves, their audience, and their refugee subjects, but the differences. Seeing ex-slaves in occupied Alexandria, Nathaniel Hawthorne whimsically speculated whether they were actually human: "So rudely were they attired,—as if their garb had grown upon them spontaneously,—so picturesquely natural in manners, and wearing such a crust of primeval simplicity (which is quite polished away from the northern black man), that they seemed a kind of creature by themselves, not altogether human, but perhaps quite as good, and akin to the fauns and rustic deities of olden times." Hawthorne's English traveling companion described a gulf between himself and the refugees: "Miserably clothed, footsore, and weary, they crouched in the hot sunlight more like animals than men." Nathaniel Parker Willis—the third member of their party—chose not even to comment on the Alexandria refugees. In contrast, Harriet Jacobs's letters show African American refugees of all colors eager for, and entitled to, full citizenship.

Nowhere in these public accounts would Jacobs discuss her struggle against the civilian and military hierarchy in the camps. Fortunately, the story of her effort to help the refugees take control of their lives in the face of the active opposition of civilian and military authorities is told in a few of her private letters to colleagues, and in the writings of others.

In mid-January 1863 when Jacobs arrived in Alexandria carrying credentials from a meeting of New York Friends, she entered a city astir with
military activity. It had been occupied by federal troops in May 1861, the
day after its citizens—like all of Virginia—had voted for Secession. Under
Union guns, half the white voters had abandoned Alexandria, which now
was transformed into a supply depot. Its railroad yards housed three
important lines, and the Army had built a seven-mile road linking the city
to Washington. On King Street, a government-built slaughterhouse was
butchering a hundred oxen a day for meat for the federal soldiers at the
nearby camps, and at the old customs house on Union Street, bakers were
supplying them with vast quantities of bread. Uniformed men filled the
streets, where hucksters sold them "anything that flashed, glittered or
was plated." Before the war, Alexandria was famous as the largest slave-
mart in the country. Months after Jacobs's arrival, *the Anglo-African*
commented that although behind Union lines, Alexandria "contains this
day more secessionists than any place of its size in the country. Its colored population all testify to this fact, as they receive more insults in that
place in one week, than they do in Washington during a whole year."

The city was filled with sickness. "May I never again behold the misery I have witnessed," Jacobs wrote. "The small pox raged fearfully—
death met you at every turn. From the 20th of October to the 4th of
March, 800 refugees were buried in this town by the Government."
Despite this, Alexandria was an important medical center for the
wounded of both armies, and after the battle at Fredericksburg in December 1862, so many trains of casualties pulled into the city yards that most
of the wounded had to spend the night in the boxcars without blankets.

In the "contraband" camp, Jacobs met Julia Wilbur, a Quaker
schoolteacher she had known in Rochester who had come to the city to
work for the Rochester Ladies Anti-Slavery Society. Wilbur had grown
up on a farm near Rochester, and after moving to town to teach in 1844,
quickly involved herself in abolitionist and feminist circles. She returned
to the farm after the death of a sister left her three-year-old niece Freda
motherless, and when Freda's father took the child away, Wilbur was desolate. In October 1862, she accepted the position as agent of the Society
and arrived in Alexandria shortly before Jacobs came.

Conditions in the camp were terrible. The refugees, Jacobs wrote,
were "packed together in the most miserable quarters, dying without the
commonest necessities of life." To make matters worse, relief efforts were
in chaos: "The authorities really do not know the number of ex-slaves in

this place. We have no superintendent appointed by the Government to look after them; this we need sadly in a place like this, where the citizens are so strongly secessionist—kept down only at the point of northern bayonets. You may imagine there is little sympathy among them for these poor creatures." Wilbur reported to her Society that she found Jacobs "a very nice person, & well calculated to give personal attention to those people; to nurse the sick and care for them in various ways . . . much better than I can."

But she resented Jacobs's presence. Wilbur thought Harriet Jacobs's charge from the Quakers—to keep records of the clothing and blankets being dispensed—implied a criticism of her and of her colleague Reverend Albert Gladwin, who had been sent by New York's American Baptist Free Mission Society. She complained to her Rochester sponsors:

> We have but one room for the things, & that is not half large enough. We cannot spread them out & it is a great deal of work to look over a pile of things every time an article is wanted,—& to keep an account of every article wh. is given out, wd. take the whole time of one person. As far as we can we satisfy ourselves that persons are needy & deserving before we give them any thing, & then give what is adapted to their wants if we have it. . . . I do not wish to do any thing to make [Mrs. Jacobs] feel unpleasant. But if the N.Y. folks do not think us trusty & honest why, then, I wish they wd. send no goods to us.

Within weeks, however, Wilbur had changed her mind about both Jacobs and Gladwin. She was so shocked by Gladwin's abuse of the refugees—"threatening to flog them & scolding them as if they were animals"—that she wondered whether he had been a slave driver, "he takes to it so naturally." The goal of enabling the refugees to live independent lives was, Wilbur feared, doomed to failure because the officials "mean to give the Contrabands no chance, & then make all out of them they can." She found Gladwin's usurpation of power deeply disturbing. With the support of the military, he proclaimed that the barracks, until then used as free housing for the destitute, would be rented out to those refugees with money to pay, and that Wilbur and Jacobs would be allowed only one room to distribute relief clothing and supplies.

Then Jacobs and Wilbur learned that the doctor in charge of the smallpox hospital four miles outside the city proposed to round up all of the orphans "& *put them through the pock house.*" Jacobs was horrified, and she and Wilbur arranged to see General J. P. Slough so they could request permission to arrange space for the children at the barracks with a woman to care for them. Describing their meeting, Wilbur wrote, "Mrs. Jacobs spoke very handsomely to him, & when pleading for these Children said she 'I have been a slave myself.'" The women were vastly relieved when their request was granted. "This was," Wilbur confides, "such a great undertaking for us; we were in such a state of nervous excitement, that we were all of a tremble, & we had such a head ache too!"

Heartened by their success, two days later, Jacobs and Wilbur met with the provost marshall, who supervised the military police, to discuss abuses against the refugees. This meeting, Wilbur writes, "I dreaded more than to call on the Governor, but we composed ourselves & agreed not to cry if we could help it, & went to the Office." The women questioned the exorbitant rents and the miserly provisions for food and coal, and protested the quartering of soldiers among the women and children. "Those people need to be protected perhaps from outsiders," they argued, "but they themselves need no watching." They left encouraged that they had carried their point.

Every day from first light until full dark, Jacobs and Wilbur were on the run. They were trying to "hunt up the poor scattering families. . . . Then we want to get the orphans before Dr. B. gets them. Then we want to fix the rooms & beds &c.—Then there are sick persons that we have to see to. . . . Then we have to get places for girls, & then afterwards we want to go & see them." This cooperation made the women firm allies. Wilbur adopted Jacobs's bookkeeping system and reported that "Mrs. J," who had been talking about leaving, "says nothing more about going away. She begins to see what she can do now, & I hope she will keep well & be able to do it.—She has considerable decision of character & she does not mean to be imposed upon, by Mr. G. or Dr. B.—"

In mid-March, Jacobs mailed a long letter to L. Maria Child, confident that it would appear in the abolitionist press. Years earlier, she had composed her first piece for publication to refute claims made by the wife of the ex-President of the United States that slavery's yoke was light. Now she was writing to refute a white minister's public allegations against the black refugees. This time, instead of signing herself "A Slave" and sending her comments to a Letters column, however, as she had a decade earlier, Jacobs identified herself to her readers by name and sent her essay to the editor of her book to act as her agent and place in the press.

She begins by outlining the suffering of the people—"The misery I have witnessed must be seen to be believed." She then discusses the injustices practiced against the refugees: "In return for their kindness and ever-ready service, they often receive insults, and sometimes beatings, and so they have learned to distrust those who wear the uniform of the U. S." While Jacobs defends the people against the slanders of their detractors— "these poor refugees undoubtedly have faults, as all human beings would have, under similar circumstances"—nowhere does she address the racism and the corruption of the officials and bureaucrats controlling them. Instead, she focuses on the refugees' fundamental decency, on their kindness and generosity, and on the advances they are making: "It would do your heart good to talk with some of these people. They are quick, intelligent and full of the spirit of freedom." Outlining their progress, Jacobs sketches the recent wedding of eight couples; describes their day school, their evening school, and their sewing circle, all hugely attended; and announces arrangements for the care of the orphaned children in the camp. Voicing pride that finally, after years of agitation by blacks and their supporters, the Army has agreed to accept black troops, she sends a message of steady advancement. Jacobs urges her elite northern readers to acknowledge and aid this progress, and not to join the chorus condemning the refugees. Only at the end does she permit herself a cri de coeur: "Oh, when will the white man learn to know the hearts of my abused and suffering people!"

Jacobs was less guarded with her old pastor and friend J. Sella Martin, now working for the cause in London. Her labors, she writes, although hard, are enormously rewarding. "The memory of the past in my early life, the cruel wrongs that a slave must suffer, has served to bind me more closely to those around me; whatever I have done or may do, is a christian duty I owe to my race—I owe it to God's suffering poor. When these grateful creatures gather around me, some looking so sad and desolate, while others with their faces beaming happiness, and their condition so much improved by the blessings of freedom, I can but feel within my heart the last chain is to be broken, the accursed blot wiped out. This lightens my labours, and if any sacrifices have been made, they are forgotten."

All through the balance of the war, Jacobs worked in Alexandria as a visiting relief worker in the camp and in the hospitals. She continued to find her labors infinitely rewarding, although her friend Amy Post— never a squeamish woman—was shocked when she finally visited the city. Living conditions, Post thought, were terrible, and the work impossibly difficult: "Alexandria, Oh—horrid," she wrote home to Isaac. "I dont know how Julia & Harriet can stay their." Certainly life in the camp was hard—especially hard in the spring of 1863, with the city so nervous. In

March, the *Alexandria Gazette*, citing "information which bears every evidence of being reliable," reported that at Fairfax County, Rebel raiders had captured Union General Edwin H. Stoughton in his bed, and fearing Moseby's men, in Alexandria the provost marshall tightened security. Then, with rumors flying that 40,000 Rebels would attack that night, the military authorities ordered the city's outer fortifications strengthened, and soldiers marched male refugees to the commissary, the quartermaster depots, and the railroad to dig up the streets and build ten-foot-high stockades for defense. Alexandria had an "extremely warlike appearance. On all sides are the tented fields of the infantry. . . . In the city are the immense palisades erected around the railroad depot and near the river front, for protection against cavalry raids; and in the river the trim and fearless gunboats quietly await the presence of any threatening force."

While Alexandria prepared to repel the threatened invasion, Jacobs was packing for a special mission to the North. Like other relief workers, she routinely attempted to rescue orphans from the violence of war by trying to place them in northern homes. This trip, she was taking eight little girls with her. Promptly at 10:00 on the warm, hazy morning of May 28, 1863, Jacobs appeared in Boston at the annual meeting of the New England Anti-Slavery Society. After convening, the abolitionists adjourned until afternoon so that they could join the crowd of 20,000 people who had come to see the famous black Massachusetts 54th. The regiment's march from the railroad station to the Common was, the *Evening Transcript* reports, "perfectly triumphal." At a few minutes past ten o'clock, the men passed through the Charles Street gate into the Common. All along their route from the railroad station, "the sidewalks were crowded, and the windows and balconies were thronged. Men cheered and women waved their handkerchiefs. . . . They entered the Common at the Charles Street gate. Every place overlooking the parade ground had long been thronged with people, and hundreds who had, and thousands who had not tickets, were passed inside the lines." Led by young Colonel Robert Shaw on horseback, they passed in review before the governor, the mayor, and Senator Henry Wilson. Then "to the tune of John Brown," the men marched down State Street to the wharf, "vociferously cheered by the vast crowds that covered the sidewalks and filled the windows."

Jacobs gloried in the scene: "How proud and happy I was that day, when I saw the 54th reviewed on Boston Common! How my heart swelled with the thought that my poor oppressed race were to strike a blow for freedom! were at last allowed to help in breaking the chains, which their kindred had so long hopelessly worn!"

At a few minutes after 2:00, the abolitionists returned to their hall to discuss the astonishing developments of the past few months. The national agenda, all agreed, had changed from "UNION" to "EMAN-CIPATION AND UNION." In the evening, after a performance by the Hutchinson family (popular antislavery singers) and speeches by William Wells Brown and Edmund Quincy, Harriet Jacobs was called up to the podium. Introduced as "Linda," a former slave now engaged in refugee work in Alexandria, she mounted the platform with two of the little orphan girls. "The sight," *The Liberator* reports, "was evidently a touching one to the audience. It was stated that she purposed coming again to Boston, in course of the summer, with more of the orphan girls, for whom she desired to obtain homes. Persons in the audience at once offered to take the two girls then present."

Writing to her northern supporters, Jacobs routinely expressed her thanks and the gratitude of the refugees for help, described conditions in the camp, stressed improvements, and carefully detailed the money and items she received and dispensed. She never openly criticized Reverend Albert Gladwin, but his appointment in May as superintendent of contrabands distressed her deeply. Now she spoke freely with her Boston supporters about the problems in the Alexandria camp—and especially about Gladwin's persistent practice of crowding families into the barracks, charging them exorbitant rents, then punishing those unable to pay. Not only Jacobs, but others, too, were making complaints about conditions in Alexandria. One visitor wrote, "Some [refugees] are threatened with being put into the cars and sent to Richmond unless the rent is paid Monday morning. Others are threatened with expulsion." The superintendent was openly attacked in the pages of the *Anglo-African.* "Seeing, by his commission, that [Gladwin] had unlimited power as a magistrate, and also that a portion of his salary, which is $1,200 per annum, *comes out of the rent which the freedmen pay*, we could not help thinking that the *magistrate* might be induced at some time or another to turn the screws on the tenants for the benefit of the *landlord.*"

In addition to condemning Gladwin's rental procedures, Jacobs and Wilbur were deeply troubled by his rigorous implementation of the government policy of transporting the people to the refugee camp at Arlington. Many of the refugees, having already uprooted their lives to reach

Alexandria, wanted to stay in the city, try to locate family and friends, and settle down. Most did not want to be displaced a second time. Jacobs believed that in the refugee camp they would have little chance of becoming productive citizens, but would instead become institutionalized as dependent wards of the government. In addition, she judged conditions in the Arlington camp deplorable, and thought its administration at best negligent and at worst deliberately cruel. Wilbur concurred. "Not one in a hundred is willing to go to Arlington. The restrictions there are such that it is to them very much like going back into slavery."

The women were also concerned about the brutality routinely practiced against the refugees. In the dead of winter, Wilbur saw a man being forced naked into the shower bath, and was told that refractory women of color were punished by being stripped and showered in view of the troops: "We don't," explained a young corporal, "call them women." Another issue involved burials. While the white cemetery was well maintained, the refugees were simply "*packed* away. . . .The Potters field," Wilbur charged, "is the most heathenish looking place I ever saw. These [dead] were put in holes rather than graves, and bare covered. The poor slave. Virginia does not afford earth enough hardly to cover his remains!!" Although a new "contraband" burial ground was built, when a black solidier died, Gladwin ordered his grave dug there instead of in the Soldiers' Cemetery. His decision prompted indignant anger, and the black soldiers mounted a protest. Wilbur noted, "Mr Gladwin has buried 2 soldiers in Cold [colored] ground this P.M. Quite an excitement. The Soldiers at hos[pital] are furious, refused to go as escort. Mr. G. has caused one to be put in Slave Pen [used as a prison]."

By the time Jacobs returned to Alexandria from the meetings with her northern supporters, the Confederates were no longer directly menacing the city. A survivor of her war against Norcom, she had long ago decided she would never submit to petty tyranny. Now she felt strong enough to challenge Reverend Gladwin directly. In a private letter to Wilbur, who was summering in New York, she poured out the details of their confrontation. With new refugees arriving nightly, she was making sure she was at the barracks by 6:00 each morning, "hurrying as many as I can out among their friends before Mr. Gladwin reports them for Washington. Saturday I had 3 hrs. ahead of him, he found out that I had interfered, he came in great distress & said that I wd. be the cause of his being arrested. I requested that we both might be arrested & then I would

Harriet Jacobs in 1894. By permission.

Elijah Knox, Jacobs's half brother, in the 1890s. Courtesy of The New Bedford Whaling Museum, New Bedford, Massachusetts.

Thought to be a photograph of Joseph, Jacobs's son. By permission.

Thought to be a photograph of Louisa Matilda, Jacobs's daughter. By permission.

Deathbed codicil of Jacobs's first mistress Margaret Horniblow, willing "my negro girl Harriet" and "my bureau & work table & their contents" to Mary Matilda Norcom, her three-year-old niece, July 3, 1825. Courtesy of the North Carolina Office of Archives and History, Raleigh, North Carolina.

Mrs. James Norcom. North Carolina Museum of History. By permission.

$100 REWARD

WILL be given for the apprehension and delivery of my Servant Girl HARRIET. She is a light mulatto, 21 years of age, about 5 feet 4 inches high, of a thick and corpulent habit, having on her head a thick covering of black hair that curls naturally, but which can be easily combed straight. She speaks easily and fluently, and has an agreeable carriage and address. Being a good seamstress, she has been accustomed to dress well, has a variety of very fine clothes, made in the prevailing fashion, and will probably appear, if abroad, tricked out in gay and fashionable finery. As this girl absconded from the plantation of my son without any known cause or provocation, it is probable she designs to transport herself to the North.

The above reward, with all reasonable charges, will be given for apprehending her, or securing her in any prison or jail within the U. States.

All persons are hereby forewarned against harboring or entertaining her, or being in any way instrumental in her escape, under the most rigorous penalties of the law.

JAMES NORCOM.

Edenton, N. C. June 30   tTs2w

Advertisement for the capture of Harriet Jacobs, *American Beacon* (daily), Norfolk, Virginia, July 4, 1835. From microfilm in the collection of the North Carolina State Archives.

Dr. James Norcom. North Carolina Museum of History. By permission.

Eastern portion of North Carolina in 1770 showing Edenton, just above Albemarle Sound, and inlets offering Edenton ships passage through the Outer Banks. From *The Commerce of North Carolina, 1763–1789*, by Charles Christopher Crittenden. Yale University Press. By permission.

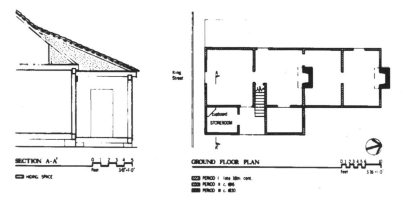

Molly Horniblow's house: reconstruction to scale of elevation and floor plan showing Jacobs's hiding space [shaded area]: 9' long, 7' wide, and 3' high. Designed and drawn by Carl R. Lounsbury, Colonial Williamsburg Foundation. By permission.

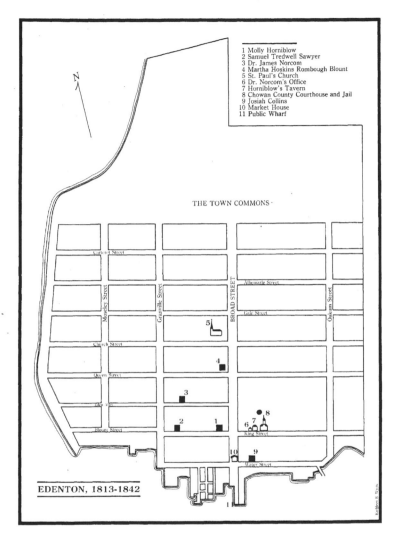

1 Molly Horniblow
2 Samuel Tredwell Sawyer
3 Dr. James Norcom
4 Martha Hoskins Rombough Blount
5 St. Paul's Church
6 Dr. Norcom's Office
7 Horniblow's Tavern
8 Chowan County Courthouse and Jail
9 Josiah Collins
10 Market House
11 Public Wharf

THE TOWN COMMONS

EDENTON, 1813-1842

Map of Edenton, North Carolina, 1813–1842. Developed by George Stevenson and drawn by Kathleen B. Wyche, North Carolina State Archives. By permission.

Lydia Maria Child in the 1860s. By permission of the Trustees of the Boston Public Library.

Amy Post in the 1860s. Rush Rhees Library, University of Rochester, Rochester, New York. By permission.

William Cooper Nell. Courtesy of the Massachusetts Historical Society.

Julia Wilbur in the 1860s. The Quaker Collection, Haverford College Library, Haverford, Pennsylvania. By permission.

Charlotte L. Forten Grimké in the 1870s. Photographs and Prints Division, Schomburg Center for Research in Black Culture, The New York Public Library; Astor, Lenox and Tilden Foundations.

Cornelia Grinnell Willis at the Old Mansion, New Bedford, Massachusetts, in 1884. Photograph by Parlow, Photographer, New Bedford. Joint Free Public Library of Morristown and Morris Township, New Jersey. By permission.

Dolls made by Jacobs for the Willis children. Photograph by the Daughters of the American Revolution Museum.

Fugitive Slave Law Convention including Frederick Douglass, Gerrit Smith, and the Edmondson sisters, Cazenovia, New York. **August 22, 1850.** Photograph by Ezra Greenleaf Weld. Courtesy of the J. Paul Getty Museum, Los Angeles, California.

INCIDENTS

IN THE

LIFE OF A SLAVE GIRL.

WRITTEN BY HERSELF.

"Northerners know nothing at all about Slavery. They think it is perpetual bondage only. They have no conception of the depth of *degradation* involved in that word, SLAVERY; if they had, they would never cease their efforts until so horrible a system was overthrown."

A WOMAN OF NORTH CAROLINA.

"Rise up, ye women that are at ease! Hear my voice, ye careless daughters! Give ear unto my speech."

ISAIAH xxxii. 9.

EDITED BY L. MARIA CHILD.

BOSTON:
PUBLISHED FOR THE AUTHOR.
1861.

Title page of the first edition of *Incidents in the Life of a Slave Girl. Written by Herself.* Boston, 1861.

Edenton April 25th

Dear Mrs Cheney.

I felt I would like to write you a line from my old home I am sitting under the old roof. twelve feet from the spot where I suffered all the crushing weight of slavery. Thank God, the bitter cup is drained of its last dreg. There is no more need of hiding places to conceal slave Mothers. yet it was little to purchase the blessings of freedom. I could have worn this poor life out there to save my children from the misery and degradation of slavery.

I had long thought I had no attachment to my old home. As I often sit here and think of those I loved of their hard struggle in life — their unfaltering love and devotion toward myself

First page of letter from Harriet Jacobs to Ednah Dow Cheney, April 25 [1867]. New England Hospital Papers, Sophia Smith Collection, Smith College, Northampton, Massachusetts. By permission.

Fugitive Slaves Crossing the Rappannock River, Virginia, August, 1862. Photograph by Timothy O'Sullivan. Library of Congress Prints and Photographs Division, Washington, D.C.

Price Birch & Co. Dealers in Slaves, 1865. Courtesy of the Alexandria Library, Alexandria, Virginia. By permission.

Laundry Day at Volusia, near Alexandria, Virginia, 1860s. Collection of Lewis and Rosalie Leigh Jr. By permission.

"Coloured School at Alexandria Va 1864 taught by Harriet Jacobs & daughter agents of New York Friends." Courtesy of the Robert Langmuir Collection of African-American Photographs. By permission.

explain why I had interfered with these people, he thought better of it & let the matter rest." When Gladwin ordered transport to carry forty of the refugees to the Arlington camp, Jacobs, hearing one of the women say, "I don't want the rations if they will let me alone" and reasoning that the people would not be transported if they were not government depen-dents, "stopped the rations knowing it was the best way to affect my pur-pose at that time. Nearly all in the Barracks were cut off, also the outside ones. Matilda with her little baby 10 wks old was cut off."

Jacobs charged that Gladwin was determined not only to expel the refugees, but to control all of the space the government provided to house them. Cataloguing the week's events, she writes that next morning, when he came to take over Wilbur's room, "I occupied it myself." He then wanted to install a stove in her room, and "he began to talk about mess-ing. I told him I didn't want to mess with them. That day I had the stove carried into the kitchen. . . . [He] had General Slough's two sons to dine with him last Sabbath, & I gave him a little Sabbath lecture before them." Gladwin was, Jacobs continues, "like a crazy man hunting up the poor refugees to send them to Washington, sent away 70 of the finest looking women & children I have seen yet. Poor Amanda came to me most heart broken, her mother was among them, & Mr. G. would not let them stay with her, I sent her to General Slough. He gave her a note to Mr. G. to let them remain with their children. Mr. G. was so angry that he slapped Amanda's little girl." Announcing her open opposition to Gladwin's regime, she declares, "I am doing all I can to make him complain of me. Last Friday I presented a document against him."

Jacobs's accusations were not, however, what prompted the Army to investigate. The Freedmen's Relief Association filed complaints by three of the camp physicians that the Alexandria refugees felt "their condition is made worse by being made free. Their present master is the hardest master of their lives." Citing Gladwin's demand of high rents for unfit housing and his practice of separating families by sending newcomers away even when they had parents or children living in Alexandria, they accused him of being "the most unfittest man for the position." But when the Army investigated, they exonerated Gladwin completely. The men making the charges had vied for Gladwin's position, and the Army con-cluded that their accusations were based on self-interest. In an adden-dum, the official document reports, "Two women, Mrs. Harriet Jacobs (colored) and Miss Julia Wilbur (White) have also been meddling with the affairs of Mr. Gladwin and endeavoring to sour the minds of the negroes against their Superintendent." "Everything," Wilbur noted, "drags but rascality. That is bold and prompt."

Early in November, Jacobs was again traveling to gather supplies when Gladwin shepherded a team of Philadelphia Friends through the camp. "They were," Wilbur writes, "led to believe that these people were very comfortably situated, & cd. have the necessaries of life, & build houses besides. . . . My pen cannot do justice to Mr. Gladwin's performance that day.—But I will say in passing, that since Mr. G. has been complained of so much, that he behaves much better." Returning to Alexandria, Jacobs rushed to reassure Wilbur that she had again spoken with their northern supporters, who would be strong allies in their effort to rid the people of Gladwin's tyrannical rule. The influential Mays had not been deceived by Gladwin on their last visit, and Sarah Russell May planned to return. Most important, "The N. Y. committee are coming in soon, and if Mr. G. can be removed, it will be done."

Jacobs well understood the importance of keeping the national leaders of the relief effort informed. The morning after her return, she wrote to Hannah Stevenson of the New England Freedmen's Aid Society that, stopping in at the barracks to see the old women and children, she had discovered that Gladwin had cleared out the furniture and sent the people away. She immediately went to General Slough, who sent for the supertintendent. Certain that in defending the people she was in the right, Jacobs was not sorry that the conflict with Gladwin had come to a head: "I had longed for this hour that I might explain before him to his superior in command how unjust he had been to these poor people. My first accusation against him was the breaking up of my old woman's home in my absence." To Gladwin's charge that she "had written all over the country and slandered him," she replied, "it was true I had written and spoke freely of him. I asked leave to state the facts." When she was finished, Wilbur reports, "There was a rich time. General S[lough] was very severe with Mr. G[ladwin]. He threatened him with the Slave pen several times. . . . Mr. G. said he would resign if these women staid here. General S. said 'very well, I will write your resignation, there are other persons who can be had.'" But Gladwin backed down. The general again granted Jacobs her barracks room for the old women and children and, Jacobs writes, "I picked up the old thread and tried to work on."

While Gladwin remained superintendent, however, the basic problems in the camp remained unresolved. When he again tried to take over Jacobs's space, Wilbur furiously catalogued his demands:

He must have an office, a sleeping room & a spare sleeping room, & a reception room, & the highest room was wanted for Miss Collier & Miss Owen, Mr. O's daughter, who has come to teach, also rooms for his men & servants &c. How many do you think he has of these? These are Mr. Owen, Secretary Hoady, the Corporal who collects rents, carries dispatches &c. Mr. Axe, who teaches at Barracks, Peter Washington & wife Susan, the latter does most of the cooking for all these, washing for some of them, & cleaning, *& is paid nothing.* Peter preaches for Mr. G[ladwin], & keeps up prayer meetings, goes for rations, saws the wood, washes dishes or cooks, makes fires or any thing else, & a boy who does errands, cleans knives & blacks boots & washes dishes.—Mr. G. pays Peter $15 a month.—Mr. O. & Miss Owen the Corporal & Mr. Axe & Peter & Susan draw full rations, wood, coal &c. Mr. Gladwin lives off of these.

Again Jacobs refused to move unless ordered by General Slough, and again Gladwin conceded. But this endless harassment was exhausting.

Over time, however, the women were gaining powerful support in their campaign against Gladwin's rule. Wilbur publicized one instance of his gouging in her annual *Report*: "I hardly think the Government is aware that it is drawing a considerable revenue from miserable rooms without windows or chimneys, or any conveniences whatever, in rents paid by these lately freed slaves, who have all their lives heretofore had their earnings appropriated by others. It is deeply mortifying to read receipts given in the name of the U. S. Government at the rate of $36 and $60 a year for one room of the above description." Influential Friends concurred. A *Report to the Executive Committee of New England Yearly Meeting of Friends* noted that "there is still a great number, who are living in very poor buildings, for which they pay a large rent, to the superintendent appointed by the government. By great efforts on the part of Friends, this rent has been reduced from what was formerly charged, but it is still large for the miserable places they occupy." Characterizing Gladwin as "harsh and tyrannical to the people under his charge, but fawning and obsequious to those in authority," the New York Committee judged him "very unsuitable for the position he occupied." Agreeing, an *Anglo-African* reporter commented: "We paid a long visit to the superintendent and hence were obliged to pay a short one to the quarters, but that visit reminded us very much of a Northerner's visit to the plantations of the South, a good while with the master, but a short time with the slave, and that short time spent in the presence of the master."

If all of this reminded Jacobs of her prolonged struggle against Dr. Norcom, she could take comfort in recalling how far she had traveled from Grandmother's attic—and in knowing that she had, after all, defeated her nemesis. Although knocked off balance in adolescence, long ago she had determined that nothing again would decenter her. Perhaps her head was filled with thoughts of petty tyrants, however, when she told Wilbur she was thinking of leaving for good in the spring.

11

Justice Will Come

~*~

A Power mightier than man is guiding this revolution, and though justice moves slowly, it will come at last. The American people will outlive this mean prejudice against complexion.
—Harriet Jacobs to L. Maria Child, March 26, 1864

In May 1863, Jacobs's old friend Amy Post joined the crowd of "loyal women" gathered in New York's Church of the Puritans to answer Susan B. Anthony's call for a Women's National Loyal League. Organizing in the wake of Lincoln's Emancipation Proclamation—which many abolitionists feared meaningless because it freed only those slaves in states rebelling against the Union—the women planned to lobby Congress for an emancipation act. After songs by the Hutchinson family and speeches by feminist Elizabeth Cady Stanton and famed abolitionist Angelina Grimké Weld, they unanimously passed a resolution creating themselves "a Loyal League, to give support to the government." Despite the federal defeat at Chancelorsville, they were not offering the government their unconditional support, but "only in so far as it makes a war for freedom." Two weeks later, the women opened up offices and began working on their goal to gather a million signatures on petitions for the abolition of slavery. In July, during the Draft Riots, their uncompromising antislavery position placed them in danger, but the women interpreted the lawlessness as proof that African Americans must not only have emancipation, but full citizenship. In October, on one of her trips to the North, Harriet Jacobs entered the national political arena when she met with League members in their rooms at the Cooper Institute.

The *Daily Tribune* reports that, with Stanton in the chair, Harriet Jacobs opened the meeting with a prayer for victory and emancipation, "invoking the Almighty to save the nation and free the slave." The women were working hard, and a few months later Senator Charles Sumner presented Congress with League petitions bearing 100,000 signatures. In the spring, the League celebrated its first anniversary at a mass meeting in New York. Responding to the news of the Confederate massacre of black troops at Fort Pillow, the women announced that they had now sent 200,000 signatures to Washington "demanding an amendment of the Constitution and an act of emancipation," and they pledged to gather 100,000 more demanding for black men "the right of suffrage . . . without which emancipation is but mockery." At this meeting, they unanimously elected Jacobs to their executive committee. She was doubtless the unnamed "mulatto member" who, the papers reported, informed the press that she had "a few words to say. She didn't see any hope for the negro until the Constitution was amended. 'Liberty, justice, equality'" she explained, "'that's where I stand, especially the equality.'"

Before Jacobs traveled north to the League meeting, the Alexandria freedmen had begun building a school and meeting house, and one of her objectives in making the trip was to gain support for their project: the establishment of a free school under black leadership. In 1812, Alexandria's African American community had founded the Washington Free School in the Alexandria Academy, and later had built the Lancastrian School. Alfred Perry had established Mount Hope Academy, a night school, in 1837, and when the mayor accused him of disobeying a local ordinance prohibiting people of color from assembling, he had hired a white man to be on the premises. He continued running his school until 1845, but when Alexandria was retroceded from the District of Columbia to Virginia a year later, the edict against African American education was made "so stern and relentless . . . that the free colored people dared only in a covert manner to teach even their own children."

Soon after the federal occupation in 1861, two black women had opened pay schools. The next year, with the support of Baptist societies, two black ministers had inaugurated a "select" school that accepted refugee children, charging them, like the other students, $1.00 a month. A little later Leland Warring, a former slave, opened a school at the Lancaster schoolhouse, but Reverend Gladwin took it over and had it moved to the Freedmen's Home, where it became the first free "contraband" school taught by whites. When Jacobs arrived in Alexandria at the beginning of 1863, nowhere in the city was there a free school under black leadership where the destitute refugees could send their children to learn.

Now, returning south from the League meeting, Jacobs brought with her $12.00 she had collected for the free school. Demonstrating that the war was opening up new opportunities for African Americans of all classes, she also brought two "colored teachers": her daughter Louisa ("an elegant girl," noted Wilbur) and Virginia Lawton, the daughter of old Boston friends. Back in Alexandria, however, she discovered that the people had run out of money and that although their building stood unfinished, a number of northern white missionaries had already applied to take charge. With construction again underway, Jacobs wrote to her northern supporters that she decided "to wait and see what was the disposition of the Freedmen to whom the Building belonged." She visited one of the trustees, who allowed he would be proud to have Louisa and Virginia Lawton teach the children, but that "the white people had made all the arrangements without consulting them." Then Jacobs acted.

Invited to the next trustees' meeting, she brought with her all the candidates vying for the school, explaining, "I wanted the colored men to learn the time had come when it was their privilege to have something to say." "I wish," Jacobs exulted to L. Maria Child, "you could have been at that meeting. Most of the people were slaves, until quite recently, but they talked sensibly, and I assure you that they put the question to vote in quite parliamentary style." When the trustees decided that Louisa was to take charge of the school with Virginia Lawton as her assistant, however, the whites refused to accept their verdict. "One gentleman arose to lay his prior claim before the people. A black man arose and said—the gentleman is out of order this meeting was called in honor of Miss Jacobs and the ladies, if the gentleman has any thing to say we will call another at another time and hear him—that man had learned a lesson for a life time."

Louisa and her mother explained that they applauded the trustees' choice not because they disapproved of white teachers, but "because our sympathies are closely linked with our oppressed race. These people, born and bred in slavery, had always been so accustomed to look upon the white race as their natural superiors and masters, that we had some doubts whether they could easily throw off the habit; and the fact of their giving preference to colored teachers, as managers of the establishment, seemed to us to indicate that even their brief possession of freedom had begun to inspire them with respect for their race." This was not, however, the end of the matter. "After this decision the poor people were tormented—first one then another would offer to take the school telling them they could not claim the Building unless a white man controlled the school." Finally, Jacobs accompanied the trustees to the authorities and received a five-year lease on the ground.

The school was named the Jacobs School, and with community control established, Jacobs and Louisa turned to the task of paying off the $180.00 owed on the building. Instead of asking their supporters in Massachusetts and New York to cover the debt, they decided to write asking them for items left over from the fund-raising fairs they had held. To the boxes and barrels that arrived, Wilbur added added some things she had received from Rochester, and they organized their own fund-raising evening. "We opened a fair with a handsome finery table," Jacobs reported, and "cleared one hundred and thirty dollars." In addition to raising the needed money, they used the fair to involve local free black women in their relief work. According to one northern supporter, by working with "the well to do—those who were free before the war, and live comfortably—[and who] so much fear on their part that this great influx of degraded contrabands would drag them all down to the same level in social estimation," Harriet and Louisa were able "to bring out their sympathies and break up this selfish, aristocratic notion." Intent on nurturing the people's self-sufficiency, Jacobs had consistently required that those earning paychecks should learn to pay for the clothing and supplies she distributed. Now she decided that the time had come for the Alexandria community to assume responsibility for the $50 needed to clear the remaining school debt: "I want them out of their contributions to pay the balance due on their building."

Eager to begin work, Louisa opened her schoolhouse doors to seventy-five students on a bright, mild morning in January 1864. She had prepared to become a teacher in her teens, and here in Alexandria was finally able to realize her vocation. She enjoyed describing her students to her northern readers. "Slavery has not crushed out the animal spirits of these children. Fun lurks in the corners of their eyes, dimples their mouths, tingles at their fingers' ends, and is, like a torpedo, ready to explode at the slightest touch." But she acknowledged that the children were also capable of belligerence. "The war-spirit has a powerful hold upon them. No one turns the other cheek for a second blow." Their generosity impressed her. "They never allow an older and stronger scholar to impose upon a younger and weaker one; and when they happen to have any little delicacies, they are very ready to share them with others." Like other committed teachers, Louisa dreamed of her students' successes: "When I look at these bright little boys, I often wonder whether there is not some Frederick Douglass among them, destined to do honor to his race in the future." In contrast to many white commentators who, discussing the freedmen's schools, speculated whether there were differences in the intellectual capacities of blacks and whites, Louisa considers that there might be differences in temperament: "I am inclined to believe their organization more restless than that of white children, the love of fun and mischief runs so warmly through their veins. . . .While the children are eager to learn, and many make astonishing progress, the duty of maintaining proper discipline is by no means easy. . . . Wholly unaccustomed to the system of a school-room, they find no lesson so difficult as the necessity of keeping quiet."

The teaching was not easy. Although Louisa was finding her labors "very encouraging," she acknowledged that "in the school they are hard." Nevertheless, she writes, "we put heart, mind, and strength freely into the work, and only regret that we have not more physical strength." Jacobs, seeing her daughter overworking in the classroom, worried about her. Louisa's health had never been robust, and now "the doctor says my daughter will have to give up; but her heart is in the work." Louisa managed to finish out the school term, but the following year gave up classroom teaching. She continued, however, to take responsibility for the Industrial Department (with classes in marketable skills such as cooking and sewing), to teach the Sunday school, and to assist her mother in less exhausting "out-of-door work."

In her letters to the North, Jacobs tried to keep her supporters current not only about the Jacobs School, but about life in Alexandria. On a cold spring morning in March 1864, she wrote to L. Maria Child that she went down to the wharf "to welcome the emigrants returned from Hayti." Historically African Americans, asserting their American roots, had rejected emigration. In the early 1860s, the Haitian-backed Haytian Emigration Bureau had actively sought recruits, and in 1862 Lincoln (who had long urged the colonization of free black people in Africa and in Central America) had signed an agreement to establish a colony of free African Americans on Ile a Vache, Haiti. Despite the strenuous opposition of the Garrisonians and a bitterly split black community, about 400 people had been transported from Fortress Monroe, at the tip of Virginia's lower peninsula, to the Ile a Vache. A little less than a year later, learning that they were suffering deprivation and terrible hardship, the President ordered a transport to return the black colonists home.

Jacobs met the shivering, ragged people down by the water. She pitied their wretchedness. "It was a bitter cold day, the snow was falling, and they were barefooted and bareheaded, with scarcely rags enough to cover them. They were put in wagons and carried to Green Heights. We did what we could for them. I went to see them next day, and found that three had died during the night. I was grieved for their hard lot." Recalling her long-held opposition to emigration schemes; remembering that, when still a fugitive slave, she had voiced the anger her "poor little indignant heart" had felt against the Colonization Society; and perhaps bitterly reliving her distress at learning that Mrs. Willis had involved the Society in her purchase, she continues: "I comforted myself with the idea that this would put an end to colonization projects. . . .They are eight miles from here, but I shall go to see them again tomorrow." Then, quickly turning to another item on her crowded political agenda: "I hope to obtain among them some recruits for the Massachusetts Cavalry." She is not interested in the bounty offered recruiters, she explains, but wants to help activists George Downing and Charles Remond, who are visiting Alexandria to sign up black troops, "because I want to do all I can to strengthen the hands of those who are battling for Freedom."

As Alexandria blossomed into spring, Jacobs took time to reflect on her experiences in the city. To her Quaker sponsors, she countered reports denying that the people were making progress: "I am convinced that the negroes are not so far behind other races as they are represented to be, if only justice is meted out to them." She has seen impressive changes in a short fifteen months: "When I came to this place, I found, in a few miserable dwellings, old foundries, old breweries, old mills, and a school house, thousands of men and women and children crowded together, the smallpox raging among them; sick from other diseases; dying, on the average, from five to seven a day, without bedding, without a change of clothing, without nourishment, without the commonest necessaries for the comfort of the sick and dying. . . . These painful sights have almost disappeared. . . . We have seven thousand colored people in our midst. . . . Not one-third are dependent on others where they can work; they are fast learning to think and act for themselves. I can see the results—it takes time for them to realize that they are free men and women." She voices her pride in what she and Louisa have accomplished: "the largest school house was built by the Freedmen, and they own it as their property. . . .

Our school progresses well, number on roll 235 scholars—too many for our accommodations. Many of the children have made astonishing progress, they read and spell in words of two and three syllables."

All was not well, however, in the divided city. Only two weeks before Jacobs sent this positive account, Wilbur had noted "a report today that Louise and Virginia [biracial women] were kidnapped last evening by Northern doctors for dissection. Queer stories afloat. Some of the colored folks are afraid of being out after dark." Alexandria continued to be tense. A British visitor wrote that the "bitterly 'secesh' white population showed their dislike of the Federal army of occupation by every means in their power." When in March, under Union guns, the loyalist Constitutional Convention voted to end chattel slavery, Wilbur jotted in her diary, "Great rejoicing in Alex. yesterday. Convention resolved that Virginia shall be a FREE State. Bells rung, & 100 guns fired, horses ran away." But the *Gazette*, reporting the clamor, commented that no one knew why the bells were chimed.

Despite the deep divisions in the city, Jacobs and Louisa decided to stay on. In the summer of 1864, as Union armies were nearing Richmond, Alexandria was again threatened. When the black refugees were drafted to defend the city against the Confederacy, stresses between the Army and the city's "secesh" population grew. Alexandria was, one reporter wrote, "now practically a military post, and the presence of soldiers forms one of the most marked features of the place." Because of the repeated raids on the Manassas Gap Railroad by Confederate partisans, trains were being run in convoys, and after Mosby attacked a federal payroll train, the Army ordered prominent local residents onto the cars as human shields.

On August 1, Jacobs and Louisa awoke early. Over the years, they had seen many celebrations on this date, but today's was to be spectacularly different. After weeks of careful planning, today would mark Alexandria's first commemoration of British West Indian Emancipation. The center of the ceremony was to be the presentation of a flag to a representative of the Colored Hospital, which had opened in February and, after receiving patients from the Colored Division of the Ninth Army Corps, was now named L'Ouverture in honor of the Haitian liberator. To organize the events, Jacobs and Louisa had collected $50.00 from the sick and wounded, worked with local women arranging a dinner and entertainment, and reached friends in Philadelphia who agreed to donate the flag. For days, Jacobs had been practicing the address she had written to deliver when she presented the banner to the hospital.

On schedule at 1:00, the band marched onto the piazza and began to play. An hour later, the convalescent soldiers marched out with four sergeants at their head and took their positions in front of the musicians. Reverend Gladwin, as superintendent of the "contraband," introduced the exercises, and after a prayer by Reverend Chauncey Leonard, the band played a stirring "Hail, Columbia." Then Harriet Jacobs spoke, ceremoniously handing the flag to the surgeon in chief. An *Anglo-African* reporter writes, "The presentation by Mrs. Jacobs was admirably done. Calm and unassuming (the peculiar characteristic of this estimable lady), she came forward, and presented to Dr. Barker a fine flag."

Formally addressing her audience of "Physicians, Soldiers, and Friends," Harriet Jacobs began by noting that thirty-one years earlier, West Indian Emancipation had compensated the slaveholders with "British gold." Today, however, she proclaimed, "we are passing through times that will secure for us a higher and nobler celebration." As if she had been preparing all her life for this moment, Jacobs delivered a political lecture to the black men in blue ranked before her.

> Soldiers, what we have got came through the strength and valor of your right arms. Three years ago this flag had no significance for you, we could not cherish it as our emblem of freedom. You then had not part in the bloody struggle for your country, your patriotism was spurned; but to-day you are in arms for the freedom of your race and the defence of your country—to-day this flag is significant to you. Soldiers you have made it the symbol of freedom for the slave. . . . Then take the dear old flag and resolve that it shall be the beacon of liberty for the oppressed of all lands, and of every soldier on American soil.

Jacobs handed the flag to Dr. Barker and, as the troops cheered, saw it raised to the top of the flagstaff while the band played "The Star Spangled Banner." After speeches and music, everyone crowded into the dining hall, where Jacobs and her women's committee served "a splendid repast." Then after more speeches, "a vote of thanks was given to Mrs. Jacobs and the ladies," and the program ended with Jacobs leading a rousing chorus of "Rally Round the Flag." The Alexandria celebration was one of many commemorations, historian David Blight has written, where even before the war was won, "blacks were preparing the script and forging the arguments for a long struggle . . . America's rebirth was one and the same with their own rebirth as 'citizens.'" John S. would have been proud.

Long before the August 1 ceremony, the establishment of the Jacobs School in the refugee settlement had signaled Jacobs's recognition by northern reformers. Her "very diligent" labors had prompted her New York Quaker sponsors to hire Louisa to assist her; the Friends had sent slates for the students; and the newly-formed New England Freedman's Aid Commission, in addition to donating money and textbooks, had sponsored Virginia Lawton's work at the school. Now the L'Ouverture flag presentation crowned Harriet Jacobs's work in Alexandria.

With the broad institutional support she had won, and with her name familiar to readers of *Incidents,* Harriet Jacobs and her mission became featured in the reform press, and Alexandria became a regular stop on the reformers' tours of the conquered South. They came to see with their own eyes—and to write about—the refugees' progress. Black leaders Frederick Douglass, George Downing, Charles Remond, J. McCune Smith, and Henry Highland Garnet; white abolitionists Theodore Parker, James Miller McKim, and Wendell Phillips Garrison; Quakers James Congdon, Benjamin Tatham, John J. Thomas, and Henry Dickinson; and relief workers Cornelia Hancock, Emily Howland, and Lucy Coleman— all trooped through the Alexandria camp.

Late in 1864, activist reverend Samuel May Jr. reported at length on his visit in the *National Anti-Slavery Standard.* Identifying Jacobs as the "Linda" of *Incidents*, May praised her as an "intelligent, judicious and invaluable friend" of the freed people, fitted "by temperament and disposition, by character and attainments, to minister to the necessities of the aged, counsel those in middle life, and influence and guide the young, among this large population so lately in slavery." The Jacobs School, he reports, shares space with the people's meeting-house which, newly lathed and plastered, has been enlarged over the summer. Now measuring sixty by twenty-eight feet, it is "an institution in which these humble parents take a very lively interest. . . . they understand that their ignorance was their weakness, and they rejoice in the hope that their children are to be lifted out of it. In this school-house Mrs. J. takes a very special satisfaction, and she will watch the teaching and the order of it with as much intelligence as interest."

Sarah Russell May followed up on this report by soliciting donations for the school in the pages of the *Standard*. From juvenile readers in Massachusetts, Pennsylvania, Kentucky, and Canada, she raised $22.65, which bought a United States map and four blackboards. In response, Louisa wrote her thanks for "the cards, pictures and slates," likening their child donors to magic benefactors who appeared in fairy tales her students had never known. "Their gifts," she poeticized, "have rippled like waves of sun light through many a little heart that never until now felt the touch of sympathy and love. Let no child think her mite too small to help some needy one."

The New York Representative Meeting of Friends not only published letters from both Harriet and Louisa Jacobs, they also noticed their work and their school in their annual *Reports* and in their new publication, *The Freedman.* In Alexandria, they wrote, "the colored people are endeavoring to work out for themselves, the problem of their capacity for self care. . . . They have erected principally at their own expense a building to be used as a school and meeting house." One delegation of New York Friends reporting on their visit found the school's management "dignified and efficient" and Jacobs's presence very important: "The new comers scarcely know who else to look to. She has evidently been the kind and thoughtful dispenser of many blessings." Other groups, too, printed first-hand reports. Three representatives of the New England Yearly Meeting detailed their visit for their readers. And the New England Freedmen's Aid Society's *Freedmen's Record* headlined "Jacobs (Linda) School, Alexandria, Va.," describing "the school-house, built mainly by her own exertions, named in her honor, and presided over by black and white teachers, working harmoniously together," and proudly announcing the Society's support of teachers Virginia Lawton and J. Stewart Banfield.

Fed by this publicity, Jacobs's personal celebrity grew. One volunteer nurse wrote home that at Washington she had met "the daughter of Mrs. Jacobs, authoress of 'Linda,'" and the reformer Caroline Severance, learning that a friend had gone to Washington, hurriedly queried, "And did you see . . . 'Linda'?" William Lloyd Garrison's son, touring the Washington area, wrote his famous father that after catching the one o'clock ferry for Alexandria, after they "landed at two, we made a call on Washington St. at the house where 'Linda' lives." In *The Liberator,* William C. Nell used Harriet and Louisa Jacobs as examples to strengthen his argument that the freed people merited full citizenship.

Years earlier, Jacobs, shaping her experiences in slavery into a representative life, had published her book. Now, to publicize the ability of the black refugees to become exemplary Americans, she arranged for a photograph to be taken of the school she had established. On a cool morning, more than a hundred students and teachers gathered in the yard next to the Jacobs School, a clapboard building with paned windows and peaked roof. All ages, shapes, sizes, and colors, they assembled themselves into crooked rows, taller children behind, younger in front, with a few holding hands. They were dressed in their best, some of the girls with aprons over their dresses, some of the boys wearing jackets, and the bigger boys sporting caps. A mounted horseman came to see as they stood with serious faces, watching the photographer who had come to take their picture. In back with some of the bigger boys stood Banfield, the teacher from New Hampshire, and in their midst stood Harriet Jacobs, her arms encircling a half-dozen small children, smiling. *The Freedman's Record* announced, "It is delightful to see this group of neatly dressed children, of all ages, and with faces of every variety of the African and mixed type, all intelligent, eager, and happy. Mrs. Jacobs's honest, beaming countenance irradiates the whole picture; and the good teacher stands in the background looking over his scholars with great complacency. It is a whole volume of answers to the skeptical and superficial questions often put as to the desire and capacity of the negro race for improvement. The picture may be seen at our office by any friends wishing to know how a freedman's school looks." Proudly, the New England Freedmen's Aid Society displayed the albumin photograph and had copies made for the local organizations supporting the Jacobs School at Alexandria. The picture had a prominent place in their offices, then was lost for a hundred years. It has only recently been found.

In February, Jacobs wrote again to her supporters. She was showing visitors around Alexandria when the convalescent soldiers at L'Ouverture came out to welcome the 111th Ohio Regiment. To her eyes this scene, like the photograph of her school, had symbolic meaning. "What a picture. the old Slave Pen within an Arms length. the Colored Soldiers behind me. the white Soldiers in front. two Ladies by my side. so deeply interested. While one of these brave Officers is relating the Noble and heroic deeds of his Men." Grand as this was, Jacobs then reminds herself—and her readers—that the struggle for equality and brotherhood is not yet over: "I had rather picture the day when I shall meet a Colored Regt. with Colored Officers. then I shall forget the wrongs to my race and be proud to call myself an American Woman."

A month earlier, Gladwin had finally been dismissed. The new superintendent moved quickly to abolish the entrenched abuses Jacobs and Wilbur had fought: rents were no longer charged for the old government buildings, and many of the destitute whom Gladwin had rejected were fed. Jacobs expressed enormous relief at his dismissal: "I feel the Colored people will have a friend in Chaplin Farree. he has done much in a short time to alleviate their sufferings. and redress their wrongs. the Authorities here wish these people to be treated as human beings. we only wanted a man with a heart."

All around them, Harriet and Louisa could see the progress. Members of Alexandria's African American community were organizing to exercise their rights. When the county court rejected a witness's testimony because of his race, the people met offering him support to appeal to a higher court for his rights as a black man. They were beginning to voice their historic demands for equality. At meetings at the Bethel and First Colored Baptist churches, they elected delegates to send to the National Convention of Colored Men in Syracuse, New York, where the Equal-Rights League was founded to obtain "a recognition of the rights of the colored people of the nation as American Citizens." Addressing the need to support the troops, local women established a Soldiers' Aid Association and, having initiated their charitable work a year earlier, they were soliciting items for a second fair. (One of their northern supporters noted, "We have made a few gay silk neckties, some fancy aprons for colored babies, highly-colored pincushions, &c. . . . The proceeds are to supply delicacies, &c., for the colored soldiers in the great dreary hospital at Alexandria appropriated to them.") The local refugee settlements—Grantville, Sumnerville, Petersburg, Newtown, Contraband Valley, Richmond, and Washington Square—were increasingly stable and self-sufficient. And the Jacobs School was thriving.

At the end of March 1865, Congress finally created the Freedmen's Bureau, charging it with the distribution of food, fuel, and clothing to destitute freedmen and with oversight over "all subjects" concerning their condition in the South. With the Bureau established and the federal government apparently committed to their future, with the people taking charge of their lives, with Gladwin gone and a humane new administration installed in the camp, Jacobs wrote to her Quaker sponsors. The time has come, she says, for her and her daughter to move on.

> The freed people here, with but a small exception, now take care of themselves; some, I may say, barely exist, but through the pinch of that existence they will learn before another season to do better. The people at one time thought me very hard, for I was always preaching to them about taking care of themselves; some would feel it was right, and act accordingly; others, that my only duty was to clothe their bodies; but they do not think so now, for many of them have learned that self-

reliance is the elevation of their race. It is pleasant to have them come
to me now.

Ten days later—on Monday, April 10—the *Gazette* announced,
"This morning early upon the news of the surrender of General Lee and
his army, the bells were rung, flags displayed, and guns fired." The war
was over. On Friday, the city held a procession to honor the raising of the
American flag over Fort Sumter. Wilbur found the parade "really very
fine." In addition to the military, it included the firemen, a model of the
ironclad *Monitor* (complete with a blacksmith and forge), a printing
press, and members of the Lodge of Colored Free Masons. But not everyone rejoiced. In the evening, when Alexandria was to have been lit in celebration, "only a few buildings were illuminated. Secesh houses all dark
as could be."

And then the news came. "How can I write it?" Wilbur mourned.
"The President was shot last night in the Theatre, & died at 7:22 this
morning! . . . Hard to believe at first. The bells have tolled since noon
Flags are at half mast. Stores are closed. Houses draped in black. Soldier
make secesh put black on their doors.—No boats leave for W[ashington]
to day. . . .Every colored face is sad. . . . Every Cabin, Shanty & shed
where they live has something black upon it. It is a touching sight."

Louisa Jacobs visited Washington a few days later to view Lincoln's
body. "Thousands," she reports, "went to look, for the first time, on their
emancipator, as he lay in state at the White House. 'Ah, child,' said an
old woman to me, 'they have killed our best friend. He was next to
God.' . . . Old Aunt Sicily, who bore the yoke of slavery for 110 years,
looked upon Mr. Lincoln with a reverential feeling, beautiful to behold
in one so aged, 'for the privilege,' she says, ' that he gave her to die free.'
The day after his assassination she said to me, 'I can't believe that such
a good man is dead. But child, they can't kill his work. They can't put
the chains on us again.'"

The war was over; the President was dead; life was moving very quickly.
Now was the time, Wilbur proposed, to see the Rebels' fallen capital. On
May 14, 1865, Jacobs started for Richmond with a friend, and next day,
a group including Wilbur and Louisa left Washington. Meeting at Fortress Monroe, the women proceeded to Richmond together.

The city they saw was in the midst of violent transitions. The day they
arrived, the newspaper praised the military rulers: "We have nothing to

complain of and much to be thankful for." Yet only six weeks earlier, the Confederate capital had been ablaze, fired by the retreating army, and "Richmond seemed in a night to have been transformed into an African city." With whites nowhere to be seen, black Richmonders had welcomed the federals with open arms and worked with them to save the city from complete destruction. From the first, the freed people challenged the customs of slavery: they no longer stepped down into the gutter to let whites use the sidewalk, they called meetings without obtaining permission from the whites, they began to press to elect black ministers in their churches, and they worked with the northern teachers who soon arrived to establish schools. But reorganizing a community takes time, and the generals in control wanted to reestablish civil government quickly. Most whites soon became eligible for federal rations by passing the loyalty test, which required their verbal acceptance of the defeat of the Confederacy and the end of slavery—but not their repudiation of the Confederacy or their acceptance of the freed people's rights. Black Richmond, however, had to work for its rations. Only two days before Jacobs's arrival, repressive measures were instituted: the Army began checking "the issues of subsistence to destitute persons," orders were issued that blacks must carry passes (signed by whites) displaying their identity and their employment, an evening curfew was imposed on blacks, and soldiers went through the city stopping African Americans, checking passes, and making arrests.

Jacobs and her friends found the streets full of Rebel soldiers. Their first day, eager to see the sights, they visited the Capitol, Jefferson Davis's home, Castle Thunder, and notorious Libby Prison. Next morning, joined by New England Freedmen's Aid Society teacher Lucy Colman, they toured the city jail and whipping post, Lumpkin's jail, Hill & Dickinson's slave auction house, and the poor house (which under the Union occupation was being used as a center for the very young, the sick, the old, and the disabled, driven away by their masters and sent off to die). Later, taking tea with the Forresters, a family of former slaves, the women drank from Jefferson Davis's cups and enjoyed spooning strawberries and ice cream from his saucers. "Sat & looked at his house," Wilbur wrote, amazed, "& tried to realize where I was." At five o'clock on Saturday morning, most of the group started back. They all had passes issued by the military, but because Jacobs had given hers to a friend, she could not travel with them. Instead, she was required to return as she had come by way of Baltimore, where passes were not necessary.

Down at the dock, Jacobs was saying her good-byes. She was wishing she could accompany her daughter and friends when Lucy Colman handed her pass to the guard and, glancing at it, he asked which of the women was her nurse. Colman quickly touched Jacobs's shoulder. After looking hard at Jacobs—who was wearing a rather elegant bonnet and good gloves—he stared at the sunbonnetted bare-handed Colman, then endorsed the document. Quickly passing her hand-basket to Jacobs, Colman rudely ordered her to step on board. Bewildered, Jacobs turned to Louisa, who repeated Colman's order and walked up the gangplank. Jacobs followed her daughter, only to be stopped by an officer who announced, "No niggers allowed in the cabin," but when Colman asserted a lady's right to be accompanied by her servant, he apologized. Later, Colman explained that her hastily written voucher had been misread. "Pass Mrs. Colman, vol. nurse, with transportation, to Richmond and return" had been read as "Pass Mrs. Colman, and nurse." Before the war, Jacobs had protested against Jim Crow. What did it mean when now, in the flush of the Union victory, she was permitted to ride in the cabin only when masked as a servant? Slavery was dead. Must the struggle continue?

12

Marching Without a Lance

༺❀༻

Be not discouraged. Deeds of mercy moveth even the heart
of a man who may hate his Brother. We must march on though with
but a broken lance, though we have no lance at all.
—Harriet Jacobs, Alexandria, July 2, 1865

In November 1865, Harriet and Louisa Jacobs stepped off the gangplank onto the dock in Savannah and walked straight into the center of the epic national struggle for black autonomy. Georgia's superintendent of education had pleaded with the New England Freedmen's Aid Society to send teachers, and the Jacobs women had come as the Society's representatives. Their voyage had begun badly. They had booked staterooms, but when they boarded, the captain told them they would have to travel in steerage. They protested, and after prolonged negotiations, were offered a compromise. They could keep their quarters if they agreed to eat there alone, and not with the other travelers. The old sense of enclosure stifling her, Jacobs refused. "I don't care about the meals, but I cannot be shut up in the stateroom." Finally the captain backed down, warning, "Southerners never would stand it to be put on an equality with colored people."

Despite his warning, the voyage passed without incident, but when their ship docked in Savannah harbor, the superintendent came aboard to tell them that they were not needed. Jacobs and her daughter sensed something amiss and instead of complying, went ashore anyway. The city rose above them on a plateau forty feet higher than the river, its steep embankment bolstered by rocks. Its terraces were white, bleached with water-stained cotton worked by pickers—women paid twenty-five cents a day, men ten dollars a week. After picking the good cotton loose and spreading it out on large canvases, the workers threw aside the damaged fibers to be swept into windrows. "There you see our blood," an old woman said. "Three hundred weight when the sun went down or three hundred lashes, sure!" Beyond the wharves and embankments, in the city's parks, cows and goats grazed freely, shaded by willow-leaf live oaks and evergreens. Savannah's Forsyth Park, on the outskirts, boasted a fountain decorated with dolphins and a crane. But it was not the shady parks that most impressed Savannah's northern visitors that November. It was the softness of the air, sweet with the scent of jasmine and flowering plum, and the bird sounds everywhere welcoming them.

Although Jacobs told the superintendent she was staying on because her sponsors wanted her to report on the condition of Savannah's freedmen, she may also have been curious about the city. Famous for its live oaks and notorious as the port of the *Wanderer*—in 1859 thought to be the last slave ship to enter an American port—Savannah was the city that General William Tecumseh Sherman had famously presented to President Lincoln as a Christmas gift in 1864. Only weeks afterward, Sherman and Secretary of War Stanton had held an historic meeting with a delegation of local black leaders. When questioned, their spokesman, Reverend Garrison Frazier, said, "The freedom, as I understand it, promised by the proclamation, is taking us from under the yoke of bondage and placing us where we can reap the fruit of our own labor, and take care of ourselves and assist the Government in maintaining our freedom." Four days later, Sherman followed the ministers' lead by issuing his famous Special Field Order Number 15, setting aside for the freedmen "Sherman's Reservation"—the rice fields and the islands off the Georgia–South Carolina coast that the planters had abandoned.

Among activists, Savannah was known for its black-led Savannah Education Association. The city's African American community had met Sherman's victorious troops with praise and thanksgiving—and with an agenda. In January, the people were organizing schools and arranging for the establishment of a freedmen's hospital. In February, the thousand black men and women gathered at the Second African Baptist Church listened, rapt, as General Rufus Saxton, speaking in the name of the federal government, pronounced them all free and promised them forty acres and a mule. Led by their ministers, the community immediately began organizing the Savannah Educational Association to establish free schools for themselves and their children. At one meeting, an observer watched, amazed: "Men and women came to the table with a grand rush—much like the charge of Union Soldiers on a rebel battery! Fast as their names could be written, by a swift penman, the Greenbacks were laid upon the table in sums from one to ten dollars, until the pile footed up the round sum of *seven hundred* and *thirty dollars.*" Within weeks, African American teachers were instructing black children in the Bryan and Oglethorpe schools.

White American Missionary Association representatives who traveled to Savannah to organize their own schools reported with surprise that "a goodly number" of the children already knew how to read and spell, and "others evinced considerable knowledge of arithmetic, geography and writing." They did not know that black schools had been operating in Savannah for decades, despite an 1817 city council ordinance that outlawed teaching slaves and free African Americans, and despite passage of a similar state law a dozen years later. Civil War nurse Susie King Taylor, now returned to the city, recalled that she had learned to read and write in the 1850s at the school on Bay Lane taught by Mrs. Mary Woodhouse and her daughter Mary Jane, free black women; later, her books wrapped in paper to mask them from the whites, she walked to Mrs. Mary Beasley's to continue her studies. Some of the secret schools operated for as long as thirty years. Officials seem to have known—and to have overlooked—the fact that James Porter was using his music classes to teach reading and writing. Among the underground teachers, only James M. Simms had been punished. Although publicly whipped, Simms had continued his work until he was fined $100; then he had gone to Boston.

Now Porter had become secretary of the Savannah Educational Association and principal of the Bryan Free School, housed in the old Bryan slave market at the corner of St. Julian and Bernard. Simms, too, was back. Recently ordained, he was serving as a missionary and as a Freedmen's Bureau superintendent of rice plantations on the river. While supporters of black autonomy cheered their work, Reverend S. W. Magill, sent to Savannah to organize the American Missionary Association schools, did not. "It will not do, of course, to leave these people to themselves," he counseled his northern brethren. "However good men they may be, they know nothing about educating. . . . I fear they will be jealous & sullen, if I attempt to place t management in t hands of our white teachers. But this must be done, in order to make t schs effective for good."

Commenting on the tensions between the northern white-led group and the local black-led organization, a representative of the New England

Freedmen's Aid Society noted "a rather peculiar feeling among the colored citizens here, in regard to the management of the schools. Among them are men of real ability and intelligence; and they have a natural and praiseworthy pride in keeping their educational institutions in their own hands. There is a jealousy of the superintendence of the white man in this matter. What they desire is assistance without control." Freedmen's Bureau Inspector of Schools John W. Alvord concurred: "Their management and teaching may not equal that of our northern instructors, but the people are ambitious to make their effort *themselves*—are proud of it—pay for it cheerfully according to their means." As the months passed, however, it was becoming increasingly obvious that Savannah's black-led schools were having funding and administrative problems, and the New England Freedmen's Aid Society, attempting to provide "assistance without control," began paying the salaries of Simms's "native teachers."

In the Georgia low country, the freedmen were planting the fields they believed their own. Up the rivers on the rice plantations (which for decades the masters had annually left to their overseers during the malarial season), the homogeneous and stable slave population shared a strong sense of community and a clear sense of autonomy. On the sea islands (abandoned by the planters during the war) black families from Beaufort, Hilton Head, and Savannah came and built settlements under the leadership of Freedmen's Bureau Agent Tunis Campbell, a black activist from the North. But the planters intended to have their land back and to restore plantation production. Although General Saxton reiterated that "the lands which have been taken possession of by this bureau have been solemnly pledged to the freedmen," President Andrew Johnson forced General Oliver O. Howard to issue Circular Number Fifteen, functionally restoring the plantations to the planters. Fearing that the Army would enforce compliance, Howard reluctantly began permitting the dispossession of black farmers who had claimed land under Sherman's order. After a military court restored St. Catherine's Island to Jacob Waldburg—in 1860 the largest landowner in Liberty County and, with 255 slaves, the second largest slaveholder—black settlers on the islands became deeply alarmed. Four days before Jacobs docked in Savannah, eighty freedmen, hearing that St. Catherine's and Ossebaw Islands had been returned to the planters, came to the city seeking refuge.

When Harriet and Louisa Jacobs arrived in Savannah in late November, both control of the schools and control of the land were at stake. This was, W.E.B. DuBois would write, the central struggle of Reconstruction, the issue that Reverend Frazier had addressed when he spoke to General Sherman of "placing us where we can reap the fruit of our labor, and take care of ourselves." Almost immediately, Harriet and Louisa began reporting to supporters in the North and in England. Their early letters seem to suggest that they might decide to settle in Savannah. Within a week, Louisa opened a school in the city poor-house, now a hospital for freedmen and refugees under the direction of their friend Major Augusta, with whom they had worked in Alexandria. They quickly became acquainted with the Savannah Education Association, reporting that it was operating "six schools in the city. Mr. Bradley is fitting up one of the slave auction rooms to open a seventh."

While Louisa was establishing her school, Jacobs, who had brought bundles of clothing with her, began distributing it to the hospital patients and organizing the convalescents to help. "If you could send me a barrel of hospital stores," she wrote the New York Quakers, "it would be very acceptable. I have nothing on hand." With Christmas coming, Louisa repeated the strategy successfully used for the Alexandria fair, and "went among the colored people," collecting $25 so that she and mother could cook a holiday dinner for the hospital patients. The meal was simple, Jacobs wrote, "everything is very high." But "every one that could crawl out of bed was at the table, both black and white." In occupied Savannah, a dinner where blacks and whites sat down together was certainly not the norm. Generally the city's white citizens, Jacobs comments, "don't seem to think colored people have any rights or wants."

But change was in the air. Work was beginning on "the erection of an Orphan Asylum and Old Folks' Home," and Jacobs informed her northern sponsors, "my daughter has applied for the situation of matron in the Asylum. I expect to take the Home." The plans made the local papers. The *Savannah National Republican*, headlining "A Great Improvement—Proposed Erection of a Freedmen's Refuge," reported "a number of substantial wooden buildings are shortly to be erected . . . on the vacant land situated in a Southeasterly direction from Forsyth Park." Although approving the new hospital, however, the paper attacked the freedmen it would serve, opining that "hundreds of [them] seem unable to comprehend such a thing as the future. Come day, go day, God send Sunday, is their motto, and they care little to provide for the wants of to-morrow." Within this hostile public climate, work on the refuge quickly became stymied, and Jacobs's Savannah letters express the heightening tensions in the city. Increasingly, they suggest the growing violence. "We shall be badly off when the military protection is withdrawn."

The occupying Union Army was certainly functioning as protection, but it could also be used by Savannah's powerful to attack black efforts at independence, both in the city and out on the plantations. Military rule had ended in Savannah shortly before Jacobs's arrival. The mayor and city fathers had just regained control when Aaron Bradley—like Jacobs, a fugitive slave who had worked with northern abolitionists—appeared and began speaking out for black autonomy. At meetings at the Second African Baptist Church, he advocated local black control of the schools and urged the people on the plantations to resist dispossession and to refuse to sign bad labor contracts with the planters. The American Missionary Association's representative complained: "We were getting along very pleasantly until this Bradley came and if he had stayed away and Mr. Alvord had not paid off the expenses of the Association and determined they should be sustained in this present shape I could have brought every thing under our control and made what is now working badly, more efficient." Bradley was promptly arrested, accused of voicing "seditious and treasonable language," quickly tried before a military commission, found guilty of using "insurrectionary language in public assemblages, inciting lawlessness and disturbance of public peace and good order," and sentenced to one year at hard labor at Fort Pulaski.

Jacobs's letters do not comment on Bradley's speeches or on his trial and sentence. Nor do they discuss the January convention of the Georgia Equal Rights and Education Association, organized to secure full citizenship rights for the freed people. They do, however, consistently address the land question. Visiting rice plantations on both sides of the river, Jacobs praises the work of the local black leader James Simms, reporting that she even has arranged "to teach an industrial department in connexion with some of his schools." She expresses concern, however, about the future of the freedmen's settlements where the schools are located: "Many of them will be turned over to their old masters the first of January."

Jacobs was eager to visit the people on the plantations, but violence ran unchecked in the countryside and, she explains to her northern supporters, "you have no protection. Things have come to such a pass, that you are not sure of it, even from our officers. The place Mr. Eberheart [state superintendent of schools] wished me to go, he refused to send a white teacher to, saying it was not a fit place for her." She could not even visit the smallpox patients, as she had in Alexandria. Here, "they are carried five miles in the country, put in tents, without stores, scarce any bedding. More have died from exposure and starvation than from the disease. I have made soup and sent it, but you are not always sure they get it."

Six weeks after arriving in Savannah, Jacobs tallied up the numbers to give her sponsors some idea of the scope of the refugee effort. The city's African American population numbered 10,500, with thousands more on the plantations on both sides of the river. James Simms was supervising 4,020 freedmen, and this group, she fears, are endangered. Although promised land, "now these people are found fault with for believing the government would help them. All the men that planted rice have done well," she reports, but "I am afraid they will not be allowed to plant again."

Two weeks later she wrote again, reporting the expulsion of the people from the plantations. Many, she explains, are refugees from Florida or South Carolina, where their masters had taken them early in the war to keep them from the Union armies. Now they are again being displaced. "It is a pitiful sight to go down to the Bluff where the poor creatures are landed. You will see crowds of them huddled around a few burning sticks, so ragged and filthy they scarce look like human beings."

At year's end, the *Savannah Daily Herald* announced that by Special Order of Brigadier General Tillson, all freedmen who refused or failed to sign contracts for their labor by January 10, 1866, "shall be hired under contract by the Authorized Agent of said Bureau." Jacobs explained to her northern audience what this meant: the planters were attempting to use the contracts to reestablish their authority over their former slaves. Many of these agreements, she writes, "are very unjust. They are not allowed to have a boat or musket. They are not allowed to own a horse, cow, or pig. Many of them already own them, but must sell them if they remain on the plantations." One master who owned 300 acres of rice land "wants to employ thirty hand; make the contract for the year, at ten dollars per month; gives them rations and four dollars a month out of their wages. When the crop is laid by, the master has two-thirds, the laborer has one-third, *deducting the pay for the rations*. Many of the freed people," she reports, "are leaving this place."

Ten days later, Jacobs reported, "In every direction the colored people are being turned from the plantations when unwilling to comply with the hard proposals of the planters. . . . The Bureau," she charged, "only assists them in making contracts," and these "are sometimes very severe and unjust." The people are not permitted to rent land or work on shares, but "must work under their former overseers. . . . They cannot leave the plantation without permission. If a friend calls to see them a fine is imposed of one dollar, and a second offence breaks the contract. They work for ten dollars and rations." On the river plantations, "the people are expecting the return of their old masters. Poor things! Some are excited; others so dispirited that they cannot work. They say, 'I can't eat, I can't sleep, for tinking of de hard time coming on me again; my heart 'pears to be all de time quiverin'; I knows 'tis trouble.' . . . On the rice plantations that I have visited, the people are badly off, God pity them. I lose sight of their rags when I see how degraded and hard-hearted slavery has made them."

Two weeks later, she wrote again. "I must tell you about my island poor; they have increased in numbers, mostly women and children. They are not allowed to plant, and are expecting every day to be driven off. These are the poor creatures from the interior of South Carolina; they did not know they were free until last month." Louisa, joining her mother's efforts to awaken their northern audience to the unfair conditions being forced on the people, indignantly detailed the contract demanded by one harsh master. "A boat, a mule, pigs and chickens, are prohibited; produce of any kind not allowed to be raised; permission must be asked to go off of the place . . . . Is this freedom, or encouragement to labor? Those who have had a taste of freedom will not make contracts with such men. Are they to be blamed, and held up as vagrants too lazy to earn a living?"

The people who resisted signing these contracts were being expelled by the Army. In mid-February, a *Savannah Daily Herald* report beginning, "There was nothing of any interest to our readers in this [Freedmen's] Court today," announced that a military squad had been sent to one plantation "to bring down some two hundred and fifty refractory negroes who refuse to make contracts."

Early in March, both Harriet and Louisa sent long letters north. Jacobs's was to L. Maria Child, who arranged to have it published in *The Independent*. For this newspaper's large northern audience, Jacobs again described the predicament of the thousands of freedmen who had land-passes allowing them to farm the land on the "Sherman reservation." "I visited some of the plantations, and I was rejoiced to see such a field of profitable labor opened for these poor people. If they could have worked these lands for two years, they would have needed no help from any one." Under Presidential Reconstruction, however, "Johnson has pardoned their old masters, and the poor loyal freedmen are driven off the soil, that it may be given back to traitors." She again condemns as unfair the contracts they are offered: "One of these laborers told me that, after working hard all the season to raise the master's crop, the share he received was only one dollar and fifty cents." Still, she tries to sound positive: "I am in hopes that something will yet be done for them by Congress; and therefore, I have earnestly exhorted them to remain on the plantations till ordered off by the authorities of the United States. But one by one the plantations have been given back to the rebels, till there are not five left." Then, dropping her public voice, she allowed herself a personal lament: "Oh, it is so discouraging!"

Louisa wrote to *The Freedmen's Record* to give her readers a sense of Savannah, where the old and new were colliding. "The old spirit of the system, 'I am the master and you are the slave,'" she explained, "is not dead in Georgia." She described a confrontation between their next door neighbors (who, though poor, had owned slaves), and their newly hired servant. The mistress struck the maid, a woman with "the look and air of one not easily crushed by circumstances." Louisa reports, "as I looked at the black woman's firey eye, her quivering form, and heard her dare her assailant to strike again, I was proud of her metal." When the mistress's husband appeared ready to hit her again, the maid "drew back, telling him that she was no man's slave; that she was as free as he, and would take the law upon his wife for striking her. He blustered, but there he stood deprived of his old power to kill her if it had so pleased him. . . . She went to the Bureau, and very soon had things made right."

Savannah's freedwomen were no longer complying with the ritualized subordination they had endured in slavery. Before the Union occupation, black people were not allowed to walk on the west side of Bull Street. Now, Louisa writes, when her friend was pushed off by a white man, "she gave him to understand that Sherman's march had made Bull Street as much hers as his." Not only access to the sidewalk, but fashion, too, was being revolutionized. Before the occupation, women of color had been forbidden to wear veils. Now they created a new style. "After the army came in, they went out with two on,—one over the face, the other on the back of the bonnet."

Life in the city was in transition, but all the changes were not necessarily empowering Savannah's black population. At the beginning of 1866, the superintendent of schools had privately proposed to reorganize the educational system and make the black school board "auxiliary only." By February, the American Missionary Association's Cooley could assert, "Now we have nearly all the schools in the Western part of the city and only the single school of Miss Jenness and that of Miss Jacobs in the Eastern part [are out of our control] if I may except a few private schools." Early in spring, he reports the total defeat of the black-led schools: "The teachers of the Savannah Educational Association have all withdrawn from that organization and are seeking employment elsewhere." He is, he writes, prepared "to place the whole management under our northern teachers and use any colored assistants in that position only." "The field is," he declared, "now virtually our own."

Louisa's Lincoln School, black-led and black-taught, survived. She had located it in the eastern section of the city where, upon first coming to Savannah, she had seen "hundreds of children . . . running in the streets that ought to be in school." When the new freedmen's hospital was built, she moved her classroom there. She and her mother also moved into Dr. Augusta's home, close to their work—and away from the supervision of whites. In Savannah, as in Alexandria, Louisa found "much to encourage me in my labors." A committed teacher, she delighted in the "bright faces" of her students. Acknowledging that her schoolroom (half of a hospital ward, with the old men on the other side of the partition) is "rough," she describes it as "large and airy." More important, "the freedmen," she assures her northern patrons, "are interested in the education of their children." She finds it odd that "the Southerners take no interest in the education of the freed people. It seems strange, when we consider how their interest must be linked in the future." A Pennsylvanian visiting at examination week wrote that he was impressed by her school, and other Northerners agreed. "I have children who could not spell when I organized the school in November, now reading well and studying Arithmetic and Geography," Louisa wrote in May. "This does not," she points out to her New England readers, "show inferiority of race." Still, "it will be a long time before things can be righted for the colored man South."

That spring, while Congress and the President warred over the shape of Reconstruction, Jacobs was appealing to her northern sponsors for seeds so the freedmen could plant. In response, the New York Quakers collected a large quantity, and L. Maria Child wrote, after hearing Jacobs's plea, "I hastened to do up, label, and send through the mail fifty four different kinds of seeds; a job which took a day." In Georgia, Jacobs was giving them out, along with information on improved methods of agriculture, to freedmen who had rented plots of land.

But the seeds of violence were sprouting like weeds throughout the former Confederacy. The *Loyal Georgian* reported that in South Carolina "five white men, disguised with masks," entered a black family's house, raped the woman, then went to a shop nearby and robbed the black owner. In Memphis, a traffic accident involving two horse-drawn hacks, one driven by a black man and the other by a white, escalated into three days of racial violence. When it was over, forty-eight were dead—forty-six of them black—five black women had been raped, and hundreds of black homes, schools, and churches were ruined or burned. The Georgia Education Association commented that "in many counties, the intelligent colored men who attempted to organize educational Associations were driven by their employers from the plantation where they were employed. Many planters would not allow the children of those in their employ to attend the schools after they were established." In Jacobs's Savannah, the *Daily News and Herald* reported in July that near the canal on Fahn Street, a dispute between black and white cartmen resulted in one black man being severely beaten and another being shot to death. As the paper describes the incident, after a shouting match, the black man called the white "a rebel son of a b——." The white man started beating him with a stick and then tried to drive away, but found himself "surrounded with an excited and angry crowd of negroes threatening him. We are informed," the story continues, "that Samuel Whitfield pulled out a revolver and threatened to shoot, some of the crowd at the time urging him to do so. The white man then rose in the wagon, and leveling his gun at the crowd fired, the load, consisting of buckshot, taking effect on the body of Whitfield."

The *Boston Freedmen's Journal* presents a different picture. From Savannah, James Simms wrote that Whitfield "and some other Colored Persons Seeig A White Man A Citty Cartman Beating another Colored Man Cartman . . . Supposing the Colored Man Beated was Dead . . . Followed the two White Men up in the Citty that they May not Make their escape. . . . They Stoped the Cart and Commanded them to Halt and Not Follow them as they Would Shoot them, yet the party with Mr Whitfield continued to follow them . . . Whereupon the Man Allen that had a gun in the Cart fired into the Party following them, and the Load Taking effect in the Breast of Mr Whitfield Killed him Almost Amediately." Amazingly, Simms continues, the beaten man is recovering and the man who beat him is being held. But, he explains to his New England audience, "the State Court . . . Will Surely Justify Any White Man in Beating or Killing a Colored Man on a Trivial offence   Such is the State of Law and Justice here."

Harriet and Louisa Jacobs—like both James Simms and the murdered Samuel Whitfield—were connected with the New England Freedmen's Aid Society. Only days after Whitfield's murder, Harriet and Louisa Jacobs tried to leave Savannah. Whether they had planned their departure long before, or decided to leave when they heard of the shooting, is not known. As usual, Louisa bought their first-class tickets for New York, but when they tried to board the steamship *Leo*, they were told they would have to travel in steerage, and this time, their protests were useless. In Boston, *The Freedmen's Record*, recording the incident, writes that the mother and daughter "were both put off the boat in a very rough manner, and compelled to remain," and comments, "We hope the matter will be followed up, and the rights of citizens in public conveyances will be secured." In contrast, the report in Savannah's *Daily News and Herald* ends—not with the hope that Jim Crow will be stopped—but by dismissing Jacobs and her daughter as troublemaking outsiders: "The women, we understand, are from the North. They had been employed in some of the colored schools of this city and were about to return North for the summer."

Leaving Alexandria, Jacobs had tried to focus on the progress. Now, leaving Savannah, she had to acknowledge the terrible truth. She could no longer keep on marching.

Jacobs's departure from Savannah marked a series of endings. Once back in New York, she traveled to Idlewild and learned that Nathaniel Parker Willis was dying. His epileptic seizures had been recurring with greater frequency and had grown increasingly violent. For much of the summer, he had stayed at home with the family, but in the fall returned to the city and his work at the *Home Journal*. Early in November, after fainting in the street, he was taken back home, and Jacobs went to Idlewild to help. She became absorbed by the demands of the sickroom, sharing the heavy nursing chores with Cornelia Willis until Willis's death in January 1867. Then, although her duty to her friend was completed, Jacobs apparently stayed on at Idlewild as she tried to map out her future.

A year earlier, when the issue of the freed people's citizenship was still unresolved, Harriet's and Louisa's co-workers in Georgia had formed an Equal Rights Association. Now in the North, Jacobs's colleagues in the Women's National Loyal League were again organizing, and at their first annual meeting since the war, the Eleventh National Woman's Rights Convention reconstituted itself as the American Equal Rights Association. Aware that New York State was facing its periodic constitutional revision, the delegates resolved to mount a campaign urging that the state constitution be changed to grant equal rights to all "without distinctions of color, sex or race."

Among the speakers was the black activist-poet Frances Ellen Watkins Harper. Harper's presentation alerted her New York audience to precisely the violence and racism that Jacobs and Louisa faced in Savannah: "You white women speak here of rights. I speak of wrongs. I, as a colored woman, have had in this country an education which has made me feel as I were in the situation of Ishmael, my hand against every man, and every man's hand against me." Then, she reversed the dominant notion that black women were backward and needed to change: "While there exists this brutal element in society which tramples upon the feeble and treads down the weak, I tell you that if there is any class of people who need to be lifted out of their airy nothings and selfishness, it is the white women of America." Now Louisa—in her middle thirties and without students to teach, a school to run, or an invalid to nurse—made a surprising decision. She would follow Harper onto the platform and speak for equal rights. She would fulfil her mother's old dream of becoming a public lecturer.

The *Standard* ran the announcement early in February: Louisa Jacobs had arrived in upstate New York and was lecturing in Herkimer County for the American Equal Rights Association. She was billed with Charles Lenox Remond, for thirty years committed to the movement—"the first black abolitionist lecturer and the most eloquent until the appearance of Frederick Douglass." Remond had spoken with her uncle in abolitionist meetings and conventions when Lulu was still a schoolgirl. Now he was back on the lecture circuit, working for the Equal Rights Association. Although never an easy man and in his late fifties suffering from poor health, Remond reported positively on the "conventions" he and Louisa were holding.

At Johnstown, where Elizabeth Cady Stanton had made their arrangements, they held a "capital" meeting with a friendly audience. But as the days passed, the weather turned against them. Severe snowstorms and bad roads were hindering their progress, and worse, they were feeling cut off from everyone and everything. "Both Miss Jacobs and myself suffer exceedingly for want of the current news," Remond writes. "I have lost for three weeks all run of the proceedings of Congress, and wonder sometimes if New York city is still extant!" Despite this sense of isolation, however, "the movement is, so far, I think, a success. . . . the word *fail* finds no place in our vocabulary." They were working their way through the Mohawk Valley, and a week later Remond reports encountering some hostility—people "harsh and malignant towards our race and their rights." Nonetheless, he and Louisa were making headway. "They can curse and call us by all manner of names on the sidewalks, upon the corner of the streets, and in the bar-rooms; but in the meeting we pay them off with both principle and compound interest."

After years as a reviled "nigger teacher" in Alexandria and Savannah, Louisa was not unaccustomed to insults. Still, it was hard to be cursed in public, and having Remond with her on those hostile sidewalks was reassuring. When, a decade earlier, her mother had dreamed that she might "do something" for the cause by lecturing in England, she had never imagined that one day her Lulu would be touring upstate New York for the movement, doing the same public work as her elders Frances Harper and Maria Stewart. (Celebrated as the first American-born woman to mount the public platform, Stewart, like Louisa, had spent the war years teaching black refugees.)

For Louisa, both the bleakness of the wind-swept countryside and the intimacy of the snug settlements brought back memories. In March and April, speaking in Syracuse, Rome, and Palmyra, she found herself quite literally walking in her uncle John's footsteps. Almost twenty years earlier—before he went west—he had addressed audiences there. Like her uncle then, and like movement lecturers now, Louisa and Remond depended on the hospitality of their supporters. More than a decade earlier when William C. Nell had spoken in Herkimer County, he had enjoyed a warm welcome from Zenas Brockett's family, with whom Louisa was then staying. Now it was she who was the traveling lecturer. Louisa took the time to walk the grounds of her old school building in Clinton, although Kellogg's Domestic Seminary had long since closed.

She also took advantage of her itinerary to renew old friendships with the family at Brockett's Bridge and to bask in their pride in her work. Then—like Nell before her—she collected their donation to the cause.

At Cohoes, famous for its cotton and knitting mills, Louisa and Remond were joined by John S.'s old fellow-lecturer Parker Pillsbury, Universalist minister Olympia Brown, and young Bessie Bisbee of Boston who, like Louisa, was new to the platform. Here the "factory girls" crowded the hall to hear Susan B. Anthony argue that women needed the vote. With it, they could put an end to their twelve-hour shifts and demand a ten-hour day—"to say nothing of the 8.—and also equal place & pay—the moment they should hold the ballot in their hands." Writing to Amy Post, Anthony enthused about these "capital" meetings and about her co-workers: "Louisa Jacobs—who was with us—promises first best.—She is everything proper & right in matter and manner—private and public—It is good to have two new helpers and *young* too—yes and good looking." The local press, which evidently did not recognize Louisa as African American, described her only as "a fair speaker . . . tall and quite dignified in appearance, a brunette, probably not thirty years of age."

At Syracuse, Stanton joined them and, with the Jacobses' old friend Samuel J. May in the chair, the audience formed its own Equal Rights Association. But as winter wore into spring, the speakers' heavy schedule—they were often addressing two meetings a day—wore them down. Pillsbury took to his bed, and Stanton's voice began to fail. At Orleans, the papers report, "in consequence of a severe cold, Mrs. Stanton was so hoarse that she was able to speak but a few minutes."

They needed better support. Privately, Anthony was complaining about their meager funds and about the half-hearted backing offered by the *Standard*—which, she protested, "does not officially plead the whole question of Suffrage as an inherent right of Woman as the Negro man." She explained to the wealthy philanthropist Gerrit Smith that the collections at their meetings "very nearly covered all the travelling & incidental expenses." But she had thought the abolitionists' Hovey Committee would donate $3,000 for salaries, and to her dismay, they covered only her wages and those of Parker Pillsbury. Anthony spells out the problem this created: the Equal Rights Association had hired Remond, Reverend Brown, and Stanton, "beside," she explains, "paying the travelling expenses of Miss Bisbee and Louisa Jacobs—daughter of Harriet Jacobs of the book '*Linda*' prepared by L. M. Child. . . . Can you not," she urges, "move some generous soul to put ten—yes twenty thousand dollars into our hands to push on our work of agitation? . . . If only we had the money we could carry the Convention up to equal suffrage without a shadow of a doubt."

Short of money or not, the Equal Rights Association speakers arguing the need to extend the franchise consistently addressed the situation of the freedwoman. In New York City, Olympia Brown asserted: "If there be any person who needs the ballot, it is the negro woman. Some say the woman is protected by father and husband, and therefore needs not the ballot. But it may be in the case of the negro woman the father may perchance be the very white man who drove her to her daily toil, and the only man whom she had known as husband has been of the white cast, who made her only the object of his lust."

Linking the freedwoman's need for the vote with her historic sexual exploitation in slavery resonated for Jacobs and Louisa. But Equal Rights speakers were also arguing that the freedwoman needed the vote not to protect her from the abuses of her white former master, but to protect her from legal marriage to her freed husband. The papers quote Anthony as saying, "Remember that in slavery the black woman has known nothing of the servitude of the marriage laws of the Northern States. She has lived so far in freedom. . . . But under the new dispensation, with legal marriage established among the black race as among the white race, it subjects the black woman to all the servitude and dependence which the white woman has hitherto suffered in the North." Making this argument, Anthony was attacking the freedman's character: "What kind of master do you give her? Not one educated to the sense of woman's equality that we have here, but one whose only idea of having any right of control over another person is that which has been taught to him by his master, which is the tyranny of the lash. Those men, suddenly raised to power, in all their ignorance, will become, as husbands, the greatest tyrants the world has yet seen." Stanton, too, was making black men a target, along with immigrants, in her stock speech "Reconstruction." "In view of the fact that the freedmen of the south and the millions of foreigners now crowding our western shores are all in the progress of events to be enfranchised, the best interests of the nation demand that we outweigh this incoming poverty ignorance & degradation, with the wealth education & refinement of the women of the republic."

Equal Rights audiences were being given mixed messages. At Utica, Remond, condemning the widespread sexual abuse of slave women by their masters, asserted that "whites have so diluted color that few can tell where the white man commences and the African leaves off." But in Rochester, the press reports that Stanton claimed the oppression of women in slavery was not as terrible as the oppression of women in marriage. "She said that the black women of the South under slavery were more free than they would be under the restraint of church marriages, liberated from chattel slavery and made slaves to their husbands. . . . even the poor slave woman understood, how much worse was the slavery of woman to man than that which they endured as chattels."

At Troy, Anthony went even further. Reversing the roles of master and slave, she identified the white master as the black slave woman's rescuer and the male black slave as her tyrant: "She has not the master to appeal to against her husband as when they were slaves. Where, then, unless the ballot is placed in her hands, is she likely to secure her privileges?"

Louisa spoke on the second day. Uncomfortable, she nervously read her remarks, asserting that the events of the war years "have a tendency to melt the American people into one great family" and stating that woman's presence at the ballot-box would not "increase public dissentions." On the contrary, she argued, "woman needs the ballot to enable her to work out her mission in life, to ensure her support and keep her from temptation." But regaining her seat, Louisa found her situation increasingly difficult. The problem was not only that she knew she was not a public speaker. The problem was also that she knew the freedwomen's condition. She had spent years working with refugees in Alexandria and Savannah—with women who had done everything they could to protect themselves, their children, and their men from their former masters. She well remembered these women coming asking to be married in church so that they could gain the security they believed free white women enjoyed. How could she share the platform with speakers who—in the name of asserting the rights of freedwomen—were attacking the freedmen? How could she face her audiences? Actually, how could she face any audiences? Perhaps the idea that she could fulfil her mother's dream of becoming a platform speaker was wrong-headed. If she were a public figure it might please her mother, but how could she live that life? Certainly she shared her mother's social conscience and her politics, but a life on the platform was not for her.

In the spring, the American Equal Rights Association held its annual meeting at the Church of the Pilgrims in New York City. Their effort to incorporate voting rights for women and African Americans into the new

New York State constitution had been a failure. Nevertheless, Anthony announced hopeful signs of progress: nine U.S. senators voted in favor of suffrage for women as well as for black men in the District of Columbia, and the legislatures of Kansas and Wisconsin had struck the words "white male" from their constitutions.

Throughout this meeting, the attacks on the freedman continued, despite the presence of black leaders like Remond, Robert and Harriet Purvis, and George T. Downing. When Downing pointedly asked "whether he had rightly understood that Mrs. Stanton and Mrs. Mott were opposed to the enfranchisement of the colored man, unless the ballot should also be accorded to women at the same time," Stanton side-stepped and renewed her assault on the freedman. "I would not trust him with all my rights; degraded, oppressed himself, he would be more despotic with the governing power than even our Saxon rulers are. I desire that we go into the kingdom together." Another white feminist, Frances D. Gage, exclaiming, "I shall speak for the slave woman at the South," recalled her refugee work. Gage asserted that "the men came to me and wanted to be married, because they said if they were married in the church, they could manage the women, and take care of their money. . . . But the women came to me and said, 'we don't want to be married in the church, because if we are our husbands will whip the children and whip us if they want to; they are no better than our old master.'" Sojourner Truth, the black evangelist and reformer, agreed: "if colored men get their rights, and not colored women theirs, you see the colored men will be masters over the women, and it will be just as bad as it was before. . . . Now colored men have the right to vote [in the District of Columbia]; and what I want is to have colored women have the right to vote."

But long-time white abolitionist Abby Kelley Foster protested that the condition of women and of former slaves were not analogous. In the South the freedman was "without wages, without family rights, whipped and beaten by thousands, given up to the most horrible outrages, without that protection which his value as property formerly gave him." Echoing Jacobs's letters from Savannah, with prescience she warned, "he is liable without farther guarantees, to be plunged into peonage." Is it not unjust, she asked, "to wish to postpone his security against present woes and future enslavement till woman shall obtain political rights?" As the meeting prepared to adjourn, Remond tried to retrieve at least minimal support for the extension of suffrage to black men. "Since this platform is the only place in this country where the whole question of human rights may now be considered, it seemed to me fitting that the right of the colored man to a vote, should have a place at the close of the meeting."

The discussion continued when the Equal Rights Association met the following year. The question was now tightly focused on the wording of the proposed Fourteenth Amendment—which, while naming the former slaves citizens, for the first time would insert the word "male" into the United States Constitution. Again Stanton and Anthony voiced their opposition to "the enfranchisement of another class of ignorant men to be lifted above their heads, to be their law-makers and Governors; to prescribe the moral code and political status of their daughters."

The debate climaxed in the spring of 1869. With full citizenship granted to blacks by the ratification of the Fourteenth Amendment, the Equal Rights Association met to discuss the proposed Fifteenth Amendment—which would award the suffrage to male freedmen—and to suggest a Sixteenth Amendment granting the vote to women. At this meeting, Stanton famously opposed extending the vote to black men and male immigrants while denying it to women: "Think of Patrick and Sambo and Hans and Yung Tung, who do not know the difference between a monarchy and a republic, who can not read the Declaration of Independence or Webster's spelling-book, making laws for Lucretia Mott, Ernestine L. Rose, and Anna E. Dickinson." And from the floor, Douglass famously responded: "When women, because they are women, are hunted down through the cities of New York and New Orleans; when they are dragged from their houses and hung upon lamp-posts; when their children are torn from their arms, and their brains dashed out upon the pavement; when they are objects of insult and outrage at every turn; when they are in danger of having their homes burnt down over their heads; when their children are not allowed to enter schools; then they will have an urgency to obtain the ballot equal to our own."

Frances Harper, one of the few black women present, joined the debate in the evening. Stanton notes that "when it was a question of race, she let the lesser question of sex go. But the white women all go for sex, letting race occupy a minor position. . . . If the nation could only handle one question, she would not have the black women put a single straw in the way, if only the men of the race could obtain what they wanted."

Harper would continue to try to work with the white feminists, but Louisa Jacobs's 1867 speaking tour for equal rights marked the last time either mother or daughter would play a public role on behalf of social change in the United States. On the murderous streets of Savannah, they had learned that the struggle for land was lost. On the angry lecture platforms in the North, they discovered that the effort to mount a struggle for equal rights was also finished—at least for the present.

13

No Cloudless Happiness

~❦~

There is no [cloudless happiness] in this life. If we only hold and
regulate the sunshine that lies within our reach we shall not be
deeply scarred by the cloud that will sometimes mar its brightness.
—Louisa Jacobs to [Cornelia] Downing, May 16, 1870

Instead of attending the Equal Rights Association meeting in New
York, in the spring of 1867, Harriet Jacobs went south to Edenton.
There she found everything changed—and not all for the better. The
freed people had planted and harvested, but were cheated out of their
crops by their contract masters; Edenton had opened a school, but the
children out on the plantations lived too far away to attend; the family
no longer owned Grandmother's house, but Ann Johnson Ramsey, Uncle
Mark's widow, was living next door with her daughter. In late April,
Jacobs wrote to Ednah Dow Cheney of the New England Freedmen's Aid
Society. "I am sitting," Jacobs began, "under the old roof twelve feet
from the spot where I suffered all the crushing weight of slavery." Then,
she was overcome by memories: "thank God the bitter cup is drained of
its last dreg. there is no more need of hiding places to conceal slave
Mothers. yet it was little to purchase the blessings of freedom. I could
have worn this poor life out there to save my Children from the misery
and degradation of Slavery." She had not thought she would feel such a
strong attachment to the old home. But now, sitting quietly, she found
herself thinking of "those I loved of their hard struggle in life—their
unfaltering love and devotion toward myself and Children. I love to sit
here and think of them. they have made the few sunny spots in that dark
sacred to me." Overwhelmed by bursts of feeling she had not expected,
she struggled for language: "the change is so great I can hardly take it all
in." It was difficult to feel any confidence in the new regime. Even in the

midst of "all these new born blessings, the old dark cloud comes over me, and I find it hard to have faith in rebels."

Jacobs had spent time out on the plantations in Virginia and Georgia, and now in Edenton, she went into the country, "distributing seed and trying to teach the women to make Yankee gardens" that could produce food from spring until late fall. Her heart hungry for Grandmother, she "hunted up all the old people, done what I could for them. I love to work for these old people. many of them I have known from Childhood." In this deeply personal letter, as in her earlier businesslike letters to the freedmen's aid societies, she reports on the condition of the people. In Edenton, too, they are being "cheated out of their crop." Here, too, "Negro suffrage is making a stir in this place. the rebels are striving to make these people feel they are their true friends." And as always, she reports on the schools. One has been organized in Edenton, and the freed people out on the plantations are eager to establish more. The churches are crowded. "the Whites say the Niggers sung and prayed until they got their freedom, and they are not satisfied. now they are singing and praying for judjment. . . . I never saw such a state of excitement the Churches have been open night and day." Then, ironically, "these people have time to think of their souls, now they are not compelled to think for the Negro."

Jacobs had come back to see whether she could still live in her old home, but this visit convinced her that she could not. Six months later her friend Julia Wilbur, now in Washington, noted, "This evening Mrs. Jacobs came to stay all night, good visit with her. Her Georgia experiences interesting. Also her visit to her old home in Edenton. Has posession of her Grandmother's property, has no desire to make her home there."

Jacobs could not go home again. She had abandoned her hopes for land and homes for her people in the South. She had given up on the possibility of an antiracist movement for equality in the North. Still, she thought, she could perhaps try "to be useful" to the freed people of Savannah. Just before Christmas in 1867, Frederick W. Chesson, writing in London, bore witness to her effort in his diary. Chesson notes, "Mrs Jacobs, the sister of my old friend John S. Jacobs, and heroine, as well as the writer, of 'the Deeper Wrong' or 'Linda' called. Both she and her daughter have come to England in connection with the Freedmen's movement."

Neither the New England Freedmen's Aid Society nor any of the Quaker groups Jacobs worked with during the war had sent her across the Atlantic. Instead, she had withdrawn all of her savings to undertake this mission for the Savannah freedmen. Almost two years earlier, she had thought she would fill the position of matron in the old folks' home being planned, and that her daughter would have charge of the orphan asylum to be attached, but the project had never gotten off the ground. Nevertheless, the community desperately needed the facility. Committed to making it a reality, Harriet and Louisa had come to England to raise the necessary money.

In her middle fifties, Jacobs must have realized that this would be her final trip abroad. Now—as years earlier, when she had tried to convince Harriet Beecher Stowe to include Lulu among her traveling party—she was eager for her daughter to experience the sense of liberation she had felt in England, when she had "laid my head on my pillow, for the first time, with the delightful consciousness of pure, unadulterated freedom" [ILSG p. 183].

She may have had another personal item on her agenda: to reconnect with her brother John S., now shipping out of London as a seaman. They had not seen each other for years, although early in the war, the Union blockade had forced his ship into New York port for three days. He had married an Englishwoman, and now had a son named for two of their uncles: heroic Joseph—lost to the family—and Mark Ramsey, whom she had sketched as the nurturing "Uncle Phillip" of *Incidents*. Jacobs and Louisa were surely eager to see John S., to meet his British wife Elleanor and her two older children William and Elleanor, and to hug little Joseph Ramsey Jacobs, now a toddler. But their hopes were dashed by the fortunes of a seaman's life. In the same diary entry announcing the appearance of Jacobs and Louisa in London, Chesson noted, "her brother is in India—has been gone twelve months and is not expected to return before next summer."

Without John S. to greet them, Jacobs and Louisa spent time between Christmas and New Year's with the Chessons, whom they fascinated with their stories. During the ten years since they had seen each other, the United States had fought its Civil War, freed its slaves, made them citizens, and extended the franchise to the freedmen. In the process, Jacobs and Louisa had created schools, hospitals, and institutions for the freed people. Jacobs told about providing health care for the black refugees in Washington, about work in Alexandria, and about Georgia—where, Chesson comments, she reported the people were "making great progress." She also spoke of her recent visit to Edenton, where she found "positions were now reversed." Ironically, as she left, her master's daughter had asked her for "something to remember her by," and her master's son "begged her to convey a letter to Mr. Grinnell's partner, asking for a situation!"

But delighted as she was to catch up with her old friends, Jacobs needed to focus on the primary purpose of her visit: raising money for black Savannah. To do this, she required support. Now—unlike ten years ago—she did not need letters of introduction from Boston abolitionists like Maria Weston Chapman. This time, she came as the author of the widely reviewed *Deeper Wrong; or Incidents in the Life of a Slave Girl*, and as the writer of a series of pieces on the Reconstruction South that had appeared in *The Freed-Man*, the organ of the British and Foreign Freed-Men's Aid Society.

Although Jacobs was able to reconnect with the Chessons, she found the old London Emancipation Society circle broken. Many of the abolitionists were less interested in the American freed people than in the aftermath of the Morant Bay affair. In October 1865, at St. Thomas-in-the-East, Morant Bay, Jamaica, 400 black settlers had protested a decision of local magistrates. When the militia intervened, the people attacked the courthouse, fifteen magistrates were killed, and there was rioting. Governor Edward John Eyre then declared martial law, and a month of bloody reprisals began. When it was over, 439 black people had been executed, 600 had been flogged, more than 1,000 homes of suspected rioters had been burned, and the primary spokesman for the black peasants in the House of Assembly, had been put to death. Appalled, the London activists protested against the government's violence and sent an agent to Jamaica to investigate. His report condemned the governor, and the Emancipation Society pushed for legal proceedings against Eyre, with Jacobs's friend Chesson protesting that "the old slave-planting interest" was conspiring "to deprive the blacks of the protection of the law; to exclude them from the franchise; to supersede their labour by the importation of coolies partly at their expense; and gradually to prepare the way for the restoration of slavery."

But British public opinion was moving in the opposite direction. The black violence at Morant Bay was strengthening racist stereotypes, and the *London Times, Standard, Morning Herald*, and *Daily Telegraph* all judged that the riots demonstrated the unfitness of black people for freedom. In the wake of Morant Bay, Sarah Parker Remond (the sister of

Louisa's Equal Rights colleague) felt a chill in Britain's racial climate. She had lived comfortably in England for most of the past decade, but now found planter interests becoming dominant. Since the Civil War, she reported, "Southern Confederates and their natural allies, those former West Indian planters, have united together to endeavour to neutralise the interest felt for the oppressed negroes, and to hold them up to scorn and contempt of the civilised world."

Jacobs's old pastor J. Sella Martin agreed. After the war, he and his wife Sarah had returned to England, where he was working as an agent of the American Missionary Association. But raising money for the southern freedmen was becoming harder and harder. Now about to leave England, he felt that the country that had welcomed him in 1861 had, seven years later, turned decidedly racist. When back in America, he announced, he would have to report "that the name of England was anti-slavery, but that rich, cultivated, aristocratic, fashionable England was pro-slavery."

Also leaving were William and Ellen Craft—who with their four children and Ellen's mother had made their Hammersmith home a center for expatriated African Americans. (Ellen's effort to find her mother—typical of the efforts of thousands of displaced freed people—was unlike many in that it had ended happily. In the wake of Sherman's march through Georgia, Ellen tried to locate her. When the Union commander at Macon sent news that Marie was living nearby, she sent passage money, and in 1865 mother and daughter were reunited in London.) Through the years, Ellen had been active in the antislavery movement, raising money for the freedmen, working in the ladies' auxiliary of the British and Foreign Freedmen's Aid Society, and supporting a girls' school in Sierra Leone. William had spent more than four years in Africa, where he attempted to establish a school and a mercantile business in Whydah, Dahomey. But he had returned to London in debt, and late in 1867, the family had to sell their home to pay their creditors. When Jacobs arrived in England, the Crafts were making plans to return to the States.

Not only were Jacobs's old friends leaving, the organizations she had come to enlist in support of her mission were disbanding. After American emancipation was proclaimed, the London Freedmen's Aid Society, which had been committed to slavery's abolition, had reorganized to aid American freedmen, and two years later, a national group formed to coordinate the work of the forty or fifty organizations that followed their lead. In 1866 this had became the National Freedmen's Aid Union. But only months after Jacobs's arrival the organization, explaining that it had never been intended as permanent, announced it was dissolving. Despite Jacobs's prominence as an author and reporter-activist, and despite her connections with the old abolitionist circles, she would have to do some creative fund-raising if she was to return with the money she needed.

Early in March, the *Anti-Slavery Reporter* published a notice urging its readers to make a "generous response" to the appeal "made by a well-known victim of Slavery, Linda Brent, now Harriet Jacob, whose narrative, entitled 'Linda,' every one should read." Perhaps to spark the recognition of her British readers by referring to her pseudonym, Jacobs signed this appeal with a conglomerate name, "Linda Jacobs." Most of the people she had successfully solicited to support her—those who publicized their willingness to collect the funds she was requesting—were doubtless familiar to the readers of the *Reporter*. Heading the list was Stafford Allen, who had agreed to become the honorary secretary of her fund-raising effort. A Quaker pharmacutical manufacturer, Allen had from its beginnings been a prominent member of the British and Foreign Anti-Slavery Society along with the forerunners Wilberforce, Sturge, and Clarkson. Also endorsing her effort was the Quaker chemist Robert Alsop. He was the active secretary of the Stoke Newington Committee for the management of the Yearly Meeting's Negro and Aborigines Fund, which supported schools in Jamaica, Antigua, Berbice, and Monrovia. Perhaps the only surprising name among her endorsers is that of a woman, Clementia Taylor, the wife of the radical M.P. Peter Taylor. Taylor, a supporter of Mazzini and the Young Italian Party, was treasurer of the London Emancipation Society, and during America's Civil War, was the first M.P. to associate himself with the federal party. More recently, he had acted as treasurer of the Jamaica Committee in the prosecution of Governor Eyre.

In her published appeal, Jacobs paints a picture of Savannah's need. "I know of the degradation of Slavery—the blight it leaves; and, thus knowing, feel how strong the necessity is of throwing around the young, who, through God's mercy, have come out of it, the most salutary influences." Despite this need, she writes, the Freedmen's Bureau has made no arrangements for orphans except that they be apprenticed, and "it not infrequently happens that the apprenticeship is to the former master. As the spirit of Slavery is not exorcised yet, the child, in many instances, is cruelly treated." Nor is there any provision for the old people. "Infirm, penniless, homeless, they wander about dependent on charity for bread and shelter." Jacobs then outlines the project. The Savannah "Society for the relief of freed orphans and aged freedmen" is raising money to buy a fifteen-acre plot on which the old people, and the children after school, could raise vegetables, fruit, and chickens to supply their needs and to sell at the market. Acknowledging the continued help of the British people since Emancipation, she thanks her readers, concluding, "It is a noble evidence of their joy at the downfall of American Slavery and the advancement of human rights. . . . Every mite will tell in the balance."

The appearance of Clementia Taylor's name endorsing Jacobs's appeal suggests that by March, Jacobs had been able to make at least one new friend in London. A month later, Kate Amberley—after noting in her journal that her parents-in-law Lady and Lord John Russell paid a call in the morning—wrote: "At 5 Mrs. Jacobs (Linda) comes to see me; she is the slave whose book I have got; she is a mulatto, a clever looking respectable woman; she wants money for a home for old negroes in Savannah Georgia, and also to sell her books." Did Jacobs feel that she was back where she had been when her narrative first was published and she had carried copies to Philadelphia, hoping that Mary Rebecca Darby Smith could introduce her to potential patrons who might buy it? Now again she was trying to sell her book to create a circle of supporters for her people's cause. But Kate Amberley's drawing room was a far cry from Smith's Philadelphia parlor. Now her people were free, and she was selling her book to raise the money they needed to care for the most vulnerable members of the community.

Kate Amberley demonstrated her support a few days later, when she invited Lady Frederick Cavendish to her home to meet Jacobs. Sandwiched among the miscellany in her diary—between mention of "a fine fish" her husband hooked but could not land and notes on a dinner conversation with Lord Clarendon concerning his interview with the Pope— is Lady Cavendish's account of this visit. Kate Amberley "had a quondam slave to trot out: a poor, respectable-looking mulatto woman, with a handsome, ladylike *white* daughter, and a book with the heart-breaking story of her life." Lady Cavendish did not mention whether she bought a copy of the book, but she certainly heard Jacobs's message. After meeting Harriet and Louisa Jacobs, she felt impelled to write, "Such things to hear about make one go on one's knees, and thank the Mighty Hand that has scorched up for ever, by means of that tremendous war, the iniquity of generations."

Still, it was not the beneficence of sympathetic aristocratic women, but the last gasp of organized philanthropy that finally answered Jacobs's plea. Early in August, the general committee of the National Freedmen's Aid Union of Great Britain and Ireland called a meeting with, the secretary recorded, "Mrs. Jacobs being present part of the time." Doubtless she had come along with Stafford Allen, a committee member, to plead the cause of the Savannah community. Although not recorded in their minutes, before taking up the question of the dissolution of their organization, the group apparently discussed the situation of the Savannah freedpeople. A month later, the Committee of the Representatives of the New York Yearly Meeting of Friends upon the Condition and Wants of the Freedmen received word that the National Freed-Men's Aid Union had voted to send one hundred pounds sterling to the committee "for use in the benevolent objects of Harriet Jacobs, and especially in the erection of a proposed asylum in Savannah, Georgia, for destitute colored widows or orphans."

Jacobs had succeeded in her mission, and it was time to go home. On her return, she learned that her people's lives had become even more precarious than when she had left eight months earlier. The Klan was riding and burning. In the same *Report* recording the receipt of the money from England, the New York Quakers announced that they have heard from Jacobs, and "On account of the unsettled state of affairs at the South, she did not deem it advisable to commence building the asylum at present."

The Savannah orphans would not have their home—and now Jacobs, too, needed to find a place to live. As the nation turned its back on the freed people, Jacobs and Louisa retreated to Boston, where they had some roots in the community. There, they learned that the elite white women who had sponsored their work in the South, had moved on to other things. In the view of this privileged group, although the war and Reconstruction had "incited the activity of women to a new phase of development, . . . the imperative demand for this activity ceased after peace was restored." Nonetheless, feeling that they wanted to remain "united by some means, and to continue such educational and social relations as would fit the women of a city," early in 1868 they founded the New England Women's Club. Among them were were reformers Ednah Dow Cheney, Julia Ward Howe, Abby W. May, and Jacobs's friend and former employer Cornelia Grinnell Willis, now living in Boston. The Club inaugurated their organization by sponsoring a public assembly, and in November they held their first meeting in their new rooms at 3 Tremont

Place. Quickly, they realized that they needed a clerk to keep track of the use of the bedrooms, and of attendance at the lunches, lectures, discussions, and the Club Tea, the social highlight of the week. The woman they hired—for "$7.00 a week, exclusive of her room," was Harriet Jacobs.

During the year that Jacobs worked for the New England Women's Club, the group concerned itself with a wide range of social reforms: "without aiming at the impossible, without repeating at every step those grandiose phrases, the race and the sex, we are yet taking into grave and affectionate consideration the needs of both, and endeavoring to answer them. . . . If we can mediate between the opposed classes of society, and help them to understand each other . . . we shall perform a task which will go far to justify our existence." Organizing themselves into a series of committees and subcommittees, they created an employment agency for women seeking work "of a higher grade than common house-service," explored the needs of local mothers and children, and investigated "the condition of needle-women in Boston." On some Mondays, the Club sponsored lectures by New England's brightest stars, including the young author Henry James (speaking on women), the sage Ralph Waldo Emerson, and writer and reformer Thomas Wentworth Higginson (Emily Dickinson's patron), as well as a report by Cheney on her recent tour of "schools for the education of the colored people" in the South.

In the fall, Jacobs left her job with the Club, but for her the highlight of the lecture season must have come in November, when the Club sponsored a talk by William Craft. Then she could enjoy a reunion with Ellen Craft and her family, just returned to America. Club minutes record that the former fugitive slave "gave an interesting account of Dahomey and his visit there." Following his talk, Cheney's Committee on Art and Literature invited "Mrs and Miss Jacobs and Mrs Crafts to attend the Club meetings of the season."

Jacobs was able to enjoy these lectures because, although no longer working for the Club, she had not left the Boston area. Some Club members—including L. Maria Child's friend Louisa Loring, feminist Abby May, and Annie Shaw, the widowed bride of Robert Gould Shaw of the martyred Massachusetts 54th—had become involved with a shelter for freedwomen and their children located in Cambridgeport. The Howard Industrial School was founded "to provide a temporary home, food, clothing, instruction, and advice, and to secure permanent places for colored women and children." In 1868, among its 463 new students were twenty-eight refugees from Alexandria. The following year, Harriet Jacobs, too, emigrated to Cambridge.

She knew she would find a welcoming community. In the 1840s, when Boston's militant blacks had boycotted the city's segregated schools, a number of African American families had moved to nearby Cambridge. During the war, Jacobs had convinced Virginia Lawton, the daughter of old friends, to join her and Louisa in Alexandria in establishing the Jacobs School. Now Virginia and her sister Mariana (who had also gone south) were back in the family's crowded old gable-roofed house at 46 Market Street with their widowed mother and their seven brothers and sisters. Even those who were not already old friends would prove welcoming. Local leaders like John J. Fatal, Patrick H. and John T. Raymond, and Joshua Bowen Smith knew Jacobs's longtime friend William C. Nell, and they may still have remembered her brother from his Boston days. And William Wells Brown, John Milton Clarke, and Lunsford Lane—all of whom, like Jacobs, had written and published their slave narratives—now made Cambridge their home.

The war had changed the town. In 1865, Harvard University (which had once bowed to racist student protests and dismissed Martin R. Delany, Isaac H. Snowden, and Daniel Laing Jr. from the Medical School) had admitted an African American student, Richard T. Greener. Five years later, Greener was awarded the first Bowdoin Prize for the best English dissertation, and the *Press* reports that celebrating commencement that year "the collation furnished by the city at dedication day" was provided by J. Milton Clarke, Cambridge's first black councilman.

Although African Americans accounted for only 12 percent of the city's residents—half the number of its foreign immigrants—Jacobs found Cambridge alive to the national struggle over the freed people's rights. In spring, the *Press* announced that the Transcendentalist educator Elizabeth Peabody and General Samuel C. Armstrong, founder of Hampton Institute, would address a meeting "for the benefit of the Cambridge Freedmen's Aid Society." A month later, 200 citizens formed a procession on Harvard Street and, led by Clary's Cornet Band, marched behind John J. Fatal through the port into Boston to join the huge celebration marking the passage of the Fifteenth Amendment. Both the black community and their white supporters furnished local audiences for touring performers and speakers. Each spring, Fisk University's famed Jubilee singers presented a concert of traditional melodies—evenings of poignant nostalgia for Jacobs, for whom the music pricked memories of Savannah, Alexandria, and long ago Edenton.

Late in 1871, Harriet Beecher Stowe came to Cambridge to visit her sister Mary Safford. Decades earlier, Mary and her husband Aaron had introduced Stowe to the Clarke brothers, and local belief was that Stowe had used Lewis Clarke as a model for the character of George Harris in *Uncle Tom's Cabin*. Jacobs had not forgotten the resentment she had felt when Stowe had proposed incorporating her life into her writings. But Jacobs had successfully told her own story instead, and now (probably through the good offices of the Saffords), she met Stowe face to face. As a gesture of reconciliation—perhaps in acknowledgment of her earlier high-handedness—Stowe inscribed a copy of *Uncle Tom's Cabin* to Jacobs as a Christmas present. It was a gift Jacobs's family would cherish for a century.

Life in Cambridge was not, however, without its problems. In the summer, members of the elite black paramilitary Shaw Guards were forcibly removed from a horsecar headed for Boston. (When the men asserted that they had objected to being Jim Crowed on a public conveyance, the police backed the driver, who claimed that he had refused them transportation because the car had been privately hired.)

Still, several of the city's churches sustained their long history of reform activity. The racially integrated Second Evangelical Congregational, called the "abolition church," had been ministered in the 1840s by Joseph C. Lovejoy, who had published the narrative of Lewis and Milton Clarke. (Reverend Lovejoy was the brother of the abolitionist martyr Elijah Lovejoy, murdered while defending his press from pro-slavery rioters in Alton, Illinois.) When after the Civil War the Second Evangelical disbanded, many of its members united with members of the Pilgrim Church to form Stearns Chapel Congregational, later reorganized as the Pilgrim Congregational Church. Then in 1873, the Bethel African Methodist Episcopal Church opened its doors.

Cambridge had a history of feminist activism. In April 1870, the *Press* covered the Middlesex County Woman Suffrage Convention, reporting that Cambridge's mayor announced himself "ready to concede the elective franchise to all persons of whatever race, color, or sex." A local leader "thought with Sojourner Truth, that if one woman could capsize the world by the eating of an apple, the women of America interested in woman suffrage could set it right side up." At the new year, a group of women meeting in Buckley's Hall organized themselves into the

Cambridge Woman Suffrage Association, and in East Cambridge, other women followed their lead. On July 4, the Massachusetts Woman Suffrage Association filled the grove at Framingham as the Anti-Slavery Society used to do, with speeches by Garrison and the others—but despite the reference to Sojourner Truth, it is not clear whether Jacobs, or any women of color, participated in these events.

In the 1872 election, black Cambridge organized to make its political presence felt. Smith, Fatal, and Clarke formed a "Grant Club" of African American voters, and the *Press* reports that when a "colored convention" was announced for Boston's Faneuil Hall, "the Cambridge delegation was full and enthusiastic. The colored people are all alive in this campaign, and furnish some of the best speakers." Although a "procession of colored persons" was stoned on Norfolk Street, Raymond campaigned for Ulysses S. Grant and vice-presidential candidate Henry Wilson by flying a flag bearing their names and providing his neighbors with a fireworks display and band music, and seventy-five members of the Cambridge Colored Grant and Wilson Club marched in the Grand Torchlight Procession in Boston. In local politics, J. Milton Clarke (who had succeeded his patron Aaron Safford) was reelected as councilman in Ward 2.

While Cambridge's activist political climate was important in Jacobs's decision to move, the city's economic growth was at least equally significant. During the war, the Boston Rolling Mill had opened at the end of Broad Canal, and in 1866, trains began running into Cambridgeport. Industries followed, bringing new jobs, and the *Press* reported that "'To let' is a sign seen less in Cambridge than in any other city around Boston." In Cambridge, Jacobs saw an opportunity to make a living as the landlady of her own boardinghouse.

The modest building she rented on Trowbridge Street was Harriet Jacobs's first real home since she had fled to Boston with Louisa a quarter century before. Then, their attempt at establishing themselves had ended with the death of Mary Stace Willis in the spring of 1845. Ten years later, newly freed, she had written, "The dream of my life is not yet realized. I do not sit with my children in a home of my own. I still long for a hearthstone of my own, however humble" [ILSG p. 201]. Now Jacobs resurrected her goal. After a quarter century, she could perhaps partially fulfil her dream, at least for her precious daughter.

Her pleasant two-storied frame house was set well back from the street behind a simple cast iron fence. Its front boasted a pediment, a projecting gable, and a comfortable porch where her boarders could relax after dinner. In the city directory, Jacobs advertised that her new enterprise was located at Trowbridge near Main, and she listed her boardinghouse in the *Harvard Directory* as ready for students and faculty.

In late June, the census taker who came to her door recorded that Jacobs was "keeping house" at 10 Trowbridge, writing that at that address were Louisa (listed as having "no occupation"), a staff of three servants (one an Irish immigrant, another the "mulatto" Sarah Iredell, doubtless from Edenton), and Joseph Pierce, an eight-year-old "mulatto" boy from Georgia. The other residents included Cornelia Willis and her family—in Cambridge probably because Grinnell, her oldest, was a student at Harvard.

Prominent members of the faculty were also Jacobs's boarders. Geologist Raphael Pumpelly, at Harvard after years in the Far East, had recently published his *Geological Researches in China, Mongolia and Japan* and was hard at work on the state geological survey of Missouri. Perhaps even better known was Christopher Langdell, originator of the "case" system of legal study and now Dean of the Law School, who had recently produced *Selection of Cases on the Law of Contracts*. They were joined by their colleague Chauncy Wright, "computer and mathematician." In 1873, when Jacobs and Louisa moved into a larger, more imposing house at 127 Mount Auburn, Professor Langdell and Eliza followed them, and Professor Adams Sherman Hill, back from Europe and newly appointed Professor of Rhetoric, joined the circle.

Settling into her new Mount Auburn Street home, with its Greek Revival pillars, its new mansard roof, and its welcoming entrance hall featuring a graceful mahogany banister curving up three flights, Jacobs felt satisfaction. She was also pleased to meet Mary Walker, who lived at the other end of the block. The two women shared both their North Carolina origins and their histories as slave mothers. Walker, "a woman of refinement and considerable beauty," had escaped from slavery in 1850 while accompanying her young mistresses on a visit from Raleigh to Philadelphia. For the next decade, she had tried to rescue her children. (Writing on her behalf, a Cambridge-based white patron had pleaded with her Raleigh owner to name his price: "Her heart is slowly breaking. She thinks of nothing but her children. . . . Her mother-heart yearns unspeakably after them and her eyes fail with looking towards the South, over the dreary interval which separates them from her.") But it was no use. Walker's master remained obdurate, and when the war broke out, she followed the Union Army south, searching for her son and daughter. Finally, Agnes and Briant were located in Raleigh and joined their mother in Cambridge.

Jacobs was known to Boston's privileged white women because of her book, her relief work in the South, and more recently, her job with the New England Women's Club. It is interesting to speculate about her new relationships with her academic boarders and their friends. Chauncy Wright lived alternate years at Jacobs's boarding house and at Walker's. His biographer writes that "on the night before he died, he was perfectly well, and stood in the door-way talking cheerfully and kindly with his land-lady (the daughter of Mary Walker), and her colored friend, Mrs. Jacobs, with whom he had boarded." When the stricken man was found next morning, his close friend Henry James was called to his side. We do not know whether Jacobs was reading James (whose first books were just appearing), or whether James had read Jacobs. But this incident makes clear that it was not a lack of acquaintance, but a conscious choice, that prompted James to ignore women like Jacobs and Walker in his writing. A few years later, Jacobs's editor L. Maria Child criticized him for this decision: " I do not deny that the pictures are well sketched; but I despise the subjects. . . . The writer who sketches shoddy fashionables wastes his talents."

Jacobs, settling into her comfortable new home and hungry for her own people, looked down the block with yearning. Mary Walker's daughter and son-in-law were living with her, and her son, his Irish wife, and their two little boys were in the neighborhood. But Harriet Jacobs found comfort knowing that she, too, had some family nearby. Her half-brother Elijah had come to live in New Bedford, not too far off. Back in Edenton, Jacobs and John S. may not have known Elijah well, but certainly they had known of him. Because his mother Theresa was a free woman, young Elijah Knox (named for his father, with the last name of his master) was born free. Jacobs's freedom-starved father finally had had a child who was not a slave. Little Elijah had been apprenticed at age eight under his mother's surname, Artis, to Robert Warren of Hertford County. (North Carolina law mandated that the courts of pleas and quarter sessions bind "all base born children of color, and all the children of free negroes and mulattoes where the parents with whom such children may live, do or shall not habitually employ his or her time in some honest, industrious occuption.") When young Elijah completed his apprenticeship on June

5, 1846, a dozen years later, the Hertford county court certified him a free man under his father's surname Knox. He was described as "a brownish yellow man about twenty two years old . . . five feet seven inches and one fourth high . . . [with] a very notable scarr on the thick part of his right leg (below the knee) occasioned by the bite of a dog; also a notable scarr on the right hip."

His precious free certificate in his hand, Elijah had struck out for nearby Sutton's Creek district in Perquimans County, where Isaac Douglas, a free man of color, had established a farm. The young carpenter Elijah Knox became his boarder and in time, courted his daughter Emily Elizabeth. Soon Elijah Nox "of color" was listed on Sutton Creek District tax rolls as a married man, the father of two. Then in 1850, Emily Elizabeth's cousin was for some reason exiled from the state of North Carolina and went north. By the end of the war Elijah, now a widower, had followed with his children. In New Bedford, Massachusetts, he remarried and began to put down deep roots.

Given the consistent support New Bedford activists had provided for Jacobs's relief work in Alexandria, it seems possible that during the war years, she and Elijah's exiled cousin—and perhaps even that she and Elijah, if he was already in Massachusetts—might have found each other. But the names her half brother and his new wife chose for their children suggest that Jacobs and Elijah may have been reunited somewhat later. When in 1871 his new wife gave birth to her first son, the baby was named Elijah Howland for his father and perhaps for his father's employer. In 1875, however, a second son was born, and family tradition holds that little William Jacob received his middle name in honor of his aunt Harriet and his uncle John S., who were using Jacobs, the name that their father had been denied.

In Cambridge Jacobs's family, like millions of other African American families broken in slavery, was partially reunited in freedom. Still, her adored uncle Joseph was gone, and the beloved son she had named for him was perhaps also lost. When after the war, young Joseph had failed to appear, Jacobs had finally taken her worries to L. Maria Child. Joseph, she explained, had gone west to the California gold fields, then on to the gold rush in Australia with his uncle, and for a time had reported "encouragingly" on his progress. Then there was silence. She had written urging him not to wait until he struck it rich but to come home, and in response, received a letter written in a strange hand. It claimed that Joseph had been sick with fever and still could not hold a pen to write, but that he did want to return. Could she send money for his passage to his friend in Melbourne? Somehow, Jacobs could. She sent $400 in gold, then waited. When Joseph did not come, she finally turned to Child for help, asking her former editor to try to reach someone in Melbourne. Child had written asking the city's clergymen to read Jacobs's appeal from their pulpits, but the search came to nothing. Now, settled with Lulu in their Cambridge home, Jacobs may have begun to feel that her Joseph might never return. Perhaps that thought was behind her decision to make the eight-year-old Georgia-born "mulatto" boy Joseph Pierce a member of her household.

Still yearning to gather family around her, Jacobs apparently wrote to London, urging John S. to come home. He must have found her appeals persuasive, for after twenty years abroad, he returned to America to live. At first, he bunked with the Lawtons in their crowded Market Street house. He soon was joined by his English wife and her children from an earlier marriage, thirteen-year-old William R. and twelve-year-old Elleanor, and by his own little Joseph Ramsey. By the end of 1873, John S. and his family were established in their own quarters in the frame row house at 11 Brewer.

Jacobs's relief was physical. She saw her brother's little Joe as the family's future, and watching him, felt the pain of loss—where was her son? But she also experienced deep pleasure. For a brief few months, Harriet Jacobs lived a version of the life she had fantasized for decades: she was in her own home with her daughter, and her beloved brother and his boisterous children were close by. It was the achievement of a lifelong dream. She recalled the surge of feeling when, years earlier, John S. had come to find her in New York City, and she remembered what she had written: "There are no bonds so strong as those which are formed by suffering together" [ILSG p. 170].

Years earlier, when Jacobs had first learned of John S.'s marriage to an English woman, she had felt unsure. Yet now she worked to knit her rainbow family together—helped her brother find a house and furnish it, helped her sister-in-law fill her closets with linens and her kitchen shelves with pots and pans. Certainly she baked Grandmother's snowball cake for her young niece and nephews. If she kept on keeping on, they might actually become a family. But then—unexpectedly—John sickened and died.

Grief smothered her. It was Louisa, and not her broken mother, who sent the terrible news to William Lloyd Garrison. With diffidence, Louisa addressed the great abolitionist, writing that to her, he is "a grateful memory," and confiding that to her dead uncle he was "revered . . . as the forerunner, the awakening power of freedom to the colored race." Telling Garrison that John S., a man who "did what he could for the same cause, . . . spoke of you in his last hours," she names her request. It would be "a great gratification to my mother and self if you could come to his funeral tomorrow (Sunday) at one o'clock." Then she respectfully added, in accordance with racial etiquette: "Perhaps I am asking too much."

By inviting Garrison to the funeral, Jacobs and her daughter guaranteed that it would be a political event commemorating John S. as a fighter for his people. A week later, Garrison recalled the gathering: "Last Sunday I attended the obsequies of one branded and held as a chattel slave from his birth, yet made in the divine image,—who, many years ago, asserted his God-given right to be free, by a successful escape to the North, where he remained till after the passage of the Fugitive Slave Law in 1850 when, knowing that there was no longer any safety for him on our soil, he took refuge under the British flag, and remained in exile until the jubilee trump was blown,—in every situation leading an upright life, exhibiting a manly spirit, and commanding the respect of all who knew him."

While it is clear that Jacobs and Louisa felt it important that John S. be remembered for his contributions to the freedom struggle, many other things about his brief time in Cambridge are unclear. Certainly the relationships between his wife and children, and his sister and niece remain obscure. We know that when John S. was buried at Mount Auburn cemetery, he was laid in ground belonging to the family of Mary Walker, Jacobs's neighbor and friend. (In the nineteenth century, burial in a friend's plot was not unusual in the event of sudden death.) And we know that two years later, Louisa bought a plot at Mount Auburn and had him reburied. She purchased land with spaces for four graves, intended, perhaps, not only for her uncle, but also for her mother, for her lost brother, and for herself. We also know that although the death certificate lists John S. as a married man and a father, the stone erected over his grave reads "Brother." All of the available evidence about his funeral, his burial, his reburial, and his monument suggests that it was Jacobs and Louisa—and not his wife—who buried and commemorated John S. This conclusion is supported by the fact that today, while both Louisa and

Harriet Jacobs lie near him, the fourth space in their plot remains empty. John S.'s widow Elleanor, who lived on until 1903, is not buried at Mount Auburn, but in an adjacent cemetery.

To this, we can add two additional bits of information. First, in the 1880 census—the first federal census in which Elleanor and her children appear—she and all three of her children, including Joseph Ramsey, are listed as "white." This designation could, of course, have been the unquestioning judgment of the census taker, and not the result of any specific inquiry. Second, in 1907, when Louisa wrote her will, she named among her heirs the children of her half-uncle Elijah, but she mentioned none of the children of her beloved uncle John S. This conspicuous omission suggests a rift between Louisa and her uncle's English wife. It is not difficult to hypothesize that, when becoming widowed soon after her arrival in Cambridge, Elleanor decided that American racism was a burden she would not willingly inflict on her children—and that she severed her connections with her husband's black family.

Still, this explanation does not account for another piece of information. Shortly after Jacobs and Louisa moved to Cambridge, a son of Jacobs's old Philadelphia friends, people of color, married a woman with whom Louisa had much in common. During these Cambridge years, Louisa grew close to her friend's bride and to the bride's sister, the products of a union between a master and a slave. But unlike Louisa's father, who had broken his promise to emancipate his slave children, their father actually did free them. According to family tradition, he then educated Julia and Cordelia, gave them $1,000, and sent them north. (Years later Louisa remembered her friends' descendants in her will.) When, after John S.'s death, members of that family visited Cambridge, they often stayed at the boardinghouse that John S.'s widow established at 11 Brewer Street. If Elleanor Jacobs wanted to break her connections with her late husband's black relatives, why did she continue to open her home to Julia, Cordelia, and their family? Was it because—although they identified as black—they appeared white?

Jacobs's grief at her son's disappearance and her brother's death was devestating. Added to this was her distress at political events: the closing of the Freedmen's Bureau, the bankruptcy of the Freedmen's Bank, and the withdrawl of federal troops from the South. A decade earlier, she had predicted, "we shall be badly off when the military protection is withdrawn." Still, she had urged that, against all odds, the struggle must continue. Now all her dreams—of a home in freedom for her children, of her people free in their homes—lay shriveled and dead. On a hot July day in 1877, writing in the autograph book of a young friend, Jacobs recorded her diminished vision. The words she chose express profound disappointment, both in her own situation and in the realities African Americans were facing in post-Reconstruction America. Instead of defiance, Jacobs's hand now traced an aphorism expressive of the resignation that had characterized her grandmother Molly: "Trust and be hopeful."

14

Remember the Poor

Remember the poor and the old over the whole world.
—Harriet Jacobs to Ednah Dow Cheney, January 4 [1882]

In Washington on a bright cold November day in 1877, Julia Wilbur wrote excitedly, "My dear old friend Mrs. Jacobs called at Off. to see me. She has come to W. to live, & Louisa is coming too." Why did Jacobs decide to leave Cambridge? Why did she decide to move to Washington? At sixty-four, she could no longer make her hands do what they had done. They could not even braid cornrows into a doll's hair—as they had for Cornelia Willis's children and as she wanted to do for John's little girl. Perhaps there had been a terrible break between her and her sister-in-law. Or perhaps it had finally become clear that in Cambridge, Louisa would not be able to pursue her goal of an independent professional life. Years earlier, another black teacher had testified to the impossibility of finding work in the United States. "I have spent all my life in educating my head, . . . the most advantageous offer I have had is to sail for Monrovia on the coast of Africa." Almost a generation later, Cambridge still had never had a black teacher, and it would be five more years before they would hire the first. Perhaps Washington was the place.

In the years after Reconstruction, the nation's capital, "an island of judicial protection from the most flagrant of legal persecutions elsewhere in the South," was "the center of the black aristocracy in the United States, 'the city' where Negroes had made greater strides than anywhere else." By 1877, however, class lines were clearly visible within the African American community. One black critic satirized the capital's "fust families" who, overwhelmed by the migration of large numbers of destitute freed people into the District, were withdrawing into a closed circle emphasizing lineage, "*decayed* respectability," and confirmation of white pedigree such as "blue veins" and "good hair."

Criticizing this elitism, the black weekly *The People's Advocate* urged the "colored aristocracy" to focus less on their personal enhancement, and to work "to elevate the moral and intellectual tone of the *whole* community." This "colored elite," it was generally agreed, controlled black appointments to federal and District government jobs, to the Freedmen's Hospital, to Howard University, and to the "colored" school system. Its members included activists who had worked with Jacobs through the old antislavery struggles and during the Civil War: Frederick Douglass, now U.S. Marshall of the District of Columbia; J. Sella Martin, now pastor of the prestigious Fifteenth Street Presbyterian Church; and Dr. Alexander T. Augusta, now on the faculty of Howard University's new medical school. If Louisa was to achieve professional status, Washington—where these men had some influence—might be the place.

The city held conflicting memories for Louisa Jacobs. It had been the site of her exile, at the age of six, from Grandmother and from Edenton, and of her subjection to the role of slave servant to her younger white half-sister Laura for months before her father took her from his Washington home to serve his Brooklyn cousins. A lifetime later, teaching in Alexandria, she had often visited the wartime capital. When she and her mother returned from England and Jacobs took work in Boston with the New England Women's Club, Louisa had decided to live in Washington— perhaps because she was encouraged by the beginnings of black public education in the nation's capital. Only four years after the first "public colored school" opened, and despite the withdrawal of almost all the money and personnel that northern associations had contributed during the war, the District of Columbia was operating fifty classrooms (called "schools"). Half of these were "colored." The three large "colored" schoolhouses each included eight classrooms, two brick schoolhouses were finished, and the new four-storied brick structure under construction on 21st Street (to be named for the militant abolitionist Senator Thaddeus Stevens) would soon house twelve more. The Stevens School would become the jewel in the crown of the "colored" elementary system, and in 1868 it was reported that "Miss Jacobs has just been placed in charge of a school in the Stevens school-house." After completing the academic year, however, Louisa had left Washington. Perhaps it was the pull of family—the same pull that would bring her beloved uncle John S. back from England—that in the spring of 1870 had prompted Louisa to join her mother in Cambridge.

Louisa's mother worried about her. Actually, she had worried about Lulu ever since she was born. Everything she had done, she had done for her children—and especially to save her daughter from "selling well" as a sexual slave, as Norcom had threatened [ILSG p. 85]. Certainly the irony was not lost on Jacobs, or on Louisa, that in order to rescue her daughter, she had had to abandon her. But when, before sending Lulu away to school, Jacobs had tried to explain, her daughter had assured her of her love.

Harriet had succeeded in educating Louisa, and she applauded her daughter's determination to build a life away from other people's laundries and kitchens and parlors and nurseries—a life broader than the life Harriet had managed to build for herself. She also knew that in America jobs were color-coded and gender-specific—some "colored," some "women's work." It was extremely rare for a woman of color to find anything but hard domestic labor. (A generation later, novelist Zora Neale Hurston would call the black woman "the mule of the world.") Jacobs had been hopeful when Louisa went west in search of a teaching position, but after a job failed to materialize, she had understood the cause: "The name of colour here retards your progress in everything." Later, after it became clear that what had appeared a dream job with Willis's sister Sara was really a nightmare, Jacobs had supported Lulu's decision to settle in Boston, where Louisa had found a job clerking in "a Large Indian Botanical Drug establishment" and was "justly esteemed very highly." Then the war came, Jacobs decided to go back south, and Louisa joined her behind the Union lines. The war finally had given her the chance to teach, and she loved the work. But her health had suffered.

Louisa Jacobs's life was in many ways a model for the literature of the color line. Her childhood mimicked early black fiction, and her young womanhood could have been model for the novels and short stories being produced by authors from William Dean Howells to Charles Waddell Chesnut and George Washington Cable, writers who were creating fiction out of the transformations of the war years. In their work, the fortunes of the older generation of freed people and their offspring were shaped, and distorted, with the older darker parent sacrificing for the younger lighter child, or with the child sacrificing for the parent—all in accord with the rigid laws of the American color line that judged that "one drop" of "black blood" made an individual inferior. Although not the daughter of a President (like William Wells Brown's fictional Clotel), Louisa was the daughter of a U.S. Congressman. Her mother offered her the unconditional love that fiction deemed appropriate for mothers, and she returned that love fully. Jacobs was sensitive to the fact that Louisa could, if she chose, sidestep the burden of racism by passing for white—and that she chose not to pass. In the job market, this decision meant that Louisa was confronted not only with the discrimination faced by all women, but in addition with the ubiquitous and relentless color line. Although Louisa had not managed to establish herself professionally, how could Harriet not feel anything but pride in her daughter, who chose to maintain her integrity as a black woman? Louisa might prove a failure in the labor market, but she was an outstanding success as a daughter.

During their Cambridge years, Jacobs and Louisa had kept up their Washington acquaintance. In 1870, Louisa had been invited to the wedding of her old friend Mark L. DeMortie to Cordelia, the daughter of another friend, George T. Downing of Washington. The marriage, performed in Chicago, was reported by the newspapers as a society affair, complete with details of the bride's clothing ("a heavy moire antique, round point lace and train three yards in length, white veil, headdress of orange blossoms, diamonds and pearls") and descriptions of the wedding gifts (silver desert spoons, mustard spoons, tea spoons, butter knife, cream ladle, sugar spoon, pie knife, fruit ladle, and candlesticks; "a full set of china containing the bride's initials"; and fine linens). President Ulysses S. Grant sent a bouquet to the bride, and among the hundred guests attending were Frederick Douglass and black Congressmen Harris of Louisiana and Revels of Mississippi, all of whom made the trip west for the occasion. Louisa, however sent her regrets.

Perhaps she had not traveled to the wedding because the trip west was too much for her, or perhaps the entire affair was too extravagant for her purse. Condemning such conspicuous consumption on the part of Washington's "black aristocracy," critics pointed to the worsening conditions for African Americans across the country. Throughout the South, armed white terrorist groups had operated freely in the election of 1876. After his inauguration the following March, when federal troops were withdrawn from the former Confederacy, President Rutherford Hayes appointed Frederick Douglass to the post of Marshal of the District of Columbia. It was, the *Nation* commented, "a sort of vicarious atonement for the abandonment of the Fifteenth Amendment." (When the President excused Douglass from the ceremonial tasks that earlier Marshals had performed, many of Washington's African American citizens felt the racial slight and concluded that Hayes did not want a prominent black presence in the White House.)

Harriet Jacobs, like numbers of other activists of all colors, welcomed Douglass's appointment. Addressing her old colleague from the Lawtons' Cambridge home at 46 Market Street, she wrote, "how anxiously I have perused the papers the last few days and how happy I was made this morning in my search to see your nomination confirmed. There is no man living," she continued, "that I would so rejoice to see hold this position at the Capital of the Nation as yourself." She ended with a heartfelt prayer: "may God bless you and hold up your hands for every emergency is the prayer of Your Sincere Friend Harriet Jacobs."

Eight months later, Jacobs and Louisa moved to the nation's capital. The city had changed from the Washington of their Alexandria years. The District's refugees Jacobs had worked with when she first went south during the war—initially housed in the old Capitol building, later moved across the street into the army barracks at Duff Green's Row, then moved again to Camp Barker in northwestern Washington, and from there shifted into the communities at Barry Farms or at Arlington—now were crowding Washington's neighborhoods and alleys. Their presence dramatized the class divisions within the black community, as, in the face of increasing segregation, African Americans formed their own organizations, from churches to social and fraternal groups to literary societies. Still, in the mid-1870s Douglass could claim that "in point of residential rights and privileges in the city of Washington, all Americans are created equal. . . . no American is now too black to call Washington his home, and no American is so mean as to deny him that right." Each April 16, the District's black community celebrated its emancipation with an elaborate parade. One spectator noted, "I saw the 1st celebration 1866, & others afterwards. The change—& improved appearance are truly wonderful! Absence of tatters & rags in the Crowd was noticeable. All orderly, & well-behaved! Many of the best people too were out to see!"

A year after the Jacobses' move to the city, Washington's citizens were disenfranchised when Congress voted to rule the District through commissioners appointed by the President. Nevertheless, few African Americans feared that they would lose the ground gained since the war. The local situation appeared positive: the Civil Rights Act of 1875 was on the books; African Americans were sitting in Congress (which controlled District legislation); black men held jobs as government clerks; a black Ohioan was Recorder of Deeds; the nine-man school board included three black members; and Frederick Douglass was U.S. Marshall for the District.

Among the old friends that Jacobs and Louisa found in Washington was Charlotte Forten. On an August evening fifteen years earlier Forten, on a visit to Boston, had noted in her diary that with her friend Sallie, she had "walked from B[oston] to Bunker Hill . . . refreshed again by the magnificent view from the top, descended, went to the Public Library and the Atheneum . . . then dined with Mrs. J[acobs]. In the afternoon S[allie] left . . . to W[orcester] whither I shall follow in a few days. Mrs. J[acobs] kind, motherly friend that she is, insists on my spending those days with her, which I will very gladly do." Finding a "motherly friend" was very important for Forten, who was a few years older than Louisa and had been only three when her mother died. She often confided to her diary her need to be nurtured. Precocious, literary, and deeply religious, the free-born Forten increasingly felt that God had chosen her to help her race. In her late teens, she had poeticized this sense of mission in "The Improvement of Colored People": "Not the great and gifted only / He appoints to do his will, / But each one, however lowly, / Has a mission to fulfill." A few years later, it seemed the Civil War might present her with an opportunity to serve—but how?

Lotte Forten had been teaching in her aunt's school in Philadelphia when the poet John Greenleaf Whittier urged her to go south to teach the freed people and provided her with a recommendation. She had traveled to Boston hoping to meet with a member of the Port Royal Commission, which was sending teachers to the freed people on the Sea Islands off South Carolina, but had been unable to get an appointment. It was then that Jacobs—whom she had doubtless met many times over the years at activist gatherings, and whose book she must have known—had decided to take her in hand. In Massachusetts raising money and supplies for the refugees, Jacobs had gone with Forten in an effort to see commission officials.

The next day—August 17, 1862, her twenty-fifth birthday—Forten had voiced her new resolve. She was now old enough to realize that the delights she had dreamed of in younger days could never be hers. But, she vowed, "if I can go to Port Royal, I will try to forget all these desires. I will pray that God in his goodness will make me noble enough to find my highest happiness in doing my duty. Since Mrs. J[acobs] has given me such sad accounts of the sufferings of the poor freed people my desire of helping them has increased. It is but little I c'ld do, I know, but that little I w'ld do with all my heart."

Two days later, Forten had finally succeeded in seeing the commission representative. Her Boston mission accomplished, she "bade farewell to my kind friend Mrs. J[acobs]" and returned to Philadelphia. Then, as weeks passed, she had voiced concern. "Have been anxious and disappointed at not hearing from Dr. P[eck]. But a letter from Mrs. J[acobs] to-day tells me that she has seen him, and that he is very sanguine about my going." When still she did not hear, Jacobs had tried to intervene, but the Boston Commission announced that "they were not sending women at present." Disappointed, Forten had made arrangements with the Philadelphia Port Royal Relief Association, and on October 22, 1862, had finally sailed from New York.

In the South, Forten had continued her correspondence with her "motherly friend." Forten's experiences among the black refugees during her year-and-a-half tenure on St. Helena's Island, South Carolina, were the most intense of her life. As Jacobs's stories of her work with the refugees had inspired Forten, now Forten, in her essay "Life on the Sea-Islands," used her experiences among the freed people to inspire the genteel New England readers of the *Atlantic Monthly*—and to enrich the literature of the Civil War. She had later returned to Boston, where she worked for the New England Branch of the Freedmen's Union Commission. When Harriet and Louisa Jacobs arrived in Washington in 1877, Forten was employed as a clerk in the Auditor's Office of the War Department, and late the next year, she married the Reverend Francis Grimké.

Jacobs remembered him well. Born into slavery in South Carolina, Francis and his brother Archibald were sons of the slave woman Nancy Weston and her master Henry Grimké (a brother of the Grimké sisters who had gone north to become famous abolitionist-feminists). After their master died, Nancy and her children were moved to Charleston, where despite "bitter poverty," she paid a dollar a month for the boys' schooling. As young teenagers, the brothers tried to resist when their white half-brother demanded they become his house servants, and during the Civil War both ran away. Archie spent much of the war in hiding in Charleston, but Frank was caught and sold by his half-brother to a Confederate officer. When the war ended, Nancy arranged for her sons to study at a freedmen's school where she was working as a housekeeper. They caught the attention of their teacher, who arranged for them to be sent north, and after four years at Lincoln University (when they met their famous feminist aunts Sarah Grimké and Angelina Grimké Weld) they began to study law there.

Then in 1872, Archie had entered Harvard Law School under Dean Christopher C. Langdell—one of Harriet Jacobs's boarders. It must have been while visiting his brother in Cambridge that Frank had knocked on the door of Jacobs's boardinghouse with a letter of introduction. Years later, he still remembered the warmth and "cordiality with which she received me and made me welcome to her pleasant and hospitable home." While his brother completed his courses at Harvard Law School, Frank studied at Princeton Theological Seminary, and upon graduation, accepted a call to the Fifteenth Street Presbyterian Church in Washington where he met Lotte Forten.

A year after Jacobs's arrival in the city, the Grimkés' popularity in Washington's black community was demonstrated by a surprise party organized to celebrate Lotte's pregnancy. A newspaper reports that the gifts, arranged in a pyramid and draped with flags, included flowers, food, and household items: "hams, canned fruit, tea, coffee, sugar etc. and last but not least a broom contributed by one of our popular school board ex-officials." Among the party-goers were Elizabeth Keckley, with whom Jacobs must have worked during the war, and J. Sella Martin, her pastor from her Boston days. It is not known whether Jacobs and Louisa were among those at the church that evening—or whether they were among those who consoled the Grimkés a few months later when their baby died. We do know, however, that Harriet Jacobs, who made her living serving others, was not a member of the city's "colored society," as were the Grimkés. Apparently neither Jacobs nor Louisa attended the Friday night gatherings at the couple's book-and-flower-filled Corcoran Street home, where works of painting and sculpture were studied and aesthetic criticism was read; nor (despite their Edenton origins) were they included in the Sunday evening get-togethers on Seventeenth Street, where Anna Julia Cooper, a generation younger than Louisa and Oberlin-educated, established her "little North Carolina colony."

Although Lotte Grimké was at the apex of Washington's black social structure, however, she sometimes felt lonely "under the condescending superiority of the 'Old Cits' cult at the Nation's Capital." Among her great friends outside the closed circle of Washington's "colored society" were Jacobs and her daughter. When, nearing the end of her life, Louisa framed her will, she would testify to the importance of this friendship, writing in her large, slanting hand, "To Mrs. Charlotte Grimké of Washington, D. C. two hundred dollars."

While not members of the exclusive Bethel Literary Society, Harriet and Louisa Jacobs might have enjoyed the organization's public sessions—the 1883 mass meeting urging federal aid to education, the symposia held that year and the next in Lincoln Hall, and the huge celebration of Frederick Douglass's seventy-first birthday. Harriet Jacobs knew both Bishop Payne (who had founded Bethel Literary Society), and a number of the speakers, including George T. Downing, Reverend Archibald Grimké, Frederick Douglass, and Dr. Charles Purvis, as well as Charlotte Forten Grimké. And both Jacobs and her daughter were interested in the topics addressed in the Literary Society's weekly sessions—from Mary Ann Shadd Carey's "Heroes of the Anti-Slavery Struggles" to "What are the Elements of True Womanhood," a discussion of "eminent women" of the "Negro race"; "The Black Woman at the South"; "The Anti-Slavery Movement Between 1820–1830"; and "Reminiscences of Anti-Slavery Men and Their Day." Both mother and daughter, who felt deeply about women and the vote, were interested in the spring 1885 debate between William Waring and Francis L. Cardozo on female suffrage.

Another old friend and staunch feminist, Julia Wilbur, who had moved to the capital early in 1865, had been joined there by her sister Frances Hartwell, a teacher at a freedmen's school in Georgetown. In Washington, Wilbur had continued her relief work with the freed people, then became the first female employee in the United States Patent Office. On her female copyist's salary—always less money, she annually noted, than was paid a man—she made a home for herself and her sister Frances, who continued to serve Washington's poor.

Still another friend from the past was Florence J. Smith, a daughter of Boston's Georgina and John J. Smith. Louisa had stayed with the family during her Boston sojourn in 1860, and Florence, then eight, must have admired their ladylike boarder. During the years before the war, the abolitionists had congregated at John Smith's barbershop on the corner of Howard and Bulfinch streets, and it was said that Senator Charles Sumner could often be found there. During Louisa's stay, the Smiths had five young children. When later the sixth was born, the little girl was named Harriet Louise—perhaps for Jacobs and her daughter. (Many years afterward, Louisa Jacobs would name this sixth child as a beneficiary in her will.) In the years since then, three of the Smith sisters had graduated from Boston Normal School, and now Florence, all grown up, was teaching in nearby Anacostia.

These old friends eased Harriet and Louisa's transition to Washington. Once settled, they began making new friends. One was Marion P. Shadd, a niece of Mary Ann Shadd Cary, the pioneering journalist who had spurred black emigration to Canada. Marion had come to Washington to study at Howard University, which had opened its doors to women two years after its founding, and in the 1870s she had obtained a teaching position at the John F. Cook School.

Another new friend was Frances Rollin Whipper—or perhaps Jacobs and Louisa had met her years earlier, as a member of William C. Nell's Boston circle. Freeborn and northern-educated, after the war Rollin had left South Carolina for Boston to write a biography of the black U.S. Major Martin Delany. Back in Charleston, she and her sisters had become influential in Radical Republican circles, and Frances had found work as a clerk for William J. Whipper, a delegate to the 1868 South Carolina Constitutional Convention. She had married her boss after a brief courtship, but theirs was not a happy family. Her husband's drinking and gambling prompted Frances to move to Washington with their three children. In the capital, she found work as a court stenographer and government clerk and continued her feminist activities.

Rollin Whipper had doubtless read *Incidents* long before meeting Jacobs, and doubtless, too, Jacobs and Louisa knew her *Life and Public Services of Martin R. Delany*, which had appeared under the name "Frank A. Rollin" in the summer of 1868. Like Jacobs, Rollin Whipper had published her book under a pseudonym, and the women had a lot to talk about. Jacobs, who always empathized with mothers, was deeply sympathetic to the problems of her friend, who was determined to teach her children to excel.

Despite the warmth of these friendships, the Jacobs' move was made difficult by the economic depression gripping the nation. On one cold December morning, Julia Wilbur noted in her diary: "poor folks having hard times—Grown men have become bootblacks, for want of other work." Not only the poor were hurting. Some weeks later, the economic downturn hit her close to home. "Such a time this P.M.! 70 or 80 dismissals! 6 from our Rooms! 37 tracers & others. Oh, dear! it made us all tremble." Government-funded Howard University was forced to slash faculty salaries in half. In addition to the shrunken federal economy, the withdrawal of northern aid groups from the schools was hurting black public education in the city, which continued to be overwhelmed by new-comers from the rural South. Even Stevens School, where Louisa had worked, was reduced to half-day sessions.

Harriet and her daughter had been hopeful that in the nation's cap-ital, where the "colored" schools employed a few black women teachers, Louisa could win a professional position. But it was not to be. Was it the economy? Was Lulu's experience in Alexandria's and Savannah's "con-traband schools" seen as a drawback? She lacked the Oberlin education of some of the younger applicants. Was this the problem? Was it her age? Her health? Or was it that preferred applicants had been born free and enjoyed the support and prestige of extended family networks, while she had been born a North Carolina slave? After endlessly rehearsing the sit-uation, Jacobs and her daughter finally abandoned the effort and decided to open another boardinghouse.

Middle-class visitors to nineteenth-century American cities found that arranging for food and shelter posed a problem, and boarding and lodging houses were a popular solution. This was especially true in the nation's capital, where numbers of prominent people needed temporary housing because elected officials held only brief tenures and, under the spoils system, appointed officials came and went at their patrons' will. As a Washington columnist noted at the beginning of one congressional session, "the hotels are filling up, and scores of strangers are wearing out the soles of their shoes looking up comfortable quarters for the winter. Washington is a city of boarding-houses, and of all cities which charge extraordinary prices for very ordinary board, it bears the palm." For prominent transients, not only housing but also food service involved special arrangements. A singular local solution was engaging a caterer. "The Washington caterer is a curious character. He is usually a colored gentleman, who supplies families and single boarders with meals at so much a month. Twenty dollars per person is the average price. For that he will bring your breakfast and dinner in a square tin box to your rooms, every morning and evening for thirty days."

Harriet and Louisa Jacobs chose the location of their new boarding-house carefully, finally deciding on K Street North West—the traditional dividing line between blacks (at the north) and whites (at the south). The house they rented at number 1409 was on a block in racial transition. After furnishing the rooms comfortably, Jacobs hired a young black man to do the heavy work, and two older women to help with the cooking.

The clients they intended to attract were white, members of the same liberal northeastern elite Jacobs had served in the Boston New England Women's Club and in her Cambridge boardinghouse, who had come down to Washington to run the country.

Their new enterprise was successful. Among their boarders were President Garfield's newly appointed Commissioner of Agriculture Dr. George Bailey Loring and his wife. A former Massachusetts congressman and an excellent speaker, Loring demonstrated his support of black higher education by presenting the closing address at graduation exercises of the Howard University Medical School. Jacobs's excellent cooking also attracted Massachusetts Congressman William Crapo and his wife, Sarah Tappan Davis Crapo, a prominent New Bedford couple whom Jacobs may have met earlier through Cornelia Grinnell Willis. Joining them around her dining room table were the Claflins. An advocate of woman suffrage, the former Governor of Massachusetts and his lady had come to Washington after his 1877 election to Congress. Long before either moved to the capital, Jacobs must have been acquainted with Mary Bucklin Davenport Claflin. A prominent member of the New England Woman's Club and a supporter of Cambridgeport's Howard Industrial School, Mary Claflin was also an intimate of Harriet Beecher Stowe.

While Jacobs was serving her excellent dinners to Washington's privileged white officials, throughout the South the freed people were facing brute violence. With the President's withdrawal of federal troops from the former Confederacy, the machinery of its state governments passed back into the hands of the white Democrats. Disenfranchisement, peonage, and terror followed. In Washington Richard Greener, now Dean of Howard University's law school, warned: "With the downfall of reconstruction a new lease on life was given to Southern barbarity and lawlessness." Nonetheless, Washington's African American leadership was caught by surprise when, following the 1879 crop failure in Mississippi and Louisiana, black families began fleeing the South, packing up and leaving for Kansas. Within months, 6,000 freed people reached the Prairie State, and a year later, there were more than twice as many. Douglass, who took an unpopular position by opposing the movement, found himself rejected by black audiences. Earlier, addressing the poverty of the freed people in the nation's capital, Sojourner Truth had urged Washington's jobless refugees to go where they could become independent farmers. Now she gave the emigrants her enthusiastic support. In Topeka, Truth saw the Kansas Exodus as part of a divine plan: "God still lives and means to see the black people in full possession of all their rights, even if the entire white population of the South has to be annihilated in the accomplishment of His purpose." In the capital, the Kansas Freedmen's Relief Association quickly organized to help the impoverished Exodusters. But little was being done to help the destitute remaining in Washington's alleys and slums.

Jacobs and Louisa, settled into their comfortable home on K Street, decided that they could, in a small way, resume their roles as relief workers. More than a dozen years earlier in impoverished Savannah, they had managed to provide a Christmas dinner for the city's destitute. Now, enlisting white patronage as they had during the war, they involved their boarder Mrs. Claflin in their new project.

On Christmas Day, 1880, Julia Wilbur scribbled in her diary: "called on Mrs. Jacobs & Louisa, 1413 K. . . . Home at noon to tell Francis [Wilbur's sister] to get a few old colored women & take them to Mrs. Jacobs' at 2 o clock to a Christmas dinner given by Mrs. Ex-Gov. Claflin of Mass. for 20 old women. So rainy that some of them cd. not go out. There were 12 women & 12 children there. Dinner set in style in elegant dining room. Mrs. C. & niece & one other Lady waited on them. It was like a foretaste of Paradise for these poor old ex slaves. Francis says it was an interesting & pathetic scene—Mrs. C. said, 'she believed she was the happiest of them all.'"

A week later, *The People's Advocate* featured the event in a front-page story. With its scene-painting and elevated tone, "Our Duty to the Poor—How We Observed it on Christmas," reads like the work of Charlotte Forten Grimké. After lines from a poem about old New England, the narrator plays on the title of Jacobs's book, writing that it gives pleasure to hear of "any incident of special liberality and thoughtfulness for the poor. Such an incident," the piece continues, "occurred in our city on Christmas Day, when two noble Christian women gave a bountiful dinner to a number of very poor aged women." Much of what follows quotes the extended blessing offered by Reverend Francis Grimké. Then, after applauding Mrs. Claflin, "a lady who, in her own home, has made her influence felt as the friend of the poor and the suffering, and who here in the Capital of the nation reaches out to you the same tender, sympathetic heart," the writer praises "Mrs. Jacobs, the best part of whose life has been devoted to the alleviating of the sufferings of the poor and oppressed, and to whose great and loving heart no sacrifice is too great to be made in the interest of humanity."

The praise was well-earned, but it came at a high price. Jacobs was working too hard. Two months after her Christmas dinner, she confided to Julia Wilbur that running the boardinghouse was inevitably involving her in doing catering jobs for her guests, and this was more than she could manage. Wilbur noted: "Mrs. J. gave us an account of the dinners of 13 courses that she got up for the Claflins on two occasions. Mrs. J. is tired of it, & almost worked to death. Louisa," she continues, is looking for a federal job. She "wants a place in a department" where she can earn a salary to free them from this endless work.

The following November when the weather again turned cold, *The Advocate* ran a letter calling attention to "the great suffering among one-third of the colored residents of this city and vicinity every winter." Declaring that many lacked housing, adequate clothing, and even food, it criticized middle-class black Washington for ignoring the poor: "*We hold ourselves too far aloof from them.*" A second letter followed, warning Washington's more affluent African Americans: "We cannot hide ourselves behind our respectability and say the stigma be not upon us or our children, but upon those beggars. . . . We cannot escape the collective charge of neglecting our poor." Again Jacobs and Louisa made plans for a holiday dinner. Using organizational skills honed in Alexandria and Savannah, they reached out for support to the white New Englanders who had backed their relief work during the war and Reconstruction.

On the morning of January 2, 1882, Julia Wilbur noted, "[Sister] Frances went out early to find some old women to go to the Dinner given by Mrs. Jacobs." In her diary entry, she registered her appreciation of the contrast between Jacobs's New Year feast for the poor and the holiday gala across the street at the executive mansion. "Afternoon," Wilbur writes,

> I went with [niece] Freda to Mrs. J's. Could look over the approaches to Executive Mansion. Fine equipages going & coming. Large crowd of citizens waited till 1 P. M. to go in. Freda & I went over at 1:30 on West side directly to Portico. Waited 10 min. & at the 2nd surge we were pushed to the door, & I went in backwards! Easy enough afterwards. President Arthur stood *too near the door.* No introducing.—He wished me 'A Happy New Year,' shook hands, & F & I stopped in the Room & saw the *Receiving* go on. . . . F & I went back to Mrs. Jacobs & lunched. Got home at 3:30. . . . Frances came at 7. She devoted the day

to the old folks, & did not go to Reception as she intended.—She dined at Mrs. J's.—Reverend Mr. Grimké was there. Mrs. J & Louise worked hard, but they enjoyed it, & they have the blessing of 15 old women.

Basking in the women's blessing, Jacobs reported on the project to her old friend and patron Ednah Dow Cheney, who had sent her clothing to distribute. Thanking her for the "nice dresses," Jacobs writes that late in the day, Reverend Grimké brought six more old women for her to feed. "I gave them a bountiful supper sent them home with the fragments very happy." She told the women that Fanny Garrison Villard had sent ten dollars toward their dinner, explaining that she "wanted these old people to know it was Mr. Garrisons daughter wh had been so true to our race." The day was a great success. "The old women was so happy after dinner they sang a hymn. and prayed for the dear friends that remembered them. and asked their dear Father to remember the poor and the old over the whole world. One old woman at the table said when I rised this mornin I asked the master to show me where to git a piece of bread but look dear sisters here is enough for all."

Jacobs and Louisa could set a bountiful table at New Year's, but times were worsening, and black Americans were losing ground. In its 1883 fall term, the United States Supreme Court declared the Civil Rights Act of 1875 unconstitutional. Black Washington responded with indignation, and more than 2,000 people crowded into Lincoln Hall to voice their righteous anger. They heard a series of impressive speakers, including Frederick Douglass, who thundered: "This decision has inflicted a heavy calamity upon seven millions of the people of this country, and left them naked and defenseless against the action of a malignant, vulgar, and pitiless prejudice from which the Constitution plainly intended to shield them. It presents the United States before the world as a nation utterly destitute of power to protect the constitutional rights of its own citizens upon its own soil." The editor of the *Grit* echoed his anger. "Our Country! Oh, what a mockery, what a farce . . . It will never be our country while the Constitution remains inoperative and the laws on the statute books are the playthings of the Supreme Court. It will never be our country so long as the black men are driven from their southern homes at the point of a shotgun, by the flames of the midnight torch and the dagger of the assassin." Soon after, when the elected officials among their boarders (and those for whom their other boarders worked) were turned out of office, the system of patronage that was Washington politics dictated that the Jacobses' boardinghouse close, "broken up," a newspaper reports, "by political changes."

On January 4, 1884, Harriet and Louisa visited Julia Wilbur with good news: Louisa's job-hunt was finally over. She had been hired at Howard University. Wilbur hurriedly recorded their success. "They had been to Howard U. all day fixing their rooms for living & school purposes. Louisa will teach Cooking and Sewing . . . in industrial Dept. added to the University." A year earlier, Howard's President Patton, entering the controversy in black higher education that would pit Booker T. Washington's support of vocational education against W.E.B. DuBois's endorsement of classical training, had inaugurated a small Industrial Department. Patton strongly supported vocational training, and the 1884 *University Catalogue* announced industrial training as a requirement for a number of students in the Preparatory and Normal Departments. "The Industrial Department is advancing on its second year with marked success. As the means are furnished, purchases of needed tools and machines will be made, and additional trades will be taught." The superintendent of the department taught tin and iron work; other male members of the faculty taught printing, shoemaking, tailoring, and carpentry; and, the *Catalogue* notes, "female pupils are instructed in Needlework and Cooking by Miss Louisa Jacobs."

One fine Sunday morning a few weeks later, Wilbur visited her friends in their new rooms. "At 10.30 A.M. Started for Howard University to spend rest of day with Mrs. Jacobs & Louisa.—Rode to near F[reedmen]'s Hospital, then walked through grove, up the Hill to Miner Hall. Mrs. J. has very pleasant rooms. Cool & quiet there. . . . After dinner we went to see where the Reservoir is to be. . . . Then we walked in grounds of Univty—There visited a while, had 'tea'—they went with us to Car. & I got home at dark. Had pleasant visit." Miner Hall, called "the dormitory," was a three-storied brick building with white-columned porches and topped by a neat row of chimneys. It contained about one hundred rooms for boarding students and was indeed "pleasant." But the Jacobses' stay at Howard did not last long. Two weeks later, Wilbur reported: "Mrs. Jacobs called for an hour or so. She is worried & harassed, because [Howard's] Pres. Patton has asked her to vacate her rooms, for a teacher & his wife.—" Soon after, mother and daughter moved from University Hill. Things could have been worse. Although Louisa was the only woman teaching in the Industrial Department, her job was not threatened, and the next year, she taught again. But in 1886, she was not rehired, and then—although both she and her mother had long ago resolved that she would not go into service—she took a job as a cook.

Earlier, after closing down her K Street boardinghouse, Jacobs had found work as a domestic for elite white families living temporarily in the nation's capital. Like her grandmother, she made extra money moonlighting. She did not bake "nice crackers" as Molly had done, but like Molly, who "had many jars of preserves" and was "in the habit of preserving fruit for many ladies in the town, and of preparing suppers for parties," she did preserve jellies and jams. Now, after leaving Miner Hall, Jacobs was hired as housekeeper by the Swedish Minister to the United States. (Wilbur, visiting her friend, marveled at Count Lewenhaupt's "elegantly furnished house," with its "old fashioned furniture & fine china, a carved oaken mantel and wood box.")

In the spring of 1885, Jacobs was searching for a building to rent so that she could establish another boardinghouse, when an astonishing event occurred. She discovered that the widow and children of James Norcom Jr., her old enemy, were living in the capital and were in need.

During his lifetime, old Dr. Norcom had always managed—through sneaks and spies in the North—to track Jacobs down. Years after Norcom was no longer his master, John S. acknowledged that "I never dared to trust myself in his power"; and for her part, Jacobs always tried to know Norcom's whereabouts. When she moved to Washington, she was no doubt aware that his son James Norcom Jr.—the young master from whom she had escaped—was living in the District.

In the years after Jacobs fled Grandmother's attic, James Norcom Jr. had lost everything. Judged "a poor debtor" in 1851, he had been granted by the court "50 lb Bacon - 1 Hoe - 1 Spade - 1 Shovel - 1 Rake 1 Plow - 1 Harrow - Trace Chanes & Gear - 1 Cart & Tackle - 1 Fork - 1 Axe - 1 Wheelbarrow" and $50.00 worth of household goods. But when the Civil War came to Edenton, his fortunes changed. Although his mother left home to "refugee" from the Yankees, James Jr. became Edenton's mayor. (He later petitioned the federal government for reparations, claiming that the Union Army had destroyed his property, and he received an endorsement from the Congressional Committee on Claims, which noted that "Mr. Norcom was a true loyal man, and that he uniformly showed himself such during the rebellion.") Yet when Jacobs visited Edenton just after the war ended, his fortunes had again reversed.

Dramatizing the changes the war had brought, the *Boston Freedmen's Record* reports that "the son of her old master came to see her. He has lost all his property, and professes to have been all through the war a good Union man, and a great friend of the negro. He asks the influence of his former slave to procure him an office under the Freedmen's Bureau."

In the half-century since Jacobs's escape from his Auburn plantation, James Norcom Jr. had buried his first wife, and wed and buried a second. By 1870, he was living in Norfolk and had married a third wife, Henrietta, a woman younger than his oldest children. A year later, he moved his new family to Washington, where he was hired as a clerk by the Navy Department. After President Hayes's inauguration, he found work in the War Department. Then Norcom died, leaving behind his young wife and her two children. In 1885, Henrietta Norcom was working to support her family as a seamstress and by taking in a boarder. But times were hard, and seamstresses were notoriously underpaid. The Norcoms needed help.

Henrietta Norcom probably had never heard of Harriet Jacobs, but the Norcom name had retained its power, and now Jacobs learned about Henrietta. After collecting some groceries and dishing up dinner, she enlisted Wilbur's sister Frances, and together they packed it all up and carried it to the family of her enemy.

Laden with food and walking to the Norcoms' house at 1011 11th Street North West, Jacobs recollected everything. She reminded herself of the Norcoms' cook who "never sent a dinner to his table without fear and trembling; for if there happened to be a dish not to his liking, he would either order her to be whipped, or compel her to eat every mouthful of it in his presence. . . . Sometimes she was locked up, away from her nursing baby, for a whole day and night." And she thought of old Mrs. Norcom's meanness: "If dinner was not served at the exact time on that particular Sunday, she would station herself in the kitchen, and wait till it was dished, and then spit in all the kettles and pans that had been used for cooking" [ILSG pp. 12, 13]. She sharply recalled her Aunt Betty's repeated miscarriages, brought on by overwork as the Norcoms' night-nurse. And she remembered that when her aunt finally gave birth to a living child, the baby died. She knew that her dear aunt had tried to protect her from Norcom's sexual harrassment and from his wife's jealous rages, and she had never forgotten that it was childless Aunt Betty who later strengthened her resolve to free her children and herself. Carrying food to the Norcoms, Jacobs could not forget that Tom Hoskins, a slave who had fled the plantation a year after she ran, had been shot and killed. Did she also remember that—unlike many slave narrators, unlike even her brother—she had not ended her book by forgiving her master?

Julia Wilbur did not hazard a guess about what Harriet Jacobs was thinking as she dished up dinner and carried it over to Henrietta Norcom. But she did comment on the intensity of her usually self-possessed friend: "Frances been with Mrs Jacobs to see, & carry food to the *Norcombs* (old Master's family) Mrs. Jacobs quite excited. A former slave relieving the family who held her in slavery.)!!—Time makes some things even."

But did things seem even to Jacobs? Fifty long years after fleeing Auburn plantation in the rain— thirty years after experiencing the torment of learning that her freedom had been not taken but bought—what was this passionate woman feeling? Her arms heavy with the food she was carrying, did she see herself completing the curve of her life? As she freely gave to the family of her dead enemy, did she feel that finally she was achieving her "victory"?

15

Unshaken by the Wind

❦

*She was no reed shaken by the wind, vacillating, easily moved
from a position. She did her own thinking.*
—Reverend Francis Grimké on Harriet Jacobs, March 1897

Jacobs began preparing for her new venture with renewed energy. She would make one last attempt to create a home by establishing another boardinghouse, and this time it would not be for whites, but for Washington's black elite. With segregation becoming institutionalized, the city was polarizing along racial lines. "The colored race," the *Star* reports, "lives as separate and as exclusive a life as in the days of slavery, and as a drop of African blood was once held to make a man a negro, so now it taints him and makes an insurmountable barrier against social recognitions." African American members of Congress and their families were subjected to "constant indignities," despite their status. When the wife of South Carolina's black representative entered the House gallery set aside for wives of members, a white Ohio Congressman's wife flounced out. In a city where Senator Blanche Bruce could be denied service in a restaurant because of his color, many thought it important to create businesses where Washington's black citizens were welcome. Certainly, as one Congressman pointed out in an interview, black public servants called to Washington needed appropriate housing.

Despite their decision to focus on the black community, in the midst of making preparations for the new boardinghouse—perhaps as an expression on some level of a continued commitment to integration—Jacobs and Louisa decided to reestablish their ties with the feminist movement. Jacobs had become acquainted with antislavery feminists in Rochester forty years earlier, working with her good friend Amy Post and other members of the Female Anti-Slavery Society. Many of them, like

Post, had been central in the Woman's Rights conventions at Rochester and Seneca Falls. Later, during the Civil War, she had worked with Stanton and Anthony in the Women's National Loyal League, and afterward Louisa had lectured with Anthony in the New York campaign for Equal Rights for All. Like many other black feminists, however, Harriet and Louisa Jacobs had stepped aside from the women's rights movement after the collapse of the Equal Rights Association. They had not, however, lost touch with Anthony, who continued to praise Jacobs as "a wonderful woman." Now, twenty years later, they again came forward.

In February 1886, on the Sunday before the scheduled opening of the eighteenth Women's Rights convention, Julia Wilbur noted, "I came home & found Mrs. Jacobs & Louisa—Then Miss Anthony came, & we had pleasant chat." Next morning, Wilbur attended the opening session. Recording the second day's deliberations in her diary, she reported an incident omitted from Stanton's *History of Woman Suffrage*. The official record reads, "Mrs. Meriwether's son, Lee, paid a handsome tribute to 'strong-minded mothers.'" But Wilbur writes that the boy used racist language in his talk, and that Robert Purvis—a long-time black supporter of women's rights—took the floor to protest. Purvis, Wilbur reports, "objected to way Boy spoke of Negroes." Neither the racist epithet from the rostrum, nor the comment from the floor protesting that epithet, however, elicited any response from the chair. Wilbur notes simply, "Then 'Mother' excused the Boy's 'slip of the tongue.'" How, one wonders, did Harriet and Louisa Jacobs respond to this incident? Or weren't they present on that first evening?

Jacobs was in attendance on the third day when, Wilbur reports, "Ch. filled almost when we got there. I sat in a side room & wrote Resolutions, so I did not hear much. . . . Mrs. Jacobs came home with us to tea." Two weeks later, she records Louisa's willingness to work again for the cause: "I sent package by F [her sister Frances] yesterday to Louisa Jacobs to distribute." Given Louisa's history of activism for equal rights, her decision to distribute women's suffrage publications is perhaps not surprising. But it is likely that both "the Boy's 'slip of the tongue'" and the convention's apparent acceptance of his racist language reminded her of the struggle that had torn apart the Equal Rights Association twenty years earlier, when feminist leaders invoked racism from the platform as black suffrage was pitted against woman suffrage.

Now as the century drew to a close, black women were voicing their objections to the overt racism that had become pervasive within the feminist movement. Jacobs's friend Charlotte Forten Grimké publicly joined this protest. It is because of the suffragists' blatant racism, she explained, that she has not involved herself in their annual Washington meetings: "These expressions have for years prevented many of us from attending the conventions held in this city. They have disgusted us. I do not hesitate to say that they can only be characterized as contemptible; for their direct effect is to strengthen a most unjust and cruel prejudice; to increase the burdens which already weigh so heavily upon a deeply wronged people. . . . While African American women," she asserts, "appreciate the value of women's suffrage quite as keenly as other women do, they will never cease to rejoice that their fathers and brothers, and sons and husbands had the right to vote conferred upon them. . . . And we would desire for ourselves no recognition that would involve injustice to such men."

It was within the context of a black community increasingly isolated and under siege, a community turning inward, that Jacobs planned her new boardinghouse. In the solid brick building she rented at 2119 K Street, Jacobs would add a chapter to the narrative of self-help within the black community. In the refugee camps, she had seen families broken by slavery and war who were reconstituting themselves—and in the process, redefining "family." In 1862, she had quoted a mother who had informally adopted an orphaned child in the camp: "The child's mother was a stranger; none of her friends cum wid her from de ole place. I took one boy down on de plantation; he is a big boy now, working mong de Unions. De Lord help me to bring up dat boy, and he will help me take care dish child." Like that refugee mother, Jacobs had brought a boy north with her from Georgia to Cambridge and on to Washington—although, to her distress, young Joseph Pierce was proving less interested in school than in the streets.

As black Americans urbanized, they were creating new communities and new social structures. The boardinghouse was one such site. In the nation's capital, where everything was notoriously overpriced, boardinghouses were more so. Protesting that "colored Congressmen were charged more than white men," one black member of the House pointed out that as segregation became entrenched, the problem of decent housing became ever more difficult. Later, novelist Pauline Hopkins would fictionalize the creation of a surrogate urban family in "Ma Smith's Lodging-House," where "musical evenings or reception nights [were arranged] that her tenants might have a better opportunity of becoming acquainted with each other. . . . It soon became noised about that very pleasant times were enjoyed in that house; and that a sick lodger had been nursed back to health, instead of being hustled into the hospital ambulance at the first sign of sickness."

Among Jacobs's first boarders at 2119 K—like her earlier location, on the north side of the street—was James C. Matthews, a black Democrat from New York whom President Cleveland had just named Recorder of Deeds. (Douglass had been appointed to the position of Recorder by President Garfield—the first black man to hold this lower, but more lucrative, position—and had continued in this post under President Arthur.) For four months, the Republican Senate refused to confirm Matthews's nomination, but President Cleveland stood by his man, and in August, after Congress adjourned, commissioned Matthews Recorder of Deeds. His appointment caused intense controversy in Washington's African American community. Although Matthews's opponents argued that no black man should support the Democratic Party, the *Bee* backed him. Writing that Republicans are "not the keepers of the Negro conscience, nor should they be the suppressor of any man's opinion," the newspaper asserts that it had been left to a Democratic president "to elucidate the theory that the color of the skin or the kink in the hair" does not affect "the texture of the brain."

Throughout the months his appointment was being debated, Matthews was the most prestigious lodger in Jacobs's new boardinghouse. Then in the fall, the Senate reconvened and voted him down. After this final rejection, Cleveland nominated Matthews's deputy James Monroe Trotter of Massachusetts to fill the position. Born into slavery, Trotter had enlisted in the Massachusetts 54th and after the war became a staunch Republican. Then in 1877, when Hayes withdrew federal troops from the South, he broke with the Republican Party. Trotter's activism among black Democrats won him the Washington appointment despite the objections from Republicans—who hated his politics—and from fellow Democrats—who hated his color.

Leaving his wife and their three children in Boston, Trotter moved into Harriet Jacobs's boardinghouse. Then in the spring, he fell seriously ill with typhoid-pneumonia. Jacobs sent for his wife, who hurried to K Street, and together they spent weeks nursing the sick man. Under the headline, "Mr. Trotter, the New Recorder, Still Lying at the Point of Death," *The Philadelphia Press* reported, "No one is admitted to his room but his wife, his physicians and his nurse. . . . He lies like a stranded bark at the mercy of the tide. But he is fortunate in his surroundings. Mrs.

Harriet Jacobs, the proprietor of the house, 2119 K Street, is a historic character, well and favorably known in this country and Europe." Identifying Jacobs as the author of "Linda" and describing her as "an exceedingly interesting narrator," the reporter detailed Jacobs's life in Washington before returning to Trotter's condition and concluding, "If good care and nursing can restore the sick man he will get along all right." (Trotter did recover, but his health was gone. In 1889, when the Republicans returned to power and turned him out, he went home to Boston a broken man. Four years later he died at the age of fifty.)

But even before Trotter left Washington, Jacobs had closed her boardinghouse when she, too, fell ill with pneumonia. At seventy-five, she was slow to recover. In the spring of 1888, Wilbur noted with telling economy, "Mrs. J. called to borrow money but we had none for her." After Jacobs's health improved, she found work, as she had earlier, as a housekeeper for New England's transplanted elite. In January 1889, Julia Wilbur wrote that the Jacobses were leaving their housekeeping jobs "to rest awhile. Mrs. Jacobs will visit Edenton, N. C., the scene of her slave life and sufferings."

On the last day of February, mother and daughter left for the South, hoping that Jacobs would benefit from the change in climate. But she sent Wilbur a discouraged letter: "Says Edenton is a forlorn place. . . .She had seen the place of her suffering for years." Long a city woman, Jacobs was feeling isolated in her old hometown, and missed the news. "She has had but 1 paper. So I put up a Star & put it in letter box for her, & I must send her more." Louisa returned to Washington after a month, but Jacobs stayed on in North Carolina for another ten days. When she did travel back, she ran into trouble. As her ship attempted to sail, it was battered by a "great storm . . . the worst," newspapers report, "that has ever visited Norfolk." Safe home at last, Jacobs reported to Wilbur, "It was fearful at Norfolk & all along the coast."

Again Jacobs found work as a housekeeper. And as before, she and Louisa made a little money by catering and by preserving and selling jams and jellies. During these years, Wilbur's diary is dotted with notes about the Jacobses's catering business. "Francis hurried to get ready for Mrs. J. & Louisa to come & make *chicken salad*"; "making 12 qts. Chicken Salad $1.25 a qt. for Mrs. Bruce's party to night." "Mrs. J. here yesterday & to day & cooked crabs." "Mrs. Jacobs called with Jellies for Mrs. Earle." Louisa tried to supplement their income by sewing, and Wilbur, who loved fashion, recorded one such attempt. Louisa came "to help me fix Polonaise" (an elaborate full-skirted overdress), but "it will not look well. I will have her make a basque [bodice]—Perhaps she will do as as well as any one. I don't expect it will be *good dressmaking*."

Louisa had no desire to become a modiste. Long before the war Jacobs, discussing Cornelia Willis's willingness to have her daughter join the household, had concluded, "Louisa would not be happy to live in that way. She wants to seek her own livelihood where she thinks she can be most useful." For the past twenty years, Louisa had searched for work appropriate to her education, but in color-coded patronage-driven Washington she had been unable to find it. Wilbur spelled out the reason Louisa's prospects were not good: "Civil Service, & her *color* both in the way." Finally in the spring of 1891, however, Louisa managed to find temporary employment in the Census Bureau, and afterward, a position in the Treasury Department.

Contemporary accounts stress the issue of the gentility of the women hired in government offices. Although one tourist charged, "they told us that we must not come here, to mingle with such people as they thought were in the Departments," the thousand female employees in the U.S. Treasury had their defenders. One wrote, "There is not another company of woman-workers in the land which numbers so many ladies of high character, intelligence, culture, and social position." If Louisa Jacobs was assigned the same task as most, she became one of the 200 underpaid women who worked side by side at long tables in the basement of the building, identifying and restoring mutilated bills.

They handled damaged currency that came, one commentator noted, "From the toes of stockings, in which they have been washed and dis-solved; from the stomachs of animals, and even of men; from the bodies of drowned and murdered human beings; from the holes of vice and of deadly disease, these fragments of money, whose lines are often utterly obliterated, whose tissues emit the foulest smells." Then at three in the afternoon, after a day's work, Louisa joined the others as "hats and shawls come down from their pegs, lunch-baskets come forth from their hiding-places, the great corridors, and porticoes, and broad streets are thronged with homeward-wending workers." But this job proved all too temporary. Jacobs again fell ill and needed full-time nursing. For a while the mother and daughter managed to scrape along, then finally decided that they had no choice but to sell their Edenton property.

Molly Horniblow had been living in the house on King Street when she wrote her will in July 1840. With her were her son Mark Ramsey, her great-grandchildren Joseph and Louisa—and her fugitive grand-daughter Harriet, hidden under the porch roof. With her son Mark unable to inherit because he was still a slave, and with her granddaughter Harriet a slave and in hiding, Molly Horniblow tried to preserve her property for her family by naming as her joint executors and legatees two of Edenton's aristocracy—Josiah Collins III and Dr. William Warren. She was counting on these elite men to disclaim her small inheritance and somehow arrange for it to pass to her son, whom she hoped to emancipate.

Molly Horniblow had apparently bought her property with the help of its owner Alfred Moore Gatlin, the Edenton attorney who had also managed her purchase and emancipation and the purchase of her son Mark Ramsey. Then in November 1842—a few months after her granddaughter finally fled north—Molly Horniblow had petitioned the North Carolina legislature for permission to free her son, noting that since slaves could neither be gifted nor inherit, while Mark remained in slavery, "there is no one to whom her property can descend." To strengthen her appeal, she had collected and appended the endorsements of more than eighty of Edenton's prominent citizens. (Dr. Norcom was not among them.) Although her petition was denied, by the time a year later Mark applied for a license to marry, he had become a free man. Later, after Molly Horniblow's death, Mark and his wife Ann continued living in her house. Then in the autumn of 1858 Mark died, and Dr. Warren took Molly's will to court for probate at the December term.

Not long after learning of her uncle's death, Harriet Jacobs had written to Josiah Collins III, asking about her grandmother's house and land. Instead of throwing her letter into the fire, Collins responded—although with an extraordinary lack of civility. Disdaining to use a standard greeting as he began his letter to a former "slave girl," refusing to address his correspondent with any formal designation at all, he opened his letter by writing "Harriet Jacobs" and after completing his message, abruptly signed himself "Josiah Collins." Collins writes that Molly Horniblow had never consulted with him about becoming her heir or her executor, but that he had learned from Dr. Warren "that her purpose in disposing of her property as she did—was the protection of the same—and the ultimate disposition of it for the benefit of her son, Mark—who at that time had not been emancipated." Collins informs Jacobs that he wants no portion of Molly's property. "Upon the settlement of the estate—should there be a balance of distribution this would come—if I understand the will rightly, to Dr Warren and myself—but neither he nor I desire to touch a copper of it."

A dozen years and a civil war later, Collins was dead, and neither his heirs nor Dr. Warren any longer renounced "a copper" of her estate. Instead, in February 1867 the heirs were awarded Grandmother's property, and Warren successfully sued to eject Uncle Mark's widow Ann Ramsey from her home. Although in her 1867 letter from Edenton Jacobs had written, "I am sitting under the old roof twelve feet from the spot where I suffered all the crushing weight of slavery," she had needed a stranger's permission to sit there. Her family no longer lived under that roof. Harriet was staying next door with her uncle's widow, the evicted Ann Ramsey.

Although she had lost Molly's house, however, Ann Ramsey owned other Edenton property. Five years after Jacobs's visit, when Ramsey was planning to remarry, she remained mindful of Jacobs's interests and created a trust directing that if her daughter died without children, the property should go to "Harriet Jacobs and her daughter Louisa." When Jacobs and Louisa visited Edenton in 1889, it is possible that Ann Ramsey Mayo was already ill. She wrote her will, and although her holdings had changed, her heirs remained the same. She carefully included her late husband's niece, "my beloved friend and kinswoman the said Harriet Jacobs." Ramsey Mayo instructed that the proceeds of one lot be divided between her daughter and Jacobs, and that her other lot be left to her daughter, but that in the event of the daughter's death, this, too, should be sold and the proceeds divided between her son-in-law and Harriet Jacobs.

Now in August 1892, selling the property that Ann Ramsey Mayo had so carefully left her, Jacobs was severing her last ties with Edenton. Since that rainy night she had fled the Norcoms, she had led a rootless life. Her inability to plant roots is emblematic of the condition of her people. For those unwilling to accept second-class status in post–Civil War America, where was there to go? The hopes that, as a young girl, Jacobs had conceived for her home and her family—the dreams that, during the war she had worked to realize for the entire South—had been murdered by the burnings and lynchings charring the former Confederacy, and by the government's betrayals of her people throughout the North.

The following spring, Wilbur scribbled a note revealing Louisa's distress—at the impossibility of finding a professional job, at her mother's physical condition, at her life: "Louisa Jacobs called. No signs of getting a place at present. Her mother very poorly. Louisa talked of the *Slave* Life & their life since. They have suffered *so much* & now are poor." Hard times were everywhere. The failure of an English bank in 1890 had occasioned the withdrawal of European finances from America, which resulted in wage cuts that sparked strikes. After the 1893 stock market collapse, unemployment reached new highs, and the following year, the armed battle between strikers and Frick's Pinkertons at Homestead inaugurated the labor wars characterizing the decade. Everywhere, unemployed workers began organizing "industrial armies." Best known was Coxey's army, which arrived in Washington on May Day, 1894, to join marchers from other states planning to lobby Congress for relief. Wilbur reported the climax in her diary: "Coxey & Browne [his press agent] & the men, paraded.—went to capitol. Brown showed fight & was arrested—Coxey was taken away by police. No speeches allowed."

But Congress was beginning to look beyond America's borders. With the century's end, the quest for foreign markets was beginning, and as historian Nell Painter writes, "Anglo-Saxonism combined variously with arguments for Anglo-American identity of interest, the white man's burden, manifest and ordinary destiny, and duty." Non-Anglo-Saxon Americans were shouldering a different burden: Native Americans faced genocide, Chinese immigrants faced exclusionary legislation, and African Americans faced increasing discrimination, repression, and violence. Twenty-five hundred lynchings were reported between 1885 and 1900. A dozen years earlier, the Supreme Court had struck down the Civil Rights Act of 1875 and destroyed protection against racial discrimination in public places. Now the State of Mississippi ratified a new constitution disfranchising African Americans. South Carolina followed, and in 1896 the United States Supreme Court, in the case of *Plessy v. Ferguson,* ruled that "separate but equal" accommodations met the requirements of the Fourteenth Amendment. The era of segregation that would rule American race matters until the civil rights movement of the 1950s and 1960s had begun.

Old, sick, and poor, Jacobs in many ways exemplified the condition of her people in the last decade of the nineteenth century, when "the barrier of caste, seemingly collapsing in the late 1860's, had become stronger than ever." With the condition of African Americans worsening dramatically, Washington's black community was organizing to collect food and fuel for their needy neighbors, but this time, Jacobs was not among those dispensing relief. In the years that were left, instead of soliciting the comfortable to help the poor, Jacobs became an object of the philanthropy of others. Her old friend Reverend Francis Grimké, back in the city after a long absence, began including her in his weekly home visits. Then in 1894 Jacobs, already suffering from various other conditions, was diagnosed with breast cancer and admitted to Washington's homeopathic hospital to undergo surgery.

Despite her advanced age, Harriet Jacobs recovered, and now Cornelia Willis came forward. Throughout her Washington years, Jacobs's connections with the Willis family had never been broken. When young Bailey Willis had arrived in the District to work for the Geological Survey, she had helped him and his bride settle into their L Street home. Later, when Lilian Willis was married in New Bedford, Jacobs was invited and was "taken into the wedding parlor on the arm of one of the family." (The bride was the baby who, a lifetime ago, Jacobs had carried in her arms as she fled the slavecatchers, setting out from New York "in a heavy snow storm, bound for New England again.")

Years earlier, discussing her many-layered relationship with Cornelia Grinnell Willis, Jacobs had written that not only "circumstances," but "love, duty, gratitude, also bind me to her side." Her choice of language is telling. All her long life, Jacobs felt the obligation of this mix of gratitude, duty, and love and remained bound to Willis who had, she testified, "bestowed the inestimable boon of freedom on me and my children." But hers was not a one-sided bond. Jacobs had also written, "God had raised me up a friend among strangers. . . . Friend! It is a common word, often lightly used. Like other good and beautiful things, it may be tarnished by careless handling; but when I speak of Mrs. Bruce as my friend, the word is sacred" [ILSG pp. 200–201]. During Jacobs's increasingly difficult last years, Willis maintained her commitment. Meeting her at Jacobs's home, Wilbur commented, "She is the friend in need of Mrs. Jacobs, & indeed, too."

With the eighty-one-year-old Jacobs recovering from surgery, Cornelia Grinnell Willis helped her and Louisa (now her mother's full-time nurse) settle into a small house on Pierce Place, where they rented out rooms. She then solicited aid from Ednah Dow Cheney, her colleague in the New England Women's Club and Jacobs's Civil War sponsor. Willis, explaining that although "the phenomenal vitality has held," Jacobs "is helpless however and still suffering from the two mortal diseases which are eating away the life," asked for help with medical expenses. But when

Cheney, ever an organizer, proposed that they mount a public benefit for Jacobs, Willis rejected the idea. "I should not like to make such a public appeal without consulting Louisa. Poor child she suffers under the obligation as she considers it, very keenly, and would only be willing under the very last pressure for her Mother's comfort."

Despite Willis's disapproval, Cheney solicited a few of the old New England activists for help. A few days later, Louisa wrote thanking her. She felt embarrassed that her nursing responsibilities caring for her mother prevented her from earning money to support them. "I am," she wrote, "always grieved and hurt at the necessity of calling on friends for aid." Expressing gratitude for the money Cheney had collected from Garrison's son and from Anna Parsons, she voices mixed feelings at being the object of their philanthropy: "while it saddens me I am glad that friends think my Mother worthy of their sympathy." Then, testifying both to her own feminism and to her awareness of Cheney's commitment to women's issues, "I know Mrs. Cheney you have felt interested in the—two Conventions held here by colored women. They have been well conducted and largely attended and the promise is of work that will tell for the elevation of the race." Black women were organizing. More than fifteen years earlier, in response to the increasingly repressive racial climate, Mary Ann Shadd Cary and other Washington women had banded together to form the Colored Women's Progressive Franchise Association, and they later launched the Colored Women's League. Then in 1895, League members met in Boston with women from throughout the country, and now, a year later, the Washington women were hosting representatives from Boston and New York to form the National Association of Colored Women.

Jacobs was beyond recovery. In the fall, she fell from her wheelchair and injured her hip, and in late February, Louisa received a long letter from Joseph Pierce—the wayward Georgia boy she and her mother had taken into their lives and into their home long ago. In Washington in his young manhood, Pierce had failed to embrace Jacobs's model of education and service. But more recently, he had written to Reverend Francis Grimké, asking him to tell Jacobs and Louisa "that at last the Lord has answered their prayers in my behalf, and that to day I am a saved man and a child of his, through the blessed Blood of Jesus Christ. . . .Though late," he continued, he would "try to make some amends for the contemptible manner in which I have behaved toward them." Now as her mother lay dying, Louisa wrote asking Joe to come. Addressing her as

"My dear Aunt Lou" and writing on Salvation Army stationery, he explains that he cannot afford the price of a ticket from Chicago to Washington. "Give my love to Ma and tell her that I believe this delay is a trial of our faith and for her to continue to pray for me."

A week later, Harriet Jacobs died in her Washington, D.C. home. When Pierce heard, he wrote immediately. "Although the news was not unexpected, I was shocked, but I very quickly realized that God, in His infinite mercy, had done for Ma, more than earthly friends could do, had given her rest. . . . I am certain that you realize that I couldn't get money to come, I tried and prayed, but it seemed as though it was intended as a punishment for not coming when I was making money instead of throwing away my money and then lying about it." Expressing concern about "Aunt Lou's" future, he promises, if "you must go to work for a living, I shall immediately give up my commission as an officer and come to you," and signs himself, "Ever yours faithfully, *Joe*." Louisa never heard from him again.

Jacobs had outlived her generation. One by one, the giants with whom she had worked for freedom had died: William C. Nell, Maria Stewart, William Lloyd Garrison, Lydia Maria Child, Sojourner Truth, Wendell Phillips, Maria Weston Chapman, Amy Post, Ellen Craft, Mary Ann Shadd Cary, and Frederick Douglass. Now she, too, was gone. Although a Boston newspaper noticed her death, the obituary it published is odd. Its subject is not named until the middle of the article, which treats Jacobs solely as the recipient of white patronage. It first identifies her in connection with her job "as nurse in the family of N. P. Willis." Then, mentioning that she "went to England, where she was hospitably entertained by the Duchess of Sutherland and many well known sympathizers with the anti-slavery cause," it notes—although it does not name—her book, "a touching little story of her life, relating therein one of the most painful histories of the well born mulatto slave at the South, and her efforts to escape from bondage." The Harriet Jacobs School and her relief work during the Civil War and Reconstruction are completely omitted. Actually, few in Boston remembered. New England Women's Club member Dr. Marie Zakrzewska saw Jacobs's death notice and sent it to Ednah Dow Cheney, but when Cheney spoke of Jacobs at the Club, "only the older members remembered her so rapidly does the world change."

Writing to Cornelia Grinnell Willis, Cheney sent her sympathy and expressed concern about Louisa. "The dear little thoughtful girl who concealed her knowledge of her mother's neighborhood and the deep longings of her heart, that she might not peril her safety or increase her grandmother's anxiety has been the same thoughtful loving child throughout her long life, and I am thankful that she has been able to be with her to the last and give her all the comfort and help that a loving daughter can and what more could she do—. . . . She ought to have a rest after this long watching."

In contrast to the newspaper obituary, the elegy delivered by Reverend Francis Grimké focuses on Jacobs's activism, on her selfless commitment to her people, and on her character. Over the years, he recalls, he enjoyed hearing her "speaking of the stirring times before the war when the great struggle for freedom was going on, and of the events immediately after the war. She was thoroughly alive to all that was transpiring, and had a most vivid recollection of the events and of the actors, the prominent men and women, who figured on the stage of action at that time. She herself at the close of the war took an active interest in, and played a most important part in caring for the freedmen, in looking out for their physical needs, and in providing schools for the training of their children."

"She impressed me," Grimké continues, "as a woman of marked individuality. There was never any danger of overlooking her, or of mistaking her for any body else. . . . She rose above the dead level of mediocrity, like the mountain peaks that shoot above the mountain range. . . . She was no reed shaken by the wind, vacillating, easily moved from a position. She did her own thinking; had opinions of her own, and held to them with great tenacity." Coupled with this was her tender heart. "How natural it seemed for her to take up in the arms of her great love, all who needed to be soothed and comforted. . . . Especially did her sympathies go out towards the poor, the suffering, the destitute. She never hesitated to share what she had, with others, to deny herself for the sake of helping a suffering fellow creature. There are hundreds, who if they had the opportunity, to day would rise up and call her blessed, to whom she has been a real sister of charity, a veritable Dorcas."

Six days after her death, Harriet Jacobs was buried in Cambridge's Mount Auburn cemetery next to her brother John. Louisa's final tribute echoes neither the newspaper's obituary nor Grimké's elegy. The words she chose for her mother's tombstone do not focus on Harriet Jacobs's relationship with the elites of the old world and the new, nor do they focus on her work for her people. Instead, they speak of her great strength and of her passionate commitment: "Patient in tribulation, fervent in spirit serving the Lord." These lines come from the Epistle to the Romans, in which Paul exhorts his readers to be "fervent in spirit; serving the Lord; Rejoicing in hope; patient in tribulation. . . . " On Jacobs's stone, however, Louisa reversed his strictures—emphasizing the trouble her mother passed through—and she omitted "Rejoicing in hope." What does this lapse signify? Does it speak to Jacobs's—or to Louisa's—lack of hope? To her despair at the condition of her people at century's end?

Feeling that "it is not fitting that a life so noble, so remarkable and so instructive, should pass away without some record," a few months after Jacobs's death, Cheney sent a long piece to the *Woman's Journal*. After recounting Jacobs's life in slavery and her long imprisonment, and touching on her later efforts "to support herself and children and to benefit humanity," Cheney praises Jacobs's book. "It should," she writes, "be carefully preserved in our libraries, for it is a wonderful record of the suffering and heroism of those never to be forgotten days." But even before her death, Harriet Jacobs had been largely forgotten. In the *History of Woman Suffrage*, Elizabeth Cady Stanton, collapsing Jacobs into her narrator "Linda," then muddling her together with a fictional character, had written, "The same love of liberty that glowed in eloquent words on the lips of Lucretia Mott, Angelina Grimké, and Mary Grew, was echoed in the brave deeds of Margaret Garner, Linda Brent, and Mrs. Stowe's Eliza." Then as years passed, memory of Jacobs became even more faint. The records of her Alexandria school were lost. Her book came to be thought the work of her editor L. Maria Child.

And so she vanished. The only black women who have come down to us from the nineteenth century are Harriet Tubman and Sojourner Truth. Tubman lives on in black culture as "the Moses of her people" who brought them out of the Egypt of southern slavery. The pentacostal Truth became the "Lybian Sibyl" of Harriet Beecher Stowe's essay and William Wetmore Story's heroic sculpture, then the "strong black woman" who "had to deliver every black woman's message." Both figures are larger than life. Both are exotics.

But "Mrs. Jacobs" was a woman like other women. This very fact may have made it difficult for most Americans to acknowledge her at the turn of the century. If "Mrs. Jacobs" was not—like Tubman and Truth—larger than life, but was actually a woman like ourselves, how could we have permitted the institution of chattel slavery? If "Mrs. Jacobs" was a woman like ourselves, how could we now permit the structures of Jim Crow to be put into place and maintained? Although a shade darker, the carefully dressed and neatly coifed "Mrs. Jacobs" of the albumin portrait looks like anyone's grandmother. And it is not only her appearance that seems unexceptional. In her lifelong struggle for a home in freedom for herself and her people, she was endorsing values accepted as mainstream, although within the contexts of American slavery, white racism, and sexism—the contexts of her life—her struggle was revolutionary. As segregation became the way not only of the South but of the nation, there was perhaps a little room in the national memory for heroic figures like a "Moses" or a "Sibyl," but there was no room for a "Mrs. Jacobs." Despite Cheney's belief that "such a life ought not to pass away without fitting record," and despite Reverend Grimké's conviction that a sketch of her life would be done "at another time, and by other hands," she was forgotten.

Jacobs had ended her Author's Preface with a prayer: "May the blessing of God rest on this imperfect effort in behalf of my persecuted people!" [ILSG p. 2]. Her book survived in a few collections, but it remained unread. The story it tells was perhaps not, in Toni Morrison's words, "a story to pass on." Male turn-of-the-century readers, it might be supposed, found it a "women's book." White female readers were perhaps put off by "Linda's" account of her scandalous sexual history. Even if black women readers valued the book, they did not command the attention of the publishing industry. *Incidents in the Life of a Slave Girl* was not republished. By the 1950s and 1960s, at the birth of the modern civil rights movement, it was generally held that that the work was a fiction by the white abolitionist L. Maria Child.

But today, Jacobs's prayer is being answered and her legacy understood. She left her book—finally acknowledged as her autobiography—now recognized as a key nineteenth-century American text. Translated and published in German, Portuguese, French, and Japanese, it is in print in a score of editions in English and is read in high schools and colleges across the country. She left her papers—the only papers of a woman held in American slavery known to have survived—now being prepared in a scholarly edition that maps out relationships among feminist and abolitionist reformers before, during, and after the Civil War. And she left the example of her life—the example of "a soul that burned for freedom and a heart nerved with determination to suffer even unto death in pursuit of that liberty which without makes life an intolerable burden."

Afterword

❦

A nd Louisa? Forever, it seemed, she had been Harriet Jacobs's caregiver. But at her mother's death, she was unable, as Ednah Dow Cheney hoped, to "have a rest after this long watching." Instead, she needed to look around her for a way to make a living and a way to make a life. What she settled on was the very institution she had worked hard to keep her mother out of: the National Home for the Relief of Destitute Colored Women and Children. Organized during the Civil War by the activist women sponsoring the work she and her mother were doing in Alexandria, the National Home had been designed as an asylum for the orphans and penniless old women refugees crowding the capital. It had a rocky start. In 1866, it was forced to relocate when its Georgetown property was restored to its Rebel owner (just as the Georgia ricefields had been turned back to the planters). But over the years, the Home had become an established refuge, and with the closing of the Freedmen's Bureau, it was annexed to Freedmen's Hospital. Although the trustees remained all white, by 1869 Sarah Martin (wife of Harriet Jacobs's old friend J. Sella Martin) was named a manager. Then in 1880, Helen Appo Cook became the first black woman to serve as secretary, and from that time forward, the home increasingly came "under the control of members of the race for whom it was founded." These women were determined to demonstrate "that with proper assistance, the colored race, is capable of great improvement, nay, of maintaining an enviable position, side by side with the dominant Caucasian."

Louisa turned to the Home at her mother's death. Now in her middle sixties, she was not looking for a handout, but for a job. Her great friend Charlotte Forten Grimké was among the elite women of color associated with the institution, and in 1898, Louisa was appointed assistant matron. The next year, she was promoted to matron –joining the staff of a superintendent, a teacher, an assistant teacher, an industrial teacher, a "kindergartner," and a physician.

Moving into the building on 8th Street out beyond Northern Boundary, Louisa found herself in a new situation, charged with caring for eleven aged women (the oldest ninety-eight) and ninety-five children (the youngest only four). Still, some things seemed familiar. She and her mother had always organized holiday celebrations for the neglected and forgotten, and now, living among the poorest of the poor, Louisa again made holiday plans. She called on the Willis daughters to help, and they responded with gifts of candy and trimmings for the tree. With Joseph Pierce lost to her, she found another young person to care for and mentor: young Loretta Simms, who had lived in the Home since she was three. Life was not easy. Year by year, donations were dwindling, and the building was falling into decay. The sewage system was inadequate, as was the heating plant: "During the bitter weather of last winter no efforts on the part of the Superintendent and her assistants could prevent real suffering of the children and old people, especially at night."

In 1903, the National Home welcomed a celebrated resident. Mrs. Lincoln's confidante and modiste Elizabeth Keckley, who had sparked the organization of aid to Civil War refugees, had fallen on hard times and moved into the institution she had helped found. That year, the vice president of the Home regretfully accepted Louisa's resignation. "I am sure both the children and Old Women will all miss you for you have endear yourself to them all. . . . you have all ways been so faithfull—" (Though she had taken a new job, Louisa demonstrated her commitment by continuing the annual donation that guaranteed her membership.)

Now Louisa moved back to Howard University's Miner Hall— although not as a member of the faculty, as a dozen years earlier. She returned as matron/preceptress at a salary of $500 a year, plus room and board. Keeping track of energetic striving young students was a challenge after living with helpless old women and rambunctious children, but she handled it well. When in 1908 she resigned, Howard University President Thirkield praised her ability to work with the students and commented on her "nobility of nature, gentleness of spirit and uniform courtesy. . . . Amid great provocation, often, in the management of such a large company of young people, you have shown a self-control and patience altogether admirable." She saved his letter all her life.

At seventy-five, Louisa was no longer a wage earner. Earlier, writing her will, she had identified the people important to her. She omitted all mention of Elleanor, William, and Joseph Ramsey, the children of her beloved uncle John S. She did, however, remember William and Elijah

Knox, the sons of her mother's half-brother Elijah. And she testified to her feeling for the Willis daughters by making Edith her executrix and leaving a bequest to Lilian. She also remembered friends from girlhood—the Philadelphia Chews, Hattie Smith, and Charlotte Forten Grimké. From her more recent life, however, she singled out only one—Loretta Simms—and she included a bequest to the National Home.

Louisa spent her last years as a companion to Edith Willis Grinnell, and at the end, she was at least partially a dependant of Edith's brother, Grinnell Willis. A lifetime earlier, her mother had tried to reject their mother's offer to buy her freedom, feeling that "such a great obligation could not be easily cancelled." It never was. The devoted daughter of an extraordinary mother, all her long life, Louisa remained bound by the same "love, duty, and gratitude" that had bound Harriet to Cornelia [ILSG pp. 199, 201]. When in 1917, Louisa Matilda Jacobs died, it was at the Brookline home of Edith Willis Grinnell, who buried her at Mount Auburn next to her uncle and her mother.

Notes

~✦~

Note on the Text

Excerpts from the correspondence have been reproduced as accurately as possible from the holographs. Jacobs routinely capitalizes important words but omits capital letters at the beginnings of sentences. Because in the early letters she also omits most punctuation, even final periods, spaces marking full stops have been inserted to aid the reader.

Abbreviations

AMA	Records of the American Missionary Association, 1846–1882
BAP	*The Black Abolitionist Papers*, ed. C. Peter Ripley, et al.
BAPM	*The Black Abolitionist Papers*, (microfilm edition) ed. George E. Carter, et al.
DAB	*Dictionary of American Biography*
DANB	*Dictionary of American Negro Biography*
DNB	*Dictionary of National Biography*
IAPFP	Isaac and Amy Post Family Papers
ILSG	*Incidents in the Life of a Slave Girl*
JWD	Julia Wilbur Diary
LMCP	*The Collected Correspondence of Lydia Maria Child, 1817–1880* ed. Patricia G. Holland
NCSA	North Carolina State Archives
NFP	Norcom Family Papers
TT	"A True Tale of Slavery"
RLASS	The Rochester Ladies Anti-Slavery Society Papers

Introduction

xv   *In my dissertation The Intricate Knot: Black Figures in American Literature, 1776–1863* (New York: New York University Press, 1972).

xvi   *While reading chronologically Incidents in the Life of a Slave Girl: Written by Herself* (Boston: For the Author, 1861); enlarged edition, ed. Jean Fagan Yellin (Cambridge: Harvard University Press, 2000). Hereafter ILSG in the text, with relevant page numbers.

xvi   *the book's author* See John Blassingame, *The Slave Community* (New York: Oxford University Press, 1972), pp. 233–34; and Jean Fagan Yellin, "Text and Contexts of Harriet Jacobs's Incidents in the Life of a Slave Girl: Written by Herself," in *The Slave's Narrative*, ed. Charles T. Davis and Henry Louis Gates Jr. (New York: Oxford University Press, 1985), p. 278, note 2.

xvi   The Narrative of James Williams *The Narrative of James Williams, Who was for Several Years a Driver on a Cotton Plantation in Alabama* (New York: Anti-Slavery Society; Boston: Isaac Knapp, 1838).

xvii   *a letter expressing her sympathy* Lydia Maria Child to Theodore Dwight Weld, December 29, 1838, in *Lydia Maria Child, Selected Letters, 1817–1860*, ed. Milton Meltzer and Patricia G. Holland (Amherst: University of Massachusetts Press, 1982), p. 105.

xviii We Are Your Sisters Dorothy Sterling, *We Are Your Sisters: Black Women in the Nineteenth Century* (New York: W. W. Norton, 1984).

xviii *Dated "Edenton April 25th"* Harriet Jacobs to Amy Post, April 25 [1867]. Isaac and Amy Post Family Papers, University of Rochester (hereafter IAPFP).

xix   *Dr. Andrew Knox* Will of Dr. Andrew Knox, May 20, 1816, Pasquotank County Original Wills, 1709–1917, North Carolina State Archives (hereafter NCSA).

xx   *the Papers project has been awarded* The Harriet Jacobs Papers Project is contracted with the University of North Carolina Press to produce a two-volume edition of the Papers, and with the backing of the Press, the North Carolina State Archives, and Pace University, has been awarded funding from the Gladys Delmas Foundation, the National Endowment for the Humanities, and the Center for the Study of the American South, and has won the endorsement of the National Historic Records Preservation Commission.

Chapter 1. So Fondly Shielded

4   *Edenton was an important port* Thomas D. Parramore, *Cradle of the Colony: The History of Chowan County and Edenton, North Carolina* (Edenton: Edenton Chamber of Commerce, 1967), pp. 5–15, 26–27.

4   "*It appears that most vessels*" Johann Schoeph, quoted in Parramore, *Cradle*, pp. 38–39.

4   *Horniblow's Tavern* Chowan County Deed Book 0–1, pp. 132, 145, 294. Office of the Register of Deeds, Chowan County Courthouse, Edenton, N.C. (hereafter Chowan Deeds); Tax Lists, 1779–82, Chowan County Tax Lists, 1717–1909. NCSA (hereafter Chowan Tax Lists).

4   *"a hundred slaves aboard"* Diary entry of Robert Hunter Jr., quoted in Thomas H. Claryton and Jean B. Anderson, *Close to the Land: The Way We Lived in North Carolina, 1820–1870* (Chapel Hill: University of North Carolina Press, 1983), p. 10. The text explains that port records indicate that eighty slaves, not a hundred, were brought.

5   *Edenton celebrated* (Edenton) *State Gazette of North Carolina,* December 3, 1789, in *Edenton: A Portrait in Words and Pictures* (Meriden, Connecticut: Meriden Gravure, 1984), p. 28.

5   *"lolling in tavern piazzas"* Parramore, *Cradle,* pp. 44–45.

5   *"to North Carolina a* blood-*sucker"* Thomas R. Butchko, *Edenton: An Architectural Portrait* (Edenton N.C.: Edenton Woman's Club, 1992), p. 18.

5   *the 1791 revolution* For Haiti (Santo Domingo), see C.L.R. James, *The Black Jacobins,* 2d ed. (New York, Vintage Books, 1963); for the influence of the Haitian revolution, see C. Duncan Rice, *The Rise and Fall of Black Slavery* (Baton Rouge: Louisiana State University Press, 1975), pp. 259–60.

6   *The* Edenton Gazette *reported Edenton Gazette,* March 22, 1811, p. 3.

6   *everyone "who has not arms"* Parramore, *Cradle,* p. 52.

6   *Over the years* Estate of Elizabeth Horniblow, 1827, Chowan Estates; Answer of James Norcom to the bills of complaint in equity of Frederick Hoskins and wife Eliza, 1834, in Estate of Elizabeth Horniblow, 1827, Chowan Estates (hereafter Answer of James Norcom). NCSA.

7   *"in many an hour"* [John S. Jacobs], "A True Tale of Slavery," first published in London, England, in *The Leisure Hour: A Family Journal of Instruction and Recreation* 10, nos. 476–79 (February 7, 14, 21, and 28, 1861), and reproduced in ILSG; the quoted passage is on p. 207. Subsequent references to this edition are labeled TT and included in the text. ILSG p. 90.

7   *Elijah was born* Death Certificate of Elijah Knox, January 15, 1907, City of New Bedford, Massachusetts; Chowan Deeds S-I, pp. 139–40, Tax List for 1781, Chowan Tax Lists; State Census of North Carolina, 1786–87, Chowan County, NCSA; Will of Andrew Knox, 1775, Perquimans County Original Wills, 1711–1909, NCSA; Estate of Andrew Knox, 1775, Perquimans County Estates Records,

1740–1930. NCSA; Sales from the Estate of Andrew Knox, 1787, Secretary of State Records—Inventories and Sales of Estates, 1712–98. NCSA.

8   *expert workmanship* See Elizabeth Vann Moore, *Guidebook to Historic Edenton and Chowan County* (Edenton, N.C.: Edenton Woman's Club, 1989); and Elizabeth Matheson, *Edenton: A Portrait, in Words and Pictures* (Edenton: Edenton Historical Commission, 1984), pp. 15, 19, 23, and 33.

8   *"tearing down"* John C. Bond's "Reminiscences attached to drawing of the Horniblow Tavern by B?V? Webb," Cupola House Papers, reel 3. NCSA.

8   *the Jon Kuners appeared* As if exposing the hidden violent center of Edenton's pleasant life, in 1823 one of Jon Kuner's celebrants committed the unthinkable reversal. He did not merely parody the slavocracy; he violated its most fundamental law by killing a white man. See Elizabeth A. Fenn, "'A Perfect Equality Seemed to Reign': Slave Society and Jonkonnu," *North Carolina Historical Review* 55, no. 2 (April 1988): 150–51. Stephen Nissenbaum, *The Battle for Christmas* (New York: Knopf, 1996), pp. 265–91; thanks to Lauren Osborne.

9   *"any person or persons"* Chowan County Miscellaneous Slave Records, 1730–1866 (CR.024.928.33) "Writ of Outlawry of Slaves, 1816"; Chowan County Criminal Records Concerning Slaves, 1816, NCSA.

10   *"with 8 children"* Edenton Gazette, December 1, 1818; April 27, 1819.

10   *Dilworth Edenton Gazette*, March 2, 1819.

11   *"On Tuesday evening"* Edenton Gazette, May 11, 1819.

11   *"gaining flesh and Strength"* Dr. James Norcom to Dr. John Norcom, May 4, 1818; and December 12, 1819, Norcom Family Papers, NCSA. (hereafter NFP).

11   *"it was common"* James H. Garrett quoted in Parramore, *Cradle*, p. 53.

12   *"Temporary booths"* and "people who have" *Harper's Magazine*, 1857; an unidentified visitor in 1861; both in Parramore, *Cradle*, pp. 66–68.

12   *Reading and spelling Acts Passed by the General Assembly of the State of North Carolina at the Session of 1830–1831* (Raleigh: Lawrence and Lemay, 1831), p. 11.

12   *"two accomplished Female Teachers"* Edenton Gazette and North Carolina General Advertiser, January 19, 1819.

13   *the precepts* Edgar W. Knight, *Public School Education in North Carolina* (Boston: Houghton Mifflin Co., 1916), p. 194. At eleven,

Margaret and her sister Mary had been given handsome prayer books with their names in gilt letters on the cover by Dr. Norcom; see James Norcom to Dear Sir, July 20, 1809, *The Pettigrew Papers*, I, 1685–1818, ed. Sarah McCulloh Lemmon (Raleigh, North Carolina: State Department of Archives and History, 1971), p. 417.

13   *"the spelling I believe"* Harriet Jacobs to Amy Post, Cornwall, New York, June 25 [1853]. IAPFP.

13   *the marriage of her daughter Eliza* Announcement of marriage of Eliza Horniblow and Frederick Hoskins of Plymouth at Edenton, May 11, 1820, *Raleigh Register* (weekly), May 26, 1820. (Hereafter *Raleigh Register*) Answer of James Norcom; "Horniblow, Elizabeth, 1827," Chowan Estates Records, 1728–1951. NCSA.

14   *For Elijah* Death Certificate of Elijah Knox, City of New Bedford, Massachusetts, January 12, 1907, vol. 12, p. 44. For Lavinia Matilda Knox's marriage to James Coffield, see *Raleigh Register* July 9, 1824.

14   *"It is my will"* Will of Margaret Horniblow, 1825, Chowan County Original Wills, 1694–1910, NCSA (hereafter Chowan Wills).

Chapter 2. My Puny Arm Felt Strong

16   *Norcom* Dr. James Norcom (1778–1850) graduated from the Medical School of the University of Pennsylvania in 1797. Information about his life comes NFP.

16   *"an imprudent and inordinant attachment"* Petition of James Norcom, November 30, 1808. James Norcom's divorce from Mary Custus, 1808. From Legislative Papers, 1808. L.P. 227. NCSA. Supporting Norcom's accusations, others testified that "so entirely did she abandon all care of his domestic offerings, as to suffer the negroes to waste the years allowance of provision, say Bacon by the middle of July," that she had been known to "come into the room where several young men . . . have been in bed, with no more clothes on, than her shift, and make use of such language accompanied with appropriate actions, as to clearly evince . . . that her only apparent wish was the gratification of that sensual passion, whose violence was so great as to destroy all reason and cool reflection," and that she had delivered a stillborn baby that was not Norcom's. Deposition of Stephen R. Hooker, September 16, 1808, Norcom Divorce legislative papers, 1808, p. 227ff.; Deposition of Mary Caskanden, August 27, 1808, and Deposition of Peggy Ferrell, August 24, 1808 in the Norcom Divorce legislative papers, 1808. L. P. 227, NCSA.

16   *"In the prime & vigour"* James Norcom. fragment. n.d., NFP.

17   *an old house in Eden Alley* For Norcom's house, see Robanna S. Knott, "Harriet Jacobs: The Edenton Biography" (Ph.D. diss.,

University of North Carolina at Chapel Hill, 1994), p. 136, note 27, citing Catherine Birshir et al., *Architects and Builders in North Carolina* (Chapel Hill: University of North Carolina Press, 1990), pp. 14–16. For Norcom's children, see NFP. The names of the slaves come from Writs of Execution on Dr. James Norcom's slaves 1828–38, compiled by George Stevenson in September 1997; the quotation is from ILSG p. 144. According to ILSG p. 9, Harriet Jacobs and her brother John entered the Norcom home together; according to TT in ILSG, p. 208, when John was in his tenth year, he was taken from his father and put into Dr. Norcom's shop. Evidently he was then housed at the Norcoms'.

18   *household chores* For the work of slave children, see, for example, *Remembering Slavery*, ed. Ira Berlin, Marc Favreau, and Steven F. Miller (New York: The New Press, 1998).

18   *"added another link"* Elijah's wife Theresa was perhaps Theresa Artis. Death Certificate of Elijah Knox, City of New Bedford, Massachusetts, January 12, 1907, vol. 12, p. 44. For Lavinia Matilda Knox's marriage to James Coffield, see *Raleigh Register* July 9, 1824. TT in ILSG, pp. 208–9.

18   *Since 1787* John S. Bassett, *Slavery in the State of North Carolina*, Johns Hopkins University Series in History and Political Science, Series XVII, nos. 7–8 (Baltimore: Johns Hopkins Press, 1899), p. 34; *Edenton Gazette*, November 10, 1812 (from the *New Bern Spectator*, October 31, 1812). For Cheapside, located between Water and West King on Broad Street, see Knott, "Harriet Jacobs."

19   *Providence would be forgotten* For the rediscovery and reconsecration of Providence, see Cemetery Location Affidavit, March 27, 2000, Real Estate Book 262, pp. 36–38, Register of Deeds, Chowan County; "Black Burial Ground Uncovered," *Chowan Herald*, March 16, 2000, and "Burial Site Restoration Under Way" (Edenton) *Daily Advance*, October 6, 2000. Alfred Churton (c. 1771—?), son of Joseph Churton, emancipated servant of William Churton, was trained as a barber but earned his living as a tailor, in Edenton's "Cheapside." Thomas Barnswell (1777—?), freeborn, was a sailor who in 1809 opened a shop on the wharf. Jeffrey G. Iredell, a barber (1774–1837), was emancipated by James Iredell in September 1812. George Bonner (c. 1752—c. 1825), a house carpenter, belonged to the Bonner and Murse families until his emancipation in 1807. In 1818, Barnswell, Churton, Iredell and Bonner jointly purchased a block of town lots, where they built a meeting house and a burying ground, and a mutual aid society. With Providence and the Humane Society, Edenton's black community was able to establish and control its own rituals of life and death. For Churton, see Emancipation of Joe, slave of William Churton, in Chowan County Court

Minutes, April 1766—March 1772, p. 366, entry for March Term 1768; Apprenticing of Alfred Churton son of Joe Churton to learn barbering, b. December 1785, in Chowan County Apprentice Bonds 1737–1809; Bill dated January 3, 1800, for tailoring done for Dr. John Cunningham in Chowan County Estates Records—Dr. John Cunningham, 1799, NCSA. For Barnswell, see deed, Thomas Barnswell, mariner, to Littlejohn and Bond of Edenton January 9, 1806, in Chowan County Deed Book C-2, p. 263; purchase of the house standing on Edenton wharf wherein he now lives, in deed, Henderson Standin to Thomas Barnswell, September 6, 1810, in Chowan County Deed Book E-2, pp. 177–78. NCSA. For Iredell, see bequest to Iredell of all the shaving implements and "everything" in the shop of James Cunningham, HD [hair dresser], in Chowan County Wills, James Cunningham, 1816, and purchase by Iredell of half the barber shop furniture at sale of Cunningham's estate in Chowan County Estates, James Cunningham 1816; Emancipation of Jeffrey G. Iredell in Chowan County Miscellaneous Slave Records, 1730–1836-Petition for Emancipation, 1812, and Chowan County Court Minutes, September Term 1812. NCSA. For George Bonner, house carpenter, fifty-five years old, emancipated by William T. Murse, Chowan County Court Minutes, June Term 1807. NCSA. For Providence, see Joint Purchase of a block of town lots in deed, John B. Blount and Bond, executors of James Norfleet, to Thomas Barnswell, Jeffrey G. Iredell, Alfred Churton, and George Bonner, July 8, 1818, in Chowan County Deed Book G-2, p. 477. NCSA. The Humane Society buried both free people and slaves; Providence meeting house was built and owned by the Society; see the execution on "one fourth part of a house called & known by the name of the Negro Baptist Providence Meeting House," September 5, 1831, in the cause Josiah Coffield vs. Alfred Churton, in Chowan Civil Action Papers, 1831, NCSA; and deed between James and Henrietta Norcom, and William W. White dated November 8, 1871, Deed Book V p. 107; deed dated January 22, 1916, in Deed Book M, p. 519, and deed dated April 12, 1939 in Deed Book No. 2, p. 433. NCSA.

20   *"twenty eight negroes" Edenton Gazette*, January 26, 1827.

21   *"almost total exclusion of light"* D. M. Wright, M.D., N. Leggett, M.D., and W. C. Warren, M.D. to A. Moore Esq., Edenton, May 24, 1845. Governor's Papers, William A. Graham, April—June 1845. (G.P. 110) NCSA.

22   *His price* For the description of a similar scene in Wilmington, North Carolina, on January 1, 1840, see James Sprunt, *Chronicles of Cape Fear River* (Raleigh: Edwards & Broughton, 1914), pp. 179–80.

22   *"It may seem rather strange"* Petition for Emancipation, 1828, Chowan County Miscellaneous Slave Records, 1730–1836, NCSA. TT in ILSG, p. 209.

23 *"stormy, terrific ways"* "The methods of establishing control over another person are based upon the systematic, repetitive infliction of psychological trauma. They are the organized techniques of disempowerment and disconnection. . . . designed to instill terror and helplessness . . . to convince the victim that the perpetrator is omnipotent, that resistance is futile, and that her life depends upon willing his indulgence through absolute compliance." L. Herman, *Trauma and Recovery* (New York: Basic, 1992), p. 77.

23 *Norcom remained unrelenting* On the dispute between Norcom and Messmore, see Dr. James Norcom to [John Norcom], April 28, 1845, NFP; State v. Daniel Messmore, 1845, and State v. John Cox & Others, 1845, Chowan County Criminal Action Papers, 1844–45, NCSA; and Mary Matilda Norcom Messmore to Maria Norcom, July 4, 1848; Dr. James Norcom at Philadelphia to Mary Matilda Norcom at Edenton, November 8, 1835; Dr. James Norcom at Edenton to Mary Matilda Norcom at Philadelphia, February 28, 1837. NFP.

24 *Like other domestic tyrants* Herman, *Trauma and Recovery,* pp. 80, 83.

24 *"Why does the slave"* Her inquiry [ILSG p. 37] recalls a poem published locally that begins, "Why do we love?" and ends, "Then do not love." *Edenton Gazette,* February 3, 1829.

25 *Mark Ramsey* Allan Ramsay (1753–99) was the son of James Ramsay. In 1786, he married Sarah Bateman (? —1791). Most of Ramsay's estate was left to nephews living in nearby counties. He directed his executors to arrange for the emancipation of his slave woman Sarah. Chowan County Court Minutes, April 1766—March 1772 (CR.024.301.6), p. 289; Chowan County Marriage Bonds, Allan Ramsay to Sarah Bateman, February 24, 1786; Chowan County Wills, Ramsay, Allan, 1799; Chowan County Estates Records, Ramsay, Allan, 1799 and Ramsay, Sarah 1791, NCSA; WPA Cemetery Survey, Inscriptions in St. Paul's Churchyard, Edenton.

25 *Were there two fugitives* Jacobs attributes Joseph's "white face" to Molly Horniblow's "Anglo-Saxon ancestors," not to the family of Joseph's father [ILSG p. 6]. While it remains speculation whether Molly's son Joseph was Churton's son, it is clear that Churton's son Joseph escaped from Josiah Collins c. 1829, and that Molly's son Joseph escaped from Josiah Collins at about the same time. Nine years later, the property was conveyed to Collins in payment for Joseph. Deeds Alfred Churton to Thomas Waff, September 22, 1829, in Chowan County Deed Book I-2, pp. 233–34; and Thomas Waff to Josiah Collins, July 20, 1838, in Chowan County Deed Book L-2, p. 452. NCSA.

26   *Auguste Cabarrus* May 20, 1798. Stephen Cabarrus of Pembroke to
      Auguste Cabarrus, for £200, a Negro girl named Rose, age eighteen
      or nineteen. Chowan County Deed Book B-2, p. 5; June Term 1808.
      Auguste Cabarrus to the Court. Petition for Emancipation of Negro
      Woman Rose. Chowan County P&Q Court Minutes, June Term
      1808; September 15, 1808. Auguste Cabarrus of Pembroke to Rose:
      "a small mulatto girl called Charlotte, age eight, and a mulatto boy
      called Leon, age six—these two, her children." Chowan County Deed
      Book D-1, pp. 194–95; December 1808. General Assembly. Upon
      petition of Rose Cabarrus, the General Assembly emancipated her
      children under the name Charlotte and Leon Green. General Assem-
      bly Session Records. March 15, 1816. NCSA. "Auguste Cabarrus of
      Pembroke to Free Negro Woman Rose . . . a Negro woman named
      Mary Sue, aged 58, mother of the aforesaid Rose."

26   *When cataloguing Cabarrus's effects* Auguste Cabarrus's death was
      reported in the *Raleigh Register* on August 6, 1819. For the suit to
      recover the watch, see papers in the action Auguste Cabarrus's
      Administrator vs. Rose Cabarrus, Chowan County Civil Actions for
      September 1820. NCSA. For the imprisonment and escape of Leon
      Cabarrus, see *Edenton Gazette*, August 14 and 21 to September 18,
      1820. For Leon Cabarrus's trial for his life in superior court, the judg-
      ment of guilt, and his sentence to whipping and imprisonment, see
      Chowan County Superior Court Minute Docket, 1809–28, p. 180,
      October Term 1820. NCSA. On January 10, 1821, Rose Cabarrus's
      home was attacked by a white mob looking for her son, and the grand
      jury presented an indictment against seven men—including Samuel
      Tredwell Sawyer, home from college. See deposition of A. G. Keys in
      cause State vs. A. G. Keys, Chowan County Criminal Action Papers,
      1820; and Chowan County Criminal Action Papers, 1821. NCSA.

26   *Major Sam* "Sawyer, Samuel T.," Entry of February 24, 1819, Faculty-
      Alumni File, University Archives, Swem Library, College of William
      and Mary.

26   *Now back home* ILSG p. 53; Samuel T. Sawyer to James C. John-
      ston. 11[?] February, 1825, Southern Historical Collection, Univer-
      sity of North Carolina. Hayes Collection, no. 324.

28   *"This is to request"* Samuel Tredwell Sawyer to Dr. James Norcom,
      July 2, 1828. NFP.

Chapter 3. A Determined Will

30   *a difficult pregnancy* According to a writ of *venditione expones*,
      Chowan County Civil Actions Concerning Slaves, 1830, on October
      5, 1830, Betty had a child. NCSA. According to ILSG, Betty had
      delivered two living children, "one of whom died in a few days, and

the other in four weeks." pp. 143–44; Sawyer and the naming of Harriet Jacobs's child is discussed in ILSG p. 62.

30   *most daily bread was cooked* See George Stevenson to Jean Fagan Yellin, February 17, 1999; Dr. James Norcom to Elizabeth Norcom, Edenton, June 26, 1846. NFP.

31   *all of Edenton was hierarchical* This discussion of Edenton's hierarchies is based on an analysis of George Stevenson. For Jane Banks and her family, see Chowan County Criminal Action Papers 1825, 1826, 1828, 1829, 1830, and 1834, NCSA; and see George Stevenson to Jean Fagan Yellin, June 20, 1997. For Judith Burke and her family, see Chowan County North Carolina Miscellaneous Papers, vol. 1, 1685–1744, p. 102; January Term 1756, Chowan County Court Minutes, 1755–61 (CR.024.301.4) p. 415; April Term, 1764, Chowan County Court Minutes, 1761–66 (CR.024.301.5) p. 193; January Term, 1767, Chowan County Court Minutes, 1766–72 (CR.024.301.6) p. 320; March Term, 1771, Chowan County Court Minutes, 1766–72, pp. 591, 594; June Term, 1771, Chowan County Court Minutes, 1766–72 (CR.024.301.6), pp. 605–6. NCSA. Also see George Stevenson to Jean Fagan Yellin, June 20 and June 28, 1997.

32   *"if they are not absolutely mean"* Edenton Gazette, November 7, 1829. The following week, newcomer Dr. J. R. Herndon exacerbated the problem by publishing an exchange of letters with Norcom, who writes that he *"has* been . . . [slandered] more than once." *Edenton Gazette*, November 15, 1829.

32   *"Medical Establishment"* Edenton Gazette, December 5, 1829.

32   *At the beginning of the new year* Edenton Gazette, January 16, 1830; the ad is dated January 1 and runs through February 20.

32   *considering a move* In ILSG, however, Jacobs makes no mention of his plans to leave Edenton—unless her references to his plan to move to Louisiana refer to this episode.

33   *When, condemning that "Tariff of Abominations"* See *The Growth of the American Republic*, ed. Samuel Eliot Morrison and Henry Steele Commager (New York: Oxford University Press, 1956), pp. 476–77.

33   *The* Gazette *lamented* "Roanoke Inlet," *Edenton Gazette*, March 13, 1830.

33   *"We have to present"* "Shocking," *Edenton Gazette*, April 22, 1830.

33   *"in March 1829"* Edenton Gazette, March 17, 1829.

33   *"NEGROES WANTED"* Edenton Gazette, August 25, 1829.

33   *on August 26, 1830* Writ dated August 26, 1830. NCSA.

34   *he was reelected* Writing to Sawyer on July 2, 1828, Norcom refers to his having been defeated in an "anterior contest," and that year

Sawyer was beaten 38–36 in his bid for election to the Assembly. The following year, however, Sawyer won election to the State House of Representatives. General Assembly Session Records, November 1830—January 1831 (Box 5), Certificates of Election-House. NCSA. Sawyer was regularly reelected thereafter, traveling to Raleigh each November, and returning to Edenton each January at the end of the session. He served as representative from Edenton 1829–30; 1830–31; 1831–32; and 1832–33. Elected to the state Senate, he served 1834–35.

34   *"the* northwest *of town" Edenton Gazette,* May 27, 1830.

34   Walker's Appeal David Walker, *Walker's Appeal, in four articles, together with a preamble to the Coloured Citizens of the World, but in Particular, and Very Expressly, to Those of the United States of America.* 1830; rpt. ed. Peter P. Hinks. University Park: Pennsylvania State University Press, 2000. For Walker, see *Dictionary of American Negro Biography,* ed. Rayford W. Logan and Michael R. Winston (New York: W. W. Norton, 1982), pp. 622–23 (hereafter DANB).

34   *Alerted to this "inflammatory" document* For the impact of Walker's *Appeal,* see John Hope Franklin, *The Free Negro in North Carolina* (New York: W. W. Norton, 1999), pp. 62–70.

34   *"emissaries have been dispersed" Edenton Gazette,* September 23, 1830.

34   *"unjustly and wantonly impugned" Edenton Gazette,* October 4, 1830.

35   *"to prevent the gaming" Edenton Gazette,* January 27, 1831.

35   *"a nullifier, a Traitor" Edenton Gazette,* August 3, 1831.

36   *"It seems that the insurrection" Edenton Gazette,* August 31, 1831.

37   *"ten likely fellows"* Thomas Hoskins to Thomas Ruffin, September 2, 1831, Thomas Ruffin Papers, NCSA; in Charles Edward Morris, "Panic and Reprisal: Reaction in North Carolina to the Nat Turner Insurrection" (master's thesis, Department of History, North Carolina State University at Raleigh, 1979), p. 25.

37   *"Since our last 19 negroes" Edenton Gazette,* September 7, 1831.

38   *"not the slightest evidence" Edenton Gazette,* November 10, 1831.

38   *"People felt"* True Bill Against Sandy of Brownrigg. NCSA. Kemp Plummer Battle, *Memories of an Old Time Tar Heel,* ed. William James Battle (Chapel Hill: University of North Carolina Press, 1945), p. 151, quoted in Thomas C. Parramore, "The Great Slave Conspiracy," *The State,* August 15, 1971, p. 19.

38   *"those persons" Edenton Gazette,* September 14, 1831.

38   *the military presence was inescapable* For the Chowan Guards, see *Edenton Gazette,* September 7; October 5, 19, and 26; November 9; and December 7, 1831. For the Cavalry Company, see *Edenton Gazette,* October 5 and November 2, 1831.

39   *"Vigilant Association" Edenton Gazette,* October 26, 1831.

39   *"a seditious publication" Edenton Gazette,* October 26, 1831.

39   *The* Boston Courier "Incendiary Publications," *Edenton Gazette,* November 23, 1831.

39   *Hatty was pregnant again* According to her gravestone at Mount Auburn cemetery, Cambridge, Massachusetts, Louisa Matilda Jacobs was born on October 11, 1836. According to Chapter 17 of ILSG, however, she was two years old when her mother went into hiding. Since Jacobs went into hiding in June 1835, the year of Louisa's birth must have been 1832 or 1833.

40   *to mark her as a whore* Norcom's biblical model was the judgment of the wicked daughters of Zion. See Isaiah 3:24.

41   *"Satinetts of various qualities" Edenton Gazette,* January 2, 1830; also see, for example, the issues of March 31, 1829, and May 11, 1831.

41   *the decapitated body* From the record that appears to be the inquest of George Cabarrus, dated September 17, 1833; Chowan County Miscellaneous Records, 1719–1916, Inquests (various dates, 1803–34). NCSA.

41   *George, his washerwoman's son* TT in ILSG p. 224; the Frenchman Stephen Cabarrus arrived in North Carolina in 1776 and acquired by marriage the estate of Pembroke on Pembroke Creek, which empties into Edenton Bay on Albemarle Sound. In his will, Stephen Cabarrus mentions George, one of the children of "Mariann the washing woman." After the death of Stephen's brother, the slaves were sold, and George was bought by John Popelston. Hurt by the bank closings, on June 20, 1829, Popelston sold George to Jonathan B. Haughton, who probably sold him to the trader in 1832 or 1833. Will of Stephen Cabarrus, 1808, Chowan Wills; Chowan County Deed Book I-2, p. 247. NCSA. For Pembroke, see "Old Pembroke," *The Economist* (Elizabeth City), April 1881.

41   *"This slave man"* [Harriet Jacobs], "A Fugitive," "Cruelty to Slaves," *New York Tribune,* July 25, 1853. She remembered the month incorrectly; it was not August, but September. The court document indicates that the inquest was conducted at Haughton & Booth's Wharf, where the body was lying. Also see TT in ILSG p. 224.

41   *instructed . . . to see* Norcom to Dr. John Norcom, January 29, 1833, NFP; TT in ILSG p. 208.

41   *commissioning a slaveholder* In the sole remaining issue of the *Edenton Gazette* for 1821, dated March 7, is an ad dated February 22 to run for four weeks. It reads: "CASH FOR NEGROES," and is signed by Thomas W. Overly, who announces that he can be found at Hoskins's Tavern.

41   *"beautiful black eyes"* Casper W. Norcom to Maria Norcom, Raleigh, March 22 [1835]. (The year has been determined from a

reference to the approaching wedding of Annie Iredell to Cadwallader Jones.) NFP.

42   *people he believed beneath her* The reference may be to the Banks family.

42   *the slaves' cabins* For a description of slave quarters in Chowan a generation later, see Allen Parker, *Recollections of Slavery Times* (Worcester, Massachusetts: Charles W. Burbank, 1895), pp. 11–13.

43   *fieldworkers' children* Parker, *Recollections,* p. 17.

43   *"the slaves' holiday"* Parker, *Recollections,* p. 58.

45   *this "wanted" ad* "$100 Reward" *American Beacon* (daily), Norfolk, Virginia., June 30—August 14, 1835 ;see ILSG p. 237. Jacobs quotes a somewhat different version, ILSG p. 97.

45   *"standing in the street"* Parramore, *Cradle,* pp. 62–63.

45   *"who studied the welfare"* It seems likely that Jacobs's protectress was Mrs. Martha Hoskins Rombough Blount (1777–1858), daughter of Richard and Winifred Hoskins, who had known Molly all her life. William Rombough, her first husband, was brother to John Horniblow's wife. In 1835, Mrs. Blount was living in her Queen Street home with three slaves of taxable age. Hiding her friend's granddaughter was dangerous: In North Carolina, punishment for harboring a runaway slave included fines and imprisonment. J.R.B. Hathaway, ed., *North Carolina Historical and Genealogical Register* (Edenton: n.p., 1900–1903), I:460–61; Tax Lists, 1819–1837, Chowan County Tax Lists, NCSA; Bassett, *Slavery in North Carolina*, p. 15.

46   *members of the household* At the death of William Blount in 1819, his will restored to his widow the slaves Venus, Abraham, Nancy, Jenny, and Charles, a boy; until his son Edmund came of age, he lent to her for her use the slaves Davy and his wife Fanny, and the girl Candace. By 1835, when Jacobs went into hiding, Mrs. Blount reported only three black taxables. If one was the faithless Jenny and the other the faithful cook, her third slave was either old Venus, Abraham, or the boy Charles. Will of William Rombough, 1808, and Will of William Blount, 1819, Chowan County Wills. Chowan County Tax List, 1835. NCSA.

46   *Molly's well* Although there were town pumps at the market, the court house, and other places, the town had no system of pipes to carry water into homes, and Edenton property owners had their own wells. One of the purposes of the property tax was to defray the cost of keeping the wells and pumps working. Molly's well was repaired in December 1833 and in August 1834. Then on June 27, 1835, again in July, and yet again on October 30, the town paid men to work on Molly's well. In 1836, it was also repaired. Town of Edenton, 1831–40, *Cupola House Papers* (Reel 3). NCSA.

46   *George Lamb, the jailer*, Richard Benbury Creecy, "*Grandfather's Tales of North Carolina History*" (Raleigh: Edwards & Broughton, 1901), pp. 132–35.

47   *Clement Hall* Baker Hoskins, Mrs. Blount's brother, had died on May 19, while Jacobs was at Auburn plantation; his family was living at Clement Hall, which is still standing about a mile north of Edenton. Obituary of Baker Hoskins, *Biblical Recorder* (Raleigh), June 17, 1835.

47   *Cabarrus Pocosin* Cabarrus Pocosin, "Snaky Swamp," lies southwest of Edenton and is visible from the shipping channel in Albemarle Sound used by east-by-northeast traffic headed for sea. "By far, the largest hideout, temporary quarters, and home for thousands of runaway slaves was the Great Dismal Swamp. The Dismal Swamp, located in southeastern Virginia and northeastern North Carolina, provided shelter, food, and refuge for slaves for more than two-hundred years." Freddie L. Parker, *Running for Freedom: Slave Runaways in North Carolina, 1775–1840* (New York: Garland, 1993), p. 33.

47   "*inhabited almost exclusively*" Robert C. McLean, ed., "A Yankee Tutor in the Old South," *North Carolina Historical Review* 47 (January 1970): 56; quoted in Parker, *Recollections,* p. 35.

47   *maroons* For maroons, see *Edenton Gazette,* March 22, 1811; March 2, 1819; and May 11, 1819.

47   "*It is very likely*" *Edenton Gazette,* May 8, 1827.

47   *access to vessels* Parker, *Recollections,* pp. 47–48. Most vessels in the port did not have North Carolina captains or crews. With luck, a runaway could arrange to be concealed or perhaps even hired; hence the warnings in slave ads of penalties for carrying off fugitives. Also see Parker, *Recollections,* p. 45.

47   *Chowan County would contain* Parker, *Recollections,* writes that by 1840, 54.7 percent of Chowan's population was slave, p. 17; also see p. 45.

48   "*great numbers of cypress trees*" J.F.D. Smyth, *A Tour in the United States of America* (London: G. Robinson, J. Robson, and J. Sewell, 1784), 1:107–8.

Chapter 4. Cunning Against Cunning

49   *concealing a fugitive slave* The penalty for harboring a runaway was different from the penalty for harboring a runaway to assist in his escape from the state. For harboring a runaway, the harborer, if sued by the owner, had to pay the state $100 and the owner $100 and damages, and he would be prosecuted. The maximum sentence was

$100 fine and 6 months imprisonment. *Revised Statutes of the State of North Carolina* (Raleigh, 1837), 1: c. 34, 573. In 1799, it had been made a capital felony to steal or to seduce away a slave. "Whoever aided a runaway to escape should on conviction pay L100 to the owner of the fugitive and, in addition, whatever damages might be incurred." *Revised Statutes of the State of North Carolina* 1:c.34s.11. In 1793 it had been made a capital felony for a ship captain "to take, or knowingly to allow others to take, a slave out of the State, without the written consent of the slave's master." John S. Bassett, *Slavery in North Carolina*, p. 15; for an instance in which this law was enforced, see *The State v. Edmund, a Slave, 15 N.C. Reports 340*, December Term 1833, pp. 290–95.

50   "*massive free-floating anxiety*" Stuart Grassian and Nancy Friedman, "Effects of Sensory Deprivation on Psychiatric Seclusion and Solitary Confinement," *International Journal of Law and Psychiatry* 8 (1986): 54, 60; see also "Isolation Experiments," in *The Oxford Companion to the Mind*, ed. Richard L. Gregory and O. L. Zangwill (New York: Oxford University Press, 1987), pp. 393–94; and Peter Watson, *War on the Mind: The Military Uses and Abuses of Psychology* (New York: Basic, 1978), pp. 266–74.

50   "*indulge in passion*" Dr. James Norcom to Dear Daughter [Mary Matilda Norcom], Philadelphia, November 8, 1835. NFP.

51   "*that horrible & almost insupportable*" Dr. James Norcom to My Dear Maria, December 6, 1840. NFP. Also see Dr. James Norcom to Dr. Physic, n.d., and to My Dear Son [Dr. John Norcom] April 7, 1841.NFP.

51   *pointless journey north* According to John Norcom to Benjamin Rush Norcom, August 10, 1835, Dr. Norcom was traveling in August 1835. NFP.

51   *Molly's well* Work was done on Molly's well in June, July, and October 1835. "Town of Edenton, 1831–1840," *Cupola House Papers*, (Reel 3). NCSA. William Rea, town constable and clerk of the market in 1832–35, was paid for the repair and cleaning of Molly's well in 1833, 1834, and 1835, and was one of the constables again in 1838. *Cupola House Papers* (Reel 3), Town of Edenton, 1831–40. NCSA. ILSG p. 119.

52   *Reverend Dr. Avery* For the Reverend John Avery, see [Joseph Blount Cheshire, ed.], *Sketches of Church History in North Carolina . . .* (Wilmington, North Carolina: Wm. L. DeRosset, Jr., Publisher, 1892), pp. 178–79, 256–58.

52   *Mrs. Bissell's will* Will of Mary Bissell, 1836, Chowan Wills. NCSA. Also see Memory F. Mitchell, "Off to Africa—With Judicial Blessing," *North Carolina Historical Review* 53 (July 1976): 269–71.

52 *the* Gazette reported "Emigration of People of Color" *Edenton Gazette*, January 26, 1827.

52 *Hon. James Iredell Jr* Mitchell "Off to Africa," p. 270; *African Repository* 2 (April 1826): 62; also see North Carolina Colonization Society, Auxiliary to the American Colonization Society, Raleigh, January 4, 1831, James Iredell Sr. and Jr. Papers, Letters, 1830, 1852, William L. Perkins LIbrary Duke University.

52 *indicted by the court* North Carolina Supreme Court ruling in favor of American Colonization Society, February 1846; superior court grand jury indictment of Captain Wright and Maria for fornication, and of Maria for hiring herself dated fall 1842; trials in March 1843. Dr. Norcom's suit against Cox, executor of the Bissell estate, awarded in 1843; Writ of *fieri facia* served on Cox; judgment levied on Maria April 1843; Maria seized under writ of *venditione exponas* and sold July 22, 1843, to James R. Lemmitt. NCSA. Upholding the legality of Maria's sale, Chief Justice Thomas Ruffin wrote, "Justice stands before generosity."

In February 1846, the Supreme Court decided in favor of the American Colonization Society bequest. Nancy had died in June 1841, Molly Mare in March 1842, and John in September 1842; Maria, sold in July 1843, apparently died soon after. Mary had reached adulthood and borne a daughter in 1848. Lucy had a son in 1850 who died at three, and a second child born December 28, 1853. Nothing is known of Priscilla. Mrs. Bissell's executor John Cox died in 1856. In 1857, Dr. William C. Warren petitioned the Court of Pleas and Quarter Sessions for an accounting from Cox's executor, and on December 1, 1859, the accounting was made. Also see Memory F. Mitchell, cited above. "John Cox, Executor of Mary Bissell vs. William J. H. B. Williams, et al.," Supreme Court Original Case Papers (reported in 39 NC 15 [1845]). NCSA. Selected documents in the estate file of Mary A. Bissell, 1835, in Chowan County Estates Records, 1728–1951, NCSA: "Estate of Mary A. Bissell in Account with John Cox, dec'd., 1835–1854"; Writ of *venditione expones* executed July 22, 1843; complaint of Dr. William C. Warren, Administrator *de bonis non cum testamentor annex* against John Cox's administration, September 1857. Indictments and writs of arrest in "State vs. Maria, a slave, commonly called Maria Bissell" and in "State vs. James Wright" in Chowan County Criminal Action Papers, 1842. NCSA.

53 *When the vestrymen* St. Paul's Vestry Minutes, vol. 2, pp. 40–41, 44, 46–49, 50, 52, 72. NCSA.

53 *"a certain person"* Chowan County Miscellaneous Records—Inquests, 1836. NCSA. TT in ILSG p. 224.

53 *During the second winter* Jane Iredell, Edenton, N. C., to James Iredell, Esq., Raleigh. PC. 67.17, Charles F. Johnson Collection. NCSA.

54   *"a suicidal perverseness"* Quoted in Parramore, *Cradle*, p. 60.

54   *"290 persons"* The Whigs had joined the anti-Van Buren coalition backing Sawyer. Dr. James Norcom to John Norcom, August 9, 1823. NFP.

54   *"the practice of treating"* "Treating at Elections," *Edenton Gazette*, July 15, 1830; also see June 3 and August 5 and 12, 1830; and "Treating at Elections," July 13, 1831.

54   *Norcom nevertheless* "The Jubilee," *Edenton Gazette*, June 15, 1831; also see "Fourth of July," July 6, 1831.

55   *"certain malign"* Samuel Tredwell Sawyer to General James N. McPherson, August 5, 1837. Ferebee-Gregory-McPherson Papers, Southern Collection, University of North Carolina; Election Returns for Member of Congress, 1837, from Chowan County Election Records, 1772–1864. NCSA.

57   *Over the years* For *Edenton Gazette* stories concerning antislavery sentiment in Massachusetts, see, for example, items concerning the (Boston) *Liberator* on October 26, 1831; and "Incendiary Publications," November 2 and November 23, 1831.

57   *In August 1838* Obituary of John S. Russell (brother-in-law of Lavinia Peyton). Undated 1861 clipping in the possession of Jean Fagan Yellin.

58   *the Astor House Hotel* The Astor House Hotel was on Broadway between Vesey and Barclay streets; Johnson Jeremiah & Co., trunkmakers, had a shop at 40 Fulton. John A. Kouwenhoven, *The Columbia Historical Portrait of New York* (Garden City, New York: Doubleday, 1953), p. 176; *Wilson's Business Directory of New-York City* (New York: H. Wilson, 1848), p. 234.

58   *boarded the 4:30 boat* In 1838, Sound steamers and overnight boats to Providence departed from Pier 1. Rail lines ran from Providence to Boston, Massachusetts, and to Stonington, Connecticut. Robert G. Albion, *The Rise of New York Port, 1815–1860* (New York: Scribner's, 1939, 1970), p. 91. Thanks to Norman Brouwer, Maritime Historian, South Street Seaport Museum, New York.

58   *Sawyer ran for reelection* Sawyer ran for reelection as a Democrat. The comment describes a speech Sawyer gave in a later election. William D. Valentine diaries, July 22, 1841, vol. 7, p. 31, Southern Historical Collection, University of North Carolina # 2148; *Edenton Gazette*, July 6, 1839; John M. Wheeler, *Historical Sketches of North Carolina*, (Baltimore: Regional Publishing Co., 1964), II:94–95.

60   *Like many slaves* Sale was a common cause for running, and family was a common destination; see Parker, *Running;* and John Hope Franklin and Loren Schweninger, *Runaway Slaves: Rebels on the Plantation* (New York: Oxford University Press, 1999). The ads do not change much through the years. See, for example, ad of James

Coffield, March 7, 1832; ad of Charles W. Mixson, February 20, 1833, ad for Josiah Price: "It is believed he is lurking in the neighborhood of Gates Court House, where he has a grandmother, and two brothers, named Jim and Peter Price, who will no doubt make exertions to conceal him"; ad of James Norcom, August 26, 1830, Lucy, who "formerly belonged to a Mr. Grice of Pasquotank County, and has relations near Elizabeth City, where no doubt she may be found."

61   *had become a communicant* For Dr. James Norcom's religious status, see Richard Rankin, *Ambivalent Churchmen and Evangelical Churchwomen: The Religion of the Episcopal Elite in North Carolina, 1800–1860* (Columbia: University of South Carolina Press 1990), pp. 60–61, 112–15; ILSG p. 145.

61   *Charles W. Mixson had advertised Edenton Sentinel and Albemarle Intelligencer*, May 1, 1841. I am grateful to Henry Watson for calling this item to my attention.

Chapter 5. Sometimes Like Freedom

63   *the details of her escape* For Jacobs's escape, see George Stevenson, "Calendar for the Escape, June 1842" and "Schooner *Skewarkey* 46 61/90th Tons," to Jean Fagan Yellin, May 13, 1998. For the *Skewarkey* and Captain James A. Wright, see "Record of Enrollments Issued and Credited in the District of Edenton, Commencing 1 January 1842," p. 323; and "Record of Register Issued and Credited in the District of Edenton Commencing 1st Jan 1842," p. 160, Bureau of Marine Inspection and Navigation (RG 41), National Archives. For Captain James O. Wright, see Chapter 4, above. For a description of the voyage of a schooner that apparently took the same route as Harriet Jacobs's escape vessel, see F. Roy Johnson, *Sail and Steam Navigation of Eastern Carolina* (Murfreesboro: Johnson, 1986), pp. 32–34. Thanks to Dan Law and apologies to George Stevenson. ILSG p. 156.

64   *"the earth was so full"* Parramore, *Cradle*, pp. 63–64.

65   *Philadelphia was big* For Jacobs's Philadelphia, see Gary B. Nash, *Forging Freedom: The Formation of Philadelphia's Black Community, 1720–1840* (Cambridge, Massachusetts: Harvard University Press, 1988), pp. 246–79; and Julie Winch, *Philadelphia's Black Elite: Activism, Accommodation, and the Struggle for Autonomy, 1784–1848* (Philadelphia: Temple University Press, 1988), pp. 152–66.

65   *the names of black folks* According to the 1850 Philadelphia census, ninety-one black residents were born in North Carolina. There is no way of knowing which, among them, were from Edenton. Population Studies Center, University of Pennsylvania to Jean Fagan Yellin, August 16, 1998. ILSG p. 159.

65   *Reverend Jeremiah Durham* Durham is named in ILSG p. 159. For
      Jeremiah Durham, see the 1838 census, Book Four, p. 589, where he
      is listed as a carter and his wife a washer, with one child attending
      school; a member of two Beneficial Societies, he attended Bethel
      meeting. 00016/75:16. Pennsylvania Anti-Slavery Census Facts.
      Book Three. Historical Society of Pennsylvania.

65   *In 1842* Emma Jones Lapsansky, "The Counter Culture of Agitation
      in Philadelphia," in *The Abolitionist Sisterhood*, ed. Jean Fagan
      Yellin and John C. Van Horne (Ithaca: Cornell University Press,
      1994), p. 92.

65   *The community supported* A Southerner (pseud.), *Sketches of the
      Higher Classes of Colored Society in Philadelphia. By a Southerner*
      (Philadelphia: Merrihew and Thompson, Printers, 1841), p. 19.
      McElroy's Philadelphia Directory for 1842 lists eight black churches;
      for the vigilance committee, see Joseph A. Borome, "The Vigilant
      Committee of Philadelphia," *Pennsylvania Magazine of History and
      Biography* 92 (July 1968): 320–51.

66   *"colored persons in distress"* The quoted phrase is taken from the
      1837 Organizing Minutes of the New York City Vigilance Commit-
      tee, quoted by Borome, "The Vigilant Committee," p. 320.

66   *constantly raising money* Borome, "The Vigilant Committee," p.
      343; Philip Lapsansky to Jean Fagan Yellin, October 11, 1985.

67   *Robert Douglass Jr.* For Robert Douglass Jr., see James Porter, *Mod-
      ern Negro Art*, (New York: Arno, 1969), p. 34; and Theresa Dicka-
      son Cederholm, *Afro-American Artists: A Bio-Bibliographical
      Directory* (Boston: Trustees of The Boston Public Library, 1973), p.
      81. Douglass is listed at 54 Mulberry Street in *McElroy's for 1842*, p.
      70. Visiting his studio, a friend wrote of his paintings, "he brought a
      great many home with him which he painted in Europe among which
      were, Benjamin West,—Queen Victoria, and Prince Albert." Jane
      Howell to Thomas Chandler, February 21, 1841, Michigan Histori-
      cal Collections, Bentley Historical Library, University of Michigan.

67   *Elizabeth Chew* It seems possible that, in addition to meeting Rev-
      erend Payne, Robert Purvis, and Elizabeth Chew, Jacobs also met
      Purvis's wife Harriet Forten Purvis and others of the Forten family.
      For Elizabeth and Hester Chew's membership in the Pennsylvania
      Female Anti-Slavery Society, see the 1845 list of members at the
      beginning of the Pennsylvania Female Anti-Slavery Society Minute
      Book in which first minutes are dated January 9, 1845, at the His-
      torical Society of Pennsylvania. For the women's commitment to the
      work of the Vigilance Committee, see *Ninth Annual Report of the
      Philadelphia Female Anti-Slavery Society, January 12, 1843*
      (Philadelphia: Merrihew and Thompson, Printers, 1843), pp. 10–11;
      Elizabeth Chew was also a member of the American Moral Reform

Society. In August 1839, she was among the delegates who passed a resolution stating "'That what is morally right for man to do, is morally right for woman,'" and therefore "earnestly and cordially invite women to co-operate with us in carrying out the great principles of moral reform." *The National Reformer* (Philadelphia), September 1839, pp. 140–43. For James Forten Sr., see Julie Winch, *A Gentleman of Color: The Life of James Forten* (New York: Oxford University Press, 2003).

67   *"furnish us"* Pennsylvania Female Anti-Slavery Society Minutes, Resolution September 9, 1841. Historical Society of Pennsylvania.

67   *One of these was scheduled* Pennsylvania Female Anti-Slavery Society Minutes 1839–44. Historical Society of Pennsylvania. Minutes of 6th month 23rd, 1842; that June, the Vigilance Committee system was working so well that no one could have predicted that six weeks later they would disband. But their August 1 celebration was mobbed, and Purvis's home, a target, was destroyed. Shocked and discouraged, Purvis moved his family out of the city to the safety of bucolic Byberry.

67   *Reverend Daniel A. Payne* For Daniel A. Payne (1811–93), see DANB, p. 484. For Harriet Jacobs and Payne, see Author's Preface, ILSG.

67   *"beautiful creature"* [Robert Purvis to Sydney Gay], Byberry, August 15, 1858. Gay Papers, Columbia University. I am grateful to Margaret Bacon for this letter. For Robert Purvis, see DANB, pp. 508–10; Janice Sumler Lewis, "The Fortens of Philadelphia: An Afro-American Family and Nineteenth-Century Reform" (Ph.D. diss., Georgetown, 1978); and an unpublished manuscript on Purvis by Margaret Bacon.

68   *segregated transportation* In 1838, the car into which blacks were segregated was called "the dirt car." By 1841, it was called the "Jim Crow" car. Abolitionists—and their successors—protested against "the 'negro pew' . . . wherever it may be found, whether in a gentile synagogue, a railroad car, a steamboat, or a stage coach." As the railroads expanded, black passengers were segregated into a separate car even when they bought first-class tickets, while black servants were able to travel with their employers. After activists mounted campaigns for equal accommodations in public transportation, Massachusetts railroads abolished segregation in 1842, and in New York in 1861. In Philadelphia, the struggle continued into Reconstruction. The last leg of Jacobs's trip from Philadelphia to New York City was by ferry; no tunnels or bridges had yet been built across the Hudson River. Phone conversation with Thomas Flagg, Freelance Industrial Archeologist, New York City, January 18, 2001; Carl Condit, *The Port of New York*, vol. I (Chicago: University of Chicago Press, 1980); See Louis Ruchames, "Jim Crow Railroads in

Massachusetts," *American Quarterly* 8 (1956): 61–75; Leon Litwack, *North of Slavery* (Chicago: University of Chicago Press, 1961), pp. 111–12; *Anglo-African* (New York), October 19, 1861 and July 16, 1864; "Colored People and the Philadelphia City Railroads," *The Liberator* (Boston), December 23, 1864; "Meeting of Colored People in Philadelphia," *National Anti-Slavery Standard* (New York), June 30, 1866.

68   *33 Sullivan Street* "Boarding—A few Gentlemen can be genteelly accommodated with board and lodging at 33 Sullivan Street." Ad in *The Colored American*, June 20, 1840, Apparently in 1842, a few ladies could also be accommodated.

68   *Fulton Street* For the Fulton ferry, see Norman Brouwer, "Moving People in the Port," *Seaport Magazine* (winter 1986–87): 34. For the *Fox*, which earlier had served as a Manhattan Island ferry, see Parramore, *Cradle*, p. 58.

68   *Mary Bonner Blount Tredwell* James Iredell Tredwell's mother, Helen Blair, and Margaret Hosmer Blair, Samuel Tredwell Sawyer's mother, were sisters. For Tredwell genealogy, see J.R.B. Hathaway, *The North Carolina Historical and Genealogical Register*, July 1901, vol. 2, no. 3 (rpt. Baltimore: Genealogical Publishing Company, 1970–1979), p. 459ff.

69   *Brooklyn had two African Free Schools* For Brooklyn's schools, see Robert J. Swan, "A Synoptic History of Black Public Schools in Brooklyn," in *The Black Contribution to the Development of Brooklyn*, ed. Charlene Claye Van Derzee (New Muse Community, Museum of Brooklyn, 1977), pp. 63–71.

69   *a Greek Revival row house* See Charles Lockwood, "The Old Merchant's House in New York City," *Antiques* 104, no. 6 (December 1973): 1065–67.

69   *Tredwell was facing ruin* For James Iredell Tredwell's precarious finances, see James Iredell Tredwell to James Iredell, October 28 [1828], in James Iredell Sr. and Jr. Papers, Manuscript Department, William R. Perkins Library, Duke University.

69   *shipped out on a whaler* John S. Jacobs had shipped out on the *Frances Henrietta* on August 4, 1839. TT in ILSG p. 221; Alexander Starbuck, *History of the American Whale Fishery from its Earliest Inception to the Year 1876*, 2 vols. (1878. rpt. New York: Argosy-Antiquarian, 1964), 1:354–55.

69   *"What an empire"* A. F. Rightor to Andrew McCollam, August 19, 1851, Andrew McCollam Papers, University of North Carolina at Chapel Hill, in John Hope Franklin, *A Southern Odyssey* (Baton Rouge: Louisiana State University Press, 1976), p. 21.

69   *Ladies' New York City Anti-Slavery Society* For the Ladies' New York City society, see Amy Swerdlow, "Abolition's Conservative Sisters," in

The Abolitionist Sisterhood, pp. 31–44. For the organized activities of New York black women, see Anne M. Boylan, "Benevolence and Antislavery Activity among African American Women in New York and Boston, 1820–1840," in *The Abolitionist Sisterhood*, pp. 119–38, especially pp. 121–22, 128, 134, and 136; and Anne M. Boylan, *The Origins of Women's Activism* (Chapel Hill: University of North Carolina Press, 2002).

70   *"when I first came North"* Harriet Jacobs to Amy Post, Cornwall, Orange County [1852?] IAPFP. ILSG p. 254.

70   *the American writer Nathaniel Parker Willis* Rufus Rockwell Wilson, *New York in Literature* (Elmira, New York: Primavera, 1947), p. 30. Researching his book on landscape, on the banks of Owego Creek Willis had exclaimed, "Here I would have a home!" *American Scenery. From Drawings by W. H. Bartlett. The Literary Department by N. P. Willis, Esq.*, 2 vols. (London: George Virtue, 1838). This was originally published serially. Boston, Philadelphia, and London editions followed in 1840. For Willis, see Henry A. Beers, *Nathaniel Parker Willis* (1885, rpt. New York: AMS, 1969); the quotation is on p. 262.

71   *Harriet's brother John* TT in ILSG p. 221; Robert H. Piper, son of activists William (1786–1870) and Amelia Piper, worked on the ship *Jefferson* in 1841. "Index of Blacks of New Bedford as Surveyed from the New Bedford City Directories, 1838–1845," comp. Judith Downey, New Bedford Whaling Museum; Marilyn Baily, "Index of Activist Black Women" (manuscript); James de T. Abajian, *Blacks in selected Newspapers, Census and Other Sources . . .* (Boston: G. Kittall, 1977), III, p. 70; "Deaths Registered in the City of New Bedford," *Vital Records*, 4:35, Free Public Library of the City of New Bedford. Thanks to the late Marilyn Baily, to Judith Downey of the New Bedford Whaling Museum, and to Joan E. Barney of the Free Public Library of the City of New Bedford.

71   *petitioned to free Uncle Mark* Bond of Marcus Ramsey for his marriage to Ann Johnson, November 22, 1843, in Chowan County Marriage Bonds, 1741–1868, NCSA; will of Ann Ramsey Mayo, 1890, in Chowan County Wills, 1694–1904. NCSA. See also George Stevenson to Jean Fagan Yellin, January 16 and September 16, 1997. For Molly Horniblow's November 30, 1842 petition to free Mark Ramsey, see North Carolina General Assembly Session Records, November, 1842—January 1843, Box 6, Petitions, NCSA; thanks to Harry L. Watson.

72   *George Latimer* For the Latimer case, see Benjamin Quarles, *Black Abolitionists* (New York: Oxford University Press, 1969), pp. 193–95.

72   *picking up the pieces of their lives* Sometime before November 22, 1843 when Marcus Ramsey and Charles Johnson entered into a bond

for the marriage of Ramsey to Ann Johnson, the second daughter of Gustavus Adolphus Johnson (1790–1842), Molly had managed to free Mark. Gustavus Adolphus Johnson, the son of a slave woman by Charles Johnson of Bandon Plantation north of Edenton, was manumitted by his father by private act of the North Carolina Assembly in 1795 and, at his father's death, gained an inheritance under the guardianship of Samuel Tredwell Johnson. He was taught by tutors, trained as a cabinetmaker, and in 1814 purchased and married Elizabeth. They had three children. Johnson manumitted the members of his family in 1822; three younger children were born free. Molly Horniblow was listed as communicant in St. Paul's Church Register in 1843. Chowan County Marriage Bonds, NCSA; Sketch of Charles Johnson in William S. Powell, ed., *Dictionary of North Carolina Biography* (Chapel Hill: University of North Carolina Press, 1979–96). "Bill to Emancipate a mulatto boy by the name of Gustavus Adolphus Johnson in the County of Chowan" in North Carolina General Assembly Session Records, November—December 1795—Senate Bills, December 1, 1795, NCSA; will of Charles Johnson, 1802, in Chowan County Wills, 1694–1904, NCSA; twenty-five letters and notes, 1818–25, from G. A. Johnson to Samuel Tredwell, and memorandum of "vouchers omitted in annexed account of G. A. Johnson" [1826], in Charles E. Johnson Collection, NCSA; Bill of Sale, December 30, 1813, James R. Bent to Gustavus A. Johnson, for "a certain yellow girl named Betty," in Chowan County Deed Book F-2, p. 389; Petition for Emancipation of Elizabeth, Mary, Ann, and Charles, and attendant papers, 1822, Chowan County Miscellaneous Slave Papers, 1730–1836, NCSA; Order of manumission, September Term 1822, Minutes of the Chowan County Court, 1812–1827, p. 321, NCSA; Apprentice bonds of Thomas J., William, and Elizabeth G. Johnson, February. 6, 1843, in Chowan County Apprentice Bonds, 1830–1843, NCSA; 1830 Census of Chowan County, North Carolina, p. 337, and 1840 Census of Chowan County, North Carolina, p. 207; will of Gustavus A. Johnson, 1843, in Chowan County Wills, 1694–1904, NCSA; estate of Gustavus A. Johnson, 1842, in Chowan County Estates Records, 1728–1951, NCSA. Reverend R. W. Storie, Rector, St. Paul's Parish, Edenton, North Carolina to Jean Fagan Yellin, August 24, 1981.

73   Knickerbocker The *Knickerbocker* was built in 1843. Personal communication to Jean Fagan Yellin from Mrs. Michael Sweeney, City Historian, Saratoga Springs, New York, October 23, 1985; for the Unite States Hotel, see James Silk Buckingham, *America, Historical, Statistic, and Descriptive,* 3 vols. (London: Fisher, Son, and Co., 1841), 2:435, in John Hope Franklin, *A Southern Odyssey* p. 26.

73   "*a neutral ground*" Nathaniel Parker Willis, "Ephemera," *Dashes at Life with a Free Pencil* (1845, rpt. New York: Garrett, 1969), p. 140.

73   *"a superb hotel"* "Willis, Ephemera," pp. 33, 135.

73   *"the favorite and regular resort"* "Willis, Ephemera," p. 134.

73   *Marine Pavilion* In addition to Willis and his family, the Marine
          Pavilion at Rockaway, Queens, built in 1833, hosted American writ-
          ers Henry Wadsworth Longfellow and Washington Irving. ILSG
          pp. 176–177.

74   *Joseph Blount* Hathaway, *Register*, 1:34–35, 522–23. ILSG
          p. 179.

74   *financial difficulties* At the August 1843 term of court, Dr. Norcom
          was sued for debt, and when the judgment ran against him, the sher-
          iff was ordered to seize and sell his property to satisfy the debt. The
          writ was levied on six of Norcom's slaves as well as other property.
          In November his creditor halted the sale and gave Norcom more time
          to raise the money to pay off the debt and interest. See writ of *ven-
          ditione exponas* in the suit William Benbury, Trustee, vs. James Nor-
          com, M. D., et al, in Chowan County Civil Action Papers, 1843.
          NCSA.

74   *Arent Van der Poel* Arent Van der Poel (1799–1870) was elected
          twice to the New York state legislature and twice to Congress. From
          1843 to 1850, he served as judge of the superior court. Attorney John
          Hopper (1815–64) was the son of Quaker abolitionist reformer Isaac
          T. Hopper, in 1847 founder of the New York State Vigilance Com-
          mittee. *National Cyclopedia of American Biography* (New York: J.
          T. White, 1892–1984), 11:396; Lydia Maria Child, *Letters*, p. 140;
          Quarles, *Black Abolitionists*, p. 154.

74   *the Sound steamer* Rhode Island For the Sound steamers, see *Long-
          worth's New York Registry and City Directory, 1838–1839*, p. 32.
          Completed in 1836, the *Rhode Island* was part of the fleet of the
          Rhode Island Steamboat Company, which maintained a regular
          schedule from New York to Providence. Robert G. Albion, *The Rise
          of New York Port, 1815–1860* p. 155.

75   *Boston's black community* For information on black Boston, see
          James Oliver Horton and Lois E. Horton, *Black Bostonians: Family
          Life and Community Struggle in the Antebellum North* (New York:
          Holmes & Meier, 1979).

75   *Their organizations were as varied* The African Society was founded
          in 1796, and African Lodge #459 in 1787 under the sponsorship of
          the Grand Lodge of England. (The American Masons refused the
          request of Prince Hall, a member of a British lodge, to create a black
          lodge.) The Adelphic Union Library Association was organized in
          1838. For the Histrionic Club, the Boston Philomanthean Society,
          and the Young Men's Literary Debating Society, see Horton and
          Horton, *Black Bostonians,* which cites William Wells Brown, *The
          Black Man, His Antecedents, His Genius, and His Achievements*

(New York, 1863), p. 240. The Colored Female Union Society of the Belknap Street Baptist Church was organized in 1830, the Afric-American Female Intelligence Society in 1832, the Colored Female Charitable Society in 1832, the Daughters of Zion in 1845, and the New England Temperance Society of People of Color in 1835. The Garrison Society was organized in 1833. For all, see Horton and Horton, pp. 31–35; Anne M. Boylan, "Antislavery Activity among African American Women," in *The Abolitionist Sisterhood*, pp. 136–37; and her *Origins of Women's Activism*.

75   *Possibly he recalled* See the *Edenton Gazette,* December 16, 1830, October 26, 1831, and November 2, 1831.

76   *new militant urban culture* For patterns of black migration, see Horton and Horton, *Black Bostonians,* pp. 6–7.

76   *George Latimer* For the Latimer case, see Quarles, *Black Abolitionists*, pp. 193–95; and Horton and Horton, *Black Bostonians,* p. 99.

76   *"Aid the Fugitive"* *The Liberator,* March 31, 1843.

76   *Later, the association* *The Liberator,* April 21, 1843. For debate about the convention, see *The Liberator,* August 25, 1843. For the proceedings, see *Minutes of the National Convention of Colored Citizens: Held at Buffalo. . . .* (New York: Piercy & Reed, 1843), in *Minutes of the Proceedings of the National Negro Conventions, 1830–1864,* ed. Howard Holman Bell (New York: Arno and the New York Times, 1969).

76   *"the evidences of design"* *The Liberator,* September 29, 1843; November 10, 1843.

77   *Tenth Annual Convention* The tenth annual New England Anti-Slavery Convention was held at Boston May 30—June 1, 1843. For the list of donors, see *The Liberator,* June 23, 1843.

77   *"the hub of the universe"* *The Liberator,* September 1, 1843.

77   *William C. Nell's heart* For William C. Nell, see DANB pp. 472–73; Robert P. Smith, "William Cooper Nell: Crusading Black Abolitionist," *Journal of Negro History* (July 1970); and *William Cooper Nell: Selected Writings 1832–1874,* ed. Dorothy Porter Wesley and Constance Porter Uzelac (Baltimore: Black Classic Press, 2002).

77   *(Two years later)* For the struggle over the Smith School, see John Daniels, *In Freedom's Birthplace* (1914, rpt. New York: Arno and The New York Times, 1969), pp. 446–49; and Horton and Horton, *Black Bostonians,* pp. 71–75. Also see, for example, *The Liberator,* September 4, 1846, and August 6, 1847.

77   *"Colored Help"* "Colored Help." *The Liberator*, October 25, 1843.

78   *"I labored with much success"* *Narrative of the Life and Travels of Mrs. Prince Written by Herself* (Boston: Published by the Author, 2d

ed. 1853), rpt. *Collected Black Women's Narratives*, ed. Anthony G. Barthelemy, *The Schomburg Library of Nineteenth-Century Black Women Writers*, ed. Henry Louis Gates Jr. (New York: Oxford University Press, 1988), p. 84; also see Frances Smith Foster, *Written by Herself: Literary Production by African-American Women, 1746–1892* (Bloomington: Indiana University Press, 1992), pp. 85–86.

78   *"Edenton folks"* Willis's sister Sara Payson Eldredge was living with her husband and their three little girls at "Swissdale" in Brighton, Massachusetts But sister Lucy Douglas, who had married Josiah F. Bumstead in 1823, in 1843 was at 62 Beacon Street; sister Louisa Harris, who had married Louis Dwight, was at Beacon, corner of Spruce; sister Mary Perry, who had married Joseph Jenkins in 1831, was at 2 Howard Place; and sister Julia Dan Willis was also in the city. Willis's brother Richard Storrs was abroad in 1844. Joyce W. Warren, *Fanny Fern: An Independent Woman* (New Brunswick: Rutgers University Press, 1992); *Stimpson's Boston Directory* (Boston: Charles Stimpson, 1843, 1844, 1845).

78   *"George"* Joseph Blount Skinner's body servant George was born to Polly Lowther c. 1822. George's emancipation and arrival in Boston in 1838 are not documented, but Skinner's will, written in 1850, attests that George has been freed and sent north. On September 9, 1852, George Lowther, who earned his living as a hairdresser, was married in Boston to Sarah J. F. Logan, daughter of William Logan. Lowther was elected to the House of Representatives of the Commonwealth of Massachusetts in 1873 and 1879, appointed deputy sealer of weights and measures in 1882 and 1886, and was made a messenger in the Senate Treasury in 1890. He died in Boston on October 5, 1898. *Vital Records of Chelsea, Massachusetts*, p. 191; thanks to Dolores Schueler, Boston Public Library. Will of Joseph Blount Skinner. NCSA. Chowan County Estates Records, Polly Lowther, 1864, NCSA. Record of Marriage, The Commonwealth of Massachusetts. 1860 Census, town of Milford, Worcester County, Massachusetts, p. 169. Chowan County Willis, J. D. Skinner, 1850. NCSA. Obituary of George W. Lowther, *Boston Journal*, October 7, 1898, thanks to Hon. Byron Rushing.

78   *"would mingle his tears"* Harriet Jacobs to Amy Post, Cornwall, Orange County [New York] [1852?] IAPFP.

78   *"the Eleventh Massachusetts Anti-Slavery Fair"* *The Liberator*, December 20, 1844.

78   *"several colored seamen"* *The Liberator*, February 7, 1845.

79   *"First Independent Baptist Female Society"* *The Liberator*, January 31, 1845; May 9, 1845.

79   *"three fugitives"* "Aid for the Outcasts," *The Liberator*, May 30, 1845.

Chapter 6. A Great Millstone Lifted

83   *"the day Mary Stace Willis died"* Mary Stace Willis died at the Astor House on March 25, 1845. Beers, *Nathaniel Parker Willis*, p. 176.

83   *"Boston's printing trades"* For discrimination in Boston's printing trades, see Martin Delany, *The Condition, Elevation, and Destiny of the Colored People of the United States* (1852, rpt. New York: Arno and the New York Times, 1968), pp. 27–28; Horton and Horton, *Black Bostonians*, p. 76.

84   *"international grouping of passengers"* N.R.P. Bosner, *North Atlantic Seaway*, 5 vols. (Newton Abbot: David and Charles, 1975–79); Nathaniel Parker Willis, *Famous Persons and Places* (1854, rpt. Freeport, New York: Books for Libraries Press, 1972), p. 346. Thanks to Norman Brouwer.

84   *"Some 14,000 or 15,000 black people"* Peter Fryer, *Staying Power: The History of Black People in Britain* (London: Pluto, 1984), pp. 125, 191, 207–8.

84   *"an 1833 Act of Parliament"* Fryer, *Staying Power*, pp. 203, 207, 208. While technically the Emancipation Act awarded slaves the rights and privileges of freedom, actually it established an apprentice system; only children under the age of six were immediately emancipated. Nonetheless, the act was hailed as a first step toward total emancipation. See *The Black Abolitionist Papers*, vol. 1: *The British Isles, 1830–65*, ed. C. Peter Ripley et al. (Chapel Hill: University of North Carolina Press, 1985), pp. 39–40. Hereafter BAP.

84   *"a number of African Americans"* For Paul and Remond, see BAP, 1:6–7;.for J. M. Smith, see BAP, 1:58; for Robert Douglass Jr., see BAP, 1:77; for Roper, see BAP, 1:62–63; for his *Narrative*, see 1:21, 136–37; for Grandy, see BAP, 1:8, 1:21. Douglass was in England from the autumn of 1845 until the spring of 1846; see William S. McFeely, *Frederick Douglass* (New York: Simon and Schuster, 1992), pp. 131–45; and Howard Temperley, *British Antislavery, 1833–1870* (Columbia: University of South Carolina Press, 1972), p. 195.

85   *"Liverpool"* Fryer, *Staying Power*, p. 66.

85   *"Willis fumed"* For Willis in Liverpool and London, see Willis, *Famous Persons and Places*, pp. 345–49.

85   *"I see, daily"* Willis, *Famous Persons and Places*, pp. 372–73.

86   *"Steventon, near Abingdon"* For Steventon, see Ian Yarrow, *Berkshire* (London: Robert Hale, 1952), p. 335; for Abingdon, see M. J. Thomas, *Abingdon in Camera: Portrait of a County Town 1850–1950* (Abingdon: Abingdon Area Archaeological & Historical Society in Association with The Abbey Press, 1979).

86   "*a tumbled-up, elbowy crooked old place*" Willis, *Famous Persons and Places*, p. 354.

86   "*the* utter want of hope" Willis, *Famous Persons and Places*, p. 347.

86   "*At Edenton's St. Paul's*" For Dr. James Norcom's church history, see Richard Rankin, *Ambivalent Churchmen*, pp. 114–15, 133, 137.

87   "*Harriett, her maid*" Nathaniel Parker Willis to Mrs. Stetson, November 25 [1845]. University of Iowa libraries.

87   "*Willis's niece*" *The Boston City Directory . . . from July, 1849 to July, 1850. . . .* (Boston: George Adams, 1849), p. 200, lists "Jacobs, Harriet N. dressmaker, h. 87 Charter"; in 1850, she is listed at 54 Prince. According to the 1846 *Directory*, the first issue of the weekly newspaper *The Saturday Rambler* (Boston) appeared on May 2, 1846. Alternatively, Joseph might well have been working for a New York City periodical named *The Rambler*, because on September 7, 1845, John S. wrote to his correspondent in New York, "Joseph Jacobs in the ramblers office will give you any information." [John S. Jacobs] to Friend Gay, no. 142 Nassau Street, New York City. Columbia University Libraries. Gay Collection. *The Rambler* (New York City), Dennis Hannigan, publisher, is listed under "Newspapers" as located at 138 Nassau Street in *Doggett's New-York City Directory of 1845 & 1846*, p. 429; it is listed as owned by Hannigan and Maxwell at 30 Ann Street in *Doggett's New York City Business Directory for 1846–47*, p. 172. For the May 6 wedding of Maria Louisa Dwight to William Tappan Eustis, see Reverend Abner Morse, "Willis Genealogy," *Genealogical Register*, II (Printed for the Family, 1863).

87   "*ninth annual lecture series*" The black speakers included Thomas Paul, Dartmouth graduate and son of a famous father, and Dr. James McCune Smith; *The Liberator*, October 31, 1845, p. 175.

87   "*In addition, he had taken on*" For the New England Freedom Association, see *The Liberator*, December 12, 1845; for the donation to the Massachusetts Anti-Slavery Society, see *The Liberator*, February 6, 1846.

87   "*the members of this Society*" W[illiam] C. N[ell], "Literary Progress of the Colored Young Men of Boston," *The Liberator*, March 27, 1846, p. 51.

88   "*Unlike Frederick Douglass*" For Frederick Douglass's new-found independence, see William S. McFeely, *Frederick Douglass*, especially p. 145.

88   "*hearing the talk*" "Notice," *The Liberator*, April 17, 1846; "A Free Meeting," *The Liberator*, May 22, 1846.

88   "*Monument Association*" "Meeting in Aid of the Torrey Monument," *The Liberator*, July 10, 1846; for Charles Torrey (1813–46),

see *The Letters of William Lloyd Garrison*, ed. Walter M. Merrill and Louis Ruchames. 6 vols. (Cambridge, Massachusetts: Belknap Press of Harvard University Press, 1971–1981). 3:338.

88   "*Rural Fair and Anti-Slavery Pic Nic*" "The Celebration, Fourth July, Dedham," *The Liberator*, June 19, 1846; "Celebration at Dedham," *The Liberator,* July 10, 1846. John S. Jacobs's name appears among the signers of the Anti-War Pledge in "Volunteers in the Army of Justice, Humanity, Peace and Liberty," *The Liberator*, June 5, 1846.

88   "*Later in July*" "Crowded Meeting of the Colored Population of Boston," *The Liberator*, July 24, 1846. For the campaign to "send back the money," see R. J. M. Blackett, *Building an Antislavery Wall: Black Americans in the Atlantic Abolitionist Movement, 1830–1860* (Ithaca: Cornell University Press, 1983), pp. 83ff.

89   "*the parade the next day*" "First of August in Boston," *The Liberator,* August 7, 1846.

89   "*he decided to act*" "Jonathan Walker and John S. Jacobs," *The North Star*, March 31, 1848. BAPM (microform) 05:0605.

89   "*prominent Boston citizens*" *The Liberator*, October 2 and 9, 1846.

89   "*James Tredwell died that summer*" James Tredwell died on July 25, 1846. Dr. James Norcom to [John Norcom], April 28, 1845. NFP.

90   "*a man whose origin*" Dr. James Norcom to [John Norcom], April 28, 1845. NFP.

90   "*Cut off by her family*" Daniel and Mary Matilda Norcom Messmore left Edenton in 1848. Later that year, they moved from Cincinnati, apparently to Norfolk; they eventually settled in New York. Dr. Norcom never forgave his disobedient daughter. For the letters Jacobs received, see ILSG pp. 186–87.

90   "*they have let the cat out*" John S. Jacobs to Sydney Howard Gay, Chelsea Massachusetts, June 4, 1846, Columbia University Libraries. Gay Collection.

91   "*a Belknap Street Church reception*" "Reception of Wm. Lloyd Garrison and James N. Buffum," *The Liberator,* November 27, 1846; "Great Anti-Slavery Meeting," *The Liberator,* December 4, 1846.

91   "*At the holidays*" "The Bazaar," *The Liberator,* January 1, 1847, "Reception of Frederick Douglass at the Belknap-Street Church, Boston," *The Liberator*, May 21, 1847.

91   "*West Indian Emancipation*" "Emancipation Day," *The Liberator,* August 13, 1847.

91   "*black prodigy Cleveland Lucas*" "The Lucas Family," *The Liberator*, August 28, 1847. For the Lucas family, see "Alexander Luca," DANB, p. 406. For more, see James Monroe Trotter, *Music and Some Highly Musical People* (New York: C. T. Dillingham, 1878).

91   "*sixty-six Virginia slaves*" "Emancipated Slaves," "Prompt Kindness," *The Liberator,* September 24, 1847.

91   "*at Belknap Street Church in the fall*" "Banner Presentation. *Levee.*" *The Liberator,* October 15, 1847.

91   "*National Convention held at Troy*" For the Troy convention, see *The Liberator,* July 16, September 10, and November 5, 1847; *Proceedings of the National Convention of Colored People, and Their Friends, Held in Troy, N. Y., on the 6th, 7th, 8th and 9th October, 1847* (Troy, New York, 1847); and Quarles, *Black Abolitionists,* pp. 227, 229.

92   "*three cloth dolls*" The dolls are in a private collection.

92   "*whose widow was she?*" Samuel is named in *Boyd's Directory of the District of Columbia* (Washington, D.C.) for 1885, 1888, 1894, and 1896; Elijah is named in *Boyd's* for 1886; and George is named in *Boyd's* for 1895.

93   "*the Church of the Latter Day Saints*" International Genealogical Index (R) Addendum 2. CD-Rom. 2002. Individual Record. Temple: Los Angeles. Recorder's Certificate: 00014–0162, Record File #168J4WQ records the marriage of Samuel Tredwell Sawyer to Harriet Ann Jacobs abt 1828 at Edenton, Chowan, North Carolina. Record submitted by LDS Church member, film 1903719. Sealing date Dec. 1, 1993. Additional Latter Day Saints records submitted by LDS Church member record the birth of Louisa Matilda Jacobs October 10, 1833, father Samuel Tredwell Sawyer, mother Harriet Ann Jacobs, film 1985394; and the birth of John S. Jacobs to Daniel Jacobs and Delilah Horniblow in 1815 at Edenton, Recorder's Certificate 00014-0288; record file 24Z5KN3, baptism date January 11, 1994, confirmation date February 12, 1994, Ord/initiatory date July 30, 1994, Endowment date 24, May, 1996; Sealing date July 6, 1996.

93   "*Jonathan Walker*" See Walker's *Personal Memoirs* (Boston: Bella Marsh, 1855). For an illustration of Walker's hand, see Jean Fagan Yellin, *Women and Sisters: The Antislavery Feminists in American Culture* (New Haven: Yale University Press, 1988).

93   "*That well-known sufferer*" "The Walker Meetings," *National Anti-Slavery Standard,* January 6, 1848, taken from the *Herkimer Freeman.* For John S. Jacobs's lecturing during the first six months of 1848, see *The Liberator,* February 11, March 31, April 7, April 14, May 5, May 12, May 19, May 28, and June 16, 1848.

93   "*It is seldom an evening*" Jonathan Walker, "Anti-Slavery in Western New York," East Hamilton, Madison County, New York, January 14, 1848, in *The Liberator,* February 11, 1848.

94   "*11 miles through the snow*" J. S. Jacobs, "Incidents in Western New York," Cato (Four Corners), New York, February 27, 1848, in *The Liberator,* March 13, 1848.

94   *"mobocratic spirit"* J. S. Jacobs, "Incidents in Western New York," Cato (Four Corners), New York, February 27, 1848, in *The Liberator,* March 13, 1848.

94   *"hard service"* Jonathan Walker, "Letter from Jonathan Walker," Plymouth, May 14, 1848, in *The Liberator,* May 26, 1848.

94   *100 Conventions* In June, the New England Anti-Slavery Convention resolved to hold "one hundred conventions" and raised $1,200 to spread the word. On July 14, *The Liberator* began announcing an eastern series and a western series of "One Hundred Conventions."

94   *Taking their texts* Adin Ballou, "One Hundred Conventions—Western Series," from *The Non-Resistant and Practical Christian,* in *The Liberator,* August 11, 1848.

94   *"he would prefer to see the slaves"* Adin Ballou, "One Hundred Conventions—Western Series. Narrative Concluded," from *The Non-Resistant and Practical Christian,* in *The Liberator,* August 14, 1848.

95   *"Anti-Sabbath Convention"* For the Anti-Sabbath Conventions, see *The Letters of William Lloyd Garrison,* 3:540–43. "Convention at Blackstone," *The Liberator,* August 4, 1848; G., "Anti-Sabbath Convention—Buffalo Convention," from the *Boston Daily Atlas* in *"Refuge of Oppression," The Liberator,* August 18, 1848.

95   *"John S. Jacobs"* "The Milford Convention," *The Liberator,* August 18, 1848.

95   *At the quarterly meeting* "Essex Co. A. S. Society," *The Liberator,* September 22, 1848.

96   *Boston Female Anti-Slavery Society The Liberator,* January 19, 1849.

96   *Willis's sister Sara* Charles Eldridge died on October 6, 1846; for Sarah Willis Eldridge's efforts to support her children, see Joyce Warren, *Fanny Fern,* pp. 74, 78; N. P. Willis had met Cornelia Grinnell at Washington, D.C., where he was working as a correspondent for the *National Press* and the *Morning Chronicle.* They were married on October 1, 1846. Beers, *Nathaniel Parker Willis,* pp. 287, 294.

96   *"from the necessity of the case"* "Public Meeting," *The Liberator,* February 18, 1848; Samuel May Jr., "Help for the Fugitives," *The Liberator,* March 10, 1848.

96   *Bayne's Gigantic Panoramic Painting* "Bayne's Gigantic Panoramic Painting," *The Liberator,* June 23, 1848.

96   *On the Fourth of July* "Anti-Slavery Celebration," *The Liberator,* July 4, 1848.

96   *the plight of the Edmondson family* For those captured on the *Pearl,* and for the trials of Captain Daniel Drayton, see Drayton's *Personal Memoirs* (Boston: Bella Marsh, 1855); and Harriet Beecher Stowe,

Key to Uncle Tom's Cabin (1853, rpt. New York: Arno and The New York Times, 1968), pp. 306–30.

96   *National Colored Convention* "First of August," *The Liberator,* July 28, 1848. For the 1848 Cleveland Convention, which included women, see *The Liberator* October 20, 1848, and "Report of the Proceedings of the Colored National Convention, held at Cleveland, Ohio, on Wednesday, September 6, 1848," Rochester: John Dick, at the North Star Office, 1848, in *Minutes of the Proceedings of the National Negro Conventions, 1830–1864.*

96   *"Woman's Rights Conventions" The Liberator,* August 25 and September 1, 1848.

96   *Boston's segregated Smith School* For the Smith School controversy, see Chapter 5, above.

97   *Hiram H. Kellogg's Young Ladies Domestic Seminary* The educator Hiram H. Kellogg (1803–81), born in Clinton, Oneida County, New York, graduated from Hamilton College and studied at Auburn Theological Seminary. He opened The Young Ladies' Domestic Seminary at Clinton in 1833. Nine years later, he moved to Ohio, where he became the president of Knox College. Kellogg moved back to Clinton, resumed direction of the seminary, and ran it as a co-educational institution, The Domestic Seminary and Clinton Grammar School, from 1848 to 1850, before returning west in 1851. For Kellogg, see *Hamilton Literary Monthly* 15, no. 5 (January 1881): 204. For the seminary, see Helen Neilson Rudd, *A Century of Schools in Clinton* (Clinton, New York: Clinton Historical Society, 1964), pp. 18–20; Reverend A. D. Gridley, *History of the Town of Kirkland New York* (Cambridge, Massachusetts: Riverside, 1874), pp. 141–43.

98   *Reading, Spelling, Writing Catalogue of the Domestic Seminary and Clinton Grammar School, Clinton, July, 1848* (Clinton, New York: Lewis W. Payne, Printer, 1848). Thanks to Carolyn A. Davis at the George Arents Research Library, Syracuse University; to Catherine M. Hanchett of Cortland, New York; and to Frank L. Lorenz, Hamilton College, Clinton, New York. For Mary Lyon's Mount Holyoke, see, for example, Eleanor Flexner, *Century of Struggle* (New York: Atheneum, 1970), pp. 31–36.

98   *Kellogg not only admitted* Hiram Kellogg to [Gerrit Smith], April 30, 1839. George Arents Research Library, Syracuse University.

98   *"It seems to me"* [Louisa Matilda Jacobs to John S. Jacobs], Clinton, November 5, 1849. IAPFP.

98   *"the lecturing field"* "Editorial Correspondence," *The North Star,* March 9, 1849.

99   *"Friend Jacobs"* "Editorial Correspondence," *The North Star,* March 9, 1849. Of the Avon meeting, Julia Wilbur wrote: "F. Dou-

glass and John [S.?] Jacobs came to our house & Father & I arranged an anti-Slavery meeting in E. Avon. In P.M. 14 persons present, none of the villagers.—In evening a good turnout,—very cold & stormy." Julia Wilbur Diary, February 21, 1849 hereafter JWD. For the papers of Julia Wilbur, see her diaries in The Quaker library, Haverford College, her letters in The Rochester Ladies Anti-Slavery Society papers at The Clements Library, University of Michigan, hereafter RLASS, and scattered items elsewhere, including the libraries of The University of Rochester.

99   *"he would object"* "An Anti-Slavery Tour," *The North Star*, April 20, 1849.

100   *"streets were so muddy"* "An Anti-Slavery Tour," *The North Star*, April 20, 1849.

100   *"The change was so great"* "An Anti-Slavery Tour," *The North Star*, April 20, 1849.

Chapter 7. My Mind Became Enlightened

101   *Amy and Isaac Post* Nancy A. Hewitt, "Amy Kirby Post, 'Of whom it was said, 'being dead, yet speaketh,'" *The University of Rochester Library Bulletin* 37 (1984): 13. For Post and her circle, see also Hewitt, *Women's Activism and Social Change: Rochester, New York, 1822–1872* (Ithaca: Cornell University Press, 1984); Hewitt, "Feminist Friends: Agrarian Quakers and the Emergence of Woman's Rights in America," *Feminist Studies* 12 (1986): 27–48. Hewitt is writing a biography of Post.

101   *the Douglass family's challenge* In an entry dated April 1849, Julia Wilbur wrote: "Select School in Rochester on Court St.—I boarded at [brother] Theodore's on Mortimer St.—Mary with me & went to school. Rosa Douglass came & most of the scholars left: for I would keep her, if they all left.—I kept it going 3 months." JWD. Ten-year-old Rosetta Douglass was then taught separately at Seward Seminary, a private school for girls; when Douglass protested this segregation, the principal polled the parents, and after one protested, Rosetta was asked to withdraw. Rather than send her to the substandard public school for African Americans, Douglass sent her to Albany to be educated, then in 1850 hired Phebe Thayer as her governess. Rosetta attended the Preparatory Department at Oberlin College in 1854–55. The Rochester public schools were finally desegregated in 1857. See Quarles, *Frederick Douglass* p. 108. For Rosetta Douglass's birthdate, see "Anna Murray Douglass," *Black Women in America: An Historical Encyclopedia,* ed. Darlene Clark Hine et al. (Brooklyn: Carlson, 1997).

101   *"reshaped the landscape"* Hewitt, *Women's Activism*, pp. 137–38.

102   *"where our friends"* "Address of the Executive Committee of the Western New York Anti-Slavery Society to the Abolitionists of Western New York," *The North Star*, February 25, 1848.

102   *"a rich variety"* Advertisement, "Books, . . ." *The North Star*, May 12, 1848.

102   *"to sew, knit"* "The Bazaar," *The North Star*, September 1, 1848.

102   *"had been visited by but few"* *The North Star*, December 29, 1848.

102   *Antislavery Office and Reading Room* Jane Elizabeth Jones, *The Young Abolitionists* (Boston: Anti-Slavery Office, 1848); Lysander Spooner, *Poverty: its illegal causes and legal cure* (Boston: Bela Marsh, 1846); Charles Morley, *The Power of Kindness* . . . (New York: Fowlers & Wells, 1849); Jonathan Walker, *The Branded Hand* . . . (Boston: The Anti-Slavery Office, 1845); *History of the Mexican War* (William Jay, *A Review of the Causes and Consequences of the Mexican War* [Boston: Benjamin B. Mussey & Co., 1849]?); Theodore Parker, *A Discourse Occasioned by the Death of John Quincy Adams. Delivered at the Melodeon in Boston, March 5, 1848.* (Boston: Bela Marsh, 1848); Theodore Parker, *A Sermon on the Mexican War; preached at the Melodeon, on Sunday, June 25, 1848* . . . (Boston: Coolidge and Wiley, 1848); Theodore Parker, *A Letter to the People of the United States Touching the Matter of Slavery* (Boston: James Monroe & Co. 1848); Parker Pillsbury, *The Church as it is or the Forlorn Hope of Slavery*, 2d ed. (Boston: Bela Marsh, 1847); Richard Hildreth, *Despotism in America* . . . (Boston: Whipple & Damrell, 1840); Richard Hildreth, *The Slave; or, Memoirs of Archy Moore* (Boston: John H. Eastburn, 1836)

103   *"Agent Anti-Slavery Reading Rooms"* Rochester *City Directory* 1849–50; she is not listed for 1847–48, or for 1850–51. Her brother John S. is not listed at all.

103   *given up the reading room* William C. Nell to Amy Post, June 30, 1849, IAPFP. For the Reading Room move from the first floor to the floor above, see *The North Star*, August 3, 1849; "Oysters! Oysters!" *The North Star*, November 2, 1849; also see [Louisa Matilda Jacobs to John S. Jacobs], Clinton, November 5, 1849. IAPFP.

103   *the August First celebration* "Celebration at Auburn," *The North Star*, August 10, 1849.

103   *Union Anti-Slavery Society* See the announcement of the Union Society Fair signed by E. W. Walker, President, and Mary Gibbs, Vice President, announcing their event to be held in Minerva Hall on August 1, 1848, in *The North Star*, July 21, 1848; for more on the Union Anti-Slavery Committee, see *The North Star*, December 5, 1850; concerning the Ladies Committee Anti-Slavery Festival, see *The North Star* April 24, 1851. For the work of black activist Barbara Ann Steward, who in 1853 helped organize an auxiliary of the

National Council of the Colored People in western New York state, see BAP, 4:297.

103 *both young men* See Harriet Jacobs to Amy Post, nd#83: "while we have sons to weep over we must commend them to our heavenly Father." For Jacobs as "Dah," see, for example, Jacobs to Amy Post, June 25 [1853]. IAPFP.

103 *spiritualism* See Ann Braude, *Radical Spirits: Spiritualism and Women's Rights in Nineteenth-Century America* (Boston: Beacon, 1989); Isaac Post to Amy Post, Rochester, May 22, 1849. IAPFP.

104 *"Did you frighten her"* Isaac Post to Amy Post, May 19, 1849. IAPFP.

104 *"Though impelled by a natural craving"* Amy Post, "Appendix," ILSG pp. 203–04.

104 *"in an exticy"* Isaac Post to Amy Post, Rochester, May 7, 1849. IAPFP.

104 *"I feel so happy"* Harriet Jacobs to Amy Post [May 1849]. IAPFP.

105 *Joseph disappointed his mother* Isaac Post to Amy Post, Rochester, May 22, 1849. IAPFP.

105 *"9 white men"* April 19, 1849 and June 15, 1849 entries in JWD; "Gavitt's Original Ethiopian Seranaders," *The North Star* June 29, 1849.

105 *Anti-Slavery Fair* Amy Post, "An Appeal in Behalf of the Western New York Anti-Slavery Fair," *The North Star*, June 29, 1849.

106 *"When it was finally held"* Amy Post, "Western New York Annual Anti-Slavery Fair at Rochester." *The North Star*, November 9, 1849. Harriet Jacobs's name is not among those listed on fair committees. Douglass complained: "The Fair, held in this city, during two days of the past week, realized two hundred dollars—a large part of which will be consumed in defraying the expenses attendant upon holding it. While in a financial point of view the Fair must be considered a failure, we are sorry to say, that morally, it has been far from successful." *The North Star*, February 1, 1850. See "Rules and Regulations for The Fair," n.d. IAPFP. For the postponement, see "To the Anti-Slavery Friends of Western New York and Elsewhere," *The North Star*, December 14, 1849; for Sewing Society meetings at the Douglass home, see *The North Star*, August 10 and October 19, 1849.

106 *"One hundred people"* Amy Post to Frederick Douglass, Rochester, February 2, 1850. IAPFP.

106 *Western New York State Anti-Slavery Society* For Western New York Anti-Slavery Society executive meetings at the Post home, see, for example, *The North Star*, September 21 and October 19, 1849; "The Rochester Annual Meeting," *The North Star*, November 23, 1849.

106   *"colored children"* "Colored School Meeting," *The North Star,*
       December 21, 1849. Also see "Colored School Meeting," and
       "Schools for Colored Children," both in *Rochester Daily Democrat,*
       December 14, 1849; and "Board of Education, Jan. 14, 1850,"
       Rochester Daily Advertiser.

106   *a mass meeting Rochester Republican,* September 6, 1849.

107   *"Resolved"* "Mass Meeting at Corinthian Hall," *The North Star,*
       April 12, 1850; also published in *Rochester Daily Democrat,* April
       9, 1850.

107   *the Compromise of 1850* For the Compromise of 1850 and the new
       Fugitive Slave Law, see Quarles, *Black Abolitionists,* pp. 198–99;
       also see Stanley W. Campbell, *The Slave Catchers: Enforcement of
       the Fugitive Slave Law, 1850–1860* (Chapel Hill: University of North
       Carolina Press, 1968, 1970), especially pp. 24–25.

107   *a convention of fugitive slaves* For the Cazanovia Convention, see
       Hugh C. Humphreys, "Agitate! Agitate! Agitate! The Great Cazen-
       ovia Fugitive Slave Law Convention and its Rare Daguerreotype,"
       in *Madison County Heritage,* ed. Barbara L. Evans (Oneida, New
       York: Madison County Historical Society, 1994).

108   *California* TT in ILSG p. 223; for California, see Rudolph M. Lapp,
       "The Negro in Gold Rush California," *Journal of Negro History* 49,
       no. 2 (April 1964): 81–98; and Howard H. Bell, "Negroes in Cali-
       fornia, 1849–1859," *Phylon* 28 (1967): 151–60.

108   *abolitionists praised his "resistant spirit"* For John S. Jacobs's "resis-
       tant spirit," see Sarah L. Hallowell Willis to Amy Post, October 20,
       1850. IAPFP. For the demonstration, see "Meetings of Colored Cit-
       izens," *National Anti-Slavery Standard,* October 10, 1850.

108   *"many far more deserving"* Harriet Jacobs to Amy Post, Cornwall,
       Orange County, New York [n.d.n.m.1852?] IAPFP nd #84.

109   *"The painted coffin"* Thomas N. Baker, *Sentiment and Celebrity:
       Nathaniel Parker Willis and the Trials of Literary Fame* (New York:
       Oxford University Press, 1999), p. 3; in *The North Star,* June 8,
       1849, Douglass had reprinted "The Night Funeral of a Slave" along
       with Garrison's critique, which appeared a week earlier in *The Lib-
       erator.*

109   *both marbles* For Greenough's twin sculptures, see Beers, *Nathaniel
       Parker Willis,* pp. 121–22.

109   *Cornelia Grinnell Willis* For the Nathaniel Parker Willis family, see
       Beers, *Nathaniel Parker Willis.* Willis married Cornelia Grinnell on
       October 1, 1846; their son Grinnell was born April 18, 1848, and
       that year, N. P. Willis bought the house at 198 Fourth Street in New
       York City; Lilian was born June 17, 1850. For the Grinnells, see
       Appleton's Cyclopaedia of American Biography, ed. James Grant

Wilson and John Fiske, vol. 3 (New York: Appleton, 1888); and "Charts and Chronicles of Matthew Grenelle's Descendants," comp. E. W. Grinnell, n.d., pp. 176, 177. Thanks to Judith Downey, Old Dartmouth Historical Society Whaling Museum Library. The quotation is from Beers, *Nathaniel Parker Willis*, p. 287.

110   *attempts to capture fugitive slaves* For William and Ellen Craft, see R.J.M. Blackett, "The Odyssey of William and Ellen Craft," in *Beating Against the Barriers: Biographical Essays in Nineteenth-Century Afro-American History* (Ithaca: Cornell University Press, 1986) pp. 87–138; for "Shadrach," see Gary Collison, *Shadrach Minkins: From Fugitive Slave to Citizen* (Cambridge, Massachusetts: Harvard University Press, 1997); for the above, as well as Thomas Sims, the "Christiana Massacre," and the "Jerry Rescue," see Campbell, *The Slave Catchers*.

110   *"I never go out"* Harriet Jacobs to Amy Post [1853]. Fragment. IAPFP.

110   *"boarding and lodging"* Quarles, *Black Abolitionists*, pp. 149–50; see also Leo H. Hirsch Jr., "The Negro and New York 1783 to 1865," *Journal of Negro History* 16 (1931): 382–478. For the work of the pro-Fugitive Slave Law New York merchants' Union Safety Committee, and for public meetings endorsing the new law, see Campbell, *The Slave Catchers*, pp. 56, 73–75.

111   *their country house* The location of the Grinnells' country house has not been established.

111   *Jacobs wrote to her old friend* William C. Nell to Amy Post, Boston, June 27, 1851. IAPFP.

111   *Dr. Norcom was dead* Dr. James Norcom had died at Edenton, North Carolina, on November 9, 1850. NFP.

111   *Forrest charged adultery* For the Willis's involvement in the sensational Forrest divorce, see Richard Moody, *Edwin Forrest: First Star of the American Stage* (New York: Knopf, 1960), pp. 285–332; and Beers, *Nathaniel Parker Willis*, pp. 307–21. Concerning Forrest's application for divorce, see *New York Herald*, March 28 and March 29, 1850; for Willis's defense, see *Home Journal*, April 6, 1850. For more, see William R. Alger, *Life of Edwin Forrest, the American Tragedian* (Philadelphia: J. B. Lippincott, 1877), L. Barrett, *Edwin Forrest* (Boston: J. R. Osgood, 1881); and M. J. Moses, *The Fabulous Forrest* (Boston: Little, Brown, 1929).

112   *"Gentlemen"* Moody, *Edwin Forrest*, p. 294.

112   *the widely publicized Forrest....* Moody, *Edwin Forrest*, pp. 307, 305; the trial was covered daily in the *New York Times*, December 17, 1851—January 26 and February 2, 1852.

112   *"No one could believe"* *New York Times*, January 12, 13, 1852; see also Beers, *Nathaniel Parker Willis*, p. 316.

113   *"thousands and thousands" New York Herald*, quoted in Moody, *Edwin Forrest*, p. 321.

113   *"the one circumstance"* Beers, *Nathaniel Parker Willis,* pp. 314–15. Forrest finally paid up eighteen years and five appeals later.

113   *"filled with trouble and care"* Harriet Jacobs to Amy Post, New York, February 12 [1852]. IAPFP. Robert Hughes, *The Fatal Shore: The Epic of Australia's Founding* (New York: Knopf, 1987), pp. 561–62.

113   *"vast gold-field"* For African Americans and the Australian gold rush, see E. Daniel Potts and Annette Potts, "The Negro and the Australian Gold Rushes, 1852–1857," *Pacific Historical Review* 37 (November 1968): 381–99; and E. Daniel Potts and Annette Potts, *Young America and Australian Gold: Americans and The Gold Rush of the 1850's* (St. Lucia: University of Queensland Press, 1974), especially pp. 29, 46, 57, 65–66, 151–52, 157; for the Ballarat Rebellion, after which black men were tried, see pp. 181–98.

113   *"there is five"* Harriet Jacobs to Amy Post, New York, February 12 [1852]. IAPFP.

114   *"Arrivals at City Hotels"* "Arrivals at City Hotels," *New York Evening Express*, February 28, 1852.

115   *The public drama New York Times* March 2–4, 1852. There had been an earlier postponement; see *New York Herald* July 13, 1852.

Chapter 8. Let Me Come Before the World

117   *"The freedom I had"* [Harriet Jacobs to Amy Post], quoted in Amy Post, Rochester, October 30, 1859, ILSG p. 204.

117   *"it is hard for me"* Harriet Jacobs to [Amy Post], Cornwall, December 20 [1852] n.d. #79. IAPFP.

118   *"I came this morning"* Cornelia Grinnell Willis to Elizabeth Davis Bliss Bancroft, May 3 [1852]. Library of Congress, Bancroft-Bliss Family Papers.

118   *the "cottage"* Nathaniel Parker Willis, *Outdoors at Idlewild; or, The Shaping of a Home on the Banks of the Hudson* (New York: Charles Scribner, 1855), pp. 239–41; Beers, *Nathaniel Parker Willis,* p. 328.

118   *"I have regreeted"* Harriet Jacobs to [Amy Post], Cornwall, December 20 [1852] n.d. #79. IAPFP.

119   *"my conscience approved it"* Harriet Jacobs to [Amy Post], Cornwall Orange County, New York [1852?], n.d. #84. IAPFP.

119   *"I feel that God has helped me"* Harriet Jacobs to [Amy Post], Cornwall Orange County, New York [1852?], n.d. #84. IAPFP.

119   *"Now is the time"* Harriet Jacobs to [Amy Post], Cornwall Orange County, New York [1852?], n.d. #84. IAPFP.

119   *"I should want"* Harriet Jacobs to [Amy Post], Cornwall Orange County, New York [1852?], n.d. #84. IAPFP.

120   *"Dear Amy, since I have"* Harriet Jacobs to [Amy Post], February 14 [1853]. IAPFP.

120   *"she wants to seek"* [Harriet Jacobs] to [Amy Post], Cornwall [New York] December 20 [1852]. IAPFP.

120   *"I thought if I could get her"* Harriet Jacobs to [Amy Post], February 14 [1853]. IAPFP. For Ellen Craft in England, see R.J.M. Blackett, *Beating Against the Barriers*, pp. 87–138.

120   *"as it is"* [Harriet Jacobs] to [Amy Post], March [crossed out] April 4 [1853]. IAPFP. For Stowe's *The Key to Uncle Tom's Cabin* (1853), see Yellin, "Introduction," *Uncle Tom's Cabin* (New York: Oxford World Classics, 1998), pp. 21–23, 462–81; and Joan Hedrick, *Harriet Beecher Stowe* (New York: Oxford University Press, 1994), pp. 225–32.

121   *"I had never opend"* Harriet Jacobs to Amy Post, March [crossed out] April 4 [1853]. IAPFP.

121   *"I think she did not"* Harriet Jacobs to Amy Post, March [crossed out] April 4 [1853]. IAPFP.

121   *"think dear Amy"* [Harriet Jacobs] to [Amy Post] [1853] #n.d. 80. IAPFP.

121   *"Mr Garrison Phillips"* [Harriet Jacobs] to [Amy Post] [1853] #n.d. 80. IAPFP.

122   *"feeble"* Harriet Jacobs to Amy Post, August 19 [1853]. IAPFP.

122   *"The Women of England vs. the Women of America"* Julia Tyler, "The Women of England vs. the Women of America," *New York Herald,* January 24, 1853. For the "Affectionate and Christian Address of Many Thousands of the Women of England to Their Sisters, the Women of the United States of America" (the Stafford House Address), see *A Side-Light on Anglo-American Relations, 1839–1858,* ed. Annie Heloise Abel and Frank J. Klingberg (1927, rpt. New York: A. M. Kelly, 1970), pp. 40–44, 322–24; and Howard Temperley, *British Anti-Slavery 1833–1870,* p. 226.

122   *She wrote all night* Harriet Jacobs to Amy [Post], June 25 [1853]. IAPFP.

122   *"poor as it may be"* "Letter from a Fugitive Slave," *New York Tribune,* June 21, 1853.

123   *When the letter was printed* Harriet Jacobs to Amy [Post], June 25, 1853. IAPFP.

123   *"I cannot ask the favor"* Harriet Jacobs to Amy [Post], June 25, 1853. IAPFP.

123   *"exactly as written"* It is conceivable that this letter was republished in *The North Star* on October 7, 14, 21 or November 4 or 11, 1853; these issues are missing. It appeared in the *National Anti-Slavery Standard* July 2, 1853.

123   *he sent a copy* William C. Nell to Amy Post, August 31, 1853. IAPFP.

123   *another letter* "Cruelty to Slaves," *New York Tribune,* July 25, 1853. Jacobs's letter was perhaps prompted by the annoucement that "An advertisement in a Wilmington, N. C. paper offers $25. for the head of a runaway slave!" noted in "Gleanings of News," *The North Star,* August 26, 1853. For documentation of the incident Jacobs describes, see 1833 Inquests, Chowan County, North Carolina. NCSA. "The Price of Flesh," from *The Wilmington Journal,* reprinted *New York Tribune,* July 27, 1853.

124   *composed a third* This letter has not been found. Jacobs refers to it in Harriet Jacobs to Amy Post, October 9, 1853. IAPFP. Doubtless Jacobs's letter was intended as a contribution to the renewed discussion on colonization following publication of a new book by Giles B. Stebbins. See "New Work on Colonization," *The North Star,* September 2, 1853.

124   *"dear Amy I have lost"* Harriet Jacobs to Amy Post, October 9 [1853]. IAPFP. Here, answering Post's questions about her *Tribune* letters, she writes that her first piece was factual although about a friend, not a sister, and that her second letter describes what she had seen "when the poor outlawed was brung in town with his head severed from his body." Molly Horniblow was buried in Edenton's Providence cemetery on September 4, 1853. Personal communication to Jean Fagan Yellin from Reverend R. W. Storie, Rector, St. Paul's Parish, Edenton, August 24, 1981.

124   *"I must write"* Harriet Jacobs to Amy Post, October 9 [1853]. IAPFP.

124   *"at present what we find"* William J. Wilson to Frederick Douglass, March 5, 1853, *Frederick Douglass' Newspaper,* March 11, 1853, republished in BAP, 4:140–45; Dion, "Glances at our Condition.— No. 1. Our Literature." *Frederick Douglass' Newspaper,* September 23, 1853.

125   *the creation of a permanent literature* Douglass's *Narrative* had appeared in 1845; in 1855 he produced *My Bondage and My Freedom*; Thomas Anderson, *Life and Narrative of Wiliam J. Anderson, twenty-four years a slave* (Chicago, 1857); William Green, *Narrative of Events in the Life of William Green (Formerly a Slave)* ... (Springfield, Massachusetts, 1853); William Grimes, *Life of William*

Grimes, the Runaway Slave . . . (New Haven, 1855); Daniel Peterson, *The Looking Glass: being a True Report and Narrative of the Life* . . . (New York, 1854); Austin Steward, *Twenty-two years a Slave* . . . (Rochester, 1857); John Thompson, *The life of John Thompson, a Fugitive Slave* . . . (Worcester, 1856); Levin Tilmon, *A Brief Miscellaneous Narrative of the More Early Part of the Life* . . . (Jersey City, 1854); Samuel Ringgold Ward, *Autobiography of a Fugitive Negro* . . . (London, 1855); Josephine Brown, *Biography of an American Bondman, by his Daughter* (Boston, 1856). William Wells Brown had published his slave narrative in 1846; in 1852, his *Three Years in Europe* was brought out in London; William C. Nell, *The Colored Patriots of the American Revolution* (Boston, 1855).

126   *"extensive views"* Calvert Vaux, "Villas and Cottages," quoted in Lewis Beach, "Idle-wild," *Cornwall* (Newburgh: E. M. Ruttenber & Son, 1873), pp. 83–96.

126   *"there is every where"* T. Addison Richards, "Idlewild, the Home of N. P. Willis," *Harper's New Monthly Magazine* 16, no. 92 (January 1858): 145–66; quoted passage is from p. 151.

126   *in his weekly* Home Journal *column* Nathaniel P. Willis, *Outdoors at Idlewild*, p. 515. This volume reprints selected columns Willis had published in the *Home Journal*.

126   *Picturesque Cornwall* For Cornwall, see Janet Dempsey, et al., *Images from the Past: Cornwall 1788–1920* (Cornwall, New York: Friends of the Cornwall Public Library, 1988); Lewis Beach, *Cornwall* (Newburgh, New York: E. M. Ruttenber & Son, 1873); and E. M. Ruttenber and Clark, *History of the County of Orange*. . . . (Newburgh, New York: E. M. Ruttenber & Son, 1875, 1881). Warm thanks to Kay Babbitt and to Janet Dempsey, Town Historian, Cornwall-on-Hudson, for their consistent help. For Willis's Moodna and Canterbury, see Willis, *Outdoors at Idlewild*, pp. 299–301; for Willis's Newburgh, see pp. 278–82. Harriet Jacobs wrote to Amy Post, August 7 [1855], "direct Moodna Orange County that is our New office that is near." IAPFP; the Moodna Post Office had been established October 12, 1853. See John M. Kay and Chester M. Smith Jr., *New York Postal History: The Post Offices and First Postmasters from 1775 to 1980* (State College, Pennsylvania.: American Philatelic Society, 1982), p. 230; warm thanks to Karl Kabelac.

127   *"rural tastes"* Willis, *Outdoors at Idlewild*, pp. 49–52.

127   *"broad-featured"* For Willis's Black Peter, see Willis, *Outdoors at Idlewild*, pp. 189–92, 274–76.

127   *a hundred black residents* For black Cornwall, see James W. Oberly, "The Legacy of Slavery in the Rural North: Black Cornwall, New York in the Nineteenth Century," unpublished paper delivered at a Conference on New York History, New Paltz, New York, March

1981. I am beholden to Dr. Oberly, both for this manuscript and for making his research notes available to me. For Angola Road, see Mrs. Hume, "Our Town," *Cornwall Local*, March 17, 1955.

127   *"one of the stations"* Susan Roe Caldwell, "Family History—Traditions and Memory—What I Saw in My Young Days," typescript of handwritten manuscript in the public library at Cornwall, New York; Janet Dempsey to Jean Fagan Yellin March 7, 1990. Thanks to Janet Dempsey.

128   *Nearby Newburgh* For Crèvecoeur, see *Encyclopedia Americana*; his *Letters* appeared in 1782. For Bishop James Varick (1750–1827) see DANB, pp. 616–17. For Convention delegates, see A. J. Williams-Meyers, *Long Hammering: Essays on the Forging of an African-American Presence in the Hudson River Valley* . . . (Trenton: Africa World Press, 1994), p. 122. For Alsdorf, see Kevin B. Bilati, "The Alsdorf Legacy," *Orange County Historical Society Journal* 23, no. 1 (November 1994): 30–37. For this reference I am grateful to Kevin Barrett Bilati, City Historian, Newburgh. For the Bostons, see BAP, 4:279–80. For black Poughkeepsie, see Clyde and Sally Griffen, *Natives and Newcomers* (Cambridge, Massachusetts: Harvard University Press, 1978), pp. 30–31, 77–79, 211–15. For West Indies Emancipation Day celebrations at Poughkeepsie, see John R. McKivigan and Jason H. Silverman, "Monarchial Liberty and Republican Slavery," *Americans in New York Life and History* 10 (January 1986): 17–18; *New York Tribune*, August 5, 1857; *Eagle*, August 17, 1858; *Weekly Anglo-African*, July 30, 1859; *National Anti-Slavery Standard*, August 13, 1859.

128   *"I had a long distance"* Harriet Jacobs to Amy Post, Cornwall, January 11 [1854]. IAPFP.

128   *Occasionally, in the evening* "Intolerance of Colored Persons in New York," *The Musical World and Times* 7, no. 16 (December 17, 1853): 122–23.

129   *A few months later* " The Battle against Streetcar Segregation," BAP, 4:230–33.

129   *"if I was not so tied down"* Harriet Jacobs to Amy Post, Cornwall, January 11 [1854]. IAPFP.

129   *"I have not"* Harriet Jacobs to Amy Post, Cornwall, January 11 [1854]. IAPFP.

129   *"as yet I have not"* Harriet Jacobs to Amy Post, March [1854]. IAPFP. She had apparently told Nell she was thinking of Boston, see W. C. Nell to Amy Post, February 19, 1854. IAPFP.

129   *"the Nebraska Bill"* The abolitionist Thomas Wentworth Higginson had declared in *The Liberator* that "as an agitator," he welcomed the Bill because it "only shows more clearly that there is no such thing

as peace for us, on the present terms." Jacobs was apparently echoing this idea when, playing on her friend's name, she wrote, "how is my dear old friend Mr Post I have no doubt but that he is at his Post perhaps heading a mighty Phalanx to put the Nebraska Bill through well he shall have my vote 1856." Harriet Jacobs to Amy Post, March [1854]. IAPFP.

130   "*The past two weeks*" W. C. Nell to Amy Post, June 13—July 21, 1854. IAPFP; for the Burns affair, see Albert J. Von Frank, *The Trials of Anthony Burns: Freedom and Slavery in Emerson's Boston* (Cambridge, Massachusetts: Harvard University Press, 1998).

130   "*pledging any service*" W. C. Nell to Amy Post, June 13—July 21, 1854. IAPFP.

130   "*The trouble dear Amy*" Harriet Jacobs to Amy Post, Cornwall, July 31 [1854]. IAPFP.

130   "Idlewild *associations*" See, for example, Nell to Amy Post July 31, September 15, 17, 20, and October 17, 1854. IAPFP. The quotation comes from W. C. Nell to Amy Post, September 10, 1854. IAPFP.

131   *Willis routinely filled Idlewild* Willis, *Outdoors at Idlewild*, Letter LXII, pp. 437–43.

131   "*Louisa has some business*" Harriet Jacobs to Amy Post, December 27 [1854]. IAPFP.

131   "*As Willis's health deteriorated*" By the spring of 1856, the invalided Willis had been unable for eight months to go down to New York City. Willis *The Convalescent* (New York: Charles Scribner, 1859), p. 106.

131   "*I have been very poorly*" Harriet Jacobs to Amy Post, Idlewild, August 7 [1855]. IAPFP.

131   "*Those of us who have lived*" "Speech by William Wells Brown Delivered at the City Assembly Rooms, New York, New York, May 8, 1856," BAP, 4:339–45.

131   Voices from the Spirit World See Isaac Post, *Voices from the Spirit World, Being Communication from Many Spirits* (Rochester, New York: C. H. McDonell, 1852); for William C. Nell's involvement, see for example, Nell to Amy Post, June 2, 1850, July 16, 1855, and August 12–13, 1855. IAPFP. For Willis on spiritualism, see Willis, *Rag Bag* (New York: Charles Scribner, 1855), pp. 184–94; and Willis, *The Convalescent*, pp. 303–06.

132   "*just as the spirits told me*" Harriet Jacobs to Amy Post, Idlewild, August 7 [1855]. IAPFP.

132   "*Lulu's position as governess*" Ellen Eldridge was born September 20, 1844; for Fanny Fern (Sara Payson Willis Parton), see Warren, *Fanny Fern*; for Louisa Matilda Jacobs's position in Fern's household, see Harriet Jacobs to Amy Post, Idlewild, March [1857]. IAPFP.

132   *"Fern's roman à clef"* Fanny Fern, *Ruth Hall* (New York: Mason brothers, 1855). For Fern and Nathaniel P. Willis, see Warren, *Fanny Fern* and Beers, *Nathaniel Parker Willis*; also see Harriet Jacobs's correspondence for the years 1856–58. IAPFP.

132   *"pleasant, handsome home"* The Diary of Thomas Butler Gunn, Missouri Historical Society, St. Louis. Thanks to Joyce W. Warren for this reference, and special thanks to Catherine Mach for her discoveries.

133   *"This girl"* Gunn Diary, May 23, 1858.

133   *"Louisa Jacobs"* Gunn Diary, March 16, 1859.

133   *"Inventing some transitory"* Gunn Diary, July 12, 1861.

133   *"and after tea"* William C. Nell to Amy Post, July 31—August 3, 1854. IAPFP.

134   *"I have followed you"* Harriet Jacobs to Amy Post, Idlewild, March [1857]. IAPFP. For the struggle in Kansas to which she alludes, see, for example, Louis Filler, *The Crusade Against Slavery* (New York: Harper & Brothers, 1960), pp. 219–57.

134   *"the Dred Scott decision"* For the Dred Scott decision and protest against that decision, see BAP, 4:391–94.

134   *"When I see"* Harriet Jacobs to Amy Post, Idlewild, March [1857]. IAPFP.

135   *"but not with Post"* Harriet Jacobs to Amy Post, May 18—June 8 [1857]. IAPFP. Post missed the anniversaries for the first time in years because, in the wake of her husband's bankruptcy, she was moving the family into a smaller home. See Hewitt, *Women's Activism and Social Change*, p. 185.

135   *"I have thought"* Harriet Jacobs to Amy Post, May 18—June 8 [1857]. IAPFP.

135   *"in the only spot"* Harriet Jacobs to Amy Post, June 21 [1857]. IAPFP.

136   *"there are somethings"* Harriet Jacobs to Amy Post, June 21 [1857]. IAPFP.

136   *"that I was living an Idle life"* Harriet Jacobs to Amy Post, June 21 [1857]. IAPFP.

136   *several slave narratives* BAP, 1:21; A. Chamerovzow had edited and published John Brown's, *Slave Life . . .* (London: W. M. Watts, 1855); R. D. Webb had gotten out Frederick Douglass, *Narrative . . .* (1845); Thomas Price had helped with Moses Roper's *Narrative . . .* (London: Darton, Garvey and Arton, 1838); William Farmer had promoted William Wells Brown's, *Narrative . . .* (London: C. Gilpin,

1849); and his *Three Years in Europe* . . . (London: C. Gilpin, 1852).

136   "*by identifying myself with*" Harriet Jacobs to Amy Post, June 21 [1857]. IAPFP.

Chapter 9. The Slave's Own Story

137   *Jacobs began* Harriet Jacobs to Amy Post, August 9 [1857].IAPFP.

137   "*acting as a brother should*" William C. Nell to Amy Post, September 22, 1857. IAPFP.

137   *John S. wrote* William C. Nell to Amy Post, November 10, 1857. IAPFP.

137   "*going so far from Louise*" Harriet Jacobs to Amy Post, March 1 [1858]. IAPFP.

137   "*under the protection*" Harriet Jacobs to Amy Post, March 1 [1858].IAPFP; Harriet Jacobs to Amy Post, May 3 [1858]. IAPFP; Harriet Jacobs to Miss Weston, June 28 [1858]. Boston Public Library, Weston Papers.

138   *The manuscript she carried* ILSG pp. 183, 184; Harriet Jacobs to Amy Post, Cornwall, Orange County [1852?]. IAPFP. For English racism, see Douglas A. Lorimer, *Colour, Class and the Victorians: English Attitudes To the Negro* (New York: Holmes & Meier, 1978); and James Walvin, *Black and White: The Negro and English Society, 1555–1945* (New York: Allen Lane The Penguin Press, 1973).

138   *Jacobs quickly reached people* Harriet Jacobs to Miss Weston, June 28 [1858] Boston Public Library, Weston Papers; Harriet Jacobs to Amy Post, May 3 [1858]. IAPFP. For Chapman's transatlantic circle, see Lee Chambers-Schiller, "The Cab: A Trans-Atlantic Community, Aspects of Nineteenth Century Reform" (Ph.D. diss., University of Michigan, 1963). Also see Louis Billington and Rosamund Billington, "'A Burning Zeal for Righteousness,' Women in the British Anti-Slavery Movement, 1820–1860," in *Equal or Different, Women's Politics, 1800–1914*, ed. Jane Randall (Oxford: Oxford University Press, 1987), pp. 82–111. For the Webbs, see Merrill, ed., *The Letters of William Lloyd Garrison* 2:684; 4:56; and Temperley, *British Antislavery, 1833–1870*. Thanks to Claire Taylor for her good help.

138   *the Duchess of Sutherland* In 1833, upon her husband's succession, Harriet Elizabeth Georgiana Leveson-Gower (1806–68) became Duchess of Sutherland. A close companion of Queen Victoria, she used her influence and her home to aid the antislavery movement.

Dictionary of National Biography, ed. Leslie Stephen [and Sidney Lee] v. 1–63. And supplement v. 1–3 (London: Smith, Elder & Co. 1885–1901). Hereafter DNB. 11:1031–32. For Stafford House, see Neil Burton, *British Historic Houses Handbook* (New York: Facts on File, 1982), pp. 254–55. For Jacobs as the "dusky stranger," see [Richard Webb?], "Linda; Incidents in the Life of a Slave Girl," *The Anti-Slavery Advocate* (London, May 1, 1861; for Jacobs as the Duchess's houseguest, see "A woman died in Washington" [Harriet Jacobs's obituary], *Boston Herald,* March 10, 1897.

138   *one of the truest heroines* [Richard Webb?], "Linda; Incidents in the Life of a Slave Girl." William Craft, *Running a Thousand Miles for Freedom; or, The Escape of William and Ellen Craft from Slavery* (London: William Tweedie, 1860).

138   *prevented her from seeing John S.* For Jacobs's hopes to see her brother in England and to convince him to return to the States with her, see Harriet Jacobs to Amy Post, March 1 [1858]. IAPFP, and to Miss Weston, June 28 [1858] Boston Public Library, Weston Papers. For John S.'s whereabouts during Jacobs's visit, see diary of Frederick Chesson, July 19, 1858: "Recd letter from Mr Jacobs at Malta enclosing a L5 note for his sister." Also see Chesson's diary entry for September 19, 1858: "Mr Jacobs came to tea. Since we last saw him he has been to Constantinople and the Black Sea." Raymond English Deposit; John Rylands University Library of Manchester at Deansgate, United Kingdom. Hereafter Raymond English Deposit.

138   *"a good fellow"* George Thompson to Amelia Thompson Chesson, December 24, 1857. Raymond English Deposit. George Thompson (1804–78), British abolitionist leader and Member of Parliament (1847–52) who had faced mobs in America lecturing with the Garrisonians, had recently returned from India ill and penniless. For Thompson, see DNB, 19:691; and Howard Temperley, *British Antislavery,* pp. 237–39.

139   *Amelia and Frederick Chesson* For Chesson, see "Mr. F. W. Chesson," (London) *The Athenaeum* . . . May 5, 1888; and "Obituary," *Times of London,* May 1, 1888. For the factionalism among British abolitionists in the 1850s, see Temperley, *British Antislavery, 1833–1870,* pp. 221–47.

139   *"delighted with everything"* Amelia Thompson Chesson Diary, July 23, 1858. Raymond English Deposit. At the concert, which featured Mme. Grisi, they heard the Grand Orchestra of the Royal Italian Opera; *London Times,* July 20, 1858. Weather information comes from the National Meteorological Archive, Berkshire, U.K.

139   *A few days later* Amelia Thompson Chesson Diary, July 27, 1858. Raymond English Deposit.

139 *It is unclear* For the fugitive slave named John Brown, see I. A. Chamerovzow, ed., *Slave Life in Georgia: a narrative of the life, sufferings, and escape of John Brown, a fugitive slave, now in England* (London: W. M. Watts, 1855). For Henry "Box" Brown, see BAP, 1:174–75, note 11. For the Crafts, see R.J.M. Blackett, *Building an Antislavery Wall*; Dorothy Sterling, *Black Foremothers: Three Lives* (Old Westbury, New York: Feminist Press), pp. 44–45; R.J.M. Blackett, "Fugitive Slaves in Britain: The Odyssey of William and Ellen Craft," *Journal of American Studies* 12 (April 1978): 41–68; R.J M. Blackett, *Beating Against the Barriers*, p. 104.

Julia Griffiths, who had returned to England in 1855 and in 1859 would marry the Reverend H. O. Crofts, founded "at least fourteen ladies' groups" in Great Britain before the American Civil War, according to Billington and Billington, *Equal or Different*, p. 108. Also see Blackett, *Building an Antislavery Wall*, pp. 114–15; and Erwin Palmer, "A Partnership in the Abolition Movement," *University of Rochester Library Bulletin* 26, nos. 1–2 (1970–71): 1–20.

139 *"a cheap dress for house wear"* Amelia Thompson Chesson Diary. August 15, 1858; also see virtually the same entry misdated July 19. Raymond English Deposit.

139 *Uncle Mark Ramsey had died* For the death of Mark Ramsey, see Josiah Collins to Harriet Jacobs, Somerset Place, July 23, 1859. NCSA. For Jacobs's effort to see Post at the spring 1859 New York City meeting of the American Anti-Slavery Society, see Harriet Jacobs to Amy Post, October 8 [1860]. IAPFP.

140 *"I felt"* Harriet Jacobs to Amy Post, October 8 [1860]. IAPFP.

140 *John Brown* Brown was jailed, tried, convicted of treason and of murder, and hanged on December 2, 1859. For a recent commentary, see *His Soul Goes Marching On*, ed. Paul Finkelman (Charlotte: University Press of Virginia, 1995).

140 *writer L. Maria Child* Responding to John Brown's raid, L. Maria Child wrote a series of letters that became the center of the *Correspondence Between Lydia Maria Child and Governor Wise and Mrs Mason, of Virginia* (Boston: American Anti-Slavery Society, 1860)— a best-selling abolitionist pamphlet. See Jean Fagan Yellin, *Women and Sisters* (New Haven: Yale University Press, 1989), pp. 62–64; and Carolyn Karcher, *First Woman in the Republic: A Cultural Biography of Lydia Maria Child* (Durham, North Carolina: Duke University Press, 1994), pp. 419–25.

140 *a tribute to Brown* For L. Maria Child's comment concerning Jacobs's essay on Brown, see L. Maria Child to Harriet Jacobs, Wayland, August 13, 1860. IAPFP. Jacobs's essay has not been found.

140 *"Difficulties seemed to thicken"* Harriet Jacobs to Amy Post, October 8 [1860]. IAPFP. The *Boston City Directory* for 1859 lists

Phillips and Sampson & Co., c/o S. C. Perkins, at A. K. Loring, booksellers, 13 Winter. The firm is not listed for 1860.

140   *"tremble at the thought"* Harriet Jacobs to Amy Post, October 8 [1860]. IAPFP. James Redpath, *The Public Life of Capt. John Brown* . . . (Boston: Thayer and Eldridge, 1860). Thayer and Eldridge are best known as the enthusiastic publishers of Whitman's third edition of *Leaves of Grass*. For a listing of their books, see back matter in James Redpath, *Echoes of Harper's Ferry* (Boston, 1860); thanks to Philip Lapsansky. For Child, see Karcher, *First Woman in the Republic*.

140   *"because she tells her story"* [Lydia Maria Child] to [Lucy Osgood], Wayland, August 8, 1860, Cornell University Library, Anti-Slavery Collection. L. Maria Child to Lucy [Searle], Medford, February 4, 1861.

141   *"copying a great deal of it"* Lydia Maria Child to Harriet Jacobs, August 13, 1860. IAPFP.

141   *"Under the circumstances"* Lydia Maria Child to Harriet Jacobs, September 27, 1860. IAPFP.

141   *"I am truly ashamed of it"* Harriet Jacobs to Amy Post, October 8 [1860]. IAPFP.

141   *"I am pledged"* Harriet Jacobs to Amy Post, [October 1860]. IAPFP.

142   *Nell had already heard* W. C. Nell to Amy Post, October 26, 1860. IAPFP.

142   *"especial interest"* *Anti-Slavery Bugle*, November 3, 1860.

142   *"both accauncher"* Harriet Jacobs to Amy Post, Nov. 8 [1860]. IAPFP.

142   *change public opinion Annual Report of the American Anti-Slavery Society for the Year Ending May 1, 1859* (1860), p. 41.

142   *She asked Phillips* Lydia Maria Child to Wendell Phillips, December 2, 1860, and December 9, 1860. Houghton Library, Harvard University.

142   *"My acquaintance"* William C. Nell to Wendell Phillips, December 14, 1860. Houghton Library, Harvard University.

143   *doubtless with Child's help* L. Maria Child to John Greenleaf Whittier, Medford, April 4, 1861. Library of Congress, Lydia M. Child Papers; Cornelia Grinnell Willis thanks Fields—perhaps for his involvement in the publication of *Incidents?*—in her letter to [James Thomas] Fields, Idlewild, September 13, 1861. Henry H. Huntington Library.

143   *"the long-continued and intemperate interference"* James Buchanan, "Fourth Annual Message," in *The State of the Union Messages of the Presidents, 1790–1966*, ed. Fred L. Israel (New York: Chelsea,

1966), 1:1025. E. B. Long, *The Civil War Day by Day . . .* (Garden City, New York.: Doubleday, 1971), p. 13.

143   *a $2.00 contribution* "Subscription List of the 17th National Anti-Slavery Anniversary," *The Liberator,* February 15, 1861.

143   *on December 3 The Liberator,* January 18, 1861.

143   *"lined by crowds" The Liberator* January 25, 1861.

143   *"broke down the door"* Kevin Bilali, "The Alsdorf Legacy," *Orange County Historical Society Journal* 23 (November 1, 1994): 34, citing John J. Nutt, *Newburgh, Her Institutions, Industries and Leading Citizens* (Newburgh: Ritchie & Hull, 1891), p. 128. "Newburgh Made Contributions to Union Army," *Evening News*, April 28, 1969.

144   *Only a few months after Jacobs's visit* Julie Winch, *Philadelphia's Black Elite*, pp. 148–51; also see *Emancipator,* August 25, September 1, September 8, 1842; *National Anti-Slavery Standard,* August 11, August 25, 1842; Michael Feldberg, *The Turbulent Era: Riot and Disorder in Jacksonian America* (New York: Oxford University Press, 1980); and Barome, "The Vigilant Committee of Philadelphia," pp. 326–27.

144   *"Press, Church"* Winch, *Philadelphia's Black Elite*, pp. 149–50; for Purvis's comment, see Robert Purvis to Henry C. Wright, August 22, 1842, Boston Public Library quoted in Winch, p. 39.

144   *George William Curtis* Edward Cary, *George William Curtis*, American Men of Letters series (Boston: Houghton Mifflin, 1894), pp. 126–29.

144   *bound in dark green* Bindings of this first edition vary. At the Library Company of Philadelphia, it is bound in purple, and the spine bears the title and a graphic in gold.

145   *A century later* For the early dispute over the authorship and genre of *Incidents*, see Jean Fagan Yellin, "Text and Contexts of Harriet Jacobs's *Incidents in the Life of a Slave Girl: Written by Herself,*" in *The Slave's Narrative,* ed. Charles T. Davis and Henry Louis Gates Jr. (New York: Oxford University Press, 1985), p. 278, note 2.

145   *the Willises' library* For Jacobs's access to the Willis library, see L. Maria Child to Lucy [Searle], Medford, February 4, 1861. Cornell University Library, Anti-Slavery Collection.

145   *South Ninth Street home* The 749 South Ninth Street address where Jacobs was staying in 1861 is listed in the 1860 census as the residence of John Chew, hairdresser and wig maker. Harriet Jacobs used this address in her inscription to Mary Rebecca Darby Smith in The Library Company of Philadelphia's copy of *Incidents in the Life of a Slave Girl.*

145   *"most cheerfully" The Christian Recorder,* January 11, 1861. Readers were advised to contact her at the Antislavery Office at 107 North Fifth Street.

146   *"The Slaves true Friend"* Harriet Jacobs, inscription to Mary
        Rebecca Darby Smith in The Library Company of Philadelphia's
        copy of *Incidents in the Life of a Slave Girl*. For Mary Rebecca Darby
        Smith, see *A Philadelphia Perspective: The Diary of Sidney George
        Fisher, Covering the Years 1834–1871*, ed. Nicholas Wainwright.
        (Philadelphia: Historical Society of Pennsylvania, 1967), pp.
        409–10; and Mary Rebecca Darby Smith, compiler, *Leaves from the
        Past* (Philadelphia: J. B. Lippincott, 1872).

146   *"a faithful and true witness"* *A Memorial of Sarah Pugh* (Philadel-
        phia: J. B. Lippincott, 1888), p. 100.

146   *she decided to travel* Harriet Jacobs to "Dear Lady" [Mary Rebecca
        Darby Smith], January 14 [1861], Library Company of Philadelphia.

146   *Francis Jackson* Harriet Jacobs to Francis Jackson, February 1, 1861.
        Houghton Library, Harvard University, Wendell Phillips Papers.

146   *"the Boston booksellers"* L. Maria Child to John Greenleaf Whittier,
        Medford, Massachusetts, April 4, 1861, Library of Congress, Lydia
        M. Child Papers; L. Maria Child to John Greenleaf Whittier, Med-
        ford, Massachusetts, March 14, 1861. Library of Congress, Lydia
        M. Child Papers.

146   *"'Linda'"* William C. Nell, "Linda, the Slave Girl," *The Liberator*,
        January 25, 1861.

146   *Two weeks later* "Linda," *The Liberator*, February 8, 1861.

146   *"simple and attractive"* "Incidents in the Life of a Slave Girl: the nar-
        rative of Linda Brent.—" (Salem, Ohio), *Anti-Slavery Bugle*, Febru-
        ary 9, 1861.

147   *"In New York"* *National Anti-Slavery Standard*, March 2, 1861;
        "Our Boston Correspondence," *National Anti-Slavery Standard*,
        February 16, 1861.

147   *"New Publications"* "New Publications," *National Anti-Slavery
        Standard*, February 23, 1861.

147   *"The* Weekly Anglo-African" "The Loophole of Retreat," (New
        York City) *Weekly Anglo-African*, March 30, 1861; "Linda,"
        Weekly Anglo-African, April 13, 1861.

147   *"substantially the same"* "Linda; Incidents in the Life of a Slave
        Girl," (London) *The Anti-Slavery Advocate*, May 1, 1861.

148   *"John's narrative"* [John S. Jacobs], "A True Tale of Slavery," (Lon-
        don) *The Leisure Hour: A Family Journal of Instruction and Recre-
        ation* (London) February 7, 14, 21, and 28, 1861. This text has been
        republished in ILSG pp. 207–28.

148   *"London Emancipation Committee"* The Garrisonian London
        Emancipation Committee—late in 1862 renamed the London Eman-
        cipation Society—was founded by F. W. Chesson in 1859. See R.J.M.

Blackett, *Divided Hearts: Britain and the American Civil War* (Baton Rouge: Louisiana State University Press, 2001); and Howard Temperley, *British Antislavery, 1833–1870*, pp. 254–55.

148   "The Leisure Hour" *The Leisure Hour.* See ILSG p. xxxvi.

148   *"judged* The Leisure Hour *a potential ally"* "A Word with our Readers," *The Leisure Hour,* 1, no. 1 (January 1, 1852); Louis Billington, "The Religious Periodical and Newspaper Press, 1770–1870," in *The Press in English Society from the Seventeenth to Nineteenth Centuries,* ed. Michael Harris and Alan Lee (London: Associated University Presses, 1986), p. 128.

148   *"Frederick Douglass's 1845* Narrative" Frederick Douglass, *Narrative of an American Slave* (Boston: Anti-Slavery Office), 1845; for Douglass's work as classic, see, for example, William L. Andrews, *To Tell a Free Story: The First Century of Afro-American Autobiography, 1760–1860* (Urbana: University of Illinois Press, 1986), Chapter 6.

149   *"I have no purpose"* Abraham Lincoln, "First Inaugural Address," in *Inaugural Addresses of the Presidents of the United States. . . .* (Washington, D.C.: U.S. Government Printing Office, 1989); *Civil War Day by Day,* May 24, 1861, pp. 77–78.

150   *"of overthrowing or interfering"* James McPherson, *The Struggle for Equality* (Princeton: Princeton University Press, 1964) p. 70.

150   *As fugitive slaves Civil War Day by Day,* pp. 106, 112.

150   *"You that have believed"* Harriet Jacobs to Isaac and Amy Post, June 5, 1861. IAPFP. John S. Jacobs, "A Colored American in England," *National Anti-Slavery Standard,* June 29, 1861; rpt. *The Anti-Slavery Advocate* (London), September 2, 1861.

150   *annual celebration at Abington* "Celebration of the First of August at Abington," *The Liberator,* August 9, 1861.

151   *"Many Anti-Slavery friends"* L. Maria Child to Lucy Searle, August 22, 1861. Cornell University Library Anti-Slavery Collection.

151   *"the great body"* "Celebration of the First of August at Abington," *The Liberator,* August 9, 1861.

151   *"scolding lines"* Harriet Jacobs to [Amy and Isaac Post], June 18 [1861]. IAPFP.

151   *a letter informing him* Frederick W. Chesson Diary, January 15, 1862. Raymond English Deposit.

152   *Chesson called on Tweedie* Frederick W. Chesson Diary, March 5, 1862. Raymond English Deposit. For Jacobs's London publisher William W. Tweedie, distributor of the (London) *Anti-Slavery Advocate,* see BAP, 1:330–31.

152   *"This is the act"* Frederick W. Chesson Diary, March 31, 1862. Raymond English Deposit.

152   *"The title is probably"* Frederick W. Chesson Diary, April 1, 1862. Raymond English Deposit.

152   *"This perfectly truthful"* [Amelia Thompson Chesson], "Domestic Slave-Life in the Southern States," *London Morning Star and Dial,* March 10, 1862.

152   *"We have in this country"* "Literature," *London Daily News,* March 10, 1862.

153   *"has all the interest"* "Literature," *Newcastle Daily Chronicle and Northern Counties Advertiser,* March 13, 1862.

153   *"Uncle Tom's adventures"* "Literature," *Plymouth Western Morning News,* April 5, 1862.

153   *"the heart of every female reader"* "Literary Notices," *Londonderry Standard,* March 27, 1862.

153   *"This is a most simple"* "Review," *London Anti-Slavery Reporter,* April 1, 1862.

153   *"since I have no fear"* Harriet Jacobs to Amy Post, February 14 [1853]. IAPFP.

Chapter 10. Spared for This Work

157   *In the spring of 1862* Long, *The Civil War Day by Day,* pp. 191, 192, 196, 199.

157   *the Port Royal experiment* For the Port Royal experiment, see Willie Lee Rose, *Rehearsal for Reconstruction* (Oxford: Oxford University Press, 1964, 1976); the quotation comes from C. Vann Woodword's "Introduction," p. xii.

158   *"contrabands of war"* Stanley W. Campbell, *The Slave Catchers: Enforcement of the Fugitive Slave Law, 1850–1860,* pp. 188–94.

158   *"an asylum for free negroes"* "Resolution by the Washington City Council [April, 1862]," in *Freedom: A Documentary History of Emancipation 1861–1867,* ed. Ira Berlin et al . . . series I, vol. I, *The Destruction of Slavery* (Cambridge: Cambridge University Press, 1985), p. 178.

158   *"Thousands of contrabands"* Reverend H. M. Turner, "A Call to Action," "Washington Correspondence," *Christian Recorder,* October 4, 1862.

158   *Progressive Friends* Albert J. Wahl, "The Progressive Friends of Longwood," *The Bulletin of Friends Historical Association* 42, no. 1 (spring 1953): 13–32. For the 1862 meeting, see "Tenth Yearly Meeting of Progressive Friends at Longwood, Pa.," *The Liberator,* June 20, 1862.

158   *When in late June* Pennsylvania Yearly Meeting of Progressive
        Friends, *Proceedings* (1862), p. 8, quoted in Wahl, "The Progressive
        Friends," p. 29. Thanks to Chris Densmore.

159   *Duff Green's Row* Thomas R. Johnson, "The City on the Hill: Race
        Relations in Washington, D.C. 1865–1885" (Ph.D. diss., University
        of Maryland, 1975), p. 36.

159   "*Life Among the Contrabands,*" *The Liberator*, September 5, 1862.

160   "*The first white females*" "Life Among the Contrabands," The Lib-
        erator, September 5, 1862.

160   "*where the poor creatures*" "Life Among the Contrabands," *The
        Liberator*, September 5, 1862.

161   "*Some of them*" "Life Among the Contrabands," *The Liberator*,
        September 5, 1862.

161   "*by Mrs. Jacobs*" *The Liberator*, September 5, 1862.

161   "*Mrs.*" The abolitionists conferred the title of "madam" to Elizabeth
        Keckley, probably in deference to her identity as an exclusive fash-
        ion designer.

161   "*entering the hovel*" Pennsylvania Female Anti-Slavery Society, *29th
        Annual Report* (1863), p. 13.

162   "*while she was here*" [Lydia Maria Child] to [Sarah Blake (Sturgis)
        Shaw], November 11, 1862, Houghton Library, Harvard University,
        Child Papers; Child to [Robert Folger] Wallcut, June 12, 1862, Smith
        College, Sophia Smith Collection; Child to Anna [Loring] December
        7, 1862, Schlesinger Library, Radcliffe College, Child Papers. Jacobs
        to [Elizabeth Neall] Gay, October 10 [1862?], Columbia University
        Libraries, Gay Papers. In this letter, Jacobs mentions "Mrs. Haydock."
        Hannah W. Haydock, a member of the New York Yearly Meeting,
        an active abolitionist and "a friendly helper of the colored people,
        still proscribed on account of color," died July 15, 1893, in her sev-
        enty-sixth year. *Friends' Intelligencer and Journal*, 50:456, 489.
        Jacobs also mentioned "the New York Societies that are organising";
        for these, see *Friends' Intelligencer*, November 29, 1862. For black
        women in the freedmen's aid movement, see Carol Faulkner,
        Women's Radical Reconstruction: The Freedmen's Aid Movement
        (Philadelphia: University of Pennsylvania Press, 2003), Chapter 4.

162   *refugee relief* Jacobs mentions "our little Society in Boston" in Har-
        riet Jacobs to J. Sella Martin, Alexandria, April 13 [1863], published
        as "Letter from Mrs. Jacobs," *Freed-Man's Aid Society,* MSS British
        Empire G88. p. 7; Bodleian Library at Rhodes House, Oxford, here-
        after Rhodes House; BAPM 14:0799. For this Boston group, see *The
        Liberator* of October 10 and November 5, 1862, and *Anglo-African,*
        November 12, 1862. For more, see *The Liberator,* November 21 and

December 5, 1863; and October 14, 21, and November 18, 1864. William C. Nell, announcing that a fair for "disabled colored soldiers at Alexandria" was planned for the last week in the month, wrote, "An active promoter of this event is Mrs. HARRIET A. JACOBS, whose mission in Alexandria has been frought with blessings to the friendless." See *The Liberator*, January 13, 1865.

During the war, the *Anglo-African* reported on black women's relief organizations in Brooklyn, Troy, Geneva, Albany, and Syracuse, New York; Oberlin, Ohio; Stockbridge, Massachusetts; and Hartford, Connecticut. See *Anglo-African*, January 27, March 12, April 9, July 3, and December 1, 1864; and March 4, 1865. For New Bedford contributions, see the *Anglo-African* of August 26, 1865. Also see *The Liberator* February 1, 1863. The relief work of the African Aid Society was consistently covered by the *Christian Recorder*; see, for example, *Christian Recorder*, May 3, 1863.

162   *Ladies' Contraband Relief Association* For Elizabeth Keckley (1818–1907), see *Black Women in America*, 1:672–73. In 1868, Keckley published *Behind the Scenes: or Thirty Years a Slave and Four Years in the White House*. For the broad national and international support organized by the Washington women, see *Second Annual Report of the Freedmen and Soldiers' Relief Association (Late Contraband Relief Association)*, Washington, D C., 1864 (which notes sending $50.00 to "Sick and wounded Soldiers at Alexandria, Virginia," p. 7). Also see *The Liberator*, November 21, 1863, and *Anglo-African*, January 9 and February 27, 1864.

For an earlier black Washington relief association, see "Union Relief Association," *Christian Recorder*, October 4, 1862; and "Address of the Union Relief Association of the Union Bethel Church, Washington, D.C.," *Christian Recorder*, November 8, 1862. For the Auxiliary Freedmen's Relief Association of Washington, D.C., a later black-led organization, see "Letter from James Lynch," *Christian Recorder*, February 27, 1864.

See also *First Annual Report of the National Freedmen's Relief Association of the District of Columbia* (1863); the *Third Annual Report* (1865) of the National Freedmen's Relief Association; and the *Fourth Annual Report* (1866). For the National Association for the Relief of Colored Women and Children, a white-led organization, see *Friends' Intelligencer* 20 (1863): 42; and "Relief of Contrabands in the District of Columbia; First Annual Report of the Contraband Relief Association," *The Liberator*, September 25, 1863. The *Christian Recorder* appeal, "A Call to Action," appeared October 4, 1862.

162   "*if ever I craved*" Harriet Jacobs to Amy Post, Idlewild, December 8 [1862] #050. IAPFP.

163   *"So rudely were they attired"* Nathaniel Hawthorne, "Chiefly About War Matters," *Atlantic Monthly* (July 1862), in vol. XXIII of *Works*, ed. Thomas Woodson, Claude M. Simpson, and L. Neal Smith, Centenary Edition (Columbus: Ohio State University Press, 1994), pp. 403–42.

163   *"Miserably clothed"* Edward Dicey, *Spectator of America*, ed. Herbert Mitgang (Chicago: Quadrangle, 1971), p. 154; Dicey acknowledges that "I have assumed throughout that the Negro belongs virtually to an inferior race to that of the white man." p.52. Dicey's comments were originally published as a series of articles in *The Spectator* and *Macmillan's Magazine*, then collected as *Six Months in the Federal States* (London, Cambridge: Macmillan and Company, 1863.)

163   *chose not even to comment* A search of Willis's *Home Journal* from March 15, 1862, to the end of the year, yielded no mention of his trip to Alexandria. Although he does discuss his visit to Manassas and Fortress Monroe, he makes no mention of "contrabands." Warm thanks to Carol Faulkner.

163   *in the writings of others* Most important is the diary of Julia A. Wilbur.

164   *a city astir with military activity* This description of wartime Alexandria is based on William B. Hurd, *Alexandria, Virginia, 1863–1865* (Alexandria: Fort Ward Museum, 1989); and James G. Barber, *Alexandria in the Civil War* (Lynchburg, Virginia: H. E. Howard, 1988); the quotation comes from Barber, p. 35.

164   *"contains this day"* R H[inton], "Alexandria, Va." *Anglo-African*, October 31, 1863. For "Franklin and Armfield and Price, Birch and Company, 1315 Duke Street, Alexandria, Virginia," see HUD III, p. 111, typescript in vertical file African-Americans, at Special Collections, Alexandria Library.

164   *"May I never again behold"* Harriet Jacobs to J. Sella Martin, Alexandria, April 13 [1863], "Letter from Mrs. Jacobs," *Freed-Man's Aid Society*, p. 7. Rhodes House; BAPM 14:0799.

164   *"Alexandria was an important medical center"* Barber, *Alexandria in the Civil War*, p. 42.

164   *"packed together"* Harriet Jacobs to J. Sella Martin, Alexandria, April 13 [1863]. "Letter from Mrs. Jacobs," *Freed-Man's Aid Society*, p. 7. Rhodes House; BAPM 14:0799.

164   *"The authorities really do not know"* Harriet Jacobs to J. Sella Martin, Alexandria, April 13 [1863]. "Letter from Mrs. Jacobs," *Freed-Man's Aid Society*, p. 7. Rhodes House; BAPM 14:0799.

165   *"a very nice person"* Julia Wilbur to Anna M. C. Barnes, January 15, 1863. RLASS.

165   "*We have but one room*" Julia Wilbur to Anna M. C. Barnes, January 15, 1863. RLASS.

165   "*threatening to flog them*"Julia Wilbur to Anna M. C. Barnes, February 27, 1863. RLASS.

165   "& put them through the pock house" Julia Wilbur to Anna M. C. Barnes, February 27, 1863. The smallpox hospital had been established at Claremont, the former mansion of Confederate Commander Forrest. RLASS.

166   "*Mrs. Jacobs spoke very handsomely*" Julia Wilbur to Anna M. C. Barnes, March 10, 1863. RLASS.

166   "*I dreaded more*" Julia Wilbur to Anna M. C. Barnes, March 10, 1863. RLASS. "Those people need to be protected" Julia Wilbur to Anna M. C. Barnes, March 10, 1863. RLASS.

166   "*hunt up the poor scattering families*" Julia Wilbur to Anna M. C. Barnes, March 10, 1863. RLASS.

166   *Jacobs mailed a long letter* Harriet Jacobs to L. Maria Child, March 18, 1863; published in the *National Anti-Slavery Standard* on April 18, 1863. The letter she was refuting had appeared in the *Home Evangelist* 14, no. 3 (March 3, 1863): 10. Concerning the "intellectual capacity" of the people, its author had written: "As might be expected, the intellect of these refugees is of a very low grade. The distinguishing traits of humanity are nearly effaced. We had, before, no idea of how near human beings may approximate to the brutes." Concerning their "morality," he continued: "We were assured, upon unquestionable authority, that strict honesty and integrity are almost never met with. The three vices that prevail are lying, thieving and licentiousness. Drunkenness is increasing." Warm thanks to Anne Dealy, and to Deborah van Broekhoven and Karen Soderland of the American Baptist Society.

166   "*The misery I have*"Harriet Jacobs to L. Maria Child, March 1863; published in the *National Anti-Slavery Standard* April 18, 1863. For the struggle for black troops, see John Hope Franklin, *From Slavery to Freedom*, 2d ed. (New York: Knopf, 1967), pp. 273–74.

167   "*The memory of the past*" Harriet Jacobs to [J] Sella Martin, Alexandria, April 13 [1863] "Letter from Mrs. Jacobs," *Freed-Man's Aid Society*, p. 7. Rhodes House; BAPM 14:0799. Martin had accepted a call from Boston's Joy Street Baptist Church at the end of 1859; he had sailed for London in August 1861. R.J.M. Blackett, *Beating Against the Barriers*, p. 192.

167   *a visiting relief worker* Strangely, among the "Records of Hospital Attendants, Matrons, and Nurses, 1861–1865," in the papers of the Medical Director's Office of the Army of the Potomac, "Mrs. Jacobs" is listed as being in attendance only on Leap Year Day, Feb-

ruary 29, 1864. National Archives, RG no. 94, entry 535, Records
of Adjutant General's Office 1780s—1917. Nurses. "Jacobs." Box
10. Carded Service Records of Hospital Attendants, Matrons and
Nurses, 1861–65.Mrs. Jacobs. File 1168. Feb 29/64. M[edical]
D[irector's] O[ffice] A[rmy] of P[otomac]. For the Sanitary Com-
mission, see Judith Ann Giesberg, *Civil War Sisterhood: The U. S.
Sanitary Commission and Women's Politics in Transition* (Boston:
Northeastern University Press, 2000).

167   *"Alexandria, Oh—horrid"* Amy Post to Isaac Post [December
        1863]. IAPFP. See JWD, December 10, 1863.

167   *the city so nervous* Barber, *Alexandria in the Civil War,* pp. 88, 91;
        Alexandria Gazette, October 7, 1863, in *Pen Portraits of Alexandria
        Virginia, 1739–1900*, ed. T. Michael Miller (Bowie, Maryland: Her-
        itage, 1987), p. 226.

168   *to rescue orphans* JWD, May 24, 1863. For the practice of placing
        war orphans and other refugees in the North, see Carleton Mabee,
        Sojourner Truth: Slave, Prophet, Legend (New York: New York Uni-
        versity Press, 1993), pp. 144ff. See also "Mrs. Josephine R. Griffin,"
        L. P. Brockett and Mary C. Vaughn, *Women's Work in the Civil War*
        (Philadelphia: Ziegler, McCurdy & Co., 1867), pp. 707–09.

168   *annual meeting of the New England Anti-Slavery Society National
        Anti-Slavery Standard*, June 6, 1863, p. 3. "Reception and Depar-
        ture of the 54th Regiment," *Boston Evening Transcript,* May 28,
        1863. See also *Boston Evening Journal,* May 28, 1863, quoted in
        Samuel Cornish, *The Sable Arm: Black Troops in the Union Army,
        1861–1865* (New York: Longman's, Green, 1956), p. 148; and
        "Departure of 54th Regiment of Massachusetts Volunteers," *Trav-
        eler*, reprinted in *The Liberator,* June 5, 1863, p. 2.

168   *"How proud and happy"* Harriet Jacobs to L. Maria Child, quoted
        in L. Maria Child to Francis George Shaw, October 18, 1863.
        Houghton Library, Harvard University, Child Papers.

169   *"The sight"* "New England Anti-Slavery Convention," *The Libera-
        tor,* June 5, 1863; and "New England Anti-Slavery Convention,"
        National Anti-Slavery Standard, June 6, 1863.

169   *routinely expressed her thanks* See, for example, [Letter from Har-
        riet Jacobs], May 7, 1863, *Second Report of a Committee of the Rep-
        resentatives of New York Yearly Meeting of Friends upon the
        Condition and Wants of the Colored Refugees* (1863). pp. 12–13.
        For Gladwin's appointment, see JWD, May 6, 1863.

169   *"Some [refugees]"* Samuel Shaw to Dr. J. R. Bigelow, June 14, 1863.
        National Archives RG 94, entry 360 colored troops box 15, 1863,
        G-43 letters received; R. H., Washington, October 30, 1863, "Edi-
        torial Correspondence," *Anglo-African*, November 14, 1863.

169   *In addition to condemning* According to the (Alexandria) *Gazette* of
        December 29, 1863, "Col. Greene having removed the Negro fami-
        lies from abroad in Washington to the 'freedman's Village,' will col-
        lect those from Alexandria there the first fair day. He has commenced
        the erection of fifty additional houses on Greene Heights." On
        March 3, 1864, the *Gazette* published General Slough's order that
        "all persons, known to have no reputable or visible means of sup-
        port . . . are required to leave the city of Alexandria, Va. on or before
        the 5th instl., or they will be arrested." For a condemnation of the
        refugee camp at Arlington, see *Third Report of a Committee of the
        Representatives of New York Yearly Meeting of Friends upon the
        Condition and Wants of the Colored Refugees* (1864), pp. 13–15.

170   "*Not one in a hundred*" [Julia Wilbur], *Thirteenth Annual Report
        of the Rochester Ladies' Anti-Slavery Society* (1864), p. 22.

170   "*We don't*" JWD, March 26, 1863; [Julia Wilbur], *Thirteenth
        Annual Report* (1864), p. 11.

170   "*packed away*" JWD, May 15, 1863; [Julia Wilbur],*Fourteenth
        Annual Report of the Rochester Ladies' Anti-Slavery Society* (1864)
        pp. 8–9; JWD, January 21, April 12, May 5, December 27, 1864. In
        1997, the Friends of Freedmen's Cemetery organized to preserve and
        commemorate the site, where a gas station and an office building are
        currently located. A highway marker was erected in September 2000.
        "*Freedmen's Cemetery*" (flier), Alexandria, Virginia.

170   "*hurrying as many*" Harriet Jacobs to Julia Wilbur, quoted in Julia
        Wilbur to Anna M. C. Barnes, August 8, 1863. RLASS.

171   "*I occupied it myself*" Harriet Jacobs to Julia Wilbur, quoted in Julia
        Wilbur to Anna M. C. Barnes, August 8, 1863. RLASS.

171   "*their condition is made worse*" Samuel Shaw to Dr. J. R. Bigelow,
        June 14, 1863. National Archives RG 94 entry 360 colored troops
        box 15, 1863, G-43, letters received, row 21 comp 34 shelf 2. In July,
        Drs. Bigelow, Shaw, and Graves had sent charges against Gladwin to
        the Freedmen's Relief Association in Washington; J. R. Bigelow,
        Samuel Shaw, and J. W. Graves to the Freedman's Relief Association
        Washington, D.C., July 20, 1863. National Archives, RG 94 entry
        360 colored troops box 15, 1863, G-43, letters received, row 21
        comp 34 shelf 2. Concerning Gladwin's policy of collecting rent and
        of shipping out newcomers, Graves wrote, "Mr. G. asked the privi-
        lege to collect rent, but only of those who were willing and able to
        pay now he compels them to pay." "He sends new comers from the
        front or elsewhere to Washington no matter who they are parents
        who have children here children who have parents brothers & sis-
        ters relations or friends in search of each other are given no time for
        making enquiries. . . . Husbands and wives are rudely separated and

all the family relations are respected but little if at all." J. W. Graves to Mr. Buckingham, September 12, 1863. National Archives RG 94 entry 360 colored troops box 15, 1863, G-43, letters received, row 21 comp 34 shelf 2. Despite the condemnations of Gladwin by Dr. Bigelow and his colleagues, Wilbur's papers demonstrate that she and Jacobs had no more confidence in the complainants than they had in him. Julia Wilbur to Anna M. C. Barnes, October 2, 1863, RLASS; about Bigelow, Wilbur writes: "I presume Dr. B. will remain for he makes it profitable here for himself. He has had none of the hospital fund used yet for these sick people & they die for want of nourishing food." Wilbur to Anna M. C. Barnes, October 28 [1863]. RLASS.

171   *"Two women"* National Archives, GR 94 entry 360 colored troops box 15, 1863, G-43, letters received, row 21 comp 34 shelf 2; National Archives, RG 94-entry 360, colored troops, 1863, box 15, G-43 letters received. Recd H2 DW [?] September 29; National Archives. Capt. W. Mc. L. Gwynne to Brig.Gen. J. P. Slough, October 1863 and Brig. Gen. Jno. P. Slough, October 1, 1863, and Brig. Gen. Jno. P. Slough to Asst. Adjt. General, October 1, 1863, filed with G-43, 1863, letters received, ser. 360, Colored Troops Division, RG 94 [13–29], National Archives. Gladwin was supported by letters from Capt. John C. Wyman, October 1; by Col. H. H. Wells, October 1; and Lieut. Col. Lemuel Towns, October 1, 1863; National Archives G-3, 1863. General Slough—who, Wilbur reports, was angry because the charges had not been brought to him at first—concludes that Gladwin was "persecuted by a class of would-be philanthropists who would, if possible, occupy his position," and gives the Superintendent his full support. See Julia Wilbur to Anna M. C. Barnes, October 2, 1863, RLASS. For Julia Wilbur's comment, see JWD, December 27, 1863.

172   *"They were, Wilbur writes"* JWD, October 14, 1863; Julia Wilbur to Anna M. C. Barnes, November 5, 1863. RLASS.

172   *"The N. Y. committee"* Julia Wilbur to Anna M. C. Barnes, November 20, 1863. RLASS.

172   *"I had longed for this hour"* Harriet Jacobs to Hannah E. Stevenson, March 10 [1864], Boston Public Library; Julia Wilbur to Anna M. C. Barnes, November 20, 1863, RLASS. Stevenson, a sister of the prominent Boston merchant J. Thomas Stevenson, was working with Hannah Ropes at the Union Hospital in Washington as a volunteer nurse. *Civil War Nurse: The Diary and Letters of Hannah Ropes,* ed. John R. Brumgardt, (Knoxville: University of Tennessee Press, 1980). In 1863 and 1864, Stevenson was a member of the Teachers Committee of the New England Freedmen's Aid Society, according to the Society's *Annual Reports* of 1863 and 1864. She is named among Boston's activist women in Brockett and Vaughn, *Women's*

Work in the Civil War, p. 79. In 1863, Louisa May Alcott dedicated her *Hospital Sketches* to Stevenson.

173   "*He must have an office*" Julia Wilbur to Anna M. C. Barnes, March 8, 1864. RLASS.

173   "*I hardly think*" [Julia Wilbur], *Thirteenth Annual Report* (1864) pp. 13–14, 18.

173   "*there is still a great number*" Report to the Executive Committee of New England Yearly Meeting of Friends, upon the Condition and Needs of the Freed People of Color in Washington and Virginia 1864), p. 5; *Third Report of a Committee of the Representatives of New York Yearly Meeting of Friends upon the Condition and Wants of the Colored Refugees* (1864), p. 8; R. H., "Editorial Correspondence," Washington, October 30, 1863, published in *Anglo-African*, November 14, 1863. This judgment contradicts "A Visit to Alexandria," republished from the *Evening Post* on October 30, 1863, which praises Jacobs, Wilbur and Gladwin equally.

174   "*she was thinking of leaving for good*" Julia Wilbur to Anna M. C. Barnes, March 8, 1864. RLASS.

Chapter 11. Justice Will Come

175   *Women's National Loyal League* For the Women's National Loyal League, see *The Selected Papers of Elizabeth Cady Stanton and Susan B. Anthony*, ed. Ann D. Gordon (New Brunswick: Rutgers University Press, 1997), vol. 1; *History of Woman Suffrage*, ed. Elizabeth Cady Stanton, et al. (Rochester: Susan B. Anthony, 1881), 2:50–89, 875–899; Ida Husted Harper, *The Life and Work of Susan B. Anthony* (Indianapolis: Hollenbeck, 1898), 1:225–40.

175   *they unanimously passed a resolution* Harper, *Susan B. Anthony*, 1:229; Gordon ed., *Selected Papers*, 1:493; Stanton, *History of Woman Suffrage*, 2:888–89. Long, *Civil War Day by Day*, pp. 344–48.

175   *the women opened up offices* Wendy Hammond Venet, *Neither Ballots nor Bullets* (Charlottesville: University Press of Virginia, 1991), p. 118. For the Draft Riots, see Iver Bernstein, *The New York Draft Riots: Their Significance for American Society and Politics in the Age of the Civil War* (New York: Oxford University Press, 1990).

175   "*invoking the Almighty*" "Women's Loyal National League," *New York Daily Tribune*, October 30, 1863; The *Papers of Elizabeth Cady Stanton and Susan B. Anthony* (Microfilm) ed. Patricia G. Holland and Ann D. Gordon (Wilmington, Delaware: Scholarly Resources, 1991). 45 Microfilm reels. Hereafter Stanton-Anthony Papers. 10:572. Julia Wilbur's diary records that Jacobs left Alexandria before October 25 and returned after November 6, 1863.

176   *The women were working hard* Harper, *Susan B. Anthony*, 1:235–36.

176   *In the spring* Stanton, *History of Woman Suffrage,* 2:897; "Ladies Loyal League," *New York Herald,* May 15, 1864; Stanton-Anthony Papers, 10:808; also see *New York World,* May 16, Stanton-Anthony Papers 10:809. Pleased with its work, at summer's end the League closed its offices. The following February, the Eighteenth Amendment to the Constitution was ratified, stating that "Neither slavery nor involuntary servitude, except as a punishment for crime whereof the part shall have been duly convicted, shall exist within the United States, or any place subject to their jurisdiction." For the Fort Pillow massacre, see Long, *Civil War Day by Day,* p. 484; and *New York Herald Tribune,* May 2, 1864.

176   *building a school* Alexandria African American Heritage Park Visitors Guide (n.d., n.p.), pp. 5–7; M. B. Goodwin, "Schools of the Colored Population," *Special Report of the Commissioner of Education on the Condition and Improvement of Public Schools in the District of Columbia, Submitted to the Senate, June 1868 and to the House with Additions June 13, 1870* (Washington, D.C.: U. S. Department of Education, U.S. Government Printing Office, 1871, rpt. *American Journal of Education,* vol. 19, 1870), p. 285.

176   *two black women* Mary E. Chase had opened the Columbus Street School; Sarah Gray founded the Saint Rose Institute for the "contrabands"; Reverend C. Robinson and Reverend G. W. Parker had started the select school; and Leland Waring had opened the school at Lancastrian schoolhouse; see M. B. Goodwin, "Schools of the Colored Population," pp. 285–88. For the schools run by Chase, Robinson, and Parker, see also "Alexandria," *Anglo-African,* October 31, 1863; [Julia Wilbur], *Twelfth Annual Report of the Rochester Ladies' Anti-Slavery Society* (1863), pp. 10–11. According to Wilbur, *Twelfth Report,* a Mr. Hill and a Mrs. Crouch also opened pay schools, as did Amanda Bell, a "contraband" living at the Slave Pen who charged her students fifty cents a month.

177   *two 'colored teachers'* Julia Wilbur to Anna M. C. Barnes November 20, 1863. RLASS; Virginia Lawton's father Edward B. Lawton was a friend of John S.'s and a Boston activist. Horton and Horton, *Black Bostonians,* p. 101. Both Virginia Lawton and her sister Mariana went south to teach the freed people. The 1870 census for Cambridge, Massachusetts lists Mrs. Edward B. Lawton, 48, and a number of children, including Virginia Edward? 24; Sarah 28 teacher; and Eliza 26 teacher.

177   *"to wait and see"* Harriet Jacobs to Hannah Stevenson, March 10 [1864]. Boston Public Library.

177   *"I wanted the colored men to learn"* Harriet Jacobs to Hannah Stevenson, March 10 [1864] Boston Public Library. Harriet Jacobs to L. Maria Child, March 26, 1864 published in *National Anti-Slavery Standard,* April 16, 1864.

177 "*One gentleman arose*" Harriet Jacobs to Hannah Stevenson, March 10 [1864]. Boston Public Library.

177 "*because our sympathies*" Harriet Jacobs to L. Maria Child, March 26, 1864 in *National Anti-Slavery Standard,* April 16, 1864.

177 "*After this decision*" Harriet Jacobs to Hannah Stevenson, March 10 [1864]. Boston Public Library.

178 "*We opened a fair*" Harriet Jacobs to Hannah Stevenson, March 10 [1864]. Boston Public Library. [Georganna Woolsey Bacon and Eliza Woolsey Howland], *Letters of a Family during the War for the Union 1861–1865* (New Haven: Tuttle, Morehouse & Taylor, 1899), 2:648–49. Grateful thanks to Charles F. Johnson. For Jacobs's conviction that those who could, should pay money, see *Third Report of a Committee of the Representatives of New York Yearly Meeting of Friends upon the Condition and Wants of the Colored Refugees* (1864) pp. 5–6.

178 "*Slavery has not crushed*" Harriet Jacobs and Louisa M. Jacobs to L. Maria Child, March 26, 1864, in *National Anti-Slavery Standard,* April 16, 1864; Louisa Jacobs May 14, 1864 letter in *Third Report of a Committee of the Representatives of New York Yearly Meeting of Friends upon the Condition and Wants of the Colored Refugees* (1864), p. 7.

179 "*very encouraging*" Louisa Jacobs, May 14, 1864, in *Third Report of a Committee of the Representatives of New York Yearly Meeting of Friends upon the Condition and Wants of the Colored Refugees* (1864), p. 7; Harriet Jacobs and Louisa M. Jacobs to L. Maria Child, March 26, 1864, in *National Anti-Slavery Standard,* April 16, 1864.

179 "*the doctor says*" Harriet Jacobs, [April, 1864?] in *Third Report of a Committee of the Representatives of New York Yearly Meeting of Friends upon the Condition and Wants of the Colored Refugees* (1864), p. 6.

179 *Louisa managed to finish.* "Jacobs School," Harriet Jacobs, Alexandria, January 13, 1865 in *The Freedmen's Record,* March 1865, p. 41.

179 "*to welcome the emigrants*" Harriet Jacobs to L. Maria Child, March 26, 1864 in *National Anti-Slavery Standard,* April 16, 1864. For Lincoln's emigration scheme, see BAP, 5:108; Long, *Civil War Day by Day,* pp.179, 241, 251, 292, 303, 459; and *Thirteenth Annual Report,* pp. 19–20.

180 "*It was a bitter cold day*" Harriet Jacobs to L. Maria Child, March 26, 1864 in *National Anti-Slavery Standard,* April 16, 1864.

180 "*I comforted myself*" Harriet Jacobs to Amy Post, October 9 [1853]. IAPFP. Harriet Jacobs to L. Maria Child, March 26, 1864 in *National Anti-Slavery Standard,* April 16, 1864.

180   *"I am convinced"* Harriet Jacobs letter of March 22, 1864, in "Report of Friends' Association for the Aid and Elevation of Freedmen," *Friends' Intelligencer*, 21 (1865): 179–80; Harriet Jacobs letter of May 23, 1864, "Extracts From Letters Received by the Committee," *The Freedman*, October 1864, p. 4.

181   *"a report today"* JWD, February 14, 1864; Dicey, *Spectator of America*, p. 151; JWD, March 11, 1864; *Gazette*, March 10, 1864.

181   *"now practically a military post"* *Gazette*, July 13 and 14, 1864; *Gazette* October 12, 1864. Barber, *Alexandria in the Civil War*, p. 96.

181   *On August 1* [Julia Wilbur] *Thirteenth Annual Report*, pp. 14–15.

181   *To organize the events* "Flag Presentation at L'Ouverture Hospital, Alexandria, Va." *Anglo-African*, September 3, 1864; an earlier report, published August 20, 1864, omits Jacobs's remarks. The local participants, named in both reports, are: Miss Johnson, Misses Dougans, Miss E. Land, Miss S. Beckley, Miss C. Jones, Miss M. Henry, and Miss S. C. Douglass.

182   *"The presentation"* "Flag Presentation at L'Ouverture Hospital, Alexandria, Va." *Anglo-African*, September 3, 1864.

182   *"Physicians, Soldiers, and Friends"* "Flag Presentation at L'Ouverture Hospital, Alexandria, Va." *Anglo-African*, September 3, 1864.

182   *"a splendid repast"* "Flag Presentation at L'Ouverture Hospital, at Alexandria, Va." *Anglo-African*, September 3, 1864. Speakers included Reverend Chauncey Leonard; Robert Dale Owen, at the time a member of the Freedmen's Inquiry Commission created by the War Department in 1863; Mr. Scott of Pennsylvania, and Sergeant Fairfax. For Owen, see Robert Morris, *Reading, 'Riting, and Reconstruction* (Chicago: University of Chicago Press, 1981), p. 32. "Rally Round the Flag" comes from the chorus of George F. Root, "The Battle Cry of Freedom" (1862).

182   *"blacks were preparing the script"* David W. Blight, *Race and Reunion: The Civil War in American Memory* (Cambridge, Massachusetts: Harvard University Press, 2001), pp. 28–29.

183   *"very diligent" labors Third Report of a Committee of the Representatives of New York Yearly Meeting of Friends upon the Condition and Wants of the Colored Refugees* (1864), p. 5; "Jacobs (Linda) School," *Freedmen's Record*, February 1865, p. 19.

183   *reformers' tours* For the visitors, see for example JWD for 1864: January 2, 3, 7, 12; February 15, March 12, November 20, and December 1.

183   *"intelligent, judicious"* J. S. May Jr., "The Freedmen at Alexandria," *National Anti-Slavery Standard*, November 5, 1864; republished in the *Anglo-African*, November 12, 1864.

183   *soliciting donations* "Children, Look Here," *National Anti-Slavery Standard*, November 12, 1864; "Aid for the Schools in Alexandria," *National Anti-Slavery Standard*, December 10, 1864; Harriet Jacobs, "Help for the Alexandria School," *National Anti-Slavery Standard*, December 24, 1864; Louisa Jacobs to Sarah Russell May, Alexandria, February 6, 1865, published as "The Freedmen of Alexandria," *National Anti-Slavery Standard*, February 25, 1865.

184   *"the colored people"* Third Annual Report of the Executive Board of the Friends' Association of Philadelphia and its Vicinity, for the Relief of Colored Freedmen (1864), pp. 25–26; "Present Condition," (New York) *The Freedmen* 1 (October 1864): 7–8; "Extract from the Report of One of New York Committee who Visited the Freedmen," (New York) *The Freedmen* 1 (April 1865): 22–23.

184   *"Jacobs (Linda) School"* Edward Earle, Ann B. Earle, and Guliema W. Howland, *Report to the Executive Committee of the New England Yearly Meeting of Friends, upon the Condition and Needs of the Freed People of Color in Washington and Virginia* (1864), pp. 4–5. "Jacobs (Linda) School, Alexandria, Va." *The Freedmen's Record* 1 (February 1865): 19. And see J. M. Ellis, "A Visit to the Freedmen," (Philadelphia) *Friend's Intelligencer*, (July 1865): pp. 300–02, 313–15; and *Report of the Executive Board of the Friends' Association of Philadelphia and its Vicinity for the Relief of Colored Freedmen* (Philadelphia, C. Sherman, Son & Co., printers, 1864), which also mentions Jacobs by name and notes a visit to the school, p. 26.

184   *"the daughter of Mrs. Jacobs"* See the letter of April 12, 1864, published in Amanda Akin Stearn's *The Lady Nurse of Ward E* (New York: Baker & Taylor, 1909), pp. 229–30; thanks to Jane E. Schultz of Indiana University for this reference. Caroline M. Severance to Elizabeth P. Peabody, February 4, 1865. Antioch College Library. Wendell Phillips Garrison to William Lloyd Garrison, December 11, 1864. Houghton Library, Harvard University. Thanks to Harriet Hyman Alonso for this reference. W.C.N., "General Banks—Colored Soldiers and Freedmen," *The Liberator*, April 29, 1864.

185   *"It is delightful to see"* "School at Alexandria," (Boston), *The Freedmen's Record* 1, no. 9 (September 1865): 149. Thanks to Philip Lapsansky. In Alexandria today there is no record of the Jacobs School. On September 4, 1865, in response to a request by a Colonel S. P. Lee of Alexandria, the New England Freedmen's Aid Society decided that the $150 they had voted "for groundrent and repair of the Jacobs School" could be used "towards the purchase of a new site for the School." On June 15, 1866, the Jacobs School, in operation during the 1865–66 school year under teachers Mr. Aborn and the Misses Lawton, was "considered as discontinued on the 30 June." In late July, Alexandria was hit by a violent storm bringing wind,

rain, and hail. On August 3, 1866, "Voted that Col. Lee use the whole or part of the $150 dolls voted for repairing the Jacobs school house in Alexandria (since blown down) to helping the trustees of the school to buy a lot of land on which a house shall be built for the Jacobs School." Teachers Mrs. and Miss Smith were to be sent to Alexandria. In October 1866, the New England Freedmen's Aid Society announced that they would reopen the Jacobs School, "though in a different building, and under the auspices of Col Lee, representative of the Bureau." See *Freedmen's Record* 2 (October 1866): 173. Seven months later, Julia Wilbur wrote, "Went to headquarters, saw Col. P. Lee. He talks like a copperhead. It is said he fraternizes with rebels, & does not do well by the freed people. Too bad. Too bad!" JWD, May 13, 1867.

On January 1, 1869, Alexandria had two "colored school-houses, six rooms in each: The Pitt street house, finished in April, 1867, and the Alfred street house, finished in the following November. The lots upon which these houses stand were purchased by the colored people, in 1866. They held public meetings . . . and raised the money in their poverty, paying $800 for the first lot, and about that sum for the other. The Freedmen's Bureau built the houses, which are very comfortable, and of a capacity to seat 400 scholars." These schools were staffed by ten white teachers and assistant teacher Mary M. Nickens, "colored." The Snowden School for boys on Pitt Street would remain in use until 1915, and the Hallowell School for girls on Alfred Street, until 1920. New England Freedman's Aid Society Papers, Box 1 Daily Record 1865–66, Notebook Records of the Education Committee, 1864–74, and Box 2 Teachers Committee 1864–66 and folder "Teachers Committee February 1866-September 1870." New England Freedman's Aid Society Papers, Massachusetts Historical Society. *The Freedmen's Record* 1 (December 1865): 199–202; (Alexandria) *Gazette*, March 13, 1865, July 26, and August 2, 1866; M. B. Goodwin, "Schools of the Colored Population," pp. 288–92; "George Seaton, Jr." typescript, African-American vertical file, Special Collections, Alexandria Library.

185   *the albumin photograph* "Coloured School at Alexandria Va 1864 taught by Harriet Jacobs & daughter agents of New York Friends." 6.5" x 11" albumin photograph. Courtesy of The Robert Langmuir Collection of African-American Photographs.

185   "*What a picture*" Harriet Jacobs to Samuel J. May, Alexandria, February 10 [1865]. Harriet Beecher Stowe Center.

185   *The new superintendent* [Julia Wilbur], *Fourteenth Annual Report of the Rochester Ladies* (1865), pp. 7–8. Harriet Jacobs to Samuel J. May, Alexandria, February 10 [1865]. Also see Louisa Jacobs to Sarah Russell May, February 6, 1865, published as "The Freedmen of Alexandria," *National Anti-Slavery Standard*, February 25, 1865.

Captain Ferree, she writes, "is humane and does not ignore the fact that the Freedmen are as human as other men."

186   *At meetings at the Bethel* R. D. Beckley and Sampson White represented Alexandria at Syracuse; see *Anglo-African,* October 8 and 15, 1864; and *Proceedings of the National Convention of Colored Men, held in the City of Syracuse, N. Y., October 4, 5, 6, and 7, 1864: with the Bill of Wrongs and Rights, and the Address to the American People* (Boston: J. S. Rock and Geo. L. Ruffin, 1864), pp. 5, 36; "Testimony of Colored Witnesses in Virginia," *The Liberator,* October 14, 1864, p. 168; "From Alexandria," *Anglo-African,* June 25, 1864; "Sick and Wounded Soldiers in Alexandria," *Anglo-African,* August 27, 1864; "The Work of Relieving the Sick and Wounded Soldiers and Freedmen," *Anglo-African,* March 11, 1865; [Bacon and Howland], *Letters of a Family,* 2:649–50. For Wilbur's report on the fair held in the winter for the benefit of the soldiers, see [Julia Wilbur], *Fourteenth Annual Report of the Rochester Ladies Anti-Slavery Society,* (1865), p. 8; Timothy J. Dennee, "The Freed People of Alexandria," *Alexandria Archeology* (1997); Belinda Blomberg, "Free Black Adaptive Responses to the Antebellum Urban Environment: Neighborhood Stratification in Alexandria, Virginia, 1790–1850" (Ph.D. diss., The American University, 1988), pp. 71–73. Also see "Alexandria's African-American Heritage, 1790—Present," comp. Peter K. Matthews, *Alexandria Archeology* (1991). For the *Gazette* on the contraband villages, see the issue of January 10, 1865; thanks to T. Michael Miller for this citation.

186   *At the end of March 1965* Eric Foner, *Reconstruction: America's Unfinished Revolution, 1863–1877* (New York: Harper and Row, 1984), p. 69; Harriet Jacobs, writing from Alexandria March 30, 1865, in *Fourth Report of a Committee of the Representatives of New York Yearly Meeting upon the Condition and Wants of the Colored Refugees* (1865), pp. 8–9.

187   *"This morning early"* *Gazette,* April 10, 15, 1865; JWD, April 14, 1865.

187   *"How can I write it?"* JWD April 15, 16, 1865.

187   *"Thousands"* Louisa Jacobs, Alexandria, April 27, 1865, *Fourth Report of a Committee of Representatives of New York Yearly Meeting of Friends upon the Condition and Wants of the Colored Refugees* (1865), p. 10.

187   *the women proceeded* [Julia Wilbur] *Fourteenth Annual Report of the Rochester Ladies' Anti-Slavery Society* (1865), p. 14. For Wilbur's daily account of this trip, see JWD, May 15—June 15, 1865.

187   *The city they saw* John Leyburn, "The Fall of Richmond," *Harper's New Monthly Magazine* 33 (June 1866): 92–96, quoted in John T.

O'Brien, "Reconstruction in Richmond: White Restoration and Black Protest, April-June, 1865," *The Virginia Magazine* 89 (1981): 259–81; quotation on p. 261; Patrick, *Inside Lincoln's Army* in O'Brien, p. 271. Also see Elsa Barkley Brown, "The Contested Terrain of Freedom," typescript, 1994. I am grateful to Dr. Brown for sharing her work on Richmond; for her definitive study, see "Uncle Ned's Children: Negotiating Community and Freedom in Postemancipation Richmond, Virginia" (Ph.D. diss., Kent State University, 1994). For Wilbur's account of the four weeks she spent in Richmond, see Julia A. Wilbur, "Richmond," dated Washington, June 20, 1865, published in *The Pennsylvania Freedmen's Bulletin* 1, no. 3 (August 1, 1865): 51–53.

188   *"Sat & looked"* JWD, May 19, 1865.

189   *"Pass Mrs. Colman"* Lucy Colman, *Reminiscences* (Buffalo, 1894), pp. 74–75. Thanks to Dorothy Sterling for this citation. For Colman, see Colman, *Reminiscences*. For Jacobs on Jim Crow transportation, see ILSG pp. 176–77.

Chapter 12. Marching Without a Lance

190   *Georgia's superintendent of education* G. L. Eberhart, State Superintendent of Education for Georgia, made the request, according to *The Freedmen's Record* 2 (May 1866): 91. Seven months earlier, the Society had responded to a request from Mr. Gannett by agreeing to help the Savannah Education Association by paying the salaries of their teachers. The New York Society of Friends continued to support the Jacobs women, but their commissions were from the New England Freedmen's Aid Society, and they reported to that organization.

190   *"I don't care about the meals"* "From Harriet Jacobs," Savannah, November 22, 1865, in (New York) *The Freedman*, (December 1865): 40.

190   *they were not needed* "From Savannah," *The Freedmen's Record*, (January 1866): 3.

191   *"There you see our blood"* L[ucy Chase], "A Journey Through the South," *Worcester Evening Gazette*, n.d., rpt. *Dear Ones at Home*, ed. Henry Lee Swint (Nashville: Vanderbilt University Press, 1966) p. 186. For a description of the city, also see *Memoirs of General W. T. Sherman* (New York: The Library of America, 1990), p. 708.

191   *the softness of the air* L[ucy Chase], "A Journey Through the South," p. 189.

191   *the city* For the *Wanderer*, see Daniel P. Mannix and Malcolm Cowley, *Black Cargoes: A History of the Atlantic Slave Trade 1518–1865* (New York: Viking, 1962), pp. 277–82. *Memoirs of General W. T. Sherman*, pp. 725–26. For Reverend Garrison Frazier, see James M.

Simms, *The First Colored Baptist Church in North America. . . .* (1888, rpt. New York: Negro Universities Press, 1969), pp. 261–62.

191 *Special Field Order Number 15* "The islands from Charleston south, the abandoned rice-fields along the rivers for thirty miles back from the sea, and the country bordering the St. John's River, Florida, are reserved and set apart for the settlement of the negroes now made free by the acts of war and the proclamation of the President of the United States. . . . on the islands, and in the settlements hereafter to be established, no white person whatever, unless military officers and soldiers detailed for duty, will be permitted to reside; and the sole and exclusive management of affairs will be left to the freed people themselves, subject only the United States military authority, and the acts of Congress. . . .the young and able-bodied negroes must be encouraged to enlist as soldiers in the service of the United States. . . . Whenever three respectable negroes, heads of families, shall desire to settle on land . . . the Inspector of Settlements and Plantations will . . . give them a license to settle. . . . The three parties named will subdivide the land . . . so that each family shall have a plot of not more than forty acres of tillable ground." "Special Field Orders, No. 15," January 16, 1865, *Memoirs of General W. T. Sherman*, pp. 729–30. For a useful discussion of the "Sherman reservation," see Claude F. Oubre, *Forty Acres and a Mule: The Freedmen's Bureau and Black Land Ownership* (Baton Rouge: Louisiana State University Press, 1978), pp. 46–71.

191 *black-led Savannah Education Association* Simms, *The First Colored Baptist Church*, pp. 137–38; James Lynch, "From Savannah, Ga." *Anglo-African*, January 28, 1865.

191 *forty acres and a mule* For the account of a witness, see S. W. Magill to Dear Brn, February 3, 1865, Savannah. Records of the American Missionary Association (microfilm) hereafter AMA Papers. #1935–6

191 *"Men and women came to the table"* The Freedmen of Savannah. Savannah Educational Association. January 25, 1865. AMA Papers # 19341.

192 *African American teachers* First to be established, the Bryan School was on the corner of St. Julian and Bernard streets in the old Bryan slave market; the second, Oglethorpe School, was opened on January 15, 1865, in the Stiles House on Farm street, recently a medical college and later, a Confederate hospital. See *Savannah Daily Republican,* March 20, 25, 1865.

192 *"a goodly number"* "The Freedmen of Savannah," January 25, 1865, AMA Papers #19341.

192 *black schools had been operating* Whittington B. Johnson, *Black Savannah, 1788–1864* (Fayetteville: University of Arkansas Press, 1996), p. 126. For the antebellum free black community, see Whittington B. Johnson, "Free Blacks in Antebellum Savannah," *Georgia Historical Quarterly* 64 (winter 1980): 418–31.

192 *Susie King Taylor* Susie King Taylor, *Reminiscences of My Life in Camp: with the 33d United States Colored Troops late 1st S. C. Volunteers* (Boston: By the Author, 1902), pp. 5–6. In 1862, when she was fourteen, Taylor was taken by her uncle to St. Simon's Island, where she taught school and then joined up with Company E. Following years of teaching in the camps, after the war Taylor returned to Savannah, where she taught a school in her home. Taylor, p. 54ff.

192 *secret schools* Julian Fromantin taught his school for a quarter of a century, and Jane Deveaux conducted hers for almost thirty years. W. B. Johnson, *Black Savannah, 1788–1864* pp. 127–28; Robert E. Perdue, "The Negro in Savannah, 1865–1900" (Ph.D. diss., University of Georgia, 1971), pp. 70–71.

192 *Now Porter had become Savannah Daily Republican*, March 20, 1865.

192 *"It will not do"* serial S. W. Magill to Dear Brn, February 3, 1865, Savannah. AMA Papers #19345–6.

193 *a rather peculiar feeling* "Letter from W. C. Gannett," Savannah, April 28, 1865. *The Freedmen's Record* (June, 1865):91–92.

193 *"Their management and teaching"* H. E. Alvord to O. O. Howard, September 1, 1865, Unreg. L, Commissioner, BRFAL (752:74), quoted in Ronald E. Butchart, *Northern Schools, Southern Blacks, and Reconstruction: Freedmen's Education, 1862–1875* (Westport, Connecticut: Greenwood, 1980), p. 173.

193 *"assistance without control"* "Georgia," *The Freedmen's Record* 2 (May 1866): 91. Control was what the American Missionary Association representatives had in mind when they quickly brought in four white teachers and established their free school in the Wesley Chapel. See Magill's letters of February 3 and 26, 1865; E. Cooley's letters of December 20, 1865, January 2, February 3, March 20, April 9, and May 11, 1866. For the establishment of the first American Missionary Association school, see Magill's letter of February 26, 1865, AMA # 19353.

193 *In the Georgia low country* Russell Duncan, *Freedom's Shore: Tunis Campbell and the Georgia Freedmen* (Athens: University of Georgia Press, 1986), p. 20. For Campbell, see *DANB*, pp. 160–61; R. Saxon to O. O. Howard, September 9, 1865, in Oubre, *Forty Acres*, pp. 50–51; and see Oubre, p. 38.

193   *Fearing that the Army* Duncan, *Freedom's Shore,* p. 28; *Savannah Daily Herald,* November 11, 1865.

194   *the central struggle of Reconstruction* W.E.B. DuBois, *Black Reconstruction in America: An Essay toward a History of the Part Which Black Folk Played in the Attempt to Reconstruct Democracy in America, 1860–1880* (Cleveland: World Publishing Company, 1962); Joseph P. Reidy, "Aaron A. Bradley: Voice of Black Labor in the Georgia Lowcountry," in *Southern Black Leaders of the Reconstruction Era,* ed. Howard N. Rabinowitz (Urbana: University of Illinois Press, 1982), pp. 281–308.

194   *"six schools in the city"* "From Savannah," Harriet Jacobs to *The Freedmen's Record* (January 1866):3–4.

194   *"If you could send me"* "From Harriet Jacobs," December 24, 1865, in (New York) *The Freedman* (February 1866):49–50. *"don't seem to think"* "From Harriet Jacobs," December 24, 1865, in (New York) *The Freedman* (February 1866):49–50.

194   *"the erection of an Orphan Asylum"* Work on the Orphan Asylum and Old Folks' Home was begun under the direction of Col. Hiram F. Sickles. Harriet Jacobs in *Freedmen's Record* (January 1866):3.

194   *"A Great Improvement"* *Savannah National Republican,* November 18, 1865.

195   *"We shall be badly off"* Harriet Jacobs in *Freedmen's Record* (January 1866):3

195   *Military rule had ended* Military rule ended in Savannah on November 1, 1865; on December 4, the first Georgia legislature under the new constitution met at Milledgeville. E. A. Cooley to Samuel Hunt, December 20, 1865. Savannah. AMA # 19487–8.

195   *Bradley was promptly arrested* *Savannah National Republican,* December 12, 1865 and December 14, 1865; *Savannah Daily News and Herald* December 20, 1865. After protests, Bradley was paroled on December 29, 1865, and returned to the city. He later was elected as delegate to the State Constitutional Convention of Georgia, 1867–68. Although expelled from the convention for alleged criminal acts committed in New York in the 1850s, in 1868 he was elected to the Georgia Senate; after resigning, he was reseated early in 1870. Bradley left Georgia in the mid-1870s. Information on Bradley comes from the hostile essay by E. Merton Coulter, "Aaron Alpeoria Bradley, Georgia Negro Politician," *Georgia Historical Quarterly* 5 (1967): 17–21; and from Reidy's sympathetic essay, cited above. For Bradley as the freed people's advocate, see Sara Rappaport, "The Freedmen's Bureau as a Legal Agent for Black Men and Women in Georgia: 1865–1868," *Georgia Historical Quarterly* 73 (spring 1989): 52.

195   *"to teach an industrial department"* "From Harriet Jacobs," December 9, 1865, in (New York) *The Freedman* (February 1866);

Proceedings of the Freedmen's Convention of Georgia, Assembled at Augusta, January 10th, 1866 (Augusta: Loyal Georgian, 1866); Harriet Jacobs, December 9, 1865 in (New York) *The Freedman* (February 1866). For James Simms, see Reverend James M. Simms, *The First Colored Baptist Church in North America.*

195   "*you have no protection*" Harriet Jacobs, December 9, 1865, in (New York) *The Freedman* (February 1866):49.

196   "*they are carried*" Harriet Jacobs, December 24, 1865, in (New York) *The Freedman* (February 1866):49–50.

196   "*now these people are found fault with*" Harriet Jacobs, December 24, 1865, in (New York) *The Freedman* (February 1866):49–50.

196   "*It is a pitiful sight*" "From Harriet Jacobs," January 9, 1866, in (New York) *The Freedman* (February 1866):50–51.

196   *Special Order of Brigadier General Tillson Savannah Daily Herald*, December 30, 1865-January 10, 1866; "From Harriet Jacobs," January 9, 1866, in (New York) *The Freedman* (February 1866):50–51, republished as "Savannah," (London) *The Freed-man* (May 1866):248–49. Foner, *Reconstruction*, p. 135.

196   "*In every direction*" "From Harriet Jacobs," January 19, 1866, in (New York) *The Freedman* (February 1866):51. For an analysis concluding that "the bureau facilitated the development, at least in part, of a repressive labor system in the post bellum south," see Rappaport, "The Freedman's Bureau," p. 31.

197   "*I must tell you*" "Georgia," Harriet Jacobs, February 9, 1866, in (New York) *The Freedman* (February 1866):56.

197   "*A boat, a mule*" "From Savannah," Louisa Jacobs, in *The Freedmen's Record* (March 1866): 55–56.

197   "*There was nothing*" *Savannah Daily Herald*, February 15, 1866.

197   "*I visited some of the plantations*" "Letter from L. Maria Child," Harriet Jacobs to L. Maria Child, March 8, 1866, in (New York) *The Independent*, April 5, 1866.

198   "*The old spirit of the system*" "From Savannah," Louisa Jacobs in *The Freedmen's Record*, (March 1866):55–56. For the freedwomen, see Leslie A. Schwalm, *A Hard Fight for We: Women's Transition from Slavery to Freedom in South Carolina* (Urbana: University of Illinois Press, 1997).

198   "*she gave him to understand*" "From Savannah," Louisa Jacobs in *The Freedmen's Record*, (March 1866):55–56.

199   *Life in the city was in transition* E. A. Cooley to Samuel Hunt, January 2, 1866, AMA #19546; E. A. Cooley to Hunt, February 3, 1866, AMA #19632–3; E. A. Cooley to Reverend Samuel Hunt, March 20 [1866] AMA #19737; for a letter of application, see Louis B. Toomer to Samuel Hunt, March 20, 1866, AMA #19736; E. A.

Cooley to Samuel Hunt, April 9, 1866, AMA #19785–86. By autumn, Superintendent Eberhart would write, "Although there is much to commend in the negroes, under the difficulties which they labor, I am becoming daily more impressed with their total unfitness to assist in the moral and mental elevation of their own race." G. L. Eberhart to I. Pettibone, October 19, 1866, AMA #20118. For the American Missionary Association's African American teachers, see Linda M. Perkins, "The Black Female AMA Teacher in the South, 1861–1970," in *Black Americans in North Carolina and the South*, ed. Jeffrey J. Crow and Flora J. Hatley (Chapel Hill: University of North Carolina Press, 1984).

199   "*hundreds of children*" "From Harriet Jacobs," December 9, 1865, (New York) *The Freedman*, (February 1866):49. "From Savannah," Louisa Jacobs in *The Freedmen's Record*, (March 1866):55–56.

199   *moved into Dr. Augusta's home* Louisa Jacobs to [Ednah Dow] Cheney, May 26, 1866, *The Freedmen's Record* (July 1866):133–134.

199   "*much to encourage me*" Louisa M. Jacobs to [Ednah Dow] Cheney, May 26, 1866, *The Freedmen's Record* (July 1866):133–34.

199   "*the Southerners take no interest*" Louisa M. Jacobs to [Ednah Dow] Cheney, May 26, 1866 *The Freedmen's Record* (July 1866):133–34. "Correspondence," *Pennsylvania Freedmen's Bulletin* (June 1866):1–2. In this piece, the Jacobs women are clearly identified but strangely misnamed "Phillips." For the spring examinations in the seven "colored schools of Savannah," see *Savannah Daily Herald*, March 28, 1866. The examination at Louisa Jacobs's school, "the Hospital school at the Hospital east of the park," was scheduled for Wednesday at 3 p.m.

200   "*I hastened to do up*" Lydia Maria Child to Lucy Osgood, April 1, 1866, Cornell University Library; "Correspondence," Joseph Parrish, M.D. to the Editor, *Pennsylvania Freedmen's Bulletin* (June 1866):1–2.

200   "*five white men*" "Horrible Outrage," *The Loyal Georgian*, January 27, 1866, in *The Trouble They Seen: Black People Tell the Story of Reconstruction,* ed. Dorothy Sterling (Garden City, New York: Doubleday, 1976), pp. 48–49; Foner, *Reconstruction*, pp. 261–62. For the sexual terrorism of race politics during Reconstruction, see Catherine Clinton, "Freedwomen, Sexuality, and Violence," *Georgia Historical Quarterly* 76 (summer 1992): 313–32.

200   "*in many counties*" Georgia Educational Association, *A New Plan for Educating the Freedmen of the South* (circular, n. p., [1867]), p. 1, in Ronald E. Butchart, *Northern Schools, Southern Blacks, and Reconstruction*, p. 190.

200 "*a rebel son of a b—*" "Shooting Case," *Savannah Daily News and Herald*, July 13, 1866.

200 "*and some other Colored Persons*" James M. Simms to Miss H. E. Stevenson, August 2, 1866, in *The Freedmen's Record* (September 1866):167–68, see also "Coroner's Inquest," *Savannah Daily News and Herald*, July 20, 1866.

201 "*were both put off the boat*" *The Freedmen's Record*(September 1866):161.

201 "*The women, we understand*" *Savannah Daily News and Herald*, July 20, 1866.

201 *Nathaniel Parker Willis was dying* Beers, *Nathaniel Parker Willis*, pp. 348–50.

202 *Equal Rights Association* For the Georgia Equal Rights Association, see (Augusta) *The Loyal Georgian*, January 27 and February 17, 1866.

202 *Women's National Loyal League National Anti-Slavery Standard*, November 3, 1866. At the Eleventh National Woman's Rights Convention, held at the Church of the Puritans in New York City, May 10, 1866, the group reconstituted itself the American Equal Rights Association. At this meeting, a resolution was passed that, in light of the upcoming Constitutional Convention in the State of New York, the Equal Rights Association should demand an amendment to the New York Constitution to secure equal rights to all citizens "without distinctions of color, sex, or race." Stanton, *History of Woman Suffrage*, 2:171, 175.

202 *Harper's presentation* For the full text of Harper's speech, see "Speech of Mrs. F. E. Watkins Harper," Stanton-Anthony Papers, Series I, 11:497–99; an abbreviated version appears in *A Brighter Coming Day: A Frances Ellen Watkins Harper Reader*, ed. Frances Smith Foster (New York: The Feminist Press, 1990), pp. 217–19; see also Rosalyn Terborg-Penn, *African American Women in the Struggle for the Vote, 1850–1920* (Bloomington: Indiana University Press, 1998), p. 33; and Nell Irvin Painter, *Sojourner Truth: A Life, a Symbol* (New York: W. W. Norton, 1996), pp. 224–25.

202 *Charles Lenox Remond National Anti-Slavery Standard*, February 2, 1867. A staunch feminist, at the London World Anti-Slavery Convention in 1840 Remond had refused his seat on the floor and took his place instead in the rear gallery with the women delegates who were excluded because of their sex. During the Civil War, he worked to recruit men for the Massachusetts 54th, the first black regiment from the North to see action. For Remond, see DANB and Dorothy Porter, "The Remonds of Salem, Massachusetts: A Nineteenth-Century Family Revisited," American Antiquarian Society, *Proceedings*

95 (October 1985): 259–95. The quotation is from pp. 274–75. For the Fifteenth Annual Meeting of the American Anti-Slavery Society and the "100 Conventions," see *National Anti-Slavery Standard,* May 17 and June 7, 1849.

203   *"Both Miss Jacobs and myself"* Charles Lenox Remond from Johnstown, New York, February 3, 1867 in *National Anti-Slavery Standard,* February 9, 1867.

203   *"harsh and malignant"* [Charles Lenox Remond] to [Editor], [Brockett's Bridge, Herkimer County, February 10, 1867], *National Anti-Slavery Standard,* February 16, 1867.

203   *Lulu would be touring upstate New York* Harriet Jacobs to Amy Post, February 14 [1853]. IAPFP. For Maria Stewart, see *Maria W. Stewart: America's First Black Woman Political Writer: Essays and Speeches,* ed. Marilyn Richardson (Bloomington: Indiana University Press, 1987). In Washington, D.C., in February 1864, Stewart became principal of the Third Free School, opened by the National Freedmen's Relief Association; see *Annual Report of The National Freedmen's Relief Association of The District of Columbia,* (1863/1864):4.

203   *her uncle John's footsteps* John S. Jacobs had spoken with Jonathan Walker in Rome March 3, in Palmyra March 25, and in Syracuse March 29, 1848, and in Albion March 24, 1849; see *The Liberator,* February 11, 1848 and *The North Star,* April 20, 1849. Louisa spoke in Rome February 11 and 12, in Palmyra April 5 and 6, in Syracuse March 29, and in Albion April 8 and 9, 1867. For Louisa M. Jacobs's lecturing, see the *National Anti-Slavery Standard,* February 9, 16, and March 23, 1867; and *Little Falls Journal and Courier,* January 17, 1867.

203   *Kellogg's Domestic Seminary* For Kellogg's Domestic Seminary, see Helen Neilson Rudd, *A Century of Schools in Clinton* (Clinton, New York: Clinton Historical Society, 1964), pp. 19–21.

204   *like Nell before her* William C. Nell to Amy Post, July 21, 1853. IAPFP. "Receipts from June 1, 1866 to May 1, 1867," American Equal Rights Association, *Proceedings of the First Anniversary of the American Equal Rights Association. May 9 and 10, 1867* (New York, 1867), p. 79; Stanton-Anthony Papers 12:156.

204   *At Cohoes* For Parker Pillsbury, antislavery leader, minister, editor and author of *Acts of the Anti-Slavery Apostles,* see Merrill, ed., *The Letters of William Lloyd Garrison IV,* p. 28. For Reverend Olympia Brown, the first American woman ordained by a full denominational authority, see *Notable American Women,* ed. Edward T. James et al. (Cambridge, Massachusetts: Belknap Press of Harvard University Press, 1971), 1:256–58. For Bessie Bishee, a

Boston working woman, see *New York Tribune,* November 22, 1866, Stanton-Anthony Papers 11:649.

204   *"to say nothing of the 8"* Susan B. Anthony to Anna Elizabeth Dickinson, Albany, February 18, 1867, Stanton-Anthony Papers ll:1056; Susan B. Anthony to Amy Post, Albany, New York, February 17, 1867, Stanton-Anthony Papers 11:1050.

204   *"a fair speaker"* "Impartial Suffrage," *Troy Daily Times,* February 20, 1867.

204   *its own Equal Rights Association* "Equal Rights Meeting—Formation of a Society," *Syracuse Journal,* March 30, 1867. Thanks to Patricia Finley, Onondaga County Public Library.

204   *wore them down* For the speakers' health problems, see Susan B. Anthony to Benjamin Anthony April 4; Susan B. Anthony to Mary H. Post Hallowell April 11, Stanton-Anthony Papers; *Orleans Republican,* April 11, 1867. Thanks to Charles V. Cowling at the State University of New York at Brockport.

204   *"does not officially plead"* Susan B. Anthony to Anna Elizabeth Dickinson, Palantine Bridge, New York, March 24, 1867, Stanton-Anthony Papers 12:99–:105; also see Susan B. Anthony to Gerrit Smith, Albany, March 6, 1867, Smith Papers, Syracuse University.

205   *"If there be any person"* "Equal Rights Convention," *New York Daily News,* December 8, 1866, Stanton-Anthony Papers 11:690#2.

205   *"Remember that in slavery"* "Remarks of Miss Anthony," [Pennsylvania Anti-Slavery Society, Annual Meeting], *National Anti-Slavery Standard,* December 1, 1866. Stanton-Anthony Papers 11:665.

205   *"In view of the fact"* Elizabeth Cady Stanton, "Reconstruction," Lecture for Tour of New York State, Stanton-Anthony Papers 11:769#1,2.

205   *"whites have so diluted color"* "The Equal Rights Convention," *Utica Morning Herald and Daily Gazette,* December 11, 1866, Stanton-Anthony Papers 11: 739.

206   *She said that the black women* "Equal Rights Meeting," *Rochester Union and Advertiser,* December 12, 1866. Stanton-Anthony Papers 11:789#2.

206   *"She has not the master"* "Impartial Suffrage," *Troy Daily Times,* February 19, 1867. Stanton-Anthony Papers 11:1059.

206   *have a tendency to melt* "Impartial Suffrage," *Troy Daily Times,* February 20, 1867.

206   *she knew the freedwomen's condition* For Jacobs and Louisa on freedwomen's marriages, see Harriet Jacobs to [L. Maria Child], March 18, [1863] in *National Anti-Slavery Standard,* April 10, 1863; and Harriet Jacobs to J. Sella Martin, April 13 [1863], *Freed-Man's Aid Society,* p. 7. Rhodes House; BAPM 14:0799: "I have had

a long battle about the marriage rites for the poor people, at length I carried my point. The first wedding took place in the school house."

207   *Anthony announced hopeful signs* Anthony reported in addition that the legislatures of Maine, Massachusetts, New York, Ohio, and Missouri had discussed equal suffrage; and that the Judiciary Committees of the state legislatures of New York and New Jersey had been addressed by Lucy Stone and by Stanton. "American Equal Rights Association, Proceedings of the First Anniversary. . . . May 9 and 10, 1867," pp. 5–6, Stanton-Anthony Papers, 12:156.

207   *the presence of black leaders* See Stanton, *History of Woman Suffrage,* 2:214. For Stanton's statement, see 2:214. Among the officers of American Equal Rights Association elected at the 1867 meeting to serve the following year were Frederick Douglass, Remond, Robert and Harriet Purvis and George T. Downing. Stanton, *History of Woman Suffrage,* 2:221–22.

207   *Frances D. Gage* Stanton, *History of Woman Suffrage,* 2:197.

207   *Sojourner Truth* Stanton, *History of Woman Suffrage,* 2:193.

207   *Abby Kelley Foster* Stanton, *History of Woman Suffrage,* 2:216, 225.

208   *proposed Fourteenth Amendment* Fourteenth Amendment, Section 2: "But when the right to vote at any election for the choice of electors for President and Vice-President of the United States, Representatives in Congress, the Executive and Judicial officers of a State, or members of the Legislature thereof, is denied to any of the male inhabitants of such State"; see Stanton, *History of Woman Suffrage,* 2:323.

208   *proposed Fifteenth Amendment* Fifteenth Amendment, Section 1. "The right of citizens of the United States to vote shall not be denied or abridged by the United States, or by any State, on account of race, color, or previous condition of servitude." For the proposed Sixteenth Amendment, see Stanton, *History of Woman Suffrage* 2:333.

208   *Stanton famously opposed* Stanton, *History of Woman Suffrage,* 2:347, 353, 382–83, 391–92; queried whether this terror was not also visited upon black women, Douglass replied, "Yes, yes, yes; it is true of the black woman, but not because she is a woman, but because she is black." Stanton, *History of Woman Suffrage,* 2:382.

208   *Frances Harper* For Harper, see Stanton, *History of Woman Suffrage,* 2:391–92. At the closing session, Ernestine Rose proposed that they reconstitute themselves a women's rights organization, and by the end of the anniversary week, they had organized themselves into the National Woman's Suffrage Association. According to the newspapers, Harper addressed this reconstituted group eloquently "on matters concerning her own race"—but there is no record of her speech. Stanton, *History of Woman Suffrage,* 2:397–99; *New York World* May 14, 1869, Stanton-Anthony Papers, 13:533.

Chapter 13. No Cloudless Happiness

210   *"I am sitting, Jacobs began"* Harriet Jacobs to [Ednah Dow] Cheney, Edenton, North Carolina, April 25 [1867] Smith College, Sophia Smith Collection; the bulk of this text was published as "A Word from Harriet Jacobs" in *The Freedmen's Record* 3 (August 1867):115 under a headnote explaining that Jacobs "is no longer a teacher in our employ."

211   *"distributing seed"* Harriet Jacobs to [Ednah Dow] Cheney, Edenton, North Carolina, April 25 [1867]. Smith College, Sophia Smith Collection.

211   *"This evening Mrs. Jacobs"* JWD, October 12, 1867. For Jacobs's sale of Molly Horniblow's property, see Chapter 15, below.

211   *"to be useful"* Harriet Jacobs to Amy Post, February 14 [1853]. IAPFP. Frederick W. Chesson Diary, December 1867. Raymond English Deposit.

212   *to reconnect with her brother* Harriet Jacobs to Amy Post, December 8 [1862]. IAPFP; for more on John S.'s maritime experience, see Frederick W. Chesson Diary, August 15, 1862. Raymond English Deposit.

212   *He had married an Englishwoman* John S. Jacobs's and Elleanor Ashlands's marriage certificate has not been found, nor have the birth certificates of their son William R. Jacobs, born at London c. 1859 or 1860, or of their daughter Elleanor A. Jacobs, born at London c. 1861. The birth certificate of Joseph Ramsey Jacobs lists his date of birth as May 27, 1866, the family home as 4 St. George's Place, S. George in the East [London], names the mother as Elleanor Ashland Jacobs and the father as John S. Jacobs, a ship steward. The birth was registered July 7, 1866.

212   *"her brother is in India"* Frederick W. Chesson Diary, December 23, 1867. Raymond English Deposit.

212   *"making great progress"* Frederick W. Chesson Diary, December 28, 1867. Raymond English Deposit.

213   *"the old slave-planting interest"* Frederick W. Chesson, "Jamaica and the Freed-Men's Aid Society," (London) *The Freed-Man* 7 (February 1, 1866):153. For the Morant Bay affair, see Temperley, *British Anti-Slavery*, pp. 257–58.

213   *British public opinion* For public responses to Morant Bay, see BAP, 1:570.

214   *"Southern Confederates"* Sarah Parker Remond quoted in Bolt, *The Anti-Slavery Movement*, p. 35, cited in Blackett, *Beating Against the Barriers*, p. 232. For Sarah Parker Remond, see Ruth Bogin, "Sarah Parker Remond: Black Abolitionist from Salem," *Essex Institute Historical Collections* 110, no. 2 (April 1974); and Dorothy Burnett

Porter, "The Remonds of Salem, Massachusetts: A Nineteenth-Century Family Revisited."

214   *"that the name of England"* Blackett, *Beating Against the Barriers*, p. 251.

214   *William and Ellen Craft* In December 1868, after Jacobs returned to America, William Craft began a speaking tour of England and Scotland to raise money to buy a plantation in Georgia, where the Crafts planned to establish a freedmen's cooperative. In August 1869 the family sailed for Boston, leaving their two younger sons Brougham and William Jr. behind to finish their schooling. Blackett, *Beating Against the Barriers*, pp. 119–23; Dorothy Sterling, *Black Foremothers: Three Lives* (Old Westbury: The Feminist Press, 1979), pp. 1–59.

214   *organizations she had come to enlist* Howard Temperley, *British Antislavery, 1833–1870*, pp. 260–61.

215   *"a generous response"* "Savannah Freedmen's Orphan Asylum," *Anti-Slavery Reporter* (London) March 2, 1868.

215   *Stafford Allen* For Stafford Allen (1806–89), see *The Annual Monitor for 1890, or Obituary of the Members of the Society of Friends in Great Britain and Ireland for the Year 1889*, new series no. 48 (London: Samuel Harris & Co., 1889), pp. 3–12; for Allen and the British and Foreign Anti-Slavery Society, see Howard R. Temperley, "The British and Foreign Anti-Slavery Society, 1839–1868" (Ph.D. diss., Yale University, 1960), Appendix I.

215   *Robert Alsop* For Robert Alsop (1803–76), see *The Annual Monitor for 1877, or Obituary of the Members of the Society of Friends in Great Britain and Ireland for the Year 1876* (London: Samuel Harris & Co., 1876), pp. 155–58.

215   *Peter Taylor* For Peter Taylor (1819–91), see DNB, 19:455–56; and Frederick Bease, *Modern English Biography . . . 1851–1900 . . .* (London: Frank Cass & Co., 1965), 3:898–99. Clementina Taylor (?—April 11, 1908) is mentioned in the biographies of her husband.

215   *"I know of the degradation"* "Savannah Freedmen's Orphan Asylum," *Anti-Slavery Reporter* (London), March 2, 1868. In Savannah, no record has been found of the Society for the Relief of Freed Orphans and Aged Freedmen.

216   *Kate Amberley* For Kate Stanley Russell Amberley, wife of Lord Russell and mother of Bertrand Russell, see *The Amberley Papers: Bertrand Russell's Family Background*, ed. Bertrand Russell and Patricia Russell, 2 vols. (New York: Simon and Schuster, 1937); the quoted passage is from 2:87.

216   *"a fine fish" Diary of Lady Frederick Cavendish*, ed. John Bailey (London, 1927), 2:48. For Lady Cavendish, daughter of Lord Lyt-

tleton, niece of Gladstone, and sister and sister-in-law of bishops, see *Diary*, 1:v–vii. Thanks to Mr. and Mrs. William S. McFeeley and Henry Louis Gates Jr.

217   *"Mrs. Jacobs being present"* "Meeting of the General Committee. Friends' Institute. Friday, Aug. 7, 1868"; the final meeting of the organization was held December 4, 1868; see Papers at Rhodes House, Oxford.

217   *"for use in the benevolent objects" Eighth Report of the Committee of the Representatives of New York Yearly Meeting of Friends upon the Condition and Wants of the Freedmen.* (1869), p. 4.

217   *"On account of the unsettled state"* The committee charged the treasurer to invest the money "for the benefit of the Asylum Fund." *Eighth Report of The Committee of the Representatives of New York Yearly Meeting of Friends* (1869), p. 4.

217   *"incited the activity of women"* Julia A. Sprague, *History of the New England Women's Club* (Boston: Lee and Shepard, 1894), pp. 1–2.

217   *New England Women's Club Annual Meeting of the New England Women's Club, at Chickering's Hall, May 29, 1869* (n.p., n.d.), pp. 21–22, in the collection of the Library Company of Philadelphia; Ednah Dow Cheney, *Reminiscences* (Boston: Lee & Shepard, 1902), pp. 80–81; New England Women's Club. Arch #178. Box 1: 1v-4v 2/68–5/3/73, Schlesinger Library, Radcliffe College. See minutes of June 20, June 25, and of special meeting November 2, 1868: "Voted that the wages of our Clerk, Mrs. Jacobs, be raised to seven dollars a week, exclusive of her room." pp. 27–28.

218   *"without aiming at the impossible" Annual Meeting of the New England Women's Club . . . 1869*, pp. 17–18, 8–13, 15–16.

218   *Jacobs left her job* "The resignation of Miss Jacobs as Clerk, was accepted & Miss M. A. Whittlesey[?] Was introduced by Mrs. Severance as a lady well fitted to perform the duties of clerk and take charge of our rooms. . . ." October 2, 1869, New England Women's Club Arch # 178, Box 1: 1v-4v 2/68-5/373; for William Craft's lecture on November 8, 1869, see New England Women's Club. Arch #178. Box 4 folder 5: Meeting Notebooks, May 30, 1868—June 3, 1882; minutes of December 4, 1869, Box 1: 1v-4v 2/68-5/3/73. Schlesinger Library, Radcliffe College. For the Crafts' stay with the Haydens in Boston, see Sterling, *Black Foremothers*, pp. 49–50.

218   *Some Club members* Annie Haggerty of New York had married Robert Gould Shaw shortly before the Massachusetts 54th sailed south. For Louisa Gilman Loring, wife of Ellis Gray Loring, see *Lydia Maria Child, Selected Letters 1817–1880*, p. 30. For Abby May, see Ednah Dow Cheney, *Memoirs of Lucretia Crocker and Abby W. May* (Boston: 1893). *Second Annual Report of the Howard Industrial School Association, 1868* (Cambridge, Massachusetts:

Riverside, 1868), p. [3]; *First Annual Report of the Howard Industrial School Association*, (Cambridge, Massachusetts: Riverside, 1869), [5].

219   *when Boston's militant blacks* For the struggle against segregated schooling in Boston, see Horton and Horton, *Black Bostonians*, p. 70ff.

219   *Virginia Lawton* For Edward B. Lawton, his wife Eliza A. Lawton, and their daughters S. Virginia and E. Mariana Lawton who went south to teach, see *Cambridge City Directory for 1869* (Boston: Dudley & Greenough, 1869), p. 187; *Cambridge City Directory for 1870* (Boston : Dean Dudley & Company, 1870), p. 197; "46 Market," Architectural Inventory: Cambridge, Massachusetts, and "1880 Cambridge Census," both in the Cambridge Historical Society. For E. Mariana Lawton, and S. Virginia Lawton, see *Freedmen's Record,* 1:19, 1:48, 1:149, 1:202, 1:203; 2:88; 4:11; and *Freedmen's Journal,* 1:7, 8. Also see Horton and Horton, *Black Bostonians*, p. 101.

For John J. Fatal (1816–1904), John T. and Patrick H. Raymond (1831–92), Joshua Bowen Smith (1813–79); Lunsford Lane (c 1810—?), author of *The Narrative of Lunsford Lane* (1842), J. Milton Clarke (1820–1902) and his brother Lewis Clarke (1818–97), authors of *Narrative of the Sufferings of Lewis and Milton Clarke* (1846); and William Wells Brown (c. 1814–84), author of numerous pamphlets, plays, and books, including the landmark novel *Clotel* (1853), see Cambridge Historical Commission, "Cambridge African American History Trail" (1993); for the Clarkes and Brown, also see DANB.

219   *The war had changed the town* Varieties of Black Experience at Harvard, ed. Werner Sollors, Thomas A. Underwood, and Caldwell Titcomb (Cambridge, Massachusetts: Harvard University Department of Afro-American Studies, 1986), p 7. For Greener's award, see *Cambridge Press,* June 18, 1870; for the "collation furnished by the city" see the issue of July 2, 1870.

219   *Cambridge alive* For Cambridge in 1870, see Lois Lilley Howe, "Harvard Square in the 'Seventies and 'Eighties," *Cambridge Historical Society Publications* 29 (1943): 11–27; thanks to Charles M. Sullivan. For the evening benefit for Freedmen's Aid, see *Cambridge Press*, March 26 and April 9, 1870.

219   *the huge celebration* "The Fifteenth Amendment and the Celebration of its Passage," *Cambridge Press,* April 16, 1872. For the Fisk Jubilee Singers, see W. E. B. DuBois, *The Gift of Black Folk*, ed. Truman Nelson (New York: Washington Square, 1970), pp. 150–57; *Cambridge Press,* April 13, 1872, and March 8, 1873.

220   *Harriet Beecher Stowe* "Harriet Beecher Stowe—Chronology," (typescript), Harriet Beecher Stowe House and Library, Hartford; for Safford and Clarke, see "J. Milton Clarke and Lewis Clarke," *Cambridge African-American History Project* (Cambridge, Massachusetts: Cambridge Historical Commission, 1993). The inscribed edition of *Uncle Tom's Cabin* is in a private collection.

220   *paramilitary Shaw Guards Cambridge Press*, June 3, 1871.

220   *several of the city's churches* For the murder of Elijah Lovejoy at Alton, Illinois, see Joseph and Owen Lovejoy, *Memoir of the Rev. Elijah P. Lovejoy* (New York: J.S. Taylor, 1838), and Edward Beecher, *Narrative of the Riots at Alton* (Alton, 1838; New York: Dutton, 1965). Lewis Garrard and Milton Clarke, *Narrative of the Sufferings of Lewis Clarke, during a captivity of more than twenty-five years, among the Algerines of Kentucky; one of the so called Christian states of North America. Dictated by himself,* ed. Joseph C. Lovejoy (Boston: B. Marsh, 1846). For church history, see Lucius R. Paige, *History of Cambridge, Massachusetts, 1630–1877, with a Genealogical Register* (Boston: H. O. Houghton, 1877), pp. 326–27, 336–37; MacNair, "A Hundred Years of Church Life," Cambridge Historical Society, *Proceedings* 20 (1927–29, Published by the Society, 1934), pp. 68–70. For the Bethel African Methodist Episcopal Church of Cambridge, which closed in 1878 as its membership formed St. Paul AME, Rush AME Zion, and the First Union Baptist Church, see Cambridge, Massachusetts African-American History Project, "Timeline," June 26, 1993, pp. 46–47.

220   *history of feminist activism* "Middlesex County Woman Suffrage Convention," *Cambridge Press,* April 9, 1870; "The Woman Suffrage Movement in Cambridge," *Cambridge Press,* March 4, 1871; for East Cambridge Women's Suffrage Association, see *Cambridge Press,* April 1, 1871; announcement of Framingham July 4 meeting, see *Cambridge Press,* June 24, 1871.

221   *black Cambridge organized* Organization of "Grant Club": *Cambridge Press,* June 15, 1872; for the meeting at the corner of Norfolk and Hampshire, see *Press,* August 10, 1872; for "colored convention" see *Press,* September 7, 1872; the stoning is reported in the *Press,* September 7, 1872; Raymond's display is reported September 14, 1872, and the "Grand Torchlight Procession," on October 26, 1872. J. Milton Clarke's win is reported December 7. (In March, Clarke resigned to accept the position of messenger at the U.S. Subtreasury in Boston, where he worked with John J. Fatal; James C. Davis was elected to take his place.) See *Press,* January 25 and March 29, 1873; and "J. Milton Clarke and Lewis Clarke," Cambridge-AfricanAmerican History Project "Timeline," June 26 1993.

221   *"To let"* "Chat with Our Readers," January 8, 1870; *Cambridge Press.*

222   *In the city directory* See *Cambridge Directory for 1870*, p. 182; *Cambridge Directory for 1871*, pp. 204, 398; *Cambridge Directory for 1872*, p. 181; see *Catalogue of the Officers and Students of Harvard University, 1869–70* (Cambridge, Massachusetts, 1869).

222   *the census taker* See 1870 census, Ward 1, Cambridge, Massachusetts, taken June 18, 1870, item 34, pp. 6–7. Reading this ambiguous entry, my assumption is that the census taker listed Grinnell Willis as head of household because he was a white male over twenty-one years of age; Grinnell is not listed in the City Directory. In addition to Cornelia (who is in the 1870 City Directory), the census listing includes Lilian, Edith and Bailey Willis, and three college students (George Gould, Thomas Perry, and William Appleton), whose occupations (although not their names) are struck out. Following these are Langdell and Pumpelly and his wife Eliza. Only after listing these white people did the census taker name Jacobs and Louisa, then the servants, and finally the "mulatto" eight-year-old Joseph Pierce. For the building, see "Cambridge, Massachusetts Architectural Inventory," 10 Trowbridge; for Pumpelly at Jacobs's boarding house see 1869 Harvard University *Catalogue . . .* , p. 7; Pumpelly is listed with wife Eliza at Trowbridge near Main in the 1870 census; for Langdell at Jacobs's boardinghouse at Trowbridge near Main, see the 1870 Census.

222   *Prominent members of the faculty* For Raphael Pumpelly (1837–1923), see *Dictionary of American Biography,* 20 vols. (New York: C. Scribner's Sons, 1928–58), 8:264–66 (hereafter DAB). For Christopher Langdell (1826–1906), see DAB, 5:585–86, for Langdell at 127 Mount Auburn, see *Harvard University Catalogue . . . 1872*, p. 27; and *1873–74* p. 26. For Adams Sherman Hill, (1833–1910) at 127 Mount Auburn, see *Harvard University Catalogue . . . 1874–75*, p. 14. For Chauncy Wright (1830–75), see DAB, 10:547–48, and *Letters of Chauncy Wright*, ed. James B. Thayer (1878; rpt. New York: Burt Franklin, 1971). For Wright at Mrs. Jacobs's boardinghouse, Trowbridge near Main, see *Cambridge Directory for 1871*, p. 372. Also at Jacobs's Trowbridge boardinghouse was Frederick Pierre Dimpfel, listed as Llb, Philadelphia; see Harvard *Catalogue . . . 1871*, p. 68. For Jacobs's boardinghouse at 127 Mount Auburn, see "Cambridge Architectural Inventory," 127 Mount Auburn; and see *Cambridge Directory for 1873*, p. 407.

222   *Mary Walker* Jacobs and Walker occupied opposite ends of the block at Story and Hilliard. For Mary Walker, see Susan I. Lesley, *Recollections of my Mother* (Boston: George H. Ellis, 1889), pp. 470, 476; and *Life and Letters of Peter and Susan Lesley*, ed. Mary Lesley Ames (New York: Putnam's 1909), 1:252–53, 264, 283, 291, 294, 317, 377, and 478. Thanks to Sid Nathan. For Lesley's letter, see

Herbert G. Gutman, *The Black Family in Slavery and Freedom, 1750–1925* (New York: Pantheon, 1976), p. 183. In 1875, Walker's son Briant was listed in the Cambridge *Directory* as a gardener living at 54 Brattle, p. 419.

223 *Jacobs was known* See Cheney's remembrance of Jacobs as "a woman of great refinement and sweetness of character," whose "book should be preserved as a faithful picture of what slavery was to woman," in *Reminiscences of Ednah Dow Cheney*, pp. 80–81.

223 *"on the night before he died"* For the death of Chauncey Wright and the reference to Henry James, see *Letters of Chauncey Wright*, ed., James B. Thayer, pp. 358–59; also see Susan I. Lesley, *Recollections of my Mother*, pp. 373–74.

223 *James to ignore women* "Watch and Ward" initially appeared in *Atlantic Monthly* in 1871. James's *A Passionate Pilgrim and Other Tales* and *Transatlantic Sketches* were published in 1875. For Child's comment, see L. Maria Child to Sarah Shaw, March 20, 1879, in *Lydia Maria Child: Selected Letters*, p. 557.

223 *Her half-brother Elijah* For records naming Jacobs's father Elijah, see Chowan County Criminal Records Concerning Slaves, 1820. NCSA. Apparently Elijah witnessed an alleged attack by Dick, and when Gatlin—Dick's owner—appealed, a summons was issued to Mrs. Knox for the appearance of "her man LYDE." (Ultimately, Dick was found guilty and sentenced to twenty lashes.) The record of another appeal refers to "LYGE belonging to Mrs. Knox." Also see the July 16, 1821 issue of the *Edenton Gazette*, which lists an unclaimed letter for "Elijah Nox." For Jacobs on her father, see ILSG pp. 5, 9–10; for John S. on his father, see TT in ILSG pp. 207–8. For Jacobs's father Elijah, see Will of Dr. Andrew Knox, 1816, where he appears under the name of "Lyde," a carpenter. Pasquotank County Willis, 1709–1917. NCSA; inventory of the personal estate of Dr. Andrew Knox, 1816, Pasquotank County Estates Records, 1712–1931. NCSA; *Edenton Gazette* March 23, 1808; *Raleigh Register and North Carolina Gazette*, July 9, 1824; Estate of Sarah P. Knox, 1813, Chowan County Estates Records, 1728–1951. NCSA; death certificate of John S. Jacobs, December 19, 1871, Cambridge, Massachusetts.

For young Elijah Knox's mother Theresa, see New Bedford, Massachusetts Death Record of Elijah Knox, January 12, 1907. Also see February 1833 term: apprenticing of children Elijah Artis and Mary Artis to Robert Warren of Hertford County, minutes of the Court of Pleas and Quarter Sessions, 1830–44; freedom certificate of [Theresa's son] Elijah Knox, Hertford County 1846. NCSA.

223 *a child who was not a slave* For Elijah Knox's birth and parentage, see his Death Record. For apprenticeships, see Frederick Nash et al., eds., *Revised Statutes of the State of North Carolina*, 2 vols. (1837),

Raleigh, Chapter 5, sections 5–8. For the 1833 apprenticeship to Robert Warren of Elijah Artis and the concurrent apprenticeship of a child named Mary Artis—perhaps a sister who did not survive?—see Hertford County, Minutes of the Court of Pleas and Quarter Sessions. This early document perhaps put the children into the custody of Robert Warren by the Wardens of the Poor near the end of 1832, with their apprenticeship formalized at the next court, in February, 1833. If this Elijah is Jacobs's half brother, his mother was known as both Artis and Knox. For the completion of his apprenticeship, see "Freedman's Certificate issued to Elijah Knox, June 5, 1846, by Hertford County, North Carolina." Original document in the Old Dartmouth Historical Society-New Bedford Whaling Museum Library, New Bedford, Massachusetts.

224   *Isaac Douglas* By 1850, the hard-working Isaac Douglas owned 42 acres (16 improved), as well as a horse, 2 oxen, 13 head of cattle, and 12 swine. In his home, along with Douglas, lived his wife Martha, their 15-year-old son Harrison Sheppard, and their 17-year-old daughter, Emily Elizabeth. For the Isaac Douglas family in North Carolina, see: Perquimons County *Deed Books*, Book V, deed 94, 1824; Book BB, deed 131, 1845; Book BB, deed 141, 1844; Perquimons County Court Minutes November 1847—August 1858, 1858 February term, p. 598; Perquimons County (Original) Wills, 1711–1909, Isaac Douglas. NCSA. For Elijah Knox and the Isaac Douglas family in North Carolina, see 1850 U. S. Census, Sutton's Creek District, Perquimons County, North Carolina, pp. 35–205-06; Perquimons County Tax Lists, 1847–54; Perquimons County, *Minutes, Wardens of the Poor, 1818–1874*, pp. 232, 233, 249, 252, 286. These items represent amounts paid to Isaac Douglas (in one instance, for "services to . . . a pauper"), and to Elijah Knox, apparently for carpentry, including building a coffin for a child. NCSA.

224   *Then in 1850* For Harrison Douglas in North Carolina, see Perquimons County Marriage Bonds: Harrison Douglas and Harriet Brinkly March, 1837; Perquimons County, *Minutes, Wardens of the Poor, 1818–1874*, pp. 221, 230; Perquimons County Tax Lists, 1845–49. NCSA; for Harrison Douglas, his wife Harriet, and their children Henrietta, Edward Harrison, Evangella Harrison, William, and George in New Bedford, see 1850 U.S. Census, New Bedford, Bristol County, Massachusetts, p. 234.

224   *In New Bedford* For Elijah Knox in New Bedford, see New Bedford *Directory* for 1867: Elijah married Julia Ann Seals December 29, 1868, according to family Bible records; by 1879, the family was living in the home he had built at 183 Campbell; see Knox Papers at Old Dartmouth Historical Society-New Bedford Whaling Museum, and 1879 City Directory; according to Dr. William J. Knox Jr., John

F. moved to New York; Martha Jane Knox Morgan died in New Bedford on March 18, 1921, according to the Certificate of Death issued by the City of New Bedford.

224   *the names her half-brother and his new wife chose* According to the family Bible, William Jacob Knox was born July 30, 1875; Elijah Howland Knox had been born June 28, 1871. George Howland Jr., member of a prominent New Bedford family, "may have employed more men of color than any other white merchant in the city." He was elected mayor in 1839. Kathryn Grover, *The Fugitive's Gibraltar: Escaping Slaves and Abolitionists in New Bedford, Massachusetts* (Amherst: University of Massachusetts Press, 2001), p. 284.

224   *young Joseph had failed to appear* For the disappearance of Joseph Jacobs, see L. Maria Child to [John Fraser], Wayland [Massachusetts], November 20, 1866. *The Collected Correspondence of Lydia Maria Child, 1817–1880,* ed. Patricia G. Holland, Milton Meltzer, and Francine Krasno (Millwood, New York: Kraus Microform, 1980), 66/1746. For what may—or may not—be Joseph's death record in Australia, see "Deaths Registered in New South Wales, Australia," February 10, 1860, at West Maitland, Joseph Jacob, Sailor. This reads, "Died from wounds inflicted by himself whilst laboring under under [sic] insanity." This is the only instance in this page in which the names of the parents of a man are left blank. He was buried in Church of England Burial Ground, West Maitland. He is registered as twenty-four years old, born at Hessln Cassell, Germany, and as living for three years in New South Wales. (Jacobs's son Joseph, born in North Carolina in 1829, would have been thirty-one years old in 1860.) The name of the informant is listed as Jacob John Jacob, Collector, West Maitland. (It seems inconceivable that his uncle John S. could have been the informant and kept Jacobs ignorant of her son's fate; and the diary of Frederick Chesson testifies that by April 6, 1858, John S. had left Australia and was in London. It appears that the informant may have falsely given John S.'s name.) For Joseph Pierce, see 1870 Census, item 34, pp. 6–7, Ward 1, Cambridge, Massachusetts.

225   *he returned to America to live* For the names and ages of Elleanor's children, see census of 1880, collected July 4, 1880. For John S. at the Lawton home, see Cambridge *Directory* for 1874, p. 215. (The information for the *Directory* was, as usual, gathered in the last months of 1873.) For John S. at 11 Brewer, see his death certificate dated December 19, 1873. For his family at 11 Brewer after his death, see Cambridge City *Directory* for 1875, p. 229.

225   *she worked to knit her rainbow family together* Harriet Jacobs to Amy Post, December 8 [1862]. IAPFP.

226   *"a grateful memory"* Louisa Matilda Jacobs to William Lloyd Garrison, December 20, 1873. Boston Public Library.

226   *"Last Sunday I attended"* [Theodore Dwight Weld], *In Memory, Angelina Grimké Weld . . .* (Boston: George H. Ellis, 1880), pp. 76–77.

226   *when John S. was buried* See John S. Jacobs's death certificate, the burial record of John S. Jacobs at Mount Auburn, and the burial record of Elleanor Jacobs at Cambridge City Cemetery.

227   *additional bits of information* U. S. Census Massachusetts, Middlesex County (part) p. 12, Schedule 1, Cambridge, June 4 1880; Will of Louisa M. Jacobs, written August 2, 1907, and filed in Probate Court April 27, 1917, Norfolk Probate Court at Dedham, Massachusetts. Thanks to Dorothy Sterling and Leonard M. Lake.

227   *a son of* See the Chew-Saunders-Venning Papers at Library Company of Philadelphia; thanks to Philip Lapsansky.

227   *distress at political events* For the Freedmen's Bank, see Eric Foner, *Reconstruction,* pp. 531–32. The Bureau of Refugees, Freedmen and Abandoned Lands was established in the War Department in 1865 to continue a year after the war. In 1866, Congress passed a bill enlarging its role and making it permanent. When this was vetoed by President Johnson, Congress passed a different bill over his veto, extending the Bureau to 1868; it was later extended an additional year in unreconstructed states. Although the Bureau continued its educational work until 1872, its main work was ended in 1869. Harriet Jacobs, *Freedman's Record* (January 1866):3–4; Harriet Jacobs, July 1877, Chew-Saunders-Venning Papers, Library Company of Philadelphia.

Chapter 14. Remember the Poor

229   *"My dear old friend"* JWD, November 1, 1877. Barbara Ann Steward to Frederick Douglass, June 1, 1855 in BAP, 4:295–97. Maria Baldwin, who would graduate from the Cambridge Training School for Teachers in 1881, would be denied a job in the city's schools, then finally be appointed to teach at Agassiz Grammar School in 1887. "Maria Louise Baldwin," *Black Women in America*, 1:79–80; Cambridge African American History Project (1993).

229   *"an island of judicial protection"* Thomas R. Johnson, "The City on the Hill: Race Relations in Washington D.C. 1865–1885" (Ph.D. diss., University of Maryland, 1975), p. 367; Willard B. Gatewood, *Aristocrats of Color: The Black Elite, 1880–1920* (Bloomington: Indiana University Press, 1990), p. 39; Constance McLaughlin Green, *The Secret City: A History of Race Relations in the Nation's Capital* (Princeton: Princeton University Press, 1967), p. 121; John E. Bruce, "Washington's Colored Society," John E. Bruce Papers, Schomburg Center for Research in Black Culture, New York Public Library, quoted in Gatewood, p. 55.

230   *Criticizing this elitism The People's Advocate,* January 8, 1881, in
        Gatewood pp. 56, 59.

230   *first "public colored school" First Annual Report of the Superinten-
        dent of Colored Schools for Washington and Georgetown, D.C. for
        the Year Ending June 30, 1868,* pp. 14–15; M. B. Goodwin "Schools
        of the Colored Population," pp. 256, 289. A preparatory high school
        was organized in 1870; see Winfield S. Montgomery, *Historical
        Sketch of Education for the Colored Race in the District of Colum-
        bia, 1807–1905* (Washington, D.C.: Smith Brothers, 1907), pp.
        40–41; M. B. Goodwin, "Schools of the Colored Population,"
        Appendix C, *Special Report of the Commissioner of Education on
        the Condition and Improvement of Public Schools in the District of
        Columbia, Submitted to the Senate June, 1868, and to the House,
        with Additions June 13, 1870* (Washington, D.C.: U.S. Government
        Printing Office, 1871), p. 289; JWD, March 25, May 13, 1869.

231   *"the mule of the world"* Zora Neale Hurston, *Their Eyes Were
        Watching God* (Philadelphia: J. B. Lippincott, 1937).

231   *"The name of colour"* Harriet Jacobs to Amy Post, December 20
        [1852]. IAPFP.

231   *"a Large Indian Botanical Drug establishment"* W. C. Nell to Amy
        Post, July 8–9, 1860. IAPFP.

231   *the color line* For the literature of the color line, see, for example,
        William Dean Howells, *An Imperative Duty* (New York: Harper &
        Brothers, 1893); Charles W. Chesnutt, "Her Virginia Mammy," *The
        Wife of his Youth* (Boston: Houghton, Mifflin, 1901); George Wash-
        ington Cable, "Tite Poulette," *Old Creole Days* (New York: Scrib-
        ner's Sons, 1879); William Wells Brown, *Clotel,* and Werner Sollors,
        Neither Black nor White yet Both.

232   *reported by the newspapers as a society affair* "Fashionable Wedding
        in High Life," (Washington, D.C.) *New National Era,* May 26,
        1870, from the *New York Herald*; James H. Whyte, *The Uncivil
        Wars: Washington During the Reconstruction* (New York: Twayne,
        1958), p. 252. Louisa Matilda Jacobs to [Cordelia] Downing, May
        16, 1870. Moorland-Spingarn Library, Howard University. George
        Downing Papers.

232   *Washington's "black aristocracy" The Nation,* March 22, 1877,
        quoted in Benjamin Quarles, *Frederick Douglass,* p. 279.

233   *"how anxiously I have perused"* Harriet Jacobs to Frederick Dou-
        glass, March 18, 1877, Library of Congress, Frederick Douglass
        Papers. William S. McFeely, *Frederick Douglass* (New York: Simon
        and Schuster, 1991), pp. 290–91.

233   *"in point of residential rights"* Johnson, "The City on the Hill," p.
        36; Frederick Douglass in the *Chronicle,* November 16, 1875, in
        Johnson, pp. 290–91.

233   "*I saw the 1st celebration*" JWD, April 6, 1884; but see Frederick
Douglass's critique of the parade as "tinsel show," quoted in Green,
The Secret City, p. 127.

233   *The local situation appeared positive* Green, *The Secret City,* p. 117.

234   *Charlotte Forten.* For Charlotte Forten (1837–1914), see Gloria D.
Oden, "The Journal of Charlotte L. Forten: The Salem-Philadelphia
Years (1854–1862) Re-examined," *Essex Institute Historical Collections* 119, no. 2 (1983): 119–36; Ray Allen Billington, "A Social
Experiment: The Port Royal Journal of Charlotte L. Forten,
1862–1863," *Journal of Negro History* (July 1950): 233–64; Anna
Julia Cooper, ed., *The Life and Writings of the Grimké Family,* 2
vols. (n.p., The Author, 1951); Polly Longworth, *I, Charlotte Forten,
Black and Free* (New York: Thomas Y. Crowell, 1970); Edmund Wil-
son, *Patriotic Gore* (New York: Oxford University Press, 1962), pp.
321–57. Charlotte Forten's diary entry is dated Monday, August 11
[1862]. *The Journals of Charlotte Forten Grimké,* The Schomburg
Library of Nineteenth-Century Black Women Writers (New York:
Oxford University Press, 1988) "Sallie" has been identified as Sarah
Cassy Smith Watson, Brenda Stevenson, "Introduction," p. 25. For
Reverend Solomon Peck of the Boston Port Royal Commission, see
Willie Lee Rose, *Rehearsal for Reconstruction: The Port Royal
Experiment* (New York: Oxford University Press, 1964), pp. 88,
287. There is no corroborating reference that puts Jacobs in Boston
in August, 1862. Her trip north that summer is, however, docu-
mented. In June of that year, Jacobs was at Longwood, then in
Philadelphia and Washington, D.C. and Alexandria, then again in
Philadelphia and "home" to Idlewild to see the Willises, according
to Harriet Jacobs to William Lloyd Garrison [1862] published in *The
Liberator,* September 5, 1862. Jacobs's late September 1862 visit to
Idlewild is documented by Nathaniel Parker Willis to A. L. Dennis,
September 20, 1862, New York Historical Society; and by Willis to
Dennis October 1, 1862, Houghton Library, Harvard University. On
October 19, 1862, Jacobs wrote to [Elizabeth Neall] Gay from
Boston, saying she is going to New York in a week, and that she
hopes to go to Washington, D.C., and Alexandria in the winter.
Columbia University Libraries. Gay Papers.

234   *It was then that Jacobs* Forten, *Journals,* August 16, 1862.

234   "*if I can go to Port Royal*" Forten, *Journals,* August 17, 1862.

235   "*bade farewell*" Forten, *Journals,* August 19, September 3, 14, 15,
and October 21, 1862.

235   "'*motherly friend*'" Forten, *Journals,* November 27, 1862; for
Forten's published writings on these experiences, see Forten in *The
Liberator* December 12, 1862; "Interesting Letter from Miss Char-
lotte L. Forten, St. Helena Island, Beaufort, S. C., Nov. 27, 1862,"

The Liberator December 19, 1862; "New Year's Day on the Islands of South Carolina, 1863," *The Liberator,* January 23, 1862; "Life on the Sea Islands," Parts I and II, *Atlantic Monthly,* May and June 1864, pp. 587–96, 666–76.

235   *Francis and his brother Archibald* For Francis and Archibald Grimké, see Dickson D. Bruce Jr., *Archibald Grimké: Portrait of a Black Independent* (Baton Rouge: Louisiana State University Press, 1993), especially Chapters 1 and 2; also see Mark Perry, *Lift Up Thy Voice* (New York: Viking, 2001); and the entries in *DANB.*

236   *Jacobs's boardinghouse* Langdell's address is listed as 127 Mt. Auburn, Jacobs's boardinghouse, in the Harvard University *Catalogue* for 1872, and for 1873–74; Francis Grimké, "Eulogy of Harriet Jacobs," March 1897, Moorland-Spingarn Library,. Howard University, Francis J. Grimké Papers.

236   *"'hams, canned fruit'" The People's Advocate,* October 18, 1879; Cooper, ed., *The Life and Writings of the Grimké Family,* p. 8.

236   *"under the condescending superiority"* Cooper, ed., *The Life and Writing of the Grimké Family,* p. 11; will of Louisa M. Jacobs.

237   *Bethel Literary Society* John W. Cromwell, *History of the Bethel Literary and Historical Association* (Washington, D.C.: R. L. Pendleton, 1896); Jane Rhodes, *Mary Ann Shadd Cary: The Black Press and Protest in the Nineteenth Century* (Bloomington: Indiana University Press, 1998), p. 203.

237   *Julia Wilbur* For Wilbur, see Inez Monroe Steer, ms. written for Virginia Cragg-Gates, Quaker Collection, Haverford College; and U.S. Censuses of 1810, 1820, 1830, 1840, 1850, 1860; New York State Census of 1855; Canfield's and Warner's *Directory of the City of Rochester,* 1845–46; *Daily American Directory of the City of Rochester,* 1849–50, 1851–52; *Dewey's Rochester City Directory,* 1855–56. JWD, April 24, 1855; May 6, 1856; April 19, 1858; September 5, October 31, 1862; January 14, 1863; December 2, 1864; February 3, 1865. Freda joined Wilbur's household before 1878, JWD, December 1878. Wilbur's sister Frances Hartwell continued making visits to the poor. See, for example, JWD, February 6, 1883.

237   *Florence J. Smith.* Census Report for 1860, Massachusetts, County of Sheffield, Ward 6, p. 220; John Daniels, *In Freedom's Birthplace,* 1914 (rpt. New York: Arno, 1969), pp. 57, 100, 102, 188; "Will of Louisa M. Jacobs"; this includes a bequest to Florence Smith's sister Harriet L. Smith of Dorchester, Massachusetts. John J. and Georgiana Smith's son Hamilton, the first African American graduate of Boston University law school, worked as an investigator for the U.S. Bureau of Pensions. Hamilton Smith was a photographer; his glass plate photographs document the life of his family and friends. "150 year-old Family Photographic Portrait," *Cambridge Chronicle* March 2,

1978, at Cambridge (Massachusetts) Historical Commission; obituary of Harriet Louise Smith, *Boston Evening Transcript*, June 21, 1916. Warm thanks to Marilyn Richardson.

238   *Marion P. Shadd* Wilbur met "Mattie Shadd" at the Jacobses' home, JWD, June 24, 1882. And see JWD for May 4, 1886: "I walked to O Street School—colored—1000 pupils. Miss Mattie Shadd Principal. Quite a sight to see them all out at noon, well-dressed & well-behaved." While teaching was generally accepted as a "woman's profession," college training was generally seen as a male privilege. For Howard's few female graduates in this period, see Rayford Logan, *Howard University, The First 100 Years, 1867–1967* (New York: New York University Press, 1969), p. 98. Marion Shadd would become principal of the Lincoln School, then the first Washington woman appointed Assistant Superintendent of Schools. See *Who's Who in Colored America* 1(1927): 181; and G. Smith Wormley, "Educators in the First Half Century of the Public Schools in the District of Columbia," *Journal of Negro History* 17 (1932): 131. For her aunt Mary Ann Shadd Cary, at this time a practicing attorney in Washington, see Dorothy Sterling, ed., *We Are Your Sisters: Black Women in the Nineteenth Century*, p. 406; and Jim Bearden and Linda Jean Butler, *Shadd: The Life and Times of Mary Ann Shadd Cary* (Toronto: NC Press Ltd, 1977).

238   *Frances Rollin Whipper* For Rollin Whipper and Harriet Jacobs, see JWD December 22, 1893. Rollin Whipper's book appeared as Frank A. Rollin [pseud.], *Life and Public Services of Martin R. Delany* (Boston: Lee and Shepard, 1868, 1883). Her sister Louisa Rollin spoke for woman suffrage from the floor of the South Carolina House of Representatives in 1869, and the following year, her sister Charlotte Rollin spoke from the chair of a woman's rights convention in Columbia, South Carolina: "We ask suffrage not as a favor, nor as a privilege, but as a right based on the ground that we are human beings, and as such entitled to all human rights." Stanton, *History of Women Suffrage*, 3:828.

238   *Rollin Whipper* Rollin Whipper's effort to raise her children alone was successful. All three graduated from Howard University. Winifred became a teacher, Ionia a doctor, and Leigh a successful actor. Sterling, *We Are Your Sisters,* p. 461.

238   "*poor folks having hard times*" JWD, December 21, 1877, and February 28, 1878; Green, *The Secret City,* p. 117; "Stevens on Stevens: A Community Perspective. An Oral History of Stevens School." Washington, D.C. (n.p., n.d.), pp. 2, 4.

239   *the Oberlin education* Oberlin's early black female students included the educator Fanny Jackson Coppin, Emma V. Brown studied at Oberlin for a time, as did Mary Jane Patterson, Edmonia Lewis, Mary Sampson Patterson, Susan Bruce, Mary Virginia Montgomery,

and Anna Julia Cooper. See Sterling, *We Are Your Sisters,* pp. 194–213, 470–72; for Cooper, see Mary Helen Washington, "Introduction," Anna Julia Cooper, *Anna Julia Cooper: A Voice From the South,* Schomburg Library of Nineteenth-Century Black Women Writers (New York: Oxford University Press, 1998), pp xxxvi–liv.

239   *"the hotels are filling up"* Frank G. Carpenter, *Carp's Washington* (New York: McGraw Hill, 1960), pp. 1, 6. Thanks to George Stevenson for this reference.

239   *the traditional dividing line* For the racial dividing lines, and for the blocks between 14th and 18th Streets undergoing transition, see Johnson, "The City on the Hill," pp. 176, 303.

239   *Jacobs hired* Washington, D.C. Census, June 2, 1880, enum. dist. 17, microfilm T9-reel 122.

240   *Among their boarders* "A Historic Character, Who Was Formerly a Slave in North Carolina," *The Philadelphia Press,* n.d.; another version of this piece appears embedded in "Washington Society: Mr. Trotter, the New Recorder, Still Lying at the Point of Death," *The Philadelphia Press,* April 8, 1887; thanks to Philip Lapsansky. JWD, March 4, 1878. For Loring, see *Encyclopedia Americana*; for Crappo, see DAB, 38:74–75; for the Claflins, see DAB, 4:110–11; *Annual Meeting of the New England Women's Club . . . May 29, 1869* (n.p, n.d.), pp. 21–22 reports that Mary Claflin served as a vice-president along with Cornelia Grinnell Willis and Ednah Dow Cheney. For Claflin and the Howard Industrial School, see *Second Annual Report of the Howard Industrial School Association, 1868* (Cambridge, Massachusetts: Riverside, 1868), p. 11. For Claflin and Stowe, see Joan D. Hedrick, *Harriet Beecher Stowe: A Life* (New York: Oxford University Press, 1994), pp. 393–94. Mary B. Claflin authored a series of books about old New England.

240   *"With the downfall of reconstruction"* Richard T. Greener, "The Emigration of Colored Citizens from the Southern States," *Journal of Social Science* 2 (May 1880): 22–23, quoted in McFeely, *Frederick Douglass,* p. 299; Nell Irvin Painter, *Sojourner Truth: A Life, a Symbol* (New York: W. W. Norton, 1996), pp. 217–19, 242–46. For the Kansas Exodus, see Nell Irvin Painter, *Exodusters: Black Migration to Kansas After Reconstruction* (New York: Norton, 1979), pp. 184–211, 245–50; For the Kansas Freedmen's Relief Association, see Robert G. Athern, *In Search of Canaan: Black Migration to Kansas, 1879–80* (Lawrence: Regents Press of Kansas, 1978).

241   *"called on Mrs. Jacobs"* "From Harriet Jacobs," (New York) *The Freedman* (February 1866):56. JWD, December 25, 1880.

241   *"Our Duty to the Poor;* "Our Duty to the Poor—How We Observed It on Christmas," dated Thursday, December 30, published in *The People's Advocate,* January 8, 1881.

242   *"Mrs. J. gave us an account"* JWD, February 25, 1881.

242   *"the great suffering"* "What Shall We Do For Our Poor," *The People's Advocate*, November 19, 1881; "The Poor," *The People's Advocate,* November 26, 1881. For the need for significant organized philanthropy in black Washington, see Green, *The Secret City,* pp. 139ff.

242   *"[Sister] Frances"* JWD, January 2, 1882 (continued on page marked January 4).

243   *"'nice dresses'"* Harriet Jacobs to [Ednah Dow] Cheney, January 4-February 19 [1882]. Boston Public Library. The "little notice of the dinner" that Jacobs mentions in this letter has not been found, perhaps because the December 24, 1881 issue of *The People's Advocate* is missing at Martin Luther King Jr. library in Washington, D.C., and at the Schomburg. Describing the White House reception during Cleveland's administration, Washington columnist Frank Carpenter writes, "The White House reception was gorgeous, gay, and giddy. . . . The crowd has never been bigger. The dear people came by the thousands. Of all classes, ages, and sizes, of all colors, sexes, and conditions, they formed long lines reaching from the White House door around the paved walk all the way to the War Department." *Carp's Washington,* pp. 49–50.

243   *"This decision has inflicted"* Quarles, *Frederick Douglass,* pp. 290–91; Frederick Douglass, *Life and Times* (Boston: De Wolfe, Fiske, 1892), Chapter VI. Peter Gilbert, ed., *The Selected Writings of John Edward Bruce: Militant Black Journalist* (New York: Arno and the New York Times, 1971), p. 23 in *City on the Hill,* p. 374; "A Historic Character," *The Philadelphia Press,* n.d.

244   *"They had been to Howard U."* JWD, January 4, 1884.

244   *"The Industrial Department"* Rayford Logan, *Howard University The First Hundred Years,* pp. 99–100. *Howard University Catalogue,* March 1884-March 1885, pp. 21, 23.

244   *"At 10:30 A.M"* JWD, May 18, 1884; Rayford Logan, *Howard University, the First Hundred Years,* p. 33; JWD, June 1, June 28, 1884. At Howard, the Jacobs's circle of acquaintances widened to include Mrs. Winn, Howard's teacher of elocution, her husband Edmund, a government clerk; and later, Miss Haskell, Mrs. DeLong, and Bessie Winam. See JWD, February 13, 1886; February 9, 1889; *Boyd's* directory for 1886, pp. 846, 937; for 1887, p. 888.

244   *her job was not threatened* By 1888, Howard Trustees made it clear that the university would not adopt the vocational program that Hampton-trained Booker T. Washington had established at Tuskeegee Institute. Instead, following the focus on classical education endorsed by Douglass and promulgated by W.E.B. DuBois, the university abandoned its Industrial Department. Logan, *Howard Uni-*

versity The First Hundred Years, pp. 116–17. Louisa Jacobs is listed in the *Howard University Catalogue* dated March 1885–March 1886, p. 21; in *Boyd's Directory* for 1885, she is listed as a teacher living at 1510 R NW, p. 490.

245   *in 1886, she was not rehired Boyd's,* 1887.

245   "*nice crackers*" ILSG pp. 6, 66; Jacobs lived at 10 LaFayette Square in 1882, and at 4 LaFayette Square in 1883. according to JWD, March 11, 1882, and March 16, 1883. Under "Foreign Legations. Sweden and Norway" Count Carl Lewenhaupt, EE and MP is listed at 1021 Connecticut Ave. in *Boyd's* for 1884; JWD, September 26, 1884.

245   *the widow and children of James Norcom Jr. Boyd's* 1872–80.

245   "*John S. acknowledged that*" TT in ILSG p. 214.

245   *James Norcom Jr. had lost everything* The household goods included "1 Rocking Chair $1.50 . . . 1 Carpet & Rug in the parlour $6.00 . . . 4 Calico Curtains $.50 . . . 1 Trunnel Bedstead & Bed & furniture $4.00 . . . 1 Washstand Basin & Eure $1.00 . . . 1 Lot old Crockery—Knives & forks, waiters, Glasses &c $6.50." (He was not allotted the cow and calf he requested.) Chowan County, Insolvent Debtors, 1851. NCSA. For Mary Norcom, see Wm. Benbury, Pltff vs. W. A. B. Norcom, [Executor] of Mary Norcom, Defdt., Chowan Superior Court, Fall Term, 1870, Chowan County Estates Records—Mary Norcom, 1869. NCSA. Despite its endorsement of Norcom's petition, the U. S. government turned down his request. July 2, 1868: Report on Claim of James Norcom. Senate Reports # 152, 40th Congress. 2nd session. In a memoir written years later, a member of the 27th Massachusetts Regiment recalled his wartime experience in "the beautiful town of Edenton" which, he noted, was "under the wise administration of Mayor James Norcom, a staunch Union man." W. P. Derby, *Bearing Arms in the Twenty-Seventh Massachusetts Regiment of Volunteer Infantry during the Civil War, 1861–1865* (Boston: Wright & Potter, 1883), p. 133.

246   "*the son of her old master*" "A Milestone of Progress," *The Freedmen's Record* (December 1865):199.

246   *he moved his new family to Washington Boyd's* 1874, 1877, 1879, 1881, 1883, 1884, 1885; 1870 U. S. Census for Norfolk, Virginia, 4th Ward 3, August 1870; Beaufort County Records, estate of John S. Hawks, 1865; Chowan County Guardian's Records 1741–1913; James, John H. and Fannie E. Norcom, 1872, for Henrietta Norcom, NCSA. 1880 U.S. Census, vol. II.I pt 3, Washington County, D. of C., E. D. 49, p. 17 sheet 115 a.

247   "*Frances been with Mrs Jacobs*" JWD, June 4, 1885. For Frances Mary Wilbur Hartwell (1819–1890), see John R. Wilbor, *The Wildbores in America: A Family Tree* (St. Paul, Minnestoa: John R. Wilbor, 1907,

1933); and the *Rochester Union Advertiser,* August 30, 1890. ILSG
p. 12; Chapters 2, 18; TT in ILSG p. 224, n. 48 p. 319; pp. 220, 221.

247   *As she freely gave* Harriet Jacobs quoted by Amy Post, Rochester
October 30, 1859 in ILSG p. 204.

Chapter 15. Unshaken by the Wind

248   *"The colored race" Star,* December 19, 1883, in Thomas R. Johnson, "The City on the Hill, p. 291; the same quotation is attributed
to the German-American newspaper *The Sentinel,* December 22,
1883, in Constance McLaughlin Green, *The Secret City,* p. 140;
James H. Whyte, *The Uncivil War,* p. 242 citing the *New York
World,* February 10, 1872; for Elliott, see *DANB;* for the incident
concerning Senator Blanche Bruce, see Johnson, p. 375 citing the
Star, September 25, 1884, and November 8, 1884; for the movement
for black businesses, see Johnson p. 389; for Congressman Joseph
Hayne Rainey's interview, see Whyte, pp. 24–43 citing *Georgetown
Courier,* June 18, 1874; for Rainey, see *DANB.*

248   *reestablish their ties with the feminist movement* Jacobs probably
first met Susan B. Anthony when, in the fall of 1849, Anthony
returned to Rochester after closing her Canajoharie school for vacation. Ida Husted Harper, *The Life and Work of Susan B. Anthony,*
1:55. For the Women's National Loyal League, see the *New York
Daily Tribune,* October 30, 1863; Stanton, *History of Women Suffrage,* 2:897 from *National Anti-Slavery Standard,* May 28, 1864;
New York World, May 16, 1864, *New York Herald,* May 15, 1864.
For Jacobs and the Equal Rights Association, see Chapter 11, above;
for Louisa's work with Anthony in the New York State campaign,
see Chapter 12, above. For Jacobs's ongoing relationship with
Anthony, see Susan B. Anthony to Helen Frances Garrison Villard,
Riggs House, Washington, D.C. 1884, Houghton Library, Harvard
University. Thanks to Ann Gordon and the staff of the Stanton-
Anthony Papers.

249   *Anthony, who continued to praise* Susan B. Anthony to Helen
Frances Garrison Villard, Washington, D.C. 1884 [after February
12]. Houghton Library, Harvard University. Thanks to Ann Gordon
and the staff at the Stanton-Anthony Papers.

249   *"I came home"* JWD, February 14, 1886; A few years earlier, Wilbur
had noted that she played host to both Jacobs and Anthony: "At 2
Mrs. Jacobs came.—At 3 Miss Anthony come. Had dinner (potfire)
at 3,30—We had pleasant visit with them. Mrs. J. left at dusk. Miss
A. left at 9.—She told us about Wendell Phillips funeral—& Lucy
Stone—& F. Douglass—& many other interresting things: Not much
of her trip to Europe—No time to talk of that.—Her mind is on the
Cause she has been so long fighting. It is marvelous how well she

keeps up her enthusiasm." JWD, February 17, 1884. Stanton, *History of Woman Suffrage,* 4:72; JWD, February 18, 1886.

249   "*Ch. filled almost*" JWD, February 19, 1886, March 7, 1886. Historian Rosalyn Terborg-Penn lists African American activists who worked within the American Woman Suffrage Association as: Charlotte Forten, Frances Ellen Watkins Harper, Mrs. K. Harris, Caroline Remond Putnam, Charlotte Rollin, Louisa Rollin, Josephine St. Pierre Ruffin, Sojourner Truth, and Frances Rollin Whipper. She names African American activists working within the National Woman Suffrage Association as: Naomi Talbert Anderson, Mrs. Beatty, Mary Ann Shadd Cary, Hatty Purvis, and Charlotte E. Ray. *African American Women in the Struggle for the Vote, 1850–1920* (Bloomington: Indiana University Press, 1998), p. 42.

250   "*These expressions have for years*" In 1898 Helen Cook, president of the black Washington Woman's League, condemned feminist speakers who objected to permitting freedmen to vote while denying votes to women. Should not the feminists, she argued, stop their attacks on the freedmen, stop repeating "the old formula" that freedmen were less qualified to vote than elite white women? Should they not instead present arguments "basing the claims of women wholly on right and justice?" Cook and Forten Grimké are quoted in *African American Women and the Vote, 1837–1965,* ed. Ann D. Gordon et al. (Amherst: University of Massachusetts Press, 1997), p. 5; the references to Helen A. Cook, "A Letter to Miss Anthony," come from *Washington Post,* February 19, 1898 and Charlotte F. Grimké, letter to the editor, *Washington Post,* February 24, 1898.

250   *Jacobs would add a chapter* For budding black capitalism, see Johnson, "The City on the Hill," pp. 389ff.; JWD, February 25, 1881.

250   "*The child's mother*" Harriet Jacobs to [William L. Garrison], *The Liberator,* September 5, 1862; also see Harriet Jacobs to [L. Maria Child] from Alexandria, March 18, 1863 in *National Anti-Slavery Standard,* April 18, 1863.

250   "*colored Congressmen*" Joseph Rainey in *New National Era,* June 18, 1874, quoted in Whyte, *The Uncivil War,* p. 242. Pauline Hopkins, *Contending Forces,* 1900, rpt. The Schomburg Library of Nineteenth-Century Black Women Writers (New York: Oxford University Press, 1988), pp. 102–03; thanks to Carla Peterson for this fictional parallel to Jacobs's boardinghouse.

251   *James C. Matthews* For Matthews, see "Honorable James C. Matthews," Reverend William J. Simmons, *Men of Mark, Eminent, Progressive and Rising* (rpt. New York: Arno and the New York Times, 1968), pp. 964–77; also see Carpenter, *Carp's Washington,* p. 244.

251   "*not the keepers*" *Washington Bee,* March 13, 1886; "Honorable James C. Matthews," Reverend William J. Simmons, *Men of Mark*

p. 972; "A Historic Character, Who Was Formerly a Slave in North Carolina," *Boyd's* for 1887, p. 606.

251   *James Monroe Trotter* For Trotter, see *DANB*, pp. 602–03; see also Stephen R. Fox, *The Guardian of Boston: William Monroe Trotter* (New York: Atheneum, 1970), pp. 3–13; for Trotter and the "Mugwumps," reform-minded Republicans, see Fox, pp. 11–12.

251   *"Mr. Trotter, the New Recorder"* "A Historic Character"; *Boyd's* for 1888, p. 865; "Washington Society. Mr. Trotter, the New Recorder, Still Lying at the Point of Death."

252   *"Mrs. J. called"* JWD, June 18, 1888. Wilbur frequently lent out money at interest to friends; see for example, JWD, March 14, 1882, September 24 and December 5, 1885, March 7 and September 8, 1886. On August 20, 1888 Jacobs was working in the home of the *Washington Post*'s Charles Nordhoff; see JWD; for Nordhoff, see *National Cyclopedia of American Biography* (New York: J. T. White, 1892–1894), 11. JWD, January 25, 1889.

252   *"Says Edenton is a forlorn place"* JWD, February 27, 1889 and February 15, 1889. Wilbur notes that day by day, she sent Jacobs papers: March 16, 17, 29. "The Great Storm," *Norfolk Landmark*, April 19, 1889; JWD, April 10, 1889.

252   *Wilbur's diary is dotted with notes* In 1890, Jacobs was working in the home of Hon. Henry L. Dawes at 1632 Rhode Island; see Cornelia Grinnell Willis to Lilian, January 14, 1890 in a private collection; JWD, February 11, May 2, August 9, 1889; re: sewing, see JWD, May 20, 21, 1889.

253   *"Louisa would not be happy"* Harriet Jacobs to Amy Post, December 20 [1852]. See JWD, April 3, 1891. The Civil Service Act of 1883 required applicants to take competitive examinations; appointments of qualified candidates were apportioned among the states, according to population. Louisa would have been competing with other Massachusetts candidates for a job. It is likely that the color barrier would have blocked her from the attention of the Massachusetts delegation in Congress, as well as in finding employment in the private sector. While the Republican Party held power, a few government positions were set aside as "Negro jobs." These included, in addition to the top posts of Recorder of Deeds, Marshall of the District of Columbia, Register of the Treasury, and the ministers to Liberia and to Haiti, some appointments in the Customs Service and in the Post Office; see *We Are Your Sisters,* ed. Dorothy Sterling, p. 426. Later, on March 30, 1893, the Treasury Department received a letter from Hon. William W. Crapo of New Bedford, recommending Louisa Jacobs for "unclassified service" in a federal department. "Her integrity, fidelity and intelligence commend her. Both of these women [Louisa Jacobs and her mother], rendered efficient service during the

War among the Freedmen, and in the hospitals, and schools, which entitle them to favorable consideration. They are worthy and deserving." RG56. National Archives.

Regarding the Census Bureau, see JWD entries of April 9, April 28, June 12, June 18, 1891; regarding the Treasury Department, see JWD entries of November 26 and December 23, 1891. Federal records include RG 29. Records of the Bureau of the Census. Administrative Records of the Census Office: Records of the Eleventh Census. Records of the First Division-Appointments: Alphabetical List of Employees for the 11th Census, 1889–1894. Vol. 1 PI-161. Entry 89. National Archives.

253   *"they told us"* Mary E. Clemmer Ames, *Ten Years in Washington: Life and Scenes in the National Capital, as a Woman Sees Them* (Hartford, Connecticut: A. D. Worthington & Co., 1873), pp. 365, 357–58, 354. Comparing the wages and hours of male and female Treasury employees, Ames pointed out that "for the same hours and the same toil, her stipend is one-fourth smaller than his smallest." p. 355.

253   *"From the toes of stockings"* Ames, *Ten Years in Washington,* pp. 354–55.

253   *she wrote her will* "Molly Horniblow," Chowan County Wills, 1694–1910, Book C, p. 431; Josiah Collins to Harriet Jacobs, Somerset Place, Lake Scuppernong, North Carolina, July 23, 1859. NCSA.

254   *bought her property* Molly Horniblow's mistress died in August 1827, and her will was proved in December court; on December 12, Gatlin acquired the southern end of Lot 14 with its house. At the New Year's auction a few weeks later, Molly Horniblow and her son Mark Ramsey were sold; on April 10, 1828, Molly's new mistress Hannah Pritchard successfully petitioned for her emancipation. Three years later, before he left Edenton for Tallahassee, Florida, Gatlin sold the lot to Molly Horniblow for $1.00. Register of Deeds, Chowan County, Deed Book I-1, p. 307. North Carolina General Assembly Session Records, November 1842–January, 1843, Box 6, Petitions. NCSA. General Assembly Session Records, November 1842–January 1843, "Petitions" *Journals of the General Assembly of the State of North Carolina its Session in 1842–43* (Raleigh: Thomas J. Lemay, 1843), p. 108; House of Commons, pp. 660, 684; Bond of Marcus Ramsey for his marriage to Ann Johnson, November 22, 1843, in Chowan County Marriage Bonds, 1740–1868. NCSA. Burial Certificate of Molly Horniblow, September 4, 1853, attested August 24, 1981 by Reverend R. W. Storie, Rector, St. Paul's Parish, Edenton, North Carolina; Josiah Collins to Harriet Jacobs, Somerset Place Lake Scuppeanong, North Carolina, July 23, 1859. "Molly Horniblow," Chowan County wills, 1694–1910, Book C p. 431. NCSA. In the August Term, 1859, Molly Horniblow's lot was described as "now occupied by Ann Ramsey"; proved December 14

1865. Register of Deeds, Chowan County, A.H. Bond and Elizabeth Clayton, Deed Book R-3, p. 149. NCSA.

254   *Harriet Jacobs* Josiah Collins to Harriet Jacobs, Somerset Place, Lake Scuppernong, North Carolina, July 23, 1859. NCSA.

255   *in February 1867* To satisfy a judgment, Warren's half was sold, and in October, 1870, both halves of Molly's property were bought in the names of the children of Robert G. Mitchell. Two years later, the building was judged in bad condition, with its fences more or less gone. Petition in *ex parte* proceeding, "R. G. Shelborne, guardian *ad litem* . . . to the Court," January 30, 1872, in guardianship of Robert, Pauline, and Howard Mitchell, 1869, Chowan County Guardian's Records, 1741–1913. NCSA. In October, 1888, the Mitchells apparently became concerned that they had never received a deed to the property, and a deed was issued. Judgment and order in the action, R. R. Felton vs. Josiah Collins, et al., Fall Term 1888, Chowan County Superior Court Minutes Docket, 1886–99, p. 131. NCSA; deed, John C. Bond, Clerk of Superior Court, to Robert, Pauline, and Howard Mitchell, October 5, 1888, Chowan County, Deed Book A, p. 435. NCSA. Then in 1890, they found an undated deed, which they offered for probate and registration on May 12, 1890. Deed, William R. Skinner, Special Commissioner in Felton vs. Collins, to Robert, Pauline, and Howard Mitchell, Chowan Deed Book B-2, p. 262. NCSA. Harriet Jacobs to [Ednah Dow] Cheney, April 25 [1867], Smith College, Sophia Smith Collection. For Ann Ramsey's purchase of the property adjoining Molly Horniblow's property after the death of Mark Ramsey, see Deed, Henry E. Roscoe to Ann Ramsey, November 5, 1859, Chowan Deed Book 9, p. 527. NCSA.

255   *"Harriet Jacobs and her daughter Louisa"* Register of Deeds Chowan County, Deed of Trust to W. D. Pruden, Book T-2, p. 71. Chowan County wills, 1694–1938. NCSA. Ann Ramsey Mayo died sometime before December, 1890.

255   *severing her last ties* Shortly before Mark Ramsey's death, his barber shop was burned in a fire, and when Ramsey rebuilt, he located his new building partly on the old site, and partly on adjoining land he had bought; see Josiah Collins to Harriet Jacobs Lake Scuppernong, North Carolina, July 23, 1859. NCSA. In the spring of 1892, Harriet and Louisa Jacobs hired William J. Leary to sue Ann Ramsey Mayo's son-in-law executor to recover $10 in rent. The court ordered that Jacobs be put in possession of the property and recover rent and court costs. Later that year, on August 29, 1892, Jacobs and Louisa sold this property to Emma Woodward Leary, their lawyer's wife. Deed Book C, p. 1891, NCSA.

255   *"Louisa Jacobs called"* JWD, April 12, 1893; for Coxey's army, see Nell Painter, *Standing at Armageddon: The United States,*

1877–1919 (New York: W. W. Norton, 1987), pp. 116–21; JWD, May 1, 1894; also see entries of April 19, 20, 23, 26 and May 12, 1894.

256 *Anglo-Saxonism* Painter, *Standing,* pp. 150, 164; Green, *The Secret City,* p. 125.

256 *"the barrier of caste"* Green, *The Secret City,* pp. 127, 145. "Visits 1893" notebook, pages 2, 4, 8, 11, 14, 16, Box 40–42, folder 1 802, Moorland-Springarn Library, Howard University, Francis J. Grimké Papers. Julia Wilbur's diary chronicles Jacobs's illnesses: see March 5, 1892, February 14, December 22 and 28, 1893. Listed under "Dispensaries," the Homeopathic Dispensary and Emergency Hospital was located at 625 Massachusetts Avenue NW; see *Boyd's* for 1894, p. 1103. Learning of her friend's condition, Julia Wilbur wrote, "She has suffered for a long time, and it is decided now that she has cancer. We are so sorry for Louisa too.—" JWD, May 23, 1894. For Jacobs's illness and recovery, also see JWD, May 28, June 3, 17, and 20, and August 4, 1894.

257 *"taken into the wedding parlor"* "A Historic Character"; JWD, November 22, 1884, May 5, 1885; *Boyd's* for 1885 lists Bailey Willis "geol sur, 2125 L nw"; ILSG p. 199; for the May 20, 1886 marriage of Lilian Willis to Robert A. Boyt, see William M. Emery, *The Howland Heirs* (New Bedford, Massachusetts: E. Anthony and Sons, 1919).

257 *"She is the friend"* JWD, May 5, 1885.

257 *"the phenomenal vitality"* Cornelia Willis to Ednah Dow Cheney, June 26, 1896 and July 5, 1896; also see Cornelia Willis to Ednah Dow Cheney January 27, 1897. Boston Public Library.

258 *"I am," she wrote "always grieved"* Louisa M. Jacobs to Ednah Dow Cheney, July 22, 1896. Boston Public Library. Anna Q. T. Parsons of 50 Thornton Street, Roxbury, is listed as a Lifetime Member of the New England Women's Club, New England Women's Club Papers, Box 10–39, Schlesinger Library, Radcliffe College. In 1897, William Lloyd Garrison had four living sons: George Thompson Garrison, William Lloyd Garrison Jr., Wendell Phillips Garrison, and Francis Jackson Garrison. It is not known which of these is referred to here.

258 *"I know Mrs. Cheney"* Louisa Jacobs to [Ednah Dow] Cheney, July 22, 1896. Boston Public Library.

258 *Black women were organizing* Mary Ann Shadd Cary Papers, Moorland-Springarn Library, Howard University, folder 5: Colored Women's Professional Assn., Minutes of the first meeting. Colored Women's Professional Franchise Assn.; Mary Church Terrell, "What the Colored Woman's League Will Do (written especially for *Ringwood's Journal"*) *The American Journal of Fashion* (Cleveland, Ohio, May and June 1893, no. 2, nos. 7 & 8), microfilm, Bethune

Museum; Elizabeth L. Davis, "The First Conference: History of the National Association of Colored Women," *Lifting as They Climb* (Washington, D.C.: National Association of Colored Women's Clubs, 1933), pp. 19–20. For Mary Ann Shadd Cary, see Jane Rhodes, *Mary Ann Shadd Cary*; and Jim Bearden and Linda Jean Butler, *Shadd*.

258   *"that at last the Lord"* Cornelia Grinnell Willis to Ednah Dow Cheney, January 27, 1897, Boston Public Library; Joseph Pierce to Reverend Francis Grimké, August 19, 1893, Moorland-Spingarn Library, Howard University, Francis J. Grimké papers; Joseph Pierce to [Louisa Jacobs], February 28, 1897. Private collection.

259   *"Although the news"* Joseph Pierce to [Louisa Jacobs], March 19, 1897. Private collection. Louisa saved this letter her whole life, writing on the reverse in her spidery hand, "Joe's last letter to me."

259   *One by one* William C. Nell died in 1874, Maria Stewart and William Lloyd Garrison in 1879, Lydia Maria Child the following year, and Sojourner Truth in 1883. Wendell Phillips died in 1884, Maria Weston Chapman in 1885, Amy Post in 1889, Ellen Craft in 1891, Mary Ann Shadd Cary in 1893, and Frederick Douglass in 1895. Still alive at Jacobs's death were Elizabeth Keckley (d. 1907), Frances Ellen Watkins Harper (d. 1911), and Harriet Tubman, who lived on until 1913.

259   *"as nurse"*. [Harriet Jacobs obituary], *Boston Herald*, March 10, 1897; thanks to the late Dr. William J. Knox.

259   *only the older members* Ednah Dow Cheney to Cornelia Grinnell Willis, March 12, 1897. Private collection.

259   *"The dear little thoughtful girl"* Ednah Dow Cheney to Cornelia Grinnell Willis, March 12, 1897. Private collection.

260   *"speaking of the stirring times"* Francis J. Grimké, Eulogy of Harriet Jacobs, Moorland-Spingarn Library, Howard University Francis J. Grimké Papers. Thanks to Dorothy Sterling.

260   *"She impressed me"* Francis J. Grimké, Eulogy of Harriet Jacobs, Moorland-Spingarn Howard University, Francis J. Grimké Papers.

261   *"Patient in"* Romans 12:11–12. Tombstone of Harriett Jacobs, Lot 4389, Clethra Path, Mount Auburn Cemetery, Cambridge, Massachusetts. Thanks to the Mount Auburn staff.

261   *Feeling that "it is not"* E.D.C. "Mrs. Harriet Jacobs," *Woman's Journal*, May 1897. Thanks to Kate Culkin.

261   *"The same love of liberty"* Stanton, *History of Woman Suffrage*, 1:324.

262   *Truth became* Nell I. Painter, *Sojourner Truth*, p. 272. For Tubman, see Sarah Bradford, *Harriet Tubman, the Moses of her People* ([1886], 1916).

262   *Despite Ednah Dow Cheney's* Ednah Dow Cheney to Cornelia Grinnell Willis, March 12, 1897. Private collection. Francis J. Grimké Eulogy of Harriet Jacobs, Moorland-Spingarn Library, Howard University, Francis J. Grimké Papers.

262   *"a story to pass on"* Toni Morrison, *Beloved* (New York: Knopf, 1987).

262   *And she left the example* Harriet Jacobs to Amy Post, October 9 [1853]. IAPFP.

Afterword

263   *"have a rest"* "The dear thoughtful little girl who concealed her knowledge of her mother's neighborhood and the deep longings of her heart, that she might not peril her safety" had been "the same thoughtful loving child throughout her long life." Ednah Dow Cheney to Cornelia Grinnell Willis, March 12, 1897. Private collection.

263   *It had a rocky start* The founders of the National Home were activists—white abolitionists and Quakers like the Passamore Williamsons, the Thathams, Gulielma Breed, Emily Howland, and the young widow of hero Robert Gould Shaw; activist black women like Maria Remond, wife of Louisa's fellow-lecturer Charles Lenox Remond; prominent writers like Harriet Beecher Stowe and E.D.E.N. Southworth, and the Jacobs's New England Freedman's Aid Society colleague Ednah Dow Cheney; National Association for the Relief of Destitute Colored Women and Children, *Fifty Years of Good Works* (Washington, D.C.: Smith Brothers, 1914), pp. 13, 15.

264   *Life was not easy. 37th Annual Report of the National Association for the Relief of Destitute Colored Women and Children . . . 1900* (Washington, D.C.: Smith Brothers, 1900), p. 10.

264   *Elizabeth Keckley* In 1907 Keckley died in her sleep at the Home.

264   *"I am sure"* By 1906, the women were no longer in control; the Board of Charities admitted and removed children, and schooling became impossible. Mrs. A. M. Edgar to Louisa Matilda Jacobs, July 9, 1903. Private collection.

264   *"'nobility of nature'"* Wilbur P. Thirkield to Louisa Matilda Jacobs, June 17, 1908. Private collection.

264   *writing her will* "Will of Louisa M. Jacobs." August 2, 1908.

265   *When in 1917* Grinnell Willis to Louisa M. Jacobs, January 5, 1913. Private collection. Death Certificate of Louisa M. Jacobs, April 5, 1917, Records, Town Clerk, Brookline, Massachusetts.

Select Bibliography

Albion, Robert G. *The Rise of New York Port, 1815–1860.* 1939; rpt. New York: Scribner's, 1970.

American Missionary Association. Records of the American Missionary Associiation, 1846–1882. Microfilm.

Ames, Mary E. Clemmer. *Ten Years in Washington: Life and Scenes in the National Capital, as a Woman Sees Them.* Hartford, Conn.: A. D. Worthington & Co., 1873.

Andrews, William L. *To Tell a Free Story: The First Century of Afro-American Autobiography, 1760–1860.* Urbana: University of Illinois Press, 1986.

Bacon, Georganna, and Eliza Woolsey Howland. *Letters of a Family during the War for the Union, 1861–1865.* New Haven: Tuttle, Morehouse & Taylor, 1899.

Barber, James G. *Alexandria in the Civil War.* Lynchburg, Va.: H. E. Howard, 1988.

Bassett, John S. *Slavery in the State of North Carolina.* Johns Hopkins University Series in History and Political Science, Series XVII, nos. 7–8. Baltimore: Johns Hopkins Press, 1899.

Bearden, Jim, and Linda Jean Butler. *Shadd: The Life and Times of Mary Ann Shadd Cary.* Toronto: NC Press Ltd., 1977.

Beers, Henry A. *Nathaniel Parker Willis.* 1885; rpt. New York: AMS, 1969.

Berlin, Ira, et al., eds. *Freedom: A Documentary History of Emancipation 1861–1867,* series I, vol. I, *The Destruction of Slavery.* New York: Cambridge University Press, 1985.

Billington, Louis, and Rosamund Billington. "A Burning Zeal for Righteousness: Women in the British Anti-Slavery Movement, 1820–1860." In *Equal or Different, Women's Politics, 1800–1914.* ed. Jane Randall. Oxford: Oxford University Press, 1987.

Blackett, R. J. M. *Beating Against the Barriers: The Lives of Six Nineteenth-Century Afro-Americans.* Ithaca: Cornell University Press, 1986.

———. *Building an Antislavery Wall: Black Americans in the Atlantic Abolitionist Movement, 1830–1860.* Ithaca: Cornell University Press, 1983, 1989.

———. *Divided Hearts: Britain and the American Civil War.* Baton Rouge: Louisiana State University Press, 2001.

Blight, David W. *Race and Reunion: The Civil War in American Memory*. Cambridge, Mass.: Harvard University Press, 2001.

Bogin, Ruth. "Sarah Parker Remond: Black Abolitionist from Salem." *Essex Institute Historical Collections* 110, no. 2 (April 1974).

Bolt, Christine. *The Anti-Slavery Movement and Reconstruction: A Study in Anglo-American Cooperation, 1833–77*. London and New York: Oxford University Press, 1969.

Borome, Joseph A. "The Vigilant Committee of Philadelphia." *Pennsylvania Magazine of History and Biography* 92 (July 1968): 320–51.

Boylan, Anne M. *The Origins of Women's Activism: New York and Boston, 1797–1840*. Chapel Hill: University of North Carolina Press, 2002.

Braude, Ann. *Radical Spirits: Spiritualism and Women's Rights in Nineteenth-Century America*. Boston: Beacon, 1989.

Brockett, L. P., and Mary C. Vaughn. *Women's Work in the Civil War*. Philadelphia: Ziegler, McCurdy, & Co., 1867.

Brown, Elsa Barkley. "Uncle Ned's Children: Negotiating Community and Freedom in Postemancipation Richmond, Virginia." Ph.D. diss., Kent State University, 1994.

Bruce, Dickson D., Jr. *Archibald Grimké: Portrait of a Black Independent*. Baton Rouge: Louisiana State University Press, 1993.

Butchart, Ronald E. *Northern Schools, Southern Blacks, and Reconstruction: Freedmen's Education, 1862–1875*. Westport, Conn.: Greenwood, 1980.

Campbell, Stanley W. *The Slave Catchers: Enforcement of the Fugitive Slave Law, 1850–1860*. Chapel Hill: University of North Carolina Press, 1968, 1970.

Carpenter, Frank G. *Carp's Washington*. Arranged and Edited by Frances Carpenter. New York: McGraw Hill, 1960.

Carter, George E., et al., eds., *Black Abolitionist Papers, 1830–1865*. Sanford, North Carolina. Microfilming Corporation of America, 1981. Microfilm.

Chambers-Schiller, Lee. "The Cab: A Trans-Atlantic Community, Aspects of Nineteenth Century Reform." Ph.D. diss., University of Michigan, 1963.

Cheney, Ednah Dow. *Reminiscences*. Boston: Lee & Shepard, 1902.

Chesson, Amelia Thompson. Diaries. Raymond English Deposit. John Rylands University Library of Manchester at Deansgate. United Kingdom.

Chesson, Frederick. Diaries. Raymond English Deposit. John Rylands University Library of Manchester at Deansgate. United Kingdom.

Clinton, Catherine. "Freedwomen, Sexuality, and Violence." *Georgia Historical Quarterly* 76 (summer 1992): 313–32.

Collison, Gary. *Shadrach Minkins: From Fugitive Slave to Citizen*. Cambridge, Mass.: Harvard University Press, 1997.

Condit, Carl. *The Port of New York*. Chicago: University of Chicago Press, 1980.

Cooper, Anna Julia. *A Voice from the South. By a Black Woman of the South*. 1892; rpt. ed. Mary Helen Washington. The Schomburg Library of Nineteenth-Century Black Women Writers. New York: Oxford, 1988.

————, ed. *The Life and Writings of the Grimké Family*. 2 vols. n.p.: The Author, 1951.

Craft, William. *Running a Thousand Miles for Freedom; or, The Escape of William and Ellen Craft from Slavery*. London: William Tweedie, 1860.

Daniels, John. *In Freedom's Birthplace*. 1914; rpt. New York: Arno and the New York Times, 1969.

Dicey, Edward. *Spectator of America*. ed. Herbert Mitgang. Chicago: Quadrangle, 1971.

Dictionary of American Biography. 20 vols. New York: C. Scribner's Sons, 1928–58.

Dictionary of American Negro Biography. ed. Rayford W. Logan and Michael R. Winston. New York: W.W. Norton, 1982.

Douglass, Frederick. *Life and Times*. Boston: De Wolfe Fiske, 1892.

DuBois, W.E.B. *Black Reconstruction in America: An Essay toward a History of the Part Which Black Folk Played in the Attempt to Reconstruct Democracy in America, 1860–1880*. 1935; rpt. Cleveland: World Pub. Co., 1962.

Duncan, Russell. *Freedom's Shore: Tunis Campbell and the Georgia Freedmen*. Athens: University of Georgia Press, 1986.

Faulkner, Carol. *Women's Radical Reconstruction: The Freedmen's Aid Movement*. Philadelphia: University of Pennsylvania Press, 2003.

Fern, Fanny. *Ruth Hall: A Domestic Tale of the Present Time*. 1855; rpt. ed. Joyce W. Warren. New Brunswick: Rutgers University Press, 1986

Foner, Eric. *Reconstruction: America's Unfinished Revolution, 1863–1877*. New York: Harper and Row, 1984.

Forton, Charlotte L. *The Journals of Charlotte Forten Grimké*. ed. Brenda Stevenson. The Schomburg Library of Nineteenth-Century Black Women Writers. New York: Oxford University Press, 1988.

Foster, Francis Smith. *Written by Herself, Literary Production by African-American Women, 1746–1892*. Bloomington: Indiana University Press, 1992.

————. ed. *A Brighter Coming Day: A Frances Ellen Watkins Harper Reader*. New York: The Feminist Press, 1990.

Franklin, John Hope. *A Southern Odyssey*. Baton Rouge: Louisiana State University Press, 1976.

————. *From Slavery to Freedom*. 2d ed. New York: Knopf, 1967.

————. *The Free Negro in North Carolina*. New York: W. W. Norton, 1999.

Franklin, John Hope, and Loren Schweninger. *Runaway Slaves: Rebels on the Plantation*. New York: Oxford University Press, 1999.

Fryer, Peter. *Staying Power: The History of Black People in Britain*. London: Pluto, 1984.

Gatewood, Willard B. *Aristocrats of Color: The Black Elite, 1880–1920*. Bloomington: Indiana University Press, 1990.

Giesberg, Judith Ann. *Civil War Sisterhood: The U.S. Sanitary Commission and Women's Politics in Transition*. Boston: Northeastern University Press, 2000.

Goodwin, M. B. "Schools of the Colored Population." *Special Report of the Commissioner of Education on the Condition and Improvement of Public Schools in the District of Columbia.* Washington, D.C.: U.S. Government Printing Office, 1871, *American Journal of Education,* vol. 19, 1870.

Gordon, Ann D., et al., eds. *African American Women and the Vote, 1837–1965.* Amherst: University of Massachusetts Press, 1997.

———, ed. *The Selected Papers of Elizabeth Cady Stanton and Susan B. Anthony.* New Brunswick: Rutgers University Press, 1997.

Green, Constance McLaughlin. *The Secret City: A History of Race Relations in the Nation's Capital.* Princeton: Princeton University Press, 1967.

Grimké, Charlotte L. Forten. See Forten, Charlotte L.

Grover, Kathryn. *Fugitive's Gibraltar: Escaping Slaves and Abolitionism in New Bedford, Massachusetts.* Amherst: University of Massachusetts Press, 2001.

Gunn, Thomas Butler. Diaries. Missouri Historical Society. St. Louis.

Gutman, Herbert G. *The Black Family in Slavery and Freedom, 1750–1925.* New York: Pantheon, 1976.

Harper, Ida Husted. *The Life and Work of Susan B. Anthony.* Indianapolis: Hollenbeck, 1898.

Hathaway, J.R.B., ed. *North Carolina Historical and Genealogical Register.* 3 vols. 1900–03. rpt. Baltimore: Genaeological Publishing Co., 1970–71.

Hedrick, Joan D. *Harriet Beecher Stowe: A Life.* New York: Oxford University Press, 1994.

Herman, L. *Trauma and Recovery.* New York: Basic, 1992.

Hewitt, Nancy A. *Women's Activism and Social Change: Rochester, New York, 1822–1872.* Ithaca: Cornell University Press, 1984.

Hine, Darlene Clark, et al., eds. *Black Women in America: An Historical Encyclopedia.* Brooklyn: Carlson, 1993.

Holland, Patricia G. *The Collected Correspondence of Lydia Maria Child, 1817–1880.* Millwood, New York: Kraus Microform. 1980. Microfiche.

Holland, Patricia G., and Ann D. Gordon, eds. *The Papers of Elizabeth Cady Stanton and Susan B. Anthony.* Wilmington, Delaware: Scholarly Resources, 1991. Microfilm.

Horton, James Oliver, and Lois E. Horton. *Black Bostonians: Family Life and Community Struggle in the Antebellum North.* New York: Holmes & Meier, 1979.

Incidents in the Life of a Slave Girl. See Jacobs, Harriet.

Jacobs, Harriet. *Incidents in the Life of a Slave Girl: Written by Herself.* Boston: For the Author, 1861. Cambridge: Harvard University Press, 1987–2000.

Jacobs, John S. "A True Tale of Slavery." In *The Leisure Hour: A Family Journal of Instruction and Recreation* 10, no. 476–79 (February 4, 14, 21, and 28, 1861). In *Incidents in the Life of a Slave Girl,* pp. 207–28.

James, Edward T., et al. eds. *Notable American Women*. Cambridge, Mass.: Belknap Press of Harvard University Press, 1971.

Johnson, Thomas R. "The City on the Hill: Race Relations in Washington D.C., 1865–1885." Ph.D. diss., University of Maryland, 1975.

Johnson, Whittington B. *Black Savannah, 1788–1864*. Fayetteville: University of Arkansas Press, 1996.

Karcher, Carolyn L. *The First Woman in the Republic: A Cultural Biography of Lydia Maria Child*. Durham: Duke University Press, 1994.

Knott, Robanna S. "Harriet Jacobs: The Edenton Biography." Ph.D. diss., University of North Carolina at Chapel Hill, 1994.

Lapp, Rudolph M. "The Negro in Gold Rush California." *Journal of Negro History* 49, no. 2 (April 1964): 81–98.

Lapsansky, Emma Jones. "The Counter Culture of Agitation in Philadelphia." In *The Abolitionist Sisterhood*. ed. Jean Fagan Yellin and John C. Van Horne. Ithaca: Cornell University Press, 1994.

Lesley, Susan I. *Recollections of my Mother*. Boston: George H. Ellis, 1889.

Logan, Rayford W. *Howard University, The First 100 Years, 1867–1967*. New York: New York University Press, 1969.

Long, E. B. *The Civil War Day by Day: An Almanac, 1861-1865*. Garden City, New York: Doubleday, 1971.

Mabee, Carleton. *Sojourner Truth: Slave, Prophet, Legend*. New York: New York University Press, 1993.

McFeely, William S. *Frederick Douglass*. New York: Simon and Schuster, 1992.

McPherson, James. *The Struggle for Equality*. Princeton: Princeton University Press, 1964.

Meltzer, Milton, and Patricia G. Holland, eds. *Lydia Maria Child, Selected Letters 1817–1880*. Amherst: University of Massachusetts Press, 1982.

Merrill, Walter M., and Louis Ruchames, eds. *The Letters of William Lloyd Garrison*. 6 vols. Cambridge, Mass.: Harvard University Press, 1971–81.

Mitchell, Memory F. "Off to Africa—With Judicial Blessing." *North Carolina Historical Review* 53 (July 1976): 269–71.

Moody, Richard. *Edwin Forrest: First Star of the American Stage*. New York: Knopf, 1960.

Morris, Robert. *Reading, 'Riting, and Reconstruction*. Chicago: University of Chicago Press, 1981.

Nash, Frederick, et al., eds. *Revised Statutes of the State of North Carolina*. Raleigh: Turner and Hughes. 1837.

Nash, Gary B. *Forging Freedom: The Formation of Philadelphia's Black Community, 1720–1840*. Cambridge, Mass.: Harvard University Press, 1988.

Norcom Family Papers. North Carolina State Archives.

Oden, Gloria D. "The Journal of Charlotte L. Forten: The Salem-Philadelphia Years (1854–1862) Re-examined." *Essex Institute Historical Collections* 119, no. 2 (1983): 119–36.

Oubre, Claude F. *Forty Acres and a Mule: The Freedmen's Bureau and Black Land Ownership.* Baton Rouge: Louisiana State University Press, 1978.

Painter, Nell Irvin. *Sojourner Truth: A Life, a Symbol.* New York: W. W. Norton, 1996.

———. *Standing at Armageddon : The United States, 1877–1919.* New York: W. W. Norton, 1987.

Parker, Allen. *Recollections of Slavery Times.* Worcester, Mass.: Charles W. Burbank and Co., 1895.

Parker, Freddie L. *Running for Freedom: Slave Runaways in North Carolina, 1775–1840.* New York: Garland, 1993.

Parramore, Thomas D. *Cradle of the Colony: The History of Chowan County and Edenton, North Carolina.* Edenton: Edenton Chamber of Commerce, 1967.

Perkins, Linda M. "The Black Female AMA Teacher in the South, 1861–1970." In *Black Americans in North Carolina and the South.* ed. Jeffrey J. Crow and Flora J. Hatley. Chapel Hill: University of North Carolina Press, 1984.

Porter, Dorothy Burnett. "The Remonds of Salem, Massachusetts: A Nineteenth-Century Family Revisited." In *The Proceedings of the American Antiquarian Society* 95, part 2 (October 1985): pp. 259–95.

Post, Isaac, and Amy Post. The Isaac and Amy Post Family Papers. Rush Rhees Library. University of Rochester.

Potts, Daniel E., and Annette Potts. *Young America and Australian Gold: Americans and The Gold Rush of the 1850's.* St. Lucia: University of Queensland Press, 1974.

Powell, William S., ed. *Dictionary of North Carolina Biography.* Chapel Hill: University of North Carolina Press, 1979–96.

Quarles, Benjamin. *Black Abolitionists.* New York: Oxford University Press, 1969.

Rankin, Richard. *Ambivalent Churchmen and Evangelical Churchwomen: The Religion of the Episcopal Elite in North Carolina, 1800–1860.* Columbia: University of South Carolina Press, 1993.

Ray, Charlotte E. *African American Women in the Struggle for the Vote, 1850–1920.* Bloomington: Indiana University Press, 1998.

Rhodes, Jane. *Mary Ann Shadd Cary: The Black Press and Protest in the Nineteenth Century.* Bloomington: Indiana University Press, 1998.

Richardson, Marilyn, ed. *Maria W. Stewart: America's First Black Woman Political Writer: Essays and Speeches.* Bloomington: Indiana University Press, 1987.

Ripley, C. Peter, et al., eds. *The Black Abolitionist Papers*, vol. 1: *The British Isles, 1830–65.* Chapel Hill: University of North Carolina Press, 1985.

Rochester Ladies Anti-Slavery Society Papers. Clements Library. University of Michigan.

Rose, Willie Lee. *Rehearsal for Reconstruction: The Port Royal Experiment.* Oxford: Oxford University Press, 1964, 1976.

Schwalm, Leslie A. *A Hard Fight for We: Women's Transition from Slavery to Freedom in South Carolina.* Urbana: University of Illinois Press, 1997.

Sherman, W. T. *Memoirs of General W. T. Sherman.* New York: The Library of America, 1990.

Simms, James M., *The First Colored Baptist Church in North America: Constituted at Savannah, Georgia, January 20, A.D. 1788.* 1888; rpt. New York: Negro Universities Press, 1969.

Sollors, Werner. *Neither Black nor White yet Both.* New York: Oxford University Press, 1997.

Stanton, Elizabeth Cady, et al., eds. *History of Woman Suffrage.* Rochester: Susan B. Anthony, 1881.

Sterling, Dorothy. *Black Foremothers: Three Lives.* Old Westbury, New York: The Feminist Press, 1979.

———, ed. *The Trouble They Seen: Black People Tell the Story of Reconstruction.* Garden City, New York: Doubleday, 1976.

———, ed. *We Are Your Sisters: Black Women in the Nineteenth Century.* New York: W. W. Norton, 1984.

Stowe, Harriet Beecher. *Key to Uncle Tom's Cabin.* 1853; rpt. New York: Arno and the New York Times, 1968.

Swint, Henry Lee, ed. *Dear Ones at Home.* Nashville: Vanderbilt University Press, 1966.

Temperley, Howard R. *British Antislavery, 1833–1870.* Columbia: University of South Carolina Press, 1972.

Terborg-Penn, Rosalyn. *African American Women in the Struggle for the Vote, 1850–1920.* Bloomington: Indiana University Press, 1998.

Thayer, James B., ed. *Letters of Chauncey Wright.* 1878; rpt. New York: Burt Franklin, 1971.

"True Tale of Slavery, A." See Jacobs, John S.

Venet, Wendy Hammond. *Neither Ballots nor Bullets: Women Abolitionists and the Civil War.* Charlottesville: University Press of Virginia, 1991.

Von Frank, Albert J. *The Trials of Anthony Burns: Freedom and Slavery in Emerson's Boston.* Cambridge, Mass.: Harvard University Press, 1998.

Wahl, Albert J. "The Progressive Friends of Longwood." *The Bulletin of Friends Historical Association* 42, no. 1 (spring 1953): 13–32.

Walker, David. *Walker's Appeal, in four articles, together with a preamble to the Coloured Citizens of the World, but in Particular, and Very Expressly, to Those of the United States of America.* 1830; rpt. ed. Peter P. Hinks. University Park: Pennsylvania State University Press, 2000.

Walker, Jonathan. *The Branded Hand: Trial and Imprisonment of Jonathan Walker,* 1845; rpt. New York: Arno Press, 1969.

Warren, Joyce W. *Fanny Fern: An Independent Woman.* New Brunswick: Rutgers University Press, 1992.

Wesley, Dorothy Porter, and Constance Porter Uzelac, eds. *William Cooper Nell: Selected Writings 1832–1874.* Baltimore: Black Classic Press, 2002.

Whyte, James H. *The Uncivil Wars: Washington During the Reconstruction.* New York: Twayne, 1958.

Wilbur, Julia. Diary. Friends Library. Haverford College.

[———]. *Twelfth Annual Report of The Rochester Ladies' Anti-Slavery Society.* Rochester: A. Strong. 1863.

[———]. *Thirteenth Annual Report of The Rochester Ladies' Anti-Slavery Society.* Rochester: Rochester Democrat. 1864.

[———]. *Fourteenth Annual Report of The Rochester Ladies' Anti-Slavery Society.* Rochester: William S. Falls. 1865.

Willis, Nathaniel Parker. *The Convalescent.* New York: Charles Scribner, 1859.

———. *Dashes at Life with a Free Pencil.* 1845; rpt. New York: Garrett, 1969.

———. *Famous Persons and Places.* 1854; rpt. Freeport, New York: Books for Libraries Press, 1972.

———. *Out-doors at Idlewild; or, The Shaping of a Home on the Banks of the Hudson.* New York: Charles Scribner, 1855.

———. *The Rag Bag.* New York: Charles Scribner, 1855.

Winch, Julie. *Philadelphia's Black Elite: Activism, Accommodation, and the Struggle for Autonomy, 1787–1848.* Philadelphia: Temple University Press, 1988.

Yellin, Jean Fagan. "Text and Contexts of Harriet Jacobs's *Incidents in the Life of a Slave Girl: Written by Herself.*" *The Slave's Narrative.* Ed. Charles T. Davis and Henry Louis Gates Jr. New York: Oxford University Press, 1985.

———. *Women and Sisters: The Antislavery Feminists in American Culture.* New Haven: Yale University Press, 1988.

Yellin, Jean Fagan, and John C. Van Horne, eds. *The Abolitionist Sisterhood.* Ithaca: Cornell University Press, 1994.

Index

2242569R00230

Made in the USA
San Bernardino, CA
28 March 2013